Silver in Georgian Dublin

Georgian Dublin is synonymous with a period of unprecedented expansion in the market for luxury goods. At a time when new commodities, novel technologies and fashionable imports seduced elite society, silver enjoyed an established association with gentility and prestige. Earlier studies have focused predominantly on the issue of style. This book considers the demand for silver goods in Georgian Ireland from the perspectives of makers, retailers and consumers. It discusses the practical and symbolic uses of silverware, interpreted through contemporary guild accounts, inventories, trade ephemera and culinary manuscripts. For the first time the activities of Dublin's goldsmiths and their customers are considered in the context of the British Isles, acknowledging Dublin's 'second city' status in relation to London. How did the availability of new products like English porcelain and Sheffield plate affect the demand for silver in Dublin, and how did silver imports from London affect the Dublin trade? To what extent do the practices of Dublin goldsmiths mirror their North American counterparts in seeking to infer associations with the fashionable metropolis of London? Drawing on an extensive range of documentary and object evidence, this wide-ranging analysis considers the context in which silver goods were made, used, valued and displayed in Georgian Ireland.

Alison FitzGerald is a Lecturer in the Department of History at Maynooth University, Ireland.

Silver in Georgian Dublin

Making, selling, consuming

Alison FitzGerald

Routledge
Taylor & Francis Group
LONDON AND NEW YORK

First published 2017 by Routledge

2 Park Square, Milton Park, Abingdon, Oxfordshire OX14 4RN
52 Vanderbilt Avenue, New York, NY 10017

Routledge is an imprint of the Taylor & Francis Group, an informa business

First issued in paperback 2018

Library of Congress Cataloging-in-Publication Data
Names: FitzGerald, Alison (Alison M.), author.
Title: Silver in Georgian Dublin : making, selling, consuming / Alison FitzGerald.
Description: New York : Routledge, 2016. | Series: The Histories of Material Culture and Collecting, 1700–1950 | Includes bibliographical references and index.
Identifiers: LCCN 2016003270 | ISBN 9781472427878 (alk. paper)
Subjects: LCSH: Silverwork—Economic aspects—Ireland—Dublin. | Dublin (Ireland)—Social conditions—18th century. | Dublin (Ireland)—Social conditions—19th century. | Dublin (Ireland)—Economic conditions—18th century. | Dublin (Ireland)—Economic conditions—19th century.
Classification: LCC NK7146.D83 F58 2016 | DDC 739.2/30941835—dc23
LC record available at http://lccn.loc.gov/2016003270

ISBN: 978-1-4724-2787-8 (hbk)
ISBN: 978-0-367-20022-0 (pbk)

Typeset in Sabon
by Apex CoVantage, LLC

For Product Safety Concerns and Information please contact our EU representative:
GPSR@taylorandfrancis.com
Taylor & Francis Verlag GmbH, Kaufingerstraße 24, 80331 München, Germany.

For Eva Mai

Contents

Acknowledgements

This book is a revised and expanded version of my PhD thesis, supervised by Helen Clifford and John Styles at the Royal College of Art and Victoria and Albert Museum (V&A), London. The generosity and collegiality that I experienced from my supervisors was exceptional; I hope that I can reciprocate it with my own students.

In the course of writing the book I have been helped by many people, and it is a pleasure to acknowledge warmly some of them here. I would like to thank the Irish Georgian Society, the Paul Mellon Centre for Studies in British Art, the National University of Ireland, and Maynooth University for their benevolence in providing funding towards the cost of illustrations for this volume. I am greatly indebted to Toby Barnard, Conor Lucey, Jacqueline Hill, Thomas Sinsteden and W. E. Vaughan for reading drafts of the book and for their exceptionally generous and helpful comments. Toby Barnard has followed the progress of the book from the outset, encouraged its publication, and informed its arguments through his pioneering work on the material culture of eighteenth-century Ireland. W. E. Vaughan has refined and improved its content by pithy, insightful and humorous annotations. I have enjoyed stimulating conversations with Thomas Sinsteden, who was always willing to share his encyclopaedic knowledge of Irish silver artefacts and their makers. At Ashgate, I am very grateful to Erika Gaffney and Michael Yonan (series editor) and especially to my editor Margaret Michniewicz. Her unfailing courtesy, efficiency and patience have made the process of producing this book much easier. At Routledge, I particularly appreciated the support and assistance of Felisa Salvago-Keyes and her team.

Several colleagues and friends have provided assistance in a variety of ways, which have always been appreciated and which have made the process of completing this project more enjoyable. I would like to thank the following people in particular: Robert Barker, David Beasley, Daniel Beaumont, Douglas Bennett, Carla Briggs, Kerry Bristol, Mary Broderick, Rebecca Campion, Aengus Carroll, Christine Casey, Vincent Comerford, Alan Costello, the late John Crawford, Gordon Crosskey, Frank Cullen, Jessica Cunningham, Ida Delamer, Tom Desmond, David Dickson, Tony Dove, the late Desmond FitzGerald, Knight of Glin, Philippa Glanville, Robert Heslip, Anne Hodge, Peter Kaellgren, Michael Kenny, Ronald Le Bas, Colm Lennon, Simon Lincoln, Anthony Malcomson, Elizabeth Mayes, Patricia McCarthy, Ivar McGrath, Jane Meredith, Tessa Murdoch, the late Conor O'Brien, Michael Potterton, Giorgio Riello, John Rogers, Breda Scott, Timothy Schroder, Elise Taylor, Jane Wainwright, Alex Ward, Beth Wees, Jimmy Weldon, Harry Williams-Bulkeley and Hilary Young.

My students in the History Department at Maynooth University have also contributed to this book with their stimulating questions, which have prompted me to look at familiar material from new perspectives. My immediate and extended family have always provided encouragement and distraction whenever it was needed; thanks in particular to Breda and Christine FitzGerald. John Loughman has lived with this project for as long as I have; to him and to Eva Mai, who was born while I was working on it, my final and most heartfelt thanks.

Figures

Dimensions have been cited as height before width unless specified otherwise. The following abbreviations have been used:

Diameter (diam)
Height (h)
Width (w)

Unless otherwise specified, the silver artefacts illustrated have Dublin hallmarks.

Tables

Note

Silver is weighed in troy weight: in pounds (lb.), ounces (oz.), pennyweights (dwt.) and grains. One pound troy = 12 oz. troy = 240 dwt. troy = 5,760 grains troy.

Prices are in pounds (£), shillings (s), pence (d), sterling.

The term 'plate' is used to describe articles of silver (or gold).

The term 'plated' refers to two or more layers of different metals joined to each other by plating (overlaying a base metal with silver) rather than being fused into a homogenous mass. This includes Sheffield plate: sheet metal made by fusing silver to one or both sides of an ingot of copper and rolled to sheet form.

Sterling silver refers to silver that has a fineness of 92.5 per cent pure silver.

Introduction

In 1758 the redoubtable Irish philanthropist, Lady Arbella Denny (Fig. I.1), went shopping for a silver coffee pot.[1] She was buying on behalf of friends, the pot was to be a wedding gift, and size mattered. In her words, and in no uncertain terms, too small a pot would be 'ungenteel to give'.[2] Denny's letters suggest that cost as well as craftsmanship ultimately dictated what she chose. Having checked prices with three Dublin goldsmiths, she commissioned James Holmes, the goldsmith whose estimate was neither the most nor the least expensive.[3] Buying from a shop offered her a level of customer satisfaction and the opportunity to acquire a piece that was bespoke. This book considers the production and consumption of silverware in eighteenth-century Dublin; the choices made by individuals like Denny and her peers are central to its theme.[4]

During the eighteenth century the term 'goldsmith' was used to describe craftsmen and specialist retailers involved in the manufacture, sale and repair of a wide range of goods made from silver and gold. In the world of artisans it was a trade associated by virtue of its materials and clientele with high status and gentility. Apart from jewellery, most of the objects produced by members of the Dublin goldsmiths' guild during this period were made from silver rather than gold, a pattern dictated primarily by cost. However, the guild, incorporated by Royal Charter in 1637, was called the Company of Goldsmiths of Dublin (Figs. I.2–I.3). It was possible to become a freeman or full member by service, birth or 'grace especial', and freemen included watchmakers, engravers, lapidaries and jewellers, as well as goldsmiths and silversmiths.[5] Of central concern here is the way in which the market functioned for manufacturers, retailers and consumers of silverware, otherwise known as plate. To what extent did the demand for silver objects change over time as a direct result of factors like innovative technology, changing social practice, and competition from new and fashionable commodities like English and continental porcelain or Sheffield plate, each available for the first time in the eighteenth century?[6] How did Dublin's 'second city' status relative to London in the Hanoverian empire affect its silver trade, both in terms of the demand for goods, and the way in which those goods were advertised? Were there differences in how the trade functioned in the two cities, given the fluidity of movement between them, and how keenly was the impact of parliamentary union in 1801 felt by Irish goldsmiths? Basing itself on the period 1714–1837, the book considers the expansion, apogee and ultimate decline of one of Dublin's foremost luxury trades, in a period associated with unprecedented choices available to the consumer.

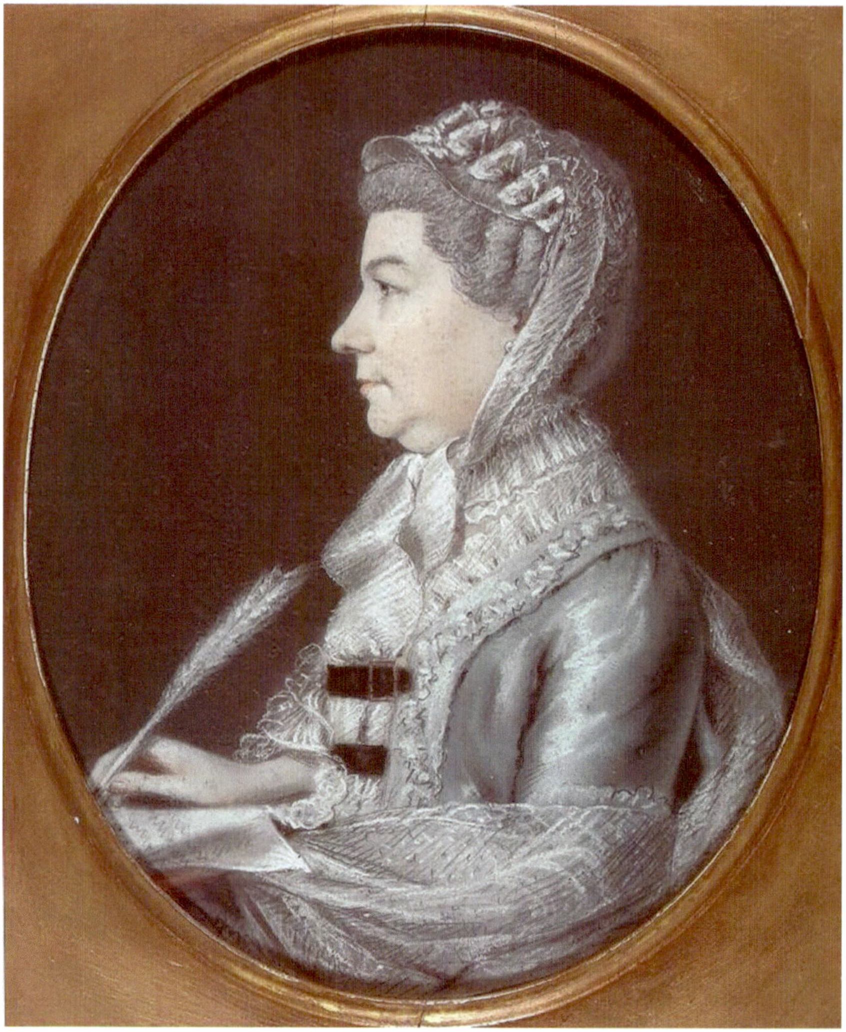

Figure I.1 Hugh Douglas Hamilton, *Portrait of Lady Arbella Denny* (1770s), pastel and graphite on paper, 24 × 19.5 cm

Source: Representative Church Body Library, Dublin. Photo credit: © Representative Church Body Library.

Historiography

A considerable amount has been written on the subject of Irish eighteenth-century silver, mostly focusing on the classification of objects by maker, date, place of origin and style. This emphasis on connoisseurship can be traced back to the nineteenth century, and is paralleled in other branches of early scholarship on the decorative arts in Ireland.[7] The recognition that hallmarks (Fig. I.4) on antique plate might be used as a research tool inspired a series of nineteenth- and early twentieth-century studies dedicated specifically to the collation and classification of maker's marks, hallmarks and date letters.[8]

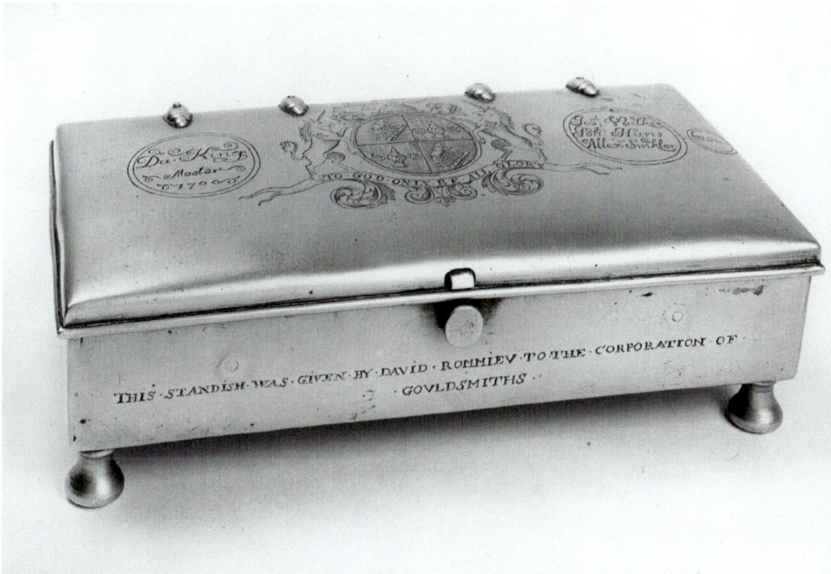

Figure I.2 David Rommieu, *Inkstand engraved with the arms of the Company of Goldsmiths of Dublin* (c.1700), brass, 7 × 24 cm

Source: Company of Goldsmiths of Dublin, Assay Office, Dublin. Photo credit: © Company of Goldsmiths of Dublin.

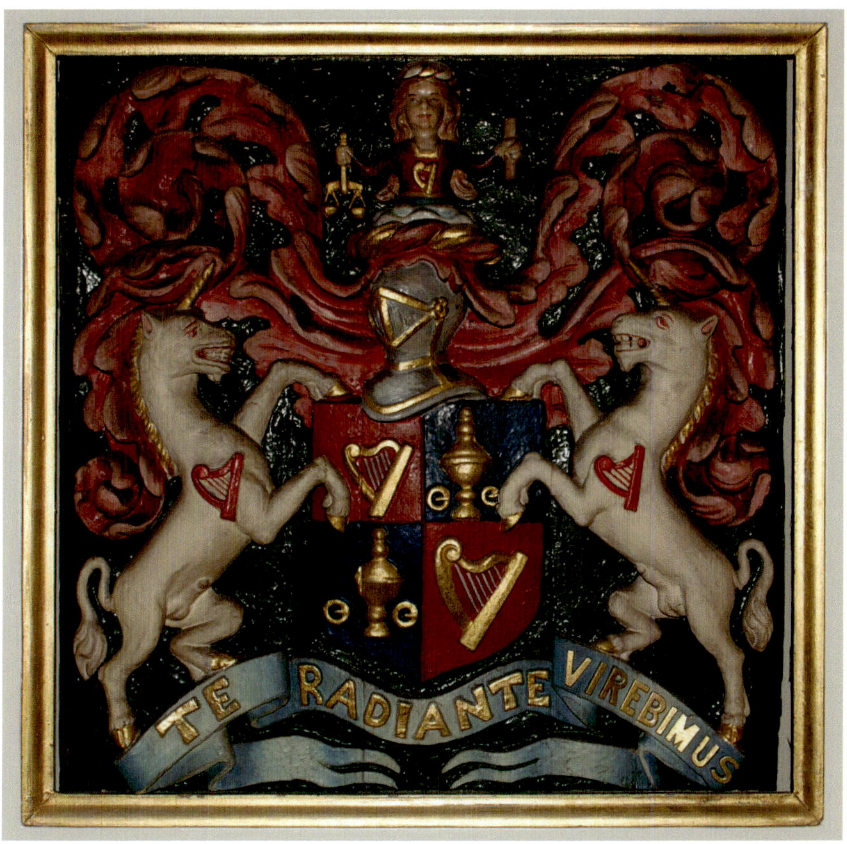

Figure I.3 Armorial of the Company of Goldsmiths of Dublin (n.d.), wood, 45 × 44 cm

Source: Company of Goldsmiths of Dublin, Assay Office, Dublin. Photo credit: © Company of Goldsmiths of Dublin.

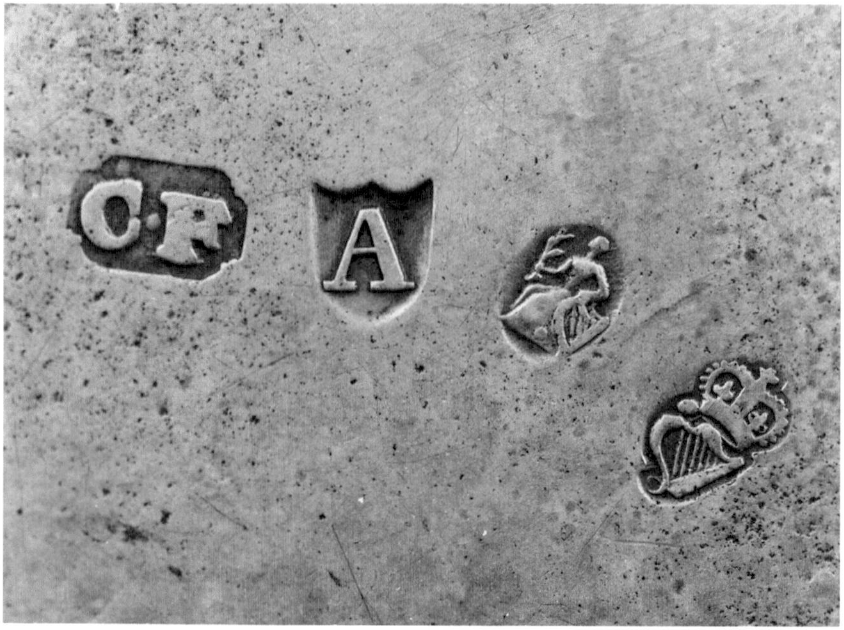

Figure I.4 Catherine Fox, *Hallmarks on the base of a salver* (1773), silver, 40.64 cm diam
Source: National Museum of Ireland, Dublin. Photo credit: © National Museum of Ireland.

In 1881, following a series of comparable publications on English silver, W.D. Waterhouse compiled a table of Dublin date letters for the period from 1638 to 1881.[9] During the decades that followed, a number of articles appeared on the subject of Irish silver, most notably by Robert Day, John Ribton Garstin, Henry Berry and Dudley Westropp.[10] These reflect a shared interest in recording the marks on antique plate, identifying the makers and dating individual objects (Fig. I.5).[11] One of the most significant publications of this kind is Charles Jackson's *English Goldsmiths and Their Marks*, first published in 1905.[12] It remains a key reference source, due to the author's inclusion of extensive lists drawn from the records of the Dublin goldsmiths' guild.[13] Jackson provides the names of apprentices, guild members and office holders within the guild.[14] More recent work by Douglas Bennett also favours a connoisseurship approach. Bennett's monograph, *Irish Georgian Silver*, was the first comprehensive survey on this subject and has been complemented by more recent surveys of Cork and Limerick silver.[15]

The value of connoisseurship as an approach to artefact analysis is indisputable. However, the dominant tendency in such studies has been to consider questions of style and authorship largely independent of other issues.[16] As a result, we know a great deal about the physical appearance of surviving objects, but less about their existence in eighteenth-century Ireland, the circumstances in which they were made and used and the values that led to 'their being constructed, traded, treasured [or] discarded'.[17] This book aims to reconstruct that context. In contrast to the work of Bennett, Jackson and Tony Sweeney, modern research on the London goldsmiths' trade has illuminated networks of subcontracting, reconstructed the physical environment

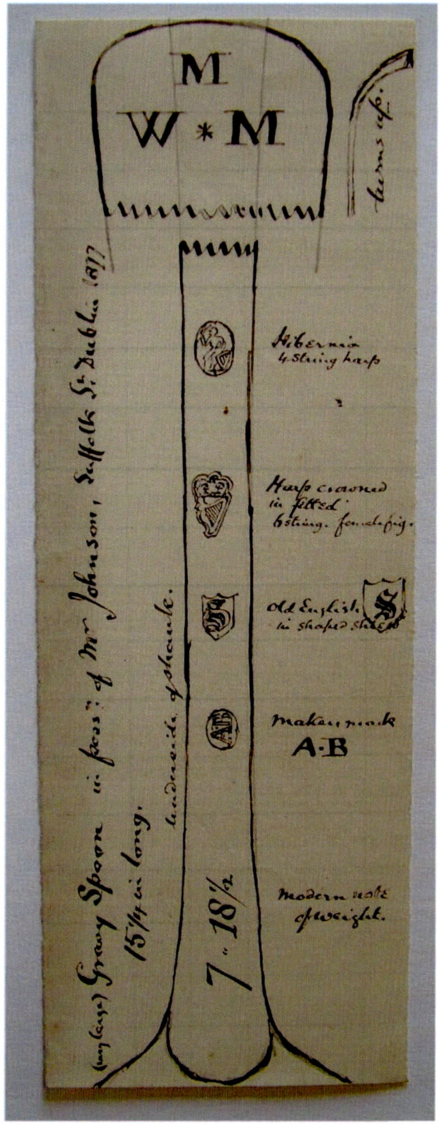

Figure I.5 John Ribton Garstin, *Hallmarks on an Irish silver spoon* (late nineteenth century), drawing, 5.6 × 16.4 cm

Source: Marsh's Library, Dublin. Photo credit: © Marsh's Library.

of goldsmiths' shops and employed Orphans' Court inventories to comment on the level of interaction between English and Huguenot goldsmiths.[18] While these studies do in some cases challenge the assumptions of connoisseurship, ultimately their approaches are complementary. Some articles on Irish eighteenth-century silver adopt a different perspective. Joseph McDonnell's work on the use of ornamental prints considers the avenues through which French designs reached Ireland, the significance of

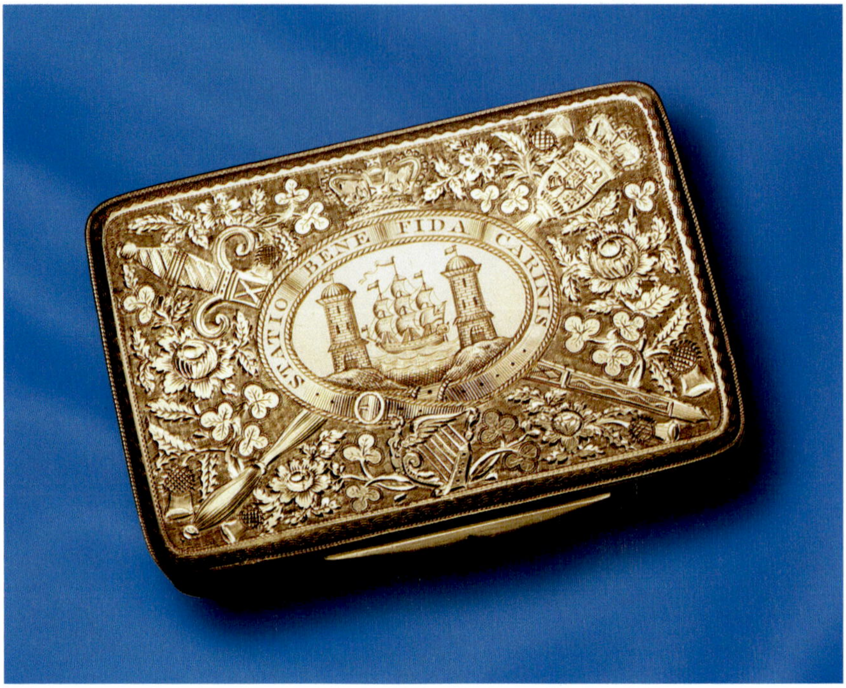

Figure I.6 Carden Terry and Jane Williams, *Freedom box* (Cork, c.1814), 2 (h) × 7 (w) × 4.7 cm diam

Source: Private collection. Photo credit: © John R. Bowen.

prints as design sources and the way in which Parisian designs were disseminated via London.[19] Thomas Sinsteden has demonstrated effectively how Dublin assay records[20] can be used to profile patterns of production, and Fiona Ahern considers the involvement of women in the trade through a case study of the Cork goldsmith Jane Williams (Fig. I.6).[21] The present study, and indeed the wider field of Irish material culture, owes much to Toby Barnard's analysis of the semiotics of objects, 'both everyday and outlandish', in particular in his seminal monograph *Making the Grand Figure: Lives and Possessions in Ireland, 1641–1770.*[22]

The Dublin-London model

The reluctance to interpret Irish goldsmiths' work contextually, and preoccupation with identification, classification and style, are only partly due to the fragmentary nature of primary sources.[23] Historians of English and North American eighteenth-century silver have access to goldsmiths' memoirs, occasional business ledgers, generous caches of trade cards and large numbers of probate inventories.[24] While fewer such sources survive for Dublin, some that do are very revealing. Dublin guild records, for example, can be more detailed for this period than comparable material for London.[25] Some exceptionally comprehensive Dublin assay ledgers survive, itemising individual objects submitted to the guild for hallmarking. These include details that London's

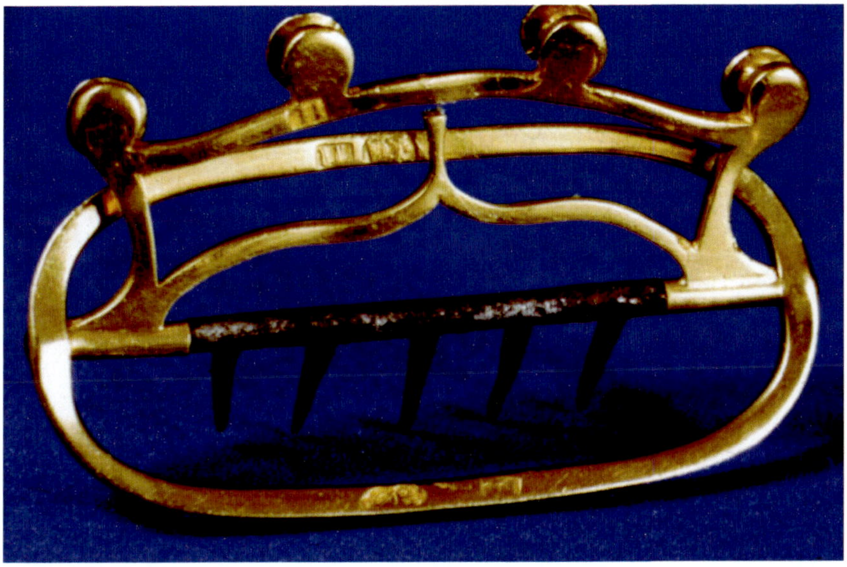

Figure I.7 John Laughlin, *Stock buckle* (c.1765), gold, 2.4 × 5 cm
Source: Private collection. Photo credit: Author's collection.

busier assay office could not have accommodated, since the quantities of goods being hallmarked there were so much greater.[26] They are used in chapters 2 and 5 to profile changes in the market for silver over time. For instance, the fact that over 24,000 buckles were assayed in 1788 (Fig. I.7), but a mere 18 in 1810, illustrates how vulnerable manufacturers could be to fashion's whims. One Dublin retailer employed a smart sales strategy to drum up business and ignite patriotism during this period. In 1784 the goldsmith William Moore advertised in the *Volunteers Journal* that 'at the request of several of his customers', he had 'adopted the following mode':

> A gentleman shall have a new pair of silver buckles every month for 4L 11s per year. – Gentlemen who do not chuse to continue the whole year shall have the first pair changed at the end of the first month for 11s 4½ d., the second for ten shillings, the third for nine, six and so on in proportion.[27]

It is more than a century since Charles Jackson first published lists of apprentice goldsmiths in eighteenth-century Dublin, but what did it mean in social terms to become a goldsmith during this period?[28] How many boys entered the trade over the course of the eighteenth century, and from what sort of backgrounds did they come?[29] Chapter 1 considers the numbers of indentured apprentices and their proportional distribution among established goldsmiths in eighteenth-century Dublin. It also examines the difficulties of setting up in business independently and the costs involved. The minutes of the Wide Streets Commission of Dublin, recording Dublin's urban expansion in the second half of the eighteenth century, offer new evidence on goldsmiths' premises and indicate the varying amounts of capital required to set up shop. For many, this was simply prohibitive.[30] Records of civic and guild admissions are used in chapter 1 to determine the numbers who trained as goldsmiths, yet never became independent masters. For all those who had street-front shops on Dublin's premier thoroughfares, there were others who remained as journeymen.

Irish silver scholarship, with a few exceptions, demonstrates a general insularity. Apart from broad references to European styles, the direct impact of London imports on the Dublin trade has not been thoroughly investigated. This seems remarkable, given the advertising rhetoric of Dublin goldsmiths, the information from customs ledgers and the inclusion of Irish clients in the order books of prominent London firms. All of these sources confirm the availability and desirability of English plate in eighteenth-century Ireland. For instance, in 1742 Joseph Leeson, son of a wealthy Dublin brewer and property developer, ordered a magnificent silver dinner service (Fig. I.8) for Russborough House in Co. Wicklow, the country seat he was building with his father's inheritance. Ambitious for a title, he was keen to surround himself with the trappings of nobility, and few possessions signified old established wealth more than plate. Like many of his Irish contemporaries, Leeson chose to buy in London.[31] This book considers why.

As David Dickson and others have observed, the sobriquet 'second city' was current in eighteenth-century Ireland and was used to characterise Dublin's complex relationship with London.[32] One individual who had spent time in both cities commented in the 1730s that Dublin was 'the largest and most populous city in the imperial dominions of Great Britain, excepting the city of London'.[33] A volume of conference

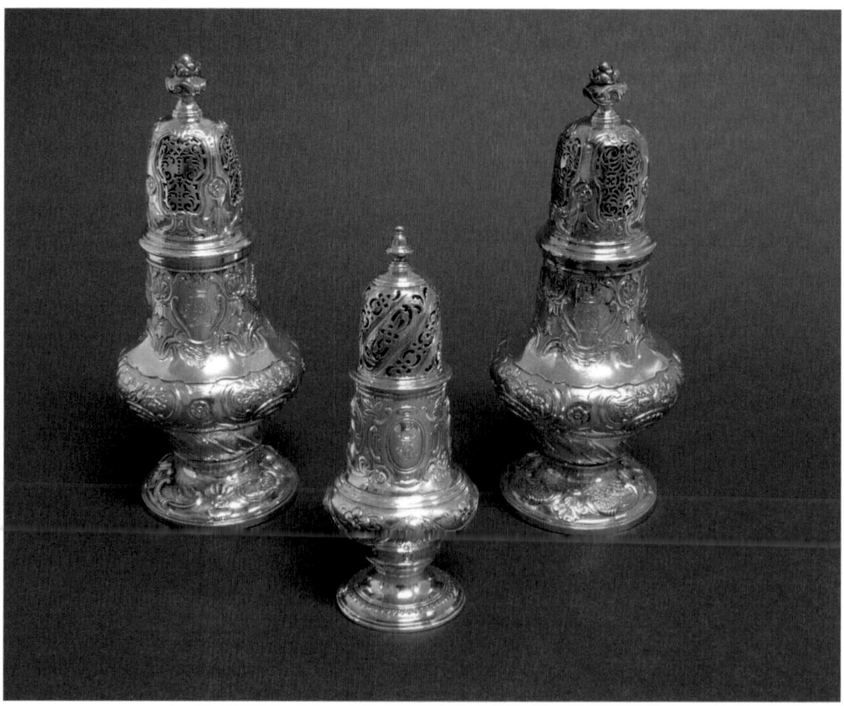

Figure I.8 George Wickes, *Casters*, one later top (London, 1742), silver

Source: National Gallery of Ireland. Photo credit: © Thomas Sinsteden.

proceedings published by the British Academy in 2001 compares the two capitals, demonstrating very effectively how their parallel histories experienced dramatic transformation in the period between 1600 and 1800.[34] From a point of marked divergence in 1600, they evolved in a manner which, by 1800, 'gave them more in common with each other than with other cities and towns in their respective islands'.[35] This circumstance, coupled with the wealth of source material for eighteenth-century London, facilitates the comparison between the goldsmiths' trade in the two capital cities. It also helps to identify patterns of continuity and change in Dublin's precious metals' trade over the course of the long eighteenth century.[36]

The population of Dublin increased from between 15,000 and 20,000 in 1600 to more than 180,000 in 1800. In London the population grew from 200,000 to almost a million during the same period, with the result that by 1800 both ranked among Europe's top ten most populous cities.[37] In the eighteenth century there were multiple parallels between them in terms of the development of cultural and leisure activities, prevalent fashions, learned organisations, and programmes of urban development. The perception that Dublin looked to London as an arbiter of taste and fashion is certainly valid.[38] In the 1730s, George Berkeley, Bishop of Cloyne, asked 'whether London is not to be considered the metropolis of Ireland?'[39] A visitor to Dublin in the 1760s observed how 'well affected to the English' the inhabitants were, noting

> their dress, fashions and diversions are taken from them; and whoever shall carry over any species of popular entertainment from London will be sure to meet with encouragement, if he has but the good fortune to be singular in his profession.[40]

Many of the characteristics that Peter Borsay identifies in arguing for London's cultural authority in an English context were also true of Dublin.[41] These include its gateway function as a port city and national capital, its population and social composition which, as Borsay writes of London, 'constituted a market unique in its size, compactness, complexity, sophistication and affluence'.[42]

Identifying whether the concerns, priorities, and authority of the goldsmiths' guild in Dublin mirrored or deviated from the example of its London counterpart helps us understand the Dublin scene. Comparing apprenticeship premiums in the two cities, profiling the origin of apprentices and considering the cost and difficulties of pursuing the trade confirms the regard in which the profession was held. In terms of production practices the two cities appear to have differed, an inevitable consequence of their vastly different sizes. Modern research on the London trade has discounted the myth of the independent maker credited with Herculean levels of productivity and skill.[43] John Styles and others have argued that the tendency for the division of labour to parallel expansion in the market was an economic reality identified by eighteenth-century commentators like Adam Smith.[44] Helen Clifford's work has shown that the London firm of goldsmiths John Parker and Edward Wakelin employed a network of 75 subcontractors in the period between 1760 and 1776.[45] It cannot be assumed that such extensive subcontracting was the norm in eighteenth-century Dublin, though it was certainly taking place. In the absence of business ledgers for Dublin goldsmiths during this period it is impossible to comment precisely on how their shops were run.[46] The fact that large numbers of objects have survived bearing a single goldsmith's mark, or that certain goldsmiths feature heavily in guild assay records, does not automatically mean that they engaged in subcontracting; extra labour could have been employed in-house, as part of a more traditional workshop model, rather than being outsourced to specialist craftsmen. The physical disparity of the two cities, and scant references to subcontracting in the records of the Dublin goldsmiths' guild, suggests that where it did occur, networks of subcontracting were more limited and less sophisticated than in London.

There were also clear differences when it came to the structure of guild membership in the two capital cities. For instance, in London the charge of quarterage, a levy payable to the guild at three-month intervals, applied only to freemen of the guild.[47] In Ireland quarterage was paid not only by freemen (Fig. I.9), but also by

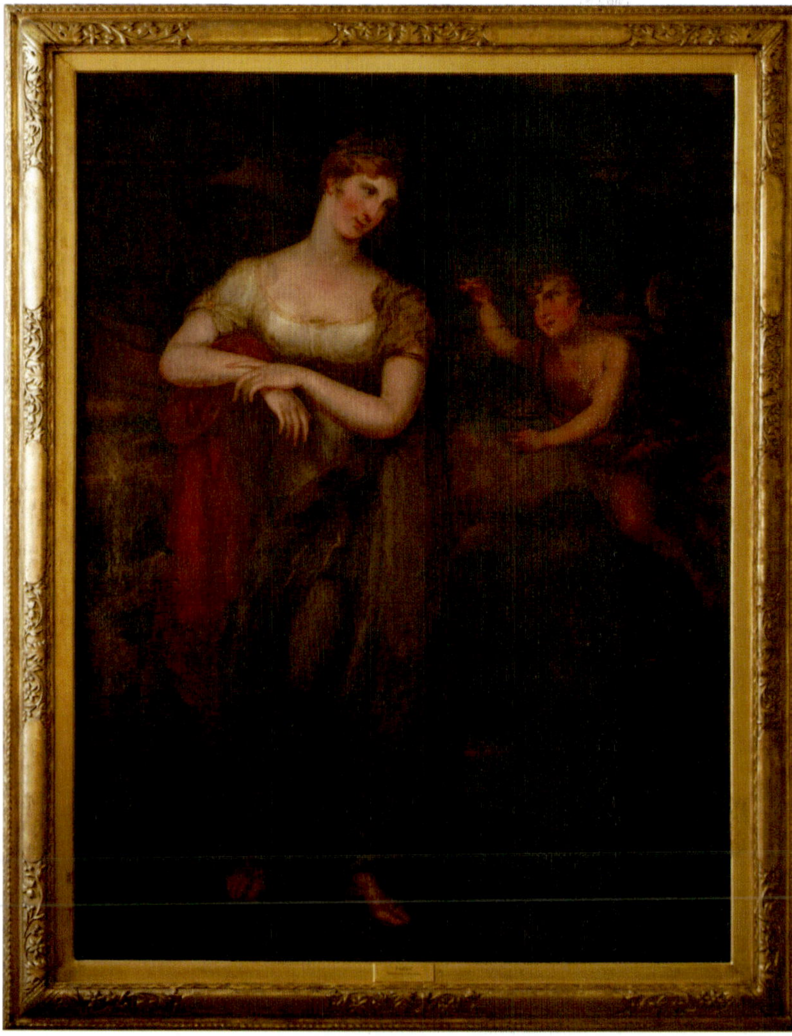

Figure I.9 Solomon Williams, *Justice* (c.1823), oil on canvas, 205 × 148 cm. This painting was presented to the goldsmiths' guild in 1823 by Williams in lieu of long arrears of quarterage owed.

Source: Company of Goldsmiths of Dublin, Assay Office, Dublin. Photo credit: © Company of Goldsmiths of Dublin.

quarter brothers (Fig. I.10), a distinct category of guild members which included Catholics, foreigners who had not been admitted to full guild membership, time-expired apprentices awaiting election as freemen, and others who were eligible to become freemen but chose not to take on the commitments and responsibilities which freedom brought.[48] Catholics were excluded from full membership until the Catholic Relief Act of 1793.[49] The perceived inequalities of the quarterage system, which applied across the Dublin guilds, was highly contentious during the eighteenth century, particularly for Catholics, who paid quarterage without enjoying the full privileges of freemen. For instance, quarter brothers were not technically entitled to keep a retail shop, though some did.[50]

The rapid expansion of Dublin and London during the eighteenth century certainly tested the boundaries of guild authority, making it harder for the goldsmiths' guilds in both capital cities to regulate the trade in a comprehensive and consistent manner. London freemen were permitted to work within the city limits, but the keen pace of urban development meant that significant numbers of craftsmen established themselves 'in holes and corners'[51] outside the boundaries in the West

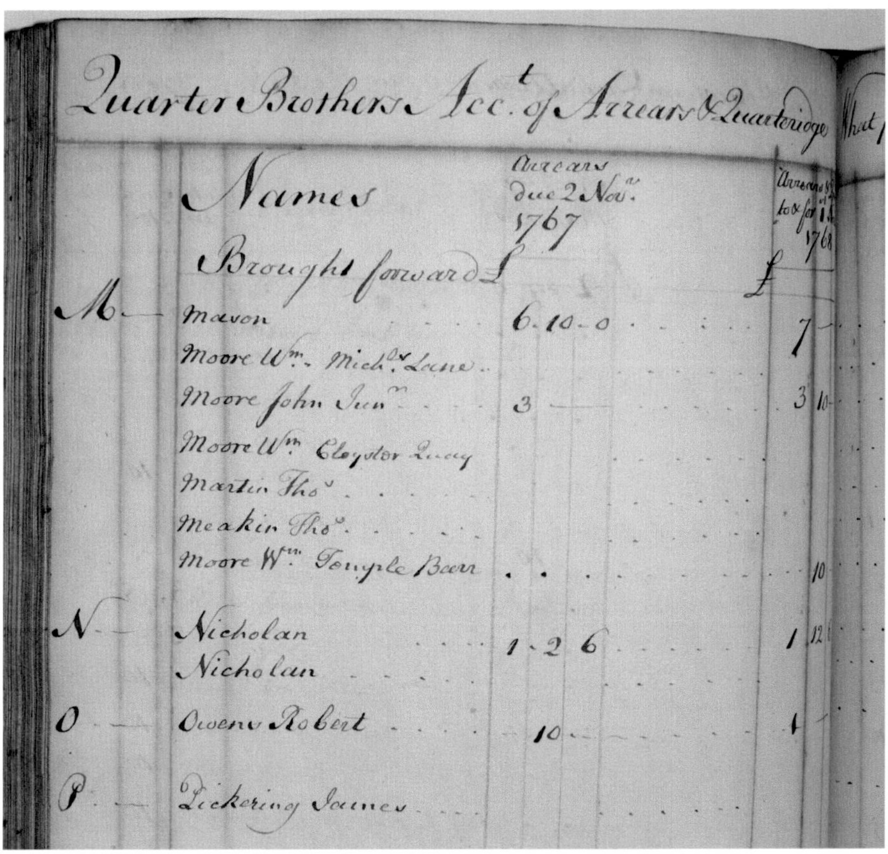

Figure I.10 Account of quarterage in arrears to the Dublin goldsmiths' guild in 1767

Source: Company of Goldsmiths of Dublin, Assay Office, Dublin. Photo credit: © Company of Goldsmiths of Dublin.

End and Westminster, where they could trade without interference from the livery companies.[52] Resentment on the part of indigenous goldsmiths towards immigrant craftsmen, who were often associated with competitive pricing and high standards of craftsmanship, exacerbated this situation. Many of these so-called aliens were highly accomplished, and practised their trades beyond the city limits. The guild's power to search for substandard wares was challenged much earlier in London than in Dublin, which suggests a greater respect for guild authority in Dublin, or at least some reluctance to embrace a free market economy. It was arguably easier to maintain jurisdiction in Dublin where the numbers and territory were smaller.[53] Between 1690 and 1715, eleven craftsmen in London declined to allow searchers into their shops. From 1715 to 1723, the last year in which a search was recorded in guild minutes, there was an average of thirteen refusals there each year.[54] By contrast, in Dublin there is evidence that searches continued throughout the eighteenth and into the nineteenth century.[55]

Despite the challenges that London's size presented when it came to regulating the sale of gold and silver wares, Judy Jowett's research has shown that the London Goldsmiths' Company operated an efficient warning system, where goldsmiths, jewellers, watchmakers, toymen, pawnbrokers and bankers were warned of recent crimes.[56] Warning carriers, operating on behalf of the guild, carried notices of stolen goods to hundreds of addresses across London and this 'ancient and obviously efficient dispersal of information from Goldsmiths' Hall shows how the Company's tentacles reached across London life unlike any other City livery company'.[57]

There is no doubt that guilds in both cities faced acute challenges during this period, as the market became bigger, craftsmen became more numerous and there were more firms that were retailers rather than manufacturers.[58] Nevertheless, it would appear that the Irish guild structure, with its dual membership of quarter brothers and freemen, allowed for a greater degree of control of the trade by the guild than its London counterpart. As Jacqueline Hill has argued, the introduction of the quarter-brother system in Dublin

> is best regarded not as a means of excluding Catholics from trade . . . it was designed to facilitate some degree of guild control over all substantial tradesmen, including Catholics, and it reflected the guilds' ability to adapt to changing conditions.[59]

While the Dublin goldsmiths' guild was prepared to relax or revise regulations gradually, there were areas where it was decidedly conservative. It agreed to allow quarter brothers to take apprentices in the early eighteenth century, but was less flexible when it came to Catholics and their right to full guild privileges.[60] This was part of a wider corporate debate, but it was also particular to the political climate of Ireland, and distinguished the agenda of the Dublin goldsmiths' guild from that of its equivalent in London.

The early minute books of the Dublin guild indicate that, in the late seventeenth century, quarter brothers were forbidden from taking apprentices – a significant drawback. The rules agreed on by the guild in 1667 specify that under no circumstances were quarter brothers allowed to engage apprentices for any length of time. Those inclined to challenge this rule risked a fine.[61] Inevitably, there were people who gambled on the consequences. In 1694, Thomas Parker was fined as a non-freeman for precisely that reason.[62] During the late seventeenth century, quarter brothers of the Dublin goldsmiths' guild were even prevented from employing journeymen, but it became impractical to enforce restrictions like these as the trade and the city expanded.[63] A minute of 1738 states that quarter brothers who kept apprentices or journeymen were obliged to pay a quarterly levy of five shillings.[64] The guild's apprenticeship ledger for the period 1752 to 1823 clearly identifies apprentices who were bound to quarter brothers, demonstrating that in this area, at least, the guild was prepared to rethink, adapt and change.[65]

There was less tolerance when it came to the Catholic question. As Hill has remarked, while 'confessionalism was an aspect of the state throughout the Crown's dominions,' in Ireland 'the minority status of the established Church of Ireland and of Protestants in general gave heightened significance to the confessional issue.'[66] While the London goldsmiths' guild complained about the encroachment of 'foreigners', in Ireland the religious question was more prominent.[67] There were intermittent periods when it came to the fore in guild proceedings. In 1697 the Dublin goldsmiths' guild met to discuss whether any of their members had 'taken to apprentice any person or persons of the popish religion'.[68] This was in the wake of the Treaty of Limerick, the official ending of the Williamite wars in Ireland, when Irish Protestants were incensed by what they regarded as the lenient terms granted to Irish Catholics and at the start of a series of laws seriously restricting Catholic access to education, property and power.[69] The guild decreed that, to prevent 'popish' apprentices gaining skills in their field, none of their brothers should take on Catholic apprentices, nor offer them any training in their specialisations of 'goldsmithing, watch-making or clock-making'.[70]

In Ireland, as the eighteenth century progressed, tensions continued to mount between an increasingly powerful Catholic middle class and a Protestant minority determinedly guarding its rights and privileges. In 1767, seventy years after their predecessors had vowed to exclude Catholics from apprenticeship, members of the goldsmiths' guild voiced concerns on the problem of 'popish' trainees. Guild minutes for 1767 reveal an official attitude of intolerance towards any free brother who trained or 'entertained' a Catholic apprentice.[71] Not only were such members seen to have been endangering the welfare of their guild, but they were also branded as abettors of popery and a bounty was to be paid for exposing and prosecuting them.

To dissuade Protestant quarter brothers from taking on Catholic apprentices, the guild recommended that applicants for guild charity or freedom could be rejected if they did not comply. A decade earlier an unfortunate woman named only as 'the widow Hutton' had been refused assistance when it emerged that she had 'brought a popish priest to her husband as he was dying'.[72]

Relief acts passed by the Irish parliament in 1778 and 1782 restored to Catholics the property rights which penal legislation had denied them. The documentation arising from these acts offers an interesting perspective on the professional profile of the Catholic merchants and traders of Dublin. It would be 1793 before a further relief act admitted Catholics to full guild membership, but the data arising from the earlier acts indicates the extent to which Catholics had advanced in various branches of Dublin trade by the late eighteenth century (and in contrast, the areas in which they were less numerous). Of 1,250 Catholics who took mandatory qualification oaths in the years between 1778 and 1782, only 3 described themselves as goldsmiths, along with a further 4 jewellers.[73] For those who valued guild privilege above religious conviction, conversion offered a potential entrée to the benefits of full guild membership. From the 1760s, converts from Catholicism were exempt from paying an entry fine to the City Corporation.[74] In 1776, John O'Neill petitioned the goldsmiths' guild for freedom.[75] It was agreed that he should be admitted free 'on producing his indentures, and also a certificate of his having conformed to the Protestant religion'.[76]

One of the Catholic goldsmiths and jewellers named in connection with the Catholic Relief Acts of 1778 and 1782 was the goldsmith Michael Cormick (Fig. I.11). He had already accused the guild of bias against Catholic quarter brothers like himself. In 1769, he was summoned before guild officials to account for a substandard silver waiter.[77] The problem arose because the piece had old hallmarks soldered into it in order to avoid the payment of duty.[78] In his defence Cormick claimed that he was being victimised as a quarter brother.[79] While this example emphasises the partisan

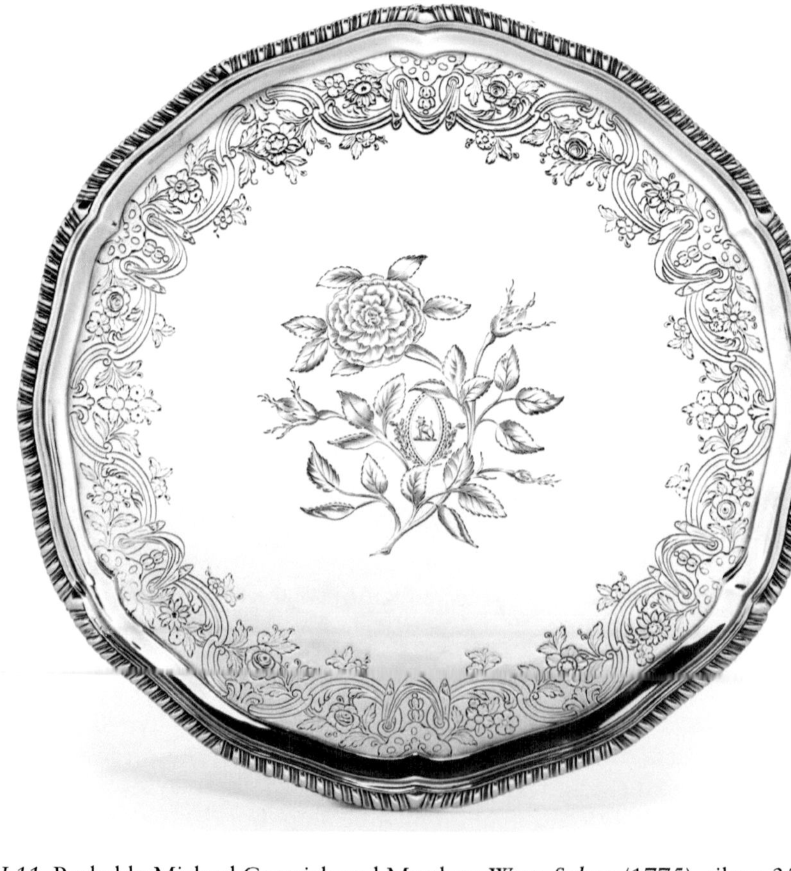

Figure I.11 Probably Michael Cormick and Matthew West, *Salver* (1775), silver, 35.5 cm diam
Photo credit: © Bonham's, London.

character of guild politics in eighteenth-century Dublin, the fact that Cormick may have pleaded religious discrimination in order to get himself out of an awkward situation cannot be discounted. Differing membership structures and confessional agendas may have distinguished the goldsmiths' trade in Dublin from its counterpart in London, but when it came to denying responsibility for substandard wares, claiming innocence and employing persuasive arguments to avoid costly fines, goldsmiths in both cities had much in common.[80]

Twenty-five years after the Relief Act of 1793 admitted Catholics to full guild membership, at least in law, the Dublin goldsmiths' firm James Henderson and Co. advertised themselves as goldsmiths 'to the Roman Catholics of Ireland'.[81] Henderson's, a firm of watchmakers, goldsmiths, jewellers and refiners, offered English stock for sale at 'very reduced prices', as well as a range of 'Irish manufactured watches, silver and jewellery'.[82] The firm's advertisement concludes by informing the public that Henderson's 'did not belong to the goldsmiths' or any other Corporation', and that, 'his partner being a Catholic', was 'consequently excluded'.[83] Evidently, despite changes to the wider context of civic politics, the goldsmiths' guild was slow to admit Catholics. Henderson's employees included 'artists highly gifted in ornamental and stained glass'. Clearly, he believed that targeting the Catholic constituency was strategically astute. By 1833, when guilds were required to return the number of Catholics admitted to guild offices, the goldsmiths' guild responded that none had been admitted free by birth or service and none had applied.[84]

A number of authors have focused on the shared material culture which bound the constituent parts of the British Atlantic world, reinforcing ties that extended beyond language and administration.[85] Aside from the flow of commodities between and within these units, the geographical proximity of Dublin to London facilitated the migration of workers and the dissemination of patterns and ideas; considering Dublin's luxury goods trade in isolation obscures these important connections. A study of the Waterford glass trade in the early nineteenth century challenges the received view of 'Irish craftsmen, creating Irish objects in a style which was distinctively Irish'.[86] This book does not dispute that national inflections can be found in Irish Georgian silver.[87] These include the lively and somewhat naive depictions of rural life which were found on Irish plate in the latter half of the eighteenth century. A sugar bowl of c.1770 (Fig. I.12) by the Dublin goldsmith Matthew West typifies this kind of chasing. Three-legged sugar bowls, like this one, and other forms such as the dish ring (Fig. I.13), though not unique to Irish eighteenth-century silver, were particularly associated with it.[88]

Nevertheless, it is essential to consider the impact of London taste on Irish consumers. In 1772, the Dublin jeweller Isaac Isaacs advertised goods of 'the very first and newest fashion'.[89] They had been made in London 'under the inspection' of his own father, whom he claimed was 'one of the principal manufacturers there in that way'. Late eighteenth-century handbills for the goldsmith John Ash of Capel Street in Dublin (Fig. I.14) advertise an extensive list of products received from his partner in London. Ash claimed they could only be sold for ready money, on account of his articles of partnership.[90] His contemporary, Ann Cormick, advertised an impressive stock of plate and specified that a London contact had been supplying her with drawings.[91]

When it came to the thorny issue of national identity, rather than seeking to distinguish their work on aesthetic grounds from that of their British counterparts, Irish goldsmiths and jewellers generally allied themselves with wider metropolitan

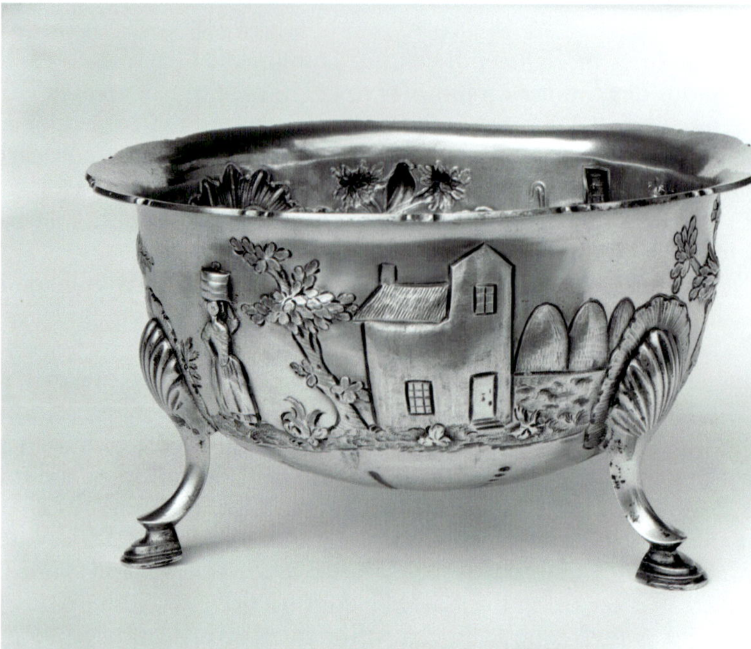

Figure I.12 Matthew West, *Three-legged sugar bowl* (c.1770), silver, 13.3 cm diam
Source: National Museum of Ireland, Dublin. Photo credit: © National Museum of Ireland.

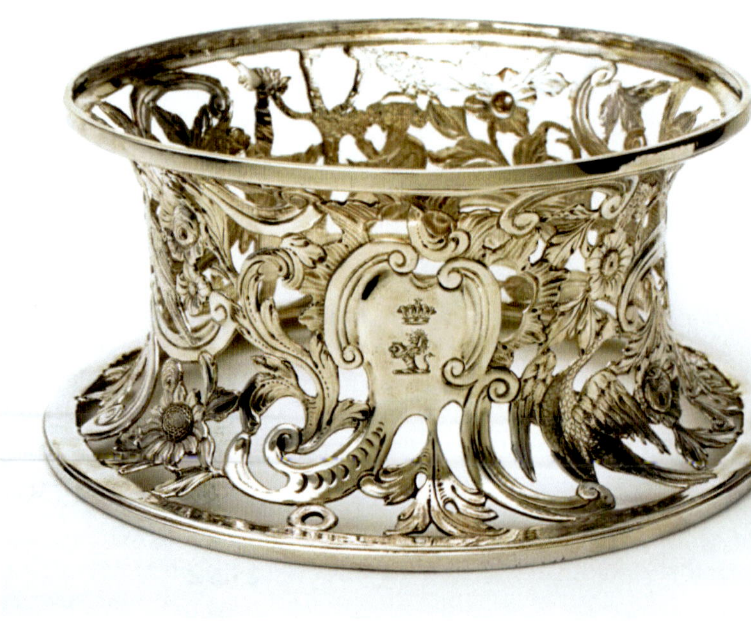

Figure I.13 Christopher Haines, *Dish ring* (1771), silver, 19 cm diam
Source: National Museum of Ireland, Dublin. Photo credit: © National Museum of Ireland.

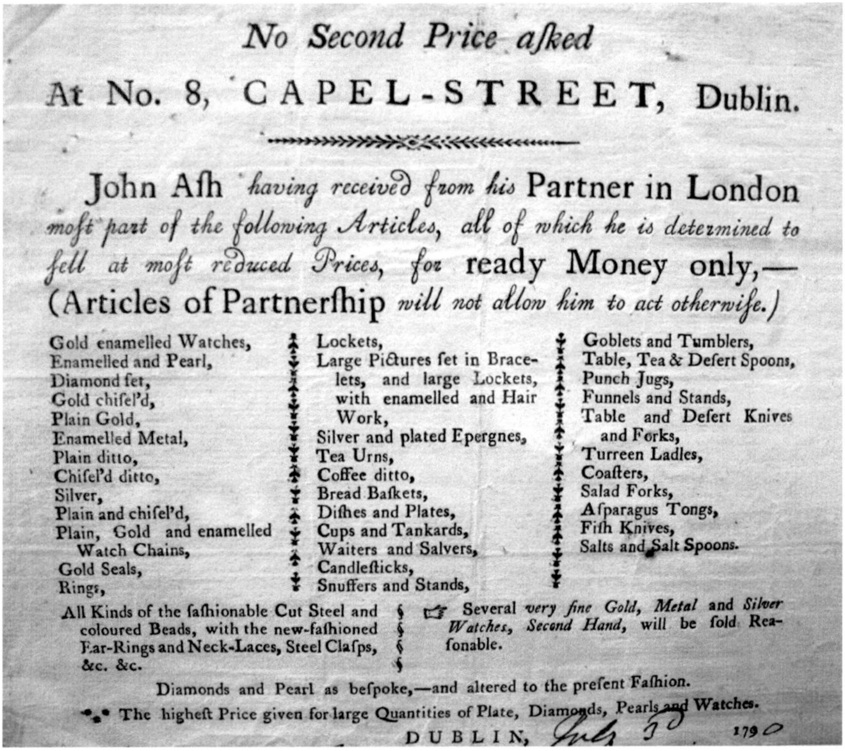

No Second Price aſked

At No. 8, CAPEL-STREET, Dublin.

John Aſh *having received from his* Partner in London *moſt part of the following Articles, all of which he is determined to ſell at moſt reduced Prices, for* ready Money only,—(Articles of Partnerſhip *will not allow him to act otherwiſe.)*

Gold enamelled Watches,
Enamelled and Pearl,
Diamond ſet,
Gold chiſel'd,
Plain Gold,
Enamelled Metal,
Plain ditto,
Chiſel'd ditto,
Silver,
Plain and chiſel'd,
Plain, Gold and enamelled Watch Chains,
Gold Seals,
Rings,

Lockets,
Large Pictures ſet in Bracelets, and large Lockets, with enamelled and Hair Work,
Silver and plated Epergnes,
Tea Urns,
Coffee ditto,
Bread Baſkets,
Diſhes and Plates,
Cups and Tankards,
Waiters and Salvers,
Candleſticks,
Snuffers and Stands,

Goblets and Tumblers,
Table, Tea & Deſert Spoons,
Punch Jugs,
Funnels and Stands,
Table and Deſert Knives and Forks,
Turreen Ladles,
Coaſters,
Salad Forks,
Aſparagus Tongs,
Fiſh Knives,
Salts and Salt Spoons.

All Kinds of the faſhionable Cut Steel and coloured Beads, with the new-faſhioned Ear-Rings and Neck-Laces, Steel Claſps, &c. &c.

☞ Several *very fine Gold, Metal* and *Silver Watches, Second Hand,* will be ſold Reaſonable.

Diamonds and Pearl as beſpoke,—and altered to the preſent Faſhion.

⁂ The higheſt Price given for large Quantities of Plate, Diamonds, Pearls and Watches.

DUBLIN, *July 30* 1790

Figure I.14 Handbill for John Ash (1790), engraving, 15.5 × 19.5 cm

Source: National Library of Ireland, Dublin. Photo credit: © National Library of Ireland.

developments. If not touting imported stock, retailers claimed that their wares were 'as good as', rather than better than, what London, or England, could offer. Patriotic rhetoric, when used by members of the goldsmiths' trade, generally reflected economic concerns rather than any claim to novelty.[92] Craftsmen, retailers and patrons moved readily across the Irish Sea. The correspondence of Birmingham metal baron Matthew Boulton (Fig. I.15) reveals how Benjamin Henfrey, an entrepreneur from provincial England, with a background in japanning,[93] became Boulton's Dublin agent in the 1780s.[94] Writing to Ann Cormick, who had advertised her English contacts in the *Volunteers Journal*, Boulton confirmed in March 1783 that an order for candlesticks had been dispatched. Ever the salesman, he assured Cormick that, should further items be needed, 'Mr Henfrey has a set of my patterns which he will of course shew you.'[95] Boulton identified Ireland as a prime market for his silverwares, not just on account of its geographical proximity, but also because the same sterling standard was in use there – Ireland was doubly convenient to such an entrepreneur.[96] Indeed, he had to remind one Dublin goldsmith to return drawings or patterns forwarded to facilitate an order. In 1777, he wrote to James Hewitt, a goldsmith and jeweller with a shop on College Green: 'When the designs are done with we should be grateful to have them carefully returned as they are expensive drawings.'[97]

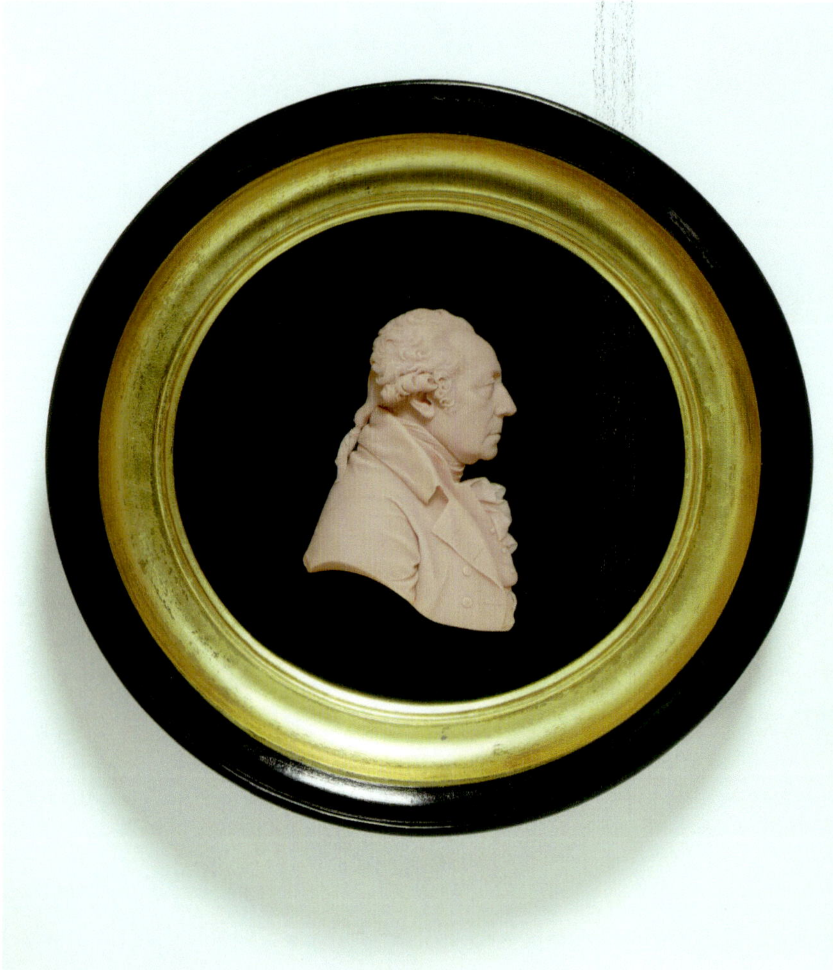

Figure I.15 Peter Rowe, *Portrait of Matthew Boulton* (1814), wax, 37 cm diam

Source: V&A, London. Given by Charles Vine. Photo credit: © V&A.

The example of Boulton also raises the question of new technology in the eighteenth century. In the second half of the century, London's pre-eminent position in the supply of precious metalwork came under pressure from the progressive and commercially aggressive industrial districts of Birmingham and Sheffield.[98] These cities and, in particular, entrepreneurs like Boulton, were producing plated wares like Sheffield plate, a copper core sandwiched between thin layers of silver (Fig. I.16), at a fraction of the cost of sterling silver. As Helen Clifford has noted:

> In terms of design, size, texture, reflective quality and visual impact Sheffield plate came up to the same standards as sterling silver, but at between twenty and thirty per cent of the cost, depending on the strength of the plating.[99]

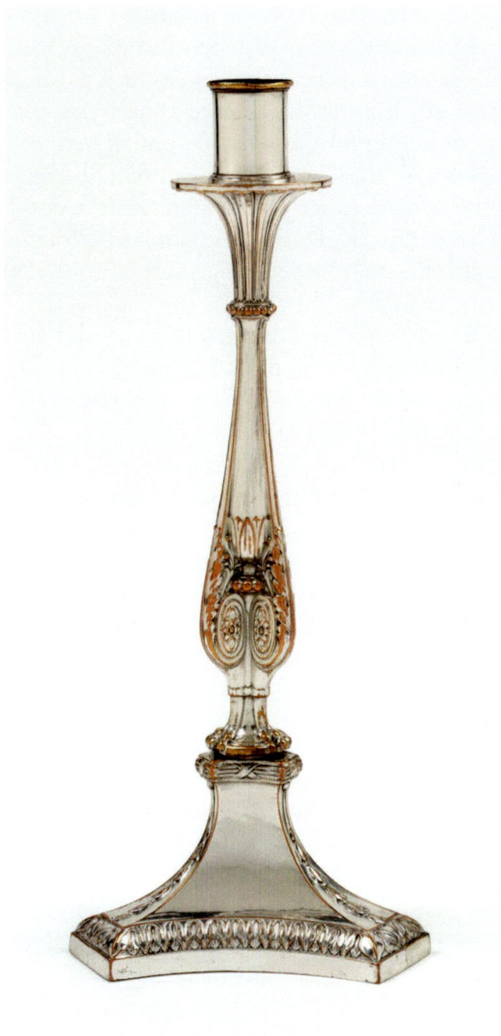

Figure I.16 Matthew Boulton, *Candlestick* (Sheffield, c.1770–75), Sheffield plate, 32.3 × 13.2 cm
Source: V&A, London. Photo credit: © V&A.

This development had important implications for goldsmiths in Dublin as well as in London. How quickly did Dublin goldsmiths respond to this innovative technology and where did the impetus come from? The existing literature on Irish silver refers only fleetingly to the (largely negative) effects of industrialisation. Matthew Boulton's correspondence clearly indicates that a number of Dublin retailers were benefiting from the sale of his wares. Some, like Jeremiah D'Olier, William Moore and Thomas Craig, were members of the Dublin goldsmiths' guild, and a primary function of guilds was to protect the interests of its members. Yet, as markets expanded, increased separation between those who were specialist retailers and those who made a living as manufacturing craftsmen was inevitable. So too, were tensions within the trade.

The danger with emphasising the convergence and divergence between Dublin and London is that, while their relationship was crucial, it was simply not a case of comparing like with like. Indeed, it could be argued that a city like Edinburgh or Philadelphia might offer a more fitting measure for Dublin. There are useful parallels to be drawn between the goldsmiths' trade in Dublin and North American cities like Boston and Philadelphia. Each reflects their peripheral status relative to London, the perceived locus of high fashion. Goldsmiths in Dublin, Boston and Philadelphia referenced London in newspaper advertisements, emphasising their connections with the metropolis while simultaneously entreating customers to shop locally. The reasons why London goldsmiths largely rejected newspaper advertising as a sales strategy while their Irish and American peers did not will be examined in chapter 4. Overall, for the reasons articulated previously, coupled with the wealth of material available, London provides the most useful model of comparison.

Nevertheless, the problematic status of 'second city' raises other issues. As cultural historians and decorative arts scholars have agreed, London was not the only point of reference for Dublin fashions.[100] Travel, printed designs and objects themselves served as conduits for the introduction of French taste, even if it was often mediated via London. For example, in 1745 the London goldsmith George Wickes supplied the Earl of Kildare with a magnificent pair of candelabra.[101] Modelled on copies first made by the Parisian goldsmith Thomas Germain, they were expensive; the high cost of making (10s per oz.) reflected the complicated casting and skilled chasing involved.[102]

While the Paris connection is not central to this account, it is still worth commenting upon briefly in this introduction, principally for what it emphasises about the London-Dublin dialogue. In a stimulating analysis of shopping in eighteenth-century Dublin, Sarah Foster proposes that 'Paris was regarded as superior to London in matters of fashion.'[103] One Dublin heiress is described evocatively as 'smoaking hot with fashion and elegance from Paris', while in 1790 the clerk of Derby's London shop lamented the trend among Irish ceramic dealers to buy in France.[104] However, in terms of the goldsmiths' trade, certain key points should be qualified. Customs ledgers, recording foreign goods exported from London and the outports to Dublin between 1700 and 1780, reveal that the trade in 'foreign' as opposed to English plate was negligible.[105] In an overwhelming majority of years, no 'foreign' plate is recorded in the export ledgers, though admittedly this does not take account of plate which could have been exported directly from France to Dublin.[106] A number of factors favoured London above Paris in terms of the physical acquisition of plate, even if continental taste was reflected in the design. For instance, many of those who were in a position to look beyond Dublin for their purchases had relatives or connections in London, or professional, convivial, family, or restorative excuses for travelling to England. Reasons for travelling to France were more limited and involved additional costs and effort. However, for retailers specialising in jewellery, which was more portable than plate, Paris was certainly more viable. One Dublin print dealer in the mid-eighteenth century highlighted the potential costs of shopping abroad. 'Mr Griffith' claimed that his French engravings 'on the best French paper' were 'as cheap as in Paris, adding the duty in London, coming that way'.[107] In a reversal of the more usual trajectory of Franco-Irish influence, the Dubliner Edward Duras became a successful manufacturer of luxury wallpapers in late eighteenth-century Bordeaux. He was enraged when an employee stole his designs, claiming that he had been robbed of 'the work of his imagination, his talents and his secrets'.[108]

Some Irish goldsmiths referred to Paris in their advertisements, seeking to emphasise their links with fashionable markets.[109] In 1791, the Dublin goldsmith and jeweller Edward Rice (Fig. I.17) advertised that his intention was to visit 'both London and Paris', and equip 'himself with the most elegant patterns in his line, that either metropolis' could produce.[110] His shop on Dublin's Capel Street (Fig. I.18), a popular location for jewellers, stocked an impressive array of diamonds, plate and

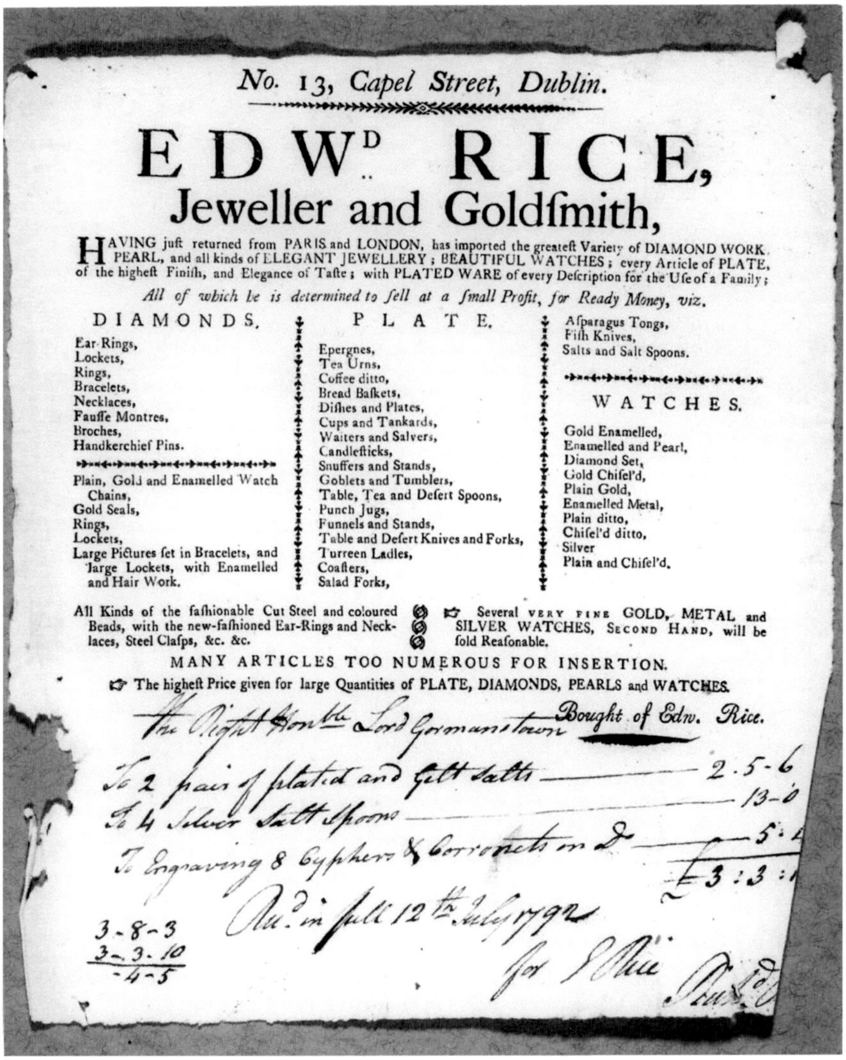
No. 13, *Capel Street, Dublin.*

EDW^{D}. RICE,

Jeweller and Goldſmith,

HAVING juſt returned from PARIS and LONDON, has imported the greateſt Variety of DIAMOND WORK, PEARL, and all kinds of ELEGANT JEWELLERY; BEAUTIFUL WATCHES; every Article of PLATE, of the higheſt Finiſh, and Elegance of Taſte; with PLATED WARE of every Deſcription for the Uſe of a Family;

All of which he is determined to ſell at a ſmall Profit, for Ready Money, viz.

DIAMONDS.
Ear-Rings,
Lockets,
Rings,
Bracelets,
Necklaces,
Fauſſe Montres,
Broches,
Handkerchief Pins.

Plain, Gold and Enamelled Watch Chains,
Gold Seals,
Rings,
Lockets,
Large Pictures ſet in Bracelets, and large Lockets, with Enamelled and Hair Work.

PLATE.
Epergnes,
Tea Urns,
Coffee ditto,
Bread Baſkets,
Diſhes and Plates,
Cups and Tankards,
Waiters and Salvers,
Candleſticks,
Snuffers and Stands,
Goblets and Tumblers,
Table, Tea and Deſert Spoons,
Punch Jugs,
Funnels and Stands,
Table and Deſert Knives and Forks,
Turreen Ladles,
Coaſters,
Salad Forks,
Aſparagus Tongs,
Fiſh Knives,
Salts and Salt Spoons.

WATCHES.
Gold Enamelled,
Enamelled and Pearl,
Diamond Set,
Gold Chiſel'd,
Plain Gold,
Enamelled Metal,
Plain ditto,
Chiſel'd ditto,
Silver
Plain and Chiſel'd.

All Kinds of the faſhionable Cut Steel and coloured Beads, with the new-faſhioned Ear-Rings and Necklaces, Steel Claſps, &c. &c.

☞ Several VERY FINE GOLD, METAL and SILVER WATCHES, SECOND HAND, will be ſold Reaſonable.

MANY ARTICLES TOO NUMEROUS FOR INSERTION.

☞ The higheſt Price given for large Quantities of PLATE, DIAMONDS, PEARLS and WATCHES.

Bought of Edw. Rice.

Figure I.17 Billhead of the Dublin goldsmith and jeweller, Edward Rice (late eighteenth century), engraving

Source: National Library of Ireland, Dublin. Photo credit: © National Library of Ireland.

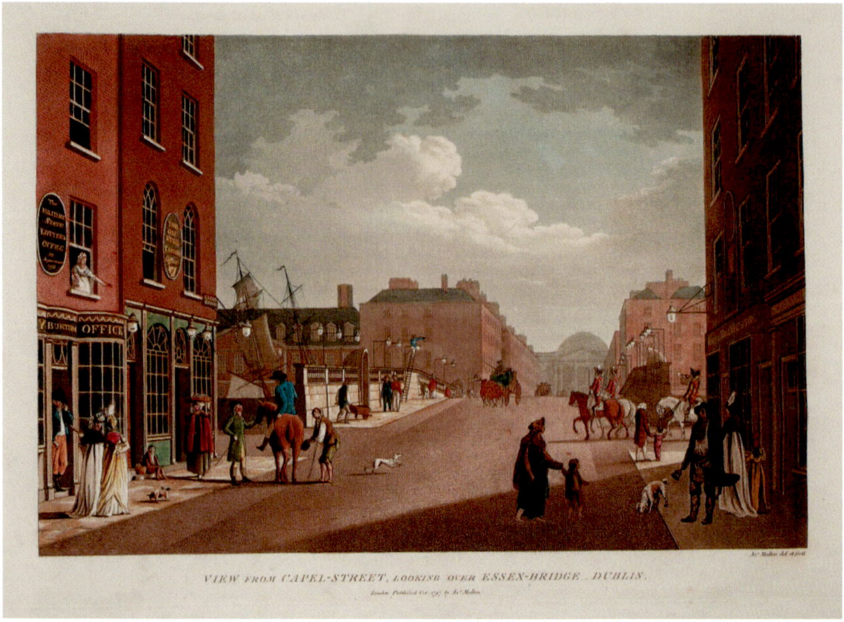

Figure I.18 James Malton, *View of Capel Street, Dublin* (1797), aquatint, 26.1 × 38.3 cm
Source: National Library of Ireland, Dublin. Photo credit: © National Library of Ireland.

watches. Some years earlier, the Cork goldsmith John Christian advertised his credentials with the résumé that he had 'wrought a considerable time in Paris, London, and Dublin'.[111]

Several factors encouraged the dissemination of French taste in Ireland, like the drawing schools of the Dublin Society, the circulation of printed designs and the migration of Huguenot craftsmen from France after the Revocation of the Edict of Nantes in 1685.[112] Joan Evans traced seventy-eight men with Huguenot names who were working as goldsmiths and jewellers in Dublin between 1710 and 1780; more recently Jessica Cunningham has made a detailed study of Dublin's Huguenot goldsmiths.[113] In the early eighteenth century, the Irish patron, Oliver St George, an assiduous purchaser of plate with a bias in favour of Huguenot goldsmiths, noted in his accounts plate obtained from the 'French man', the goldsmith David Willaume.[114] Unquestionably, French influence was reflected in Dublin silver during the eighteenth century. A pair of mid-century sauceboats (Fig. I.19), bearing the mark of the Dublin goldsmith John Hamilton, typifies many comparable examples mirroring French forms.[115] Nevertheless, the fact that similar forms are found in the work of London Huguenots Paul Crespin and Nicolas Sprimont (Fig. I.20) underscores the difficulties with determining, in the absence of concrete evidence, whether ceramics, metalwork or print served as the design catalyst for individual items of plate.

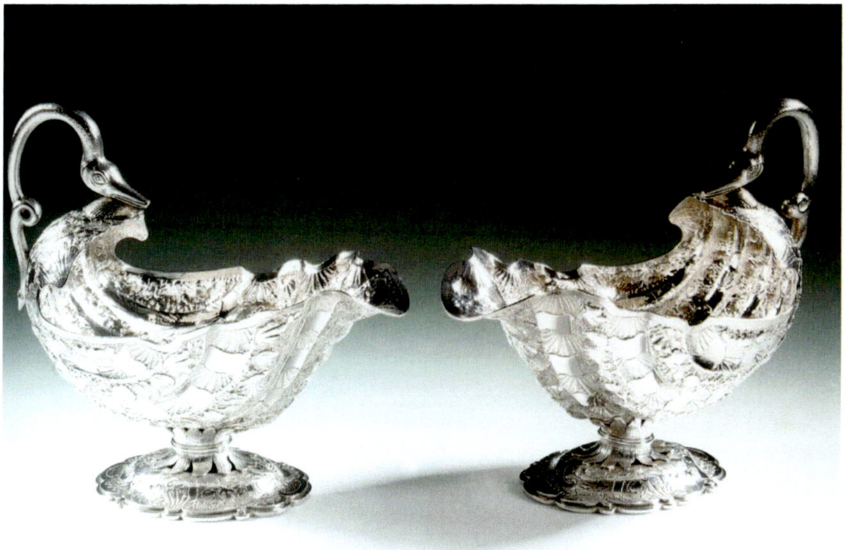

Figure I.19 John Hamilton, *Pair of sauceboats* (mid-eighteenth century), silver, 22 cm (w)
Photo credit: © Sotheby's London.

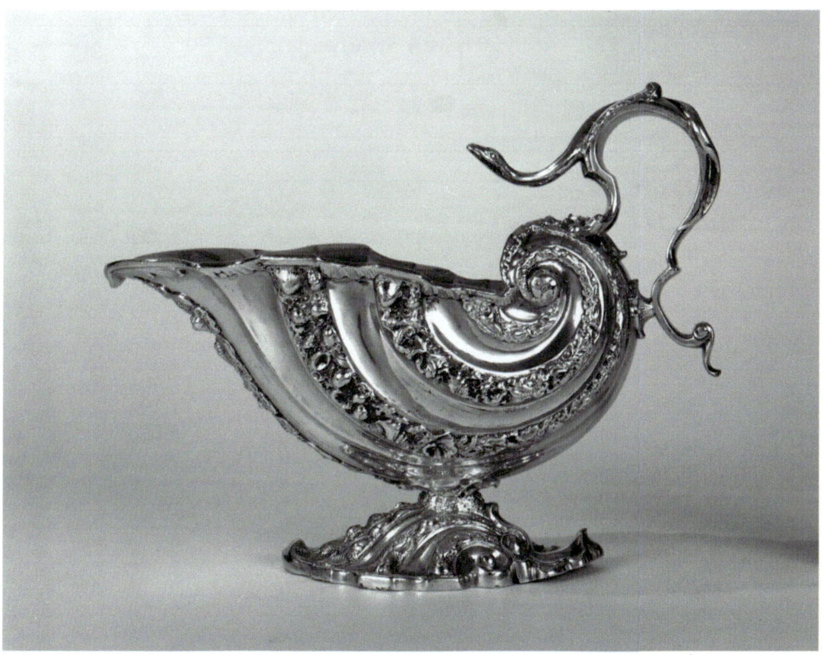

Figure I.20 Attributed to Nicholas Sprimont, *One of a pair of sauceboats, stands and ladles* (London, c.1746), silver, 17.3 × 21.4 cm
Source: V&A, London. Photo credit: © V&A.

Structure

Having set out broadly the focus of the book, it remains to expand on its structure. Chapter 1 is the first of two chapters focusing on production. It considers the various markets which Dublin goldsmiths were obliged to negotiate in establishing their businesses. These included taking on journeymen and sourcing raw materials, securing premises and surviving in a competitive and increasingly crowded market. While goldsmiths in London, Philadelphia and Dublin had the same problems, this study focuses specifically on the influences exerted over the Dublin trade by institutional forces like the guild, by parliamentary legislation and by the patriotic efforts of the Dublin Society which endeavoured to support native industry.

The places of origin, parentage and numbers of apprentices registered by the guild between 1700 and 1800 are examined. The limitations of this evidence have also been tested to reveal the circumstances of individuals who clearly operated within the trade, but did not appear in these official records. These range from the cases of negligent goldsmiths like Roger Finch, Thomas Walsh and Samuel Teare (Fig. I.21), who failed to alert the guild when they took their sons as apprentices,[116] to those who saw retail opportunities in the trade and purchased guild freedom, rather than becoming free 'by service'.[117] The guild minute books provide glimpses of a silver underworld of thefts and fraud. Inevitably, there were those who were not just lax but who knowingly broke the rules. For each of these cases, recorded in guild minutes, there must have been others whose actions went unchecked.

The Dublin apprenticeship records are remarkably rich. There is no comparably detailed information for charting apprenticeship enrolments in London. However, it is possible to identify points of similarity and difference between workshop practices in the two capitals.[118] Although goldsmiths' guilds in both cities encountered difficulties

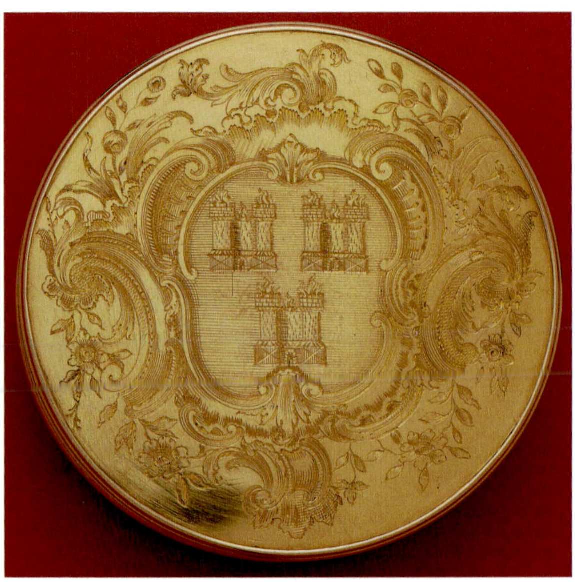

Figure I.21 Samuel Teare, *Freedom box* (c.1759), gold, 7 cm diam

Source: Royal Ontario Museum, Toronto. Photo credit: With permission of the Royal Ontario Museum © ROM.

in their efforts to regulate trade, as their physical environments expanded and production levels increased, the distinctive structure of Dublin guild membership and smaller scale of the Dublin market arguably facilitated a greater degree of corporate control. The practical repercussions of this difference may be demonstrated by the fact that the breakdown of guild control appears to have come later in Dublin than in London. Recent research of guilds in a European context contends that in the pre-industrial period, rather than obstructing economic progress, guilds in fact fostered technological and product innovation.[119] Chapter 2 considers this thesis in the context of the Dublin goldsmiths' guild.

Research on the London trade has used probate inventories to examine the contents of London goldsmiths' shops. Comparable information is not available for Dublin.[120] A notable exception in the broader area of retail history is Sarah Foster's work, which illuminates the experience of shopping in eighteenth-century Dublin.[121] Building on Foster's work, this book provides new information on the market for goldsmiths' premises, using the minutes of the Wide Streets Commission.[122] Appointed in 1758, the Commissioners had the task of investigating the best method for opening the avenue from Essex Bridge to Dublin Castle, in order to relieve traffic congestion in the city. The documented responses of local tenants, including goldsmiths, provides good evidence regarding the cost of leasing premises in the city and the consequences of securing or losing a prime location.

Equally, the ability to procure silver and other metals was crucial and not necessarily straightforward. The various sources and strategies used by goldsmiths to obtain the materials of their trade will be examined. Many advertised their demand in Dublin newspapers. In 1753, Joseph Cullen, who had recently opened a business in Skinner Row, stated that he was prepared to give 'the highest prices for bullion, old gold, and silver and all things'.[123] Later in the century, a jeweller was imprisoned, 'charged with buying and melting down the plate and rings' recently stolen from a competitor's shop.[124]

Finally, newspaper evidence from Dublin and provincial papers will be used to consider the phenomenon of retail diversification. What prompted individuals involved in such a specialised branch of luxury retailing to double-up or diversify, as purveyors of mustard, razor powder, coffin ornaments or hats? In a sector noted for exclusivity, could this sort of diversification enhance or dilute the shopping experience? Matthew Boulton had addressed this question in correspondence with the architect Robert Adam, contrasting modes of display in Paris and London: 'The great customers for plate are such as are not to be caught by shew as they walk along the street and you know that unprivate shops are only customary in London, for at Paris all their finest shops are upstairs.'[125] 'Unprivate' shops were certainly customary in Dublin too, and goldsmiths operated street-level shops on some of Dublin's finest thoroughfares.

With the scene set in chapter 1, chapter 2 deals with the production of silverware in eighteenth-century Dublin. Bert De Munck has argued in relation to early modern hallmarks that 'guild officials used marks to link the privileged status of the manufacturer to the quality of the product.'[126] One of the issues explored here is how the Dublin goldsmiths' guild interpreted its role as a quality regulator. The apparent decline in the requirement and regulation of masterpieces (pieces completed at the end of terms of apprenticeship as proof of technical facility) is counterpointed with the guild's firm opposition to petitions for a provincial assay office in Cork. Here, the unsuccessful attempt by the London goldsmiths' guild to block new assay offices in Birmingham and Sheffield offers a useful model of comparison for Dublin, which managed to maintain its assaying monopoly, despite intermittent lobbying from goldsmiths in Cork.[127]

John Forbes has used English assay books to chart fluctuations in the volume of plate assayed in London. However, it is not possible to determine from the London ledgers the extent of demand for particular types of goods, or the types of goods that individual goldsmiths were entering.[128] As analyses of British household goods for this period have shown, there is a value to mapping the profile of goods in circulation at a given moment.[129] In chapter 2, an exceptionally detailed Dublin assay book, covering the period between 1787 and 1789, is used to identify manufacturers and suppliers, to explain the terminology of eighteenth-century trade, and to consider the largest producers and the types of goods that were most in demand.[130] Since surviving objects represent just a fraction of the plate produced in eighteenth-century Dublin, this manuscript evidence is invaluable. The fact that it dates to the closing decades of the eighteenth century also opens up discussion around the availability of plated wares, which were actively competing with silver equivalents in the Dublin market by that date.

While solid empirical data may be amassed from sources like apprenticeship ledgers, guild minutes and assay records, the task of commenting on eighteenth-century consumption, particularly in an Irish context, is much more problematic. As Toby Barnard so eloquently puts it, 'Most within and almost all outside the quality obstinately elude historical resuscitation.'[131] The evidence that survives in the form of bills, receipts, accounts and inventories is often frustratingly scant or incomplete. There is a danger of imposing retrospective order on what were ultimately idiosyncratic reasons for acquiring goods. A tendency to rely on the elite emulation model, or 'trickle down' theory advanced by Thorstein Veblen, has been challenged in recent analyses of the eighteenth century.[132] A one-dimensional perspective can obscure the complex motivations that could and did inform consumer choice.

It is generally acknowledged that, at least from the end of the seventeenth century, the range of household goods available in Europe began to diversify, and that Britain's consumers enjoyed access to an unprecedented variety of such items.[133] Recent scholarship has highlighted a burgeoning consumer culture in Ireland as early as the sixteenth century.[134] By the second half of the eighteenth century, Irish goldsmiths found they were competing not only with English plate, but also with English porcelain, Sheffield plate and transfer-printed earthenware (Figs. I.22–I.23).[135]

Chapters 3 and 4 consider the consumption of plate in Georgian Dublin. What sorts of options were available to the Irish consumer who wanted to buy plate? Apart from the obvious avenue of shops, alternatives were available in the form of auctions and, less frequently, lotteries. However, there were clear advantages to favouring the fixed trade. Shops offered terms of credit, access to a bespoke service, and additional customer service in the form of maintenance and repairs. Various studies of retailing in eighteenth-century England have investigated how contemporaries perceived retailing, how advertising was deployed as a form of 'virtual display' and how shopping spaces and practices were linked to broader social structures of sociability and politeness.[136] In considering the experience of shopping for plate in Dublin, chapter 3 analyses customs data and the business accounts of London goldsmiths to assess the impact of London silver on the Irish trade. Both the larger economic trends in trade between England and Ireland and the spending patterns of individual families are explored. What, for example, possessed an Irish clergyman to order second-hand as opposed to new plate in London – could second-hand plate pass for being 'as good as new', and if so, why?

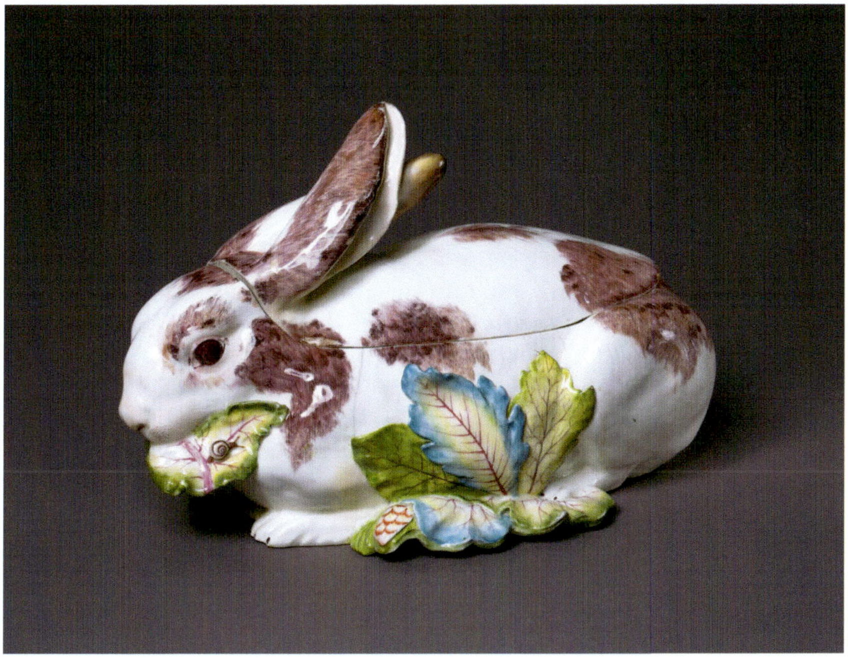

Figure I.22 Chelsea Porcelain Factory, *Tureen* (c.1755), soft-paste porcelain painted with enamels, 22.5 × 36.2 cm

Source: V&A, London. Given by Lady Charlotte Schreiber. Photo credit: © V&A.

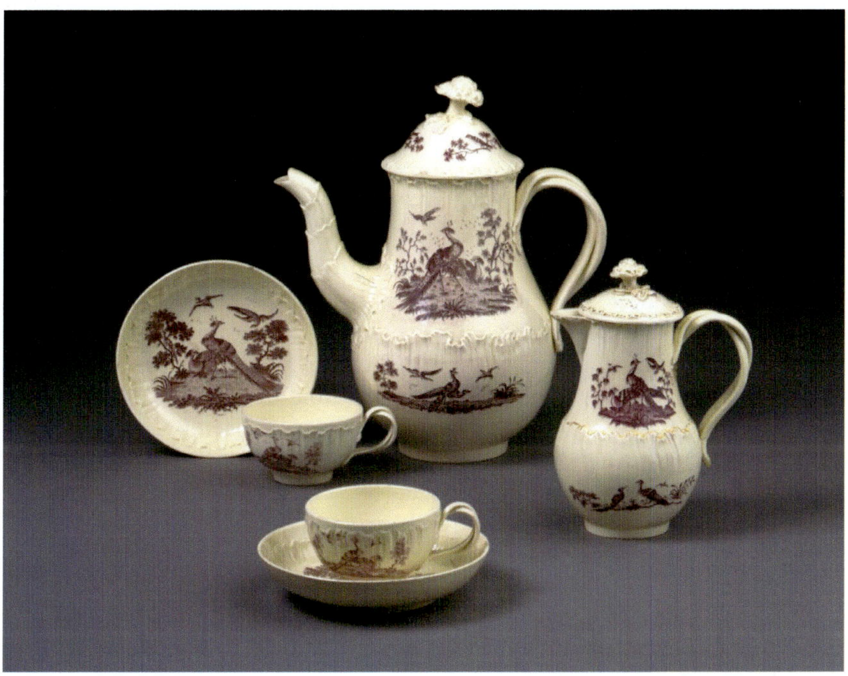

Figure I.23 Josiah Wedgwood and Sons, *Coffee service* (c.1775), creamware, 24.4 × 13.3 cm (coffee pot)

Source: V&A, London. Photo credit: © V&A.

The considerable availability of second-hand plate mediated through shops and auctions was clearly significant. Bruno Blondé and others have considered the consumption of second-hand goods in early modern Europe, the motivations to buy 'used' goods and the fact that boundaries between markets for 'old' and 'new' products were often not demarcated.[137] In an Irish context, Barnard has observed that by the 1730s 'the old or merely second-hand was in demand.'[138] It has already been acknowledged that assay records provide a much more accurate profile of the scale of silver production in Dublin than the inevitably random survival of objects. As Helen Clifford puts it, 'If we are to examine business strategies then we need to work not on the exceptional examples of silver which survive, representing the particular and the unusual, but on the typical and the usual.'[139] Complementing this analysis, chapter 3 considers currents of activity in the second-hand trade. As Blondé and others have observed, 'Studying the retentiveness of people towards "older" products is one way of grasping the "biographies of things" and, more broadly, placing the history of consumption on an essential social and cultural perspective.'[140]

Since Neil McKendrick, John Brewer and J.H. Plumb's seminal work on the birth of a consumer society,[141] several scholars have tried to find out why individuals and social groups clamoured to shop in the eighteenth century. These have included analyses of what was new,[142] the use of gendered advertising to attract custom,[143] and how local producers strove to provide new and, in some cases, innovative alternatives to imported luxuries.[144] In this context, chapter 4 deals with attitudes to silverware. Why was plate desirable in eighteenth-century Ireland? What did it mean to own, receive, or covet plate? When the Longford squire Richard Edgeworth bought a silver spoon in Dublin for his child in the mid-eighteenth century, did notions of hygiene, of status, or both motivate him? After all, the implications of being 'born with a silver spoon in one's mouth' were fairly clear.

It will be argued that the slower development of deposit banking in Dublin, the absence of a mint and the frequent shortages of coin in Ireland provided a reason to buy plate, at least in the early eighteenth century. While this is not being proposed as a major motivation for large-scale purchases, there is evidence to suggest that the association of plate with security lingered in the Irish psyche into the eighteenth century. An Irish broadsheet of 1737 alleged that, at a time when coinage was in short supply, undervalued silver coin was being channelled into plate.[145] The more general belief that plate was regarded as a sound asset is suggested by its presence in inventories of the possessions of Dublin's merchant Quaker community. As previously stated, the sources for middle-class consumption in eighteenth-century Ireland are decidedly patchy. Quaker testamentary evidence sheds valuable light on mercantile consumption. In 1716, the Dublin Quaker merchant Francis Russell set aside some of his plate, as well as cash, to provide a dowry for his daughter. She was to receive 'the Summ of Two hundred pounds Ster.g together with one Plate Tankard, one Pint Cann, Six Spoons, Two Porringers, Two Salts & One Pepper Box' when she married.[146]

Modern research on the eighteenth century has examined the value of gift exchange as a mainstay of polite culture and elite sociability. In an English context, Margot Finn examined a 'neglected tier of acquisition' by focusing on the disbursal of gifts by men.[147] Daniel Beaumont highlights the prevalence of gift exchange among the gentry of provincial Ireland and concludes that its significance should not be underrated.[148] Gifts reinforced affective bonds, defined affiliations and strengthened professional ties. Within this context, plate held a particular value, since its material worth could be calculated, readily defined and, if necessary, redeemed (Fig. I.24). As Helen Clifford has noted, a gift of plate could circumvent 'in some cases, the opprobrium of being paid in money'.[149] This is not to deny that gifts of silverware could be given purely for pleasure. Their currency within the political, confessional and professional arenas of eighteenth-century Ireland will be assessed.[150]

When silverware was given as a gift or as a bequest, it assumed an extra-material value that could equal or exceed its sterling worth. Amanda Vickery has proposed that women attached more meaning to moveable goods during this period, since they were less often in a position to apportion property. However, Irish men could and did demonstrate sentiment in the value that they placed on old, second-hand or bequeathed plate. The way in which objects were described, both in Irish testamentary records and personal accounts, will be used to assess this less tangible kind of value.

One of the most consistently expressed perceptions of plate involved its currency as a status marker. For contemporaries moving throughout Ireland, the ownership and use of silverware could represent a reliable way to form judgements about a host's refinement, taste and means. For those seeking upward mobility, or the nouveau riche, plate implied gentility. For those of lesser means, small silver objects like teaspoons or buckles were particularly highly valued for what they signified. They were also seductively portable to those inclined to pilfer. Spoons were among the most common silver items stolen by servants. Peter Wall, a servant described as 'of a middle stature, rather short and thin', with 'a round smooth face, and a few freckles, and not much bearded',

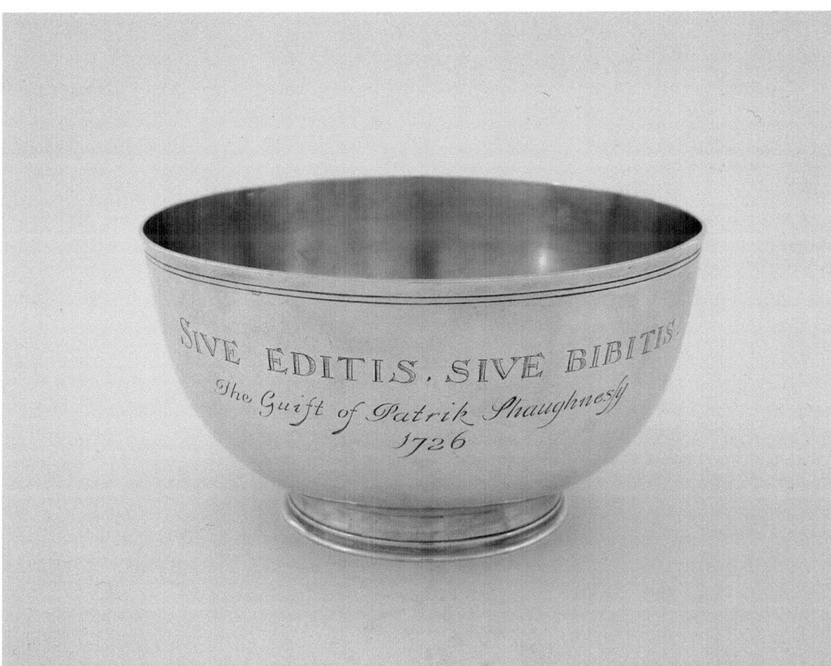

Figure I.24 William Duggan, *Bowl engraved with inscription 'The Guift of Patrik Shaughnessy'* (1726), silver, 10.25 × 18.5 cm

Source: National Museum of Ireland. Photo credit: © National Museum of Ireland.

was named in the *Dublin Intelligencer* when he stole a dozen silver spoons and other items from his master in Co. Waterford.[151] In Dublin, John Doyle was deported to the American colonies for seven years, having stolen, among other items, four silver spoons.[152]

The final chapter questions the broad generalisations that have been made about the swift decline in demand for locally produced silverware in the wake of the Act of Union. It argues for the need to consider the effects of wartime prosperity (1803 to 1815) and examines the first-hand evidence of local craftsmen, to consider the veracity of their concerns about parliamentary union. The extent to which the changing nature of fashionable society, the inevitable exodus of peers from the city, and the ascendancy of a newly empowered and increasingly wealthy middle class affected the demand for goldsmiths' work in the opening decades of the nineteenth century are all discussed. So too is the problematic question of the 'Irishness' of Irish silver. First-hand testimony from one major Irish retailer confirms that by the early nineteenth century he was importing die-stamped silver component parts for efficient assembly and 'finishing' in Dublin. These 'hybrid' wares were being hallmarked and sold as Irish, apparently without any conflict of interest on his part. This practice would be debated by the goldsmiths' guild later in the nineteenth century, but it underscores once again the importance of considering Dublin's silver trade within the broader context of the British Isles.

Notes

1 Toby Barnard, 'The Artistic and Cultural Activities of the Caldwells of Castle Caldwell, 1750–1783', *Irish Architectural and Decorative Studies* (*IADS*) 10 (2007): 100.
2 Ibid.
3 The goldsmith was abbreviated as 'Mr Holmes'. The following year Holmes, described in the *Dublin Gazette* as 'an eminent jeweller and goldsmith', married a daughter of the Revd Mr Thomas Waring, Rector of Moyra, 'a very amiable and accomplished young lady, with a considerable fortune'. *Dublin Gazette*, 26–30 December 1759. See also Douglas Bennett, *Irish Georgian Silver* (London: Cassell, 1972), 310.
4 For a good account of the shopping choices of one female consumer see Valerie Moffat, '"A Map of Her Jurisdiction", the Account Books of Meliora Adlercron of Dawson Street, Dublin, 1782–94', *IADS* 15 (2012): 128–49.
5 See Ida Delamer and Conor O'Brien, *500 Years of Irish Silver* (Wordwell: Wicklow, 2005), 17. Although jewellers and watchmakers were members of the Dublin goldsmiths' guild, this publication concentrates particularly on craftsmen and retailers who made and sold larger items of wrought silver, collectively referred to as 'plate' during this period.
6 Sheffield plate, invented by Thomas Boulsover of Sheffield in the 1740s, is a type of metal consisting of copper covered by a thin layer of silver. Products made from Sheffield plate were known as plated wares to distinguish them from their silver equivalents which were described as plate.
7 See, for example, Anna Moran, 'Manufacturing Mythology? Waterford Glass in the Early Nineteenth Century' (MA thesis, Royal College of Art, London, 2002), 4. For the burgeoning interest in antiques in Eighteenth-Century England, see Jacq Barber, 'Living with the Past: Antiques and the Middle Class Home 1870–1900' (MA thesis, Royal College of Art, London, 2000).
8 On this question, see John Culme, *The Directory of Gold and Silversmiths, Jewellers and Allied Traders 1838–1914*, vol. 1 (London: Antique Collectors' Club, 1987), xvi–xxxvi.
9 Charles James Jackson, *English Goldsmiths and Their Marks* (2nd ed., London: Macmillan, 1921), 583 reproduces this table, acknowledging it as the 'Most Nearly Accurate' template. He states that it also formed the basis of comparable tables in two important early volumes on English plate: Wilfrid Joseph Cripps, *Old English Plate* (London: John Murray,

1878) and William Chaffers, *Hallmarks on Gold and Silver Plate* (London: J. Davy & Sons, 1863). For a more recent table of Dublin date letters, see Kurt Ticher, Ida Delamer and William O'Sullivan, *Hall-marks on Dublin Silver, 1730–1772* (Dublin: National Museum of Ireland, 1968); Ida Delamer and Conor O'Brien, 'Dublin Hallmarks: A Reappraisal', *Silver Society Journal* 11 (1999): 158–67.

10 Robert Day, 'Notice of the Silver Mace of the Corporation of Castlemartyr', *Journal of the Royal Historical and Archaeological Association of Ireland* (*JRHAAI*) 8 (1888): 483; Robert Day, 'Notes on Some Early Examples of Cork Silver', *JRHAAI* 9 (1889): 127–301; John Ribton Garstin, 'The Sword and Mace of Kilkenny', *Journal of the Royal Society of Antiquaries of Ireland* (*JRSAI*) 13 (1903): 209–10; M.S.D. Westropp, 'The Goldsmiths of Cork', *Journal of the Cork Historical and Archaeological Society Journal* (*JCHAS*) 12 (1906): 37–43; M.S.D. Westropp, 'The Cork Goldsmiths, Silversmiths, Jewellers, Watchmakers and Apprentices', *JCHAS* 31 (1926): 8–13; and M.S.D. Westropp, 'The Goldsmiths of Limerick', *North Munster Antiquarian Journal* 1 (1936–39): 159–62; Materials Collected by John Ribton Garstin Towards the History of Irish Goldsmiths, late 19th century, Ms. Z.1.1.18/25, Marsh's Library, Dublin. Westropp, former keeper at the National Museum of Ireland, was not only a meticulous scholar, but also recognised the potential of certain guild records to chart fluctuations in the demand for silver.

11 In current usage, the term 'sponsor's mark' is taken to mean responsibility for a piece as opposed to guaranteed authorship.

12 Jackson, *English Goldsmiths*.

13 The lists were compiled by M.S.D. Westropp. The guild was also known as the Company of Goldsmiths of Dublin, but for clarity the term 'guild' is preferred here.

14 Jackson, *English Goldsmiths*, 644–55.

15 Bennett, *Irish Georgian Silver*. See also Tony Sweeney, *Irish Stuart Silver: Catalogue Raisonné* (Dublin: Edmund Burke, 1995). A number of museum and exhibition catalogues also deal with this subject. See, for example, Ellenor Alcorn, *English Silver in the Museum of Fine Arts, Boston. ii: Silver from 1697 Including Irish and Scottish Silver* (Boston: Museum of Fine Arts, 2000); John Teahan, *Irish Silver from the Seventeenth to the Nineteenth Century* (Washington, DC: Smithsonian Institution, 1982); and Beth Carver Wees, *English, Irish and Scottish Silver at the Sterling and Francine Clark Art Institute* (New York: Hudson Hills Press, 1997). See also Kurt Ticher, *Irish Silver in the Rococo Period* (Shannon: Irish University Press, 1972). For recent surveys of Cork and Limerick silver, see John Bowen and Conor O'Brien, *Cork Silver and Gold: Four Centuries of* Craftsmanship (Cork: Crawford Gallery, 2005); John Bowen and Conor O'Brien, eds., *A Celebration of Limerick's Silver* (Cork: Collins Press in association with the Hunt Museum, 2007).

16 An exception to this is the function of certain objects, which some authors address. See, for example, Bennett, *Irish Georgian Silver*; Wees, *English, Irish and Scottish Silver*.

17 Toby Barnard, *Making the Grand Figure: Lives and Possessions in Ireland, 1641–1770* (New Haven and London: Yale University Press, 2004), xx.

18 See, for instance, Helen Clifford, *Silver in London: The Parker and Wakelin Partnership 1760–1776* (New Haven and London: Yale University Press, 2004); Claire Walsh, 'Shop Design and the Display of Goods in the Eighteenth Century' (MA thesis, Royal College of Art, London, 1993); Emma Packer, 'Refining the Goldsmith: The London Goldsmiths' Trade Seen through Inventories, 1695–1732' (MA thesis, Royal College of Art, London, 1992).

19 Joseph McDonnell, 'Irish Rococo Silver', *Irish Arts Review Yearbook* (*IAR*) 13 (1997): 78–87. For general discussions of continental sources mediated in an Irish context during this period, see Christine Casey, 'Gaetano Brunetti', *IAR* (January 1988): 244–45; C.P. Curran, *Dublin Decorative Plasterwork of the Seventeenth and Eighteenth Centuries* (London: Alec Tiranti, 1967); Joseph McDonnell, *Irish Eighteenth-Century Stuccowork and its European Sources* (Dublin: National Gallery of Ireland, 1991); and Joseph McDonnell, 'The Influence of the French Rococo Print in Eighteenth-Century Ireland', *Bulletin of the Irish Georgian Society* (*BIGS*) 36 (1994): 63–75.

20 These are guild ledgers of goods submitted for hallmarking.

21 Thomas Sinsteden, 'Four Selected Assay Records of the Dublin Goldsmiths' Company', *Silver Society Journal* 11 (1999): 143–58; Thomas Sinsteden, 'Surviving Dublin Assay Records. Part 2 (1708–48)', *Silver Studies: The Journal of the Silver Society* 16 (2004): 87–103. On

the subject of assay records, see also Alison FitzGerald and Conor O'Brien, 'The Production of Silver in Late Georgian Dublin', *IADS* 4 (2001): 8–48; Fiona Ahern, 'Jane Williams: An Outstanding Cork Silversmith and Her Work', *Journal of the Cork Archaeological Society* (*JCAS*) 117 (2012): 31–36.

22 See, for example, Toby Barnard, 'Integration or Separation? Hospitality and Display in Protestant Ireland, 1660–1800', in *A Union of Multiple Identities: The British Isles, c.1750–c.1850*, ed. Laurence Brockliss and David Eastwood (Manchester: Manchester University Press, 1997), 127–47; Toby Barnard, 'Public and Private Uses of Wealth in Ireland, c.1660–1760', in *Luxury and Austerity*, ed. Jacqueline Hill and Colm Lennon (Dublin: University College Dublin, 1999), 66–83; Toby Barnard, *A New Anatomy of Ireland: The Irish Protestants, 1649–1770* (New Haven and London: Yale University Press, 2003); Barnard, *Making the Grand Figure*. The quotation is from Barnard, *Making the Grand Figure*, xx.

23 The term 'autograph passion' was used by Gerald Reitlinger to describe the quest for the author, which characterised late nineteenth and early twentieth-century scholarship in the fine and decorative arts. See Clifford, *Silver in London*, 9.

24 See, for example, Joseph Brasbridge, *The Fruits of Experience; or Memoir of Joseph Brasbridge Written in his 80th and 81st Year* (London: Printed for the author, 1824) and G. Fox, *Memoirs of the Late Philip Rundell Esq. Goldsmith and Jeweller to His Majesty and the Royal Family Late of the Golden Salmon, Ludgate Hill, Who by Industry and Perseverance Accumulated the Immense Fortune of One Million and a Half* (London: J. Fairburn, 1827); Garrard Ledgers, Victoria and Albert Museum, London; Banks and Heal Collection of Trade Cards, British Museum, London. The destruction of Ireland's Public Record Office in 1922 was responsible for the loss of some eighteenth-century material.

25 These are held in the Assay Office at Dublin Castle, the headquarters of the Company of Goldsmiths of Dublin.

26 For the volumes of silver being assayed in eighteenth-century London, see John Forbes, *Hallmark, A History of the London Assay Office* (London: Unicorn Press and the Goldsmiths' Company, 1999), 319.

27 *Volunteers Journal; or, Irish Herald*, 25 June 1784.

28 Jackson, *English Goldsmiths*. Revisions have been made to Jackson's work on date letters. See Delamer and O'Brien, 'Dublin Hallmarks'.

29 While a number of female goldsmiths (mostly widows) were productive in the trade, no female apprentices were registered with the guild during this period.

30 This is reinforced by the fact that the majority of goldsmiths submitted only a modest amount of silver a year. The market was dominated throughout the period by a small number of successful goldsmiths.

31 Scant evidence exists of cases where individuals ordered a complete dinner service in a single order from a Dublin goldsmith during this period.

32 David Dickson, 'Second City Syndrome: Reflections on Three Irish Cases', in *Kingdoms United? Great Britain and Ireland since 1500: Integration and Diversity*, ed. Sean Connolly (Dublin: Four Courts Press, 1999), 95–108. See also Patrick Fagan, *The Second City: Portrait of Dublin 1700–1760* (Dublin: Branar, 1986).

33 Edward Lloyd, *A Description of the City of Dublin* (1732), quoted in Fagan, *Second City*, 17. The author of the description called himself a 'citizen and silk thrower of London who has lived near twenty years in Ireland and is lately come from Dublin'.

34 Peter Clark and Raymond Gillespie, eds., *Two Capitals, London and Dublin 1500–1840* (Oxford: Oxford University Press, 2001).

35 Ibid., 1.

36 The term 'long eighteenth century' usually refers to the period from the Glorious Revolution of 1688 to the Battle of Waterloo in 1815.

37 Clark and Gillespie, *Two Capitals*, 1. For more on Dublin's population in the eighteenth century, see David Dickson, 'The Demographic Implications of Dublin's Growth, 1650–1850', in *Urban Population Development in Western Europe from the Late-Eighteenth to the Early Twentieth Century*, ed. Richard Lawton and Robert Lee (Liverpool: Liverpool University Press, 1989), 178–89; Patrick Fagan, 'The Population of Dublin in the Eighteenth Century with Particular Reference to the Proportions of Protestants and Catholics', *Eighteenth-Century Ireland* 6 (1991): 121–56.

38 When the broad cultural landscape is assessed, it is clear that a more subtle reading is required; emulative response was not entirely one-sided. Historians have observed a number of areas in which Dublin took the lead, and while this may not have typified activities within the silver trade, it is nonetheless worth qualifying. See Toby Barnard, '"Grand Metropolis" or "The Anus of the World"? The Cultural Life of Eighteenth-Century Dublin', in *Two Capitals*, ed. Clark and Gillespie, 197; John Fleming and Hugh Honour, *Penguin Dictionary of Decorative Arts* (London: Penguin, 1989), 218–19; and Peter Francis, *Irish Delftware: An Illustrated History* (London: Jonathan Horne, 2000), 10. See also William Rufus Chetwood, *A Tour through Ireland in Several Entertaining Letters* (London: J. Roberts, 1748), 191–92.

39 John Mitchel, ed., *Irish Political Economy by Jonathan Swift, Dean of St. Patrick's and George Berkeley, Bishop of Cloyne* (Dublin: Irish Confederation), 39.

40 John Bush, *Hibernia Curiosa: A Letter from a Gentleman in Dublin to His Friend at Dover in Kent, Giving a General View of the Manners, Customs, Dispositions, &c. of the Inhabitants of Ireland* (Dublin: Printed for J. Potts and J. Williams, 1769), 18.

41 Peter Borsay, 'The London Connection: Cultural Diffusion and the Eighteenth-Century Provincial Town', *London Journal* 19 (1994): 21–35; Peter Borsay, 'London, 1660–1800: A Distinctive Culture?' in Clark and Gillespie, *Two Capitals*, 167–84.

42 Borsay, 'The London Connection', 170. Both capital cities were densely populated and had a high concentration of patrons with the means to buy luxury goods.

43 Malcolm Baker, 'Roubiliac and Cheere in the 1730s and 1740s: Collaboration and Subcontracting in Eighteenth-Century English Sculptors' Workshops', *Church Monuments* 10 (1995): 90. Also see Clifford, *Silver in London*; Werner John Freundel, 'The Production and Commissioning of London-Made Private Carriages: 1740–1800' (MA thesis, Royal College of Art, London, 1999); Pat Kirkham, *The London Furniture Trade, 1700–1870* (London: Furniture History Society, 1988); Giorgio Riello, *A Foot in the Past: Consumers, Producers and Footwear in the Long Eighteenth Century* (Oxford: Oxford University Press, 2005); John Styles, 'The Goldsmiths and the London Luxury Trades, 1550–1750', in *Goldsmiths, Silversmiths and Bankers: Innovation and the Transfer of Skill 1550–1750*, ed. David Mitchell (London: Sutton, 1995), 112–20.

44 Styles, 'The Goldsmiths and the London Luxury Trades', 114. It meant that certain costs could potentially be reduced, by subcontracting manufacture to workshops in cheaper areas, availing of the attendant credit terms, and enjoying access to a network of specialisation, without paying for it on a regular or consistent basis.

45 Clifford, *Silver in London*.

46 Individual case studies of certain prominent goldsmiths such as Robert Calderwood shed some light on these issues.

47 See Jacqueline Hill, *From Patriots to Unionists: Dublin Civic Politics and Irish Protestant Patriotism, 1660–1840* (Oxford: Oxford University Press, 1997), 19–42. In London, the categories were service, redemption and patrimony. See J. P. Fallon, *Marks of London Goldsmiths and Silversmiths, c.1697–1837* (London: David & Charles, 1988), 11–12.

48 Most freemen were quarter brothers at first.

49 Maureen Wall, 'The Catholics of the Towns and the Quarterage Dispute in Eighteenth-Century Ireland', in *Catholic Ireland in the Eighteenth Century: Collected Essays of Maureen Wall*, ed. Gerard O'Brien (Dublin: Geography Publications, 1989), 62–63. In addition, see Patrick Fagan, *Catholics in a Protestant Country: The Papist Constituency in Eighteenth-Century Dublin* (Dublin: Four Courts, 1998).

50 See Bennett, *Irish Georgian Silver*, 11.

51 John Forbes, 'Search, Immigration and the Goldsmiths' Company: A Study in the Decline of Its Powers', in *Guilds, Society and Economy in London 1450–1800*, ed. Ian Anders Gadd and Patrick Wallis (London: Centre for Metropolitan History 2002), 120–23.

52 No comprehensive study of the geographical distribution of goldsmiths mapped onto the changing topography of London exists. Nevertheless, the evidence from contemporary trade cards and rate books supports this profile of suburban development. M.J. Walker, 'The Extent of the Guild Control of Trades in England, c.1660–1820: A Study Based on a Sample of Provincial Towns and London Companies' (PhD thesis, University of Cambridge, 1985), 186 clarifies the area of jurisdiction of the London livery companies in the seventeenth and

eighteenth centuries. The Goldsmiths' Company had control over members within the City but their control over the trade extended to England and Wales.

53 On the reception of immigrants in the Dublin guilds, see Edward Whelan, 'The Dublin Patriciate and the Reception of Migrants in the Seventeenth Century' (PhD thesis, National University of Ireland, Maynooth, 2008).

54 See William F. Kahl, *The Development of London Livery Companies* (Cambridge, MA: Harvard University Press, 1960), 27; and Forbes, 'Search, Immigration and the Goldsmiths' Company'.

55 Minute of 20 December 1800, Company of Goldsmiths of Dublin, Ms. 6: 299. Dublin, Assay Office.

56 Judy Jowett, 'The Warning Carriers', *Silver Studies: The Journal of the Silver Society* 18 (Special Issue), 2005.

57 Ibid., 33. A victim of crime could arrange printing of notices and ask the hall to distribute them or organise printing. A 'warning carriers' book, thought to date from the 1730s, details walks of five miles, on average, calling to over 200 addresses in the case of two of the carriers. In this way information about stolen plate could be conveyed more quickly than by using a newspaper notice.

58 The scale of the market will be examined in chapter 2. In the second half of the century, there were certainly individuals who ran large shops, yet are credited with assaying only small quantities of silverware, suggesting that they were buying in stock.

59 Hill, *From Patriots to Unionists*, 32.

60 Although their attitude was reflective of peculiar corporate agendas which were particular to Ireland, it also exemplifies the criticisms of eighteenth-century physiocrats and classical political economists, who 'regarded the privileges of guilds and urban communities as "contrary to the order of nature and the rights of the nation"; corporations of merchants or artisans "disturb order by their rivalries and jealousies" and "form jealous little republics, which disregard the general interest of the kingdom"'; see Antony Black, *Guilds and Civil Society in European Political Thought from the Twelfth Century to the Present* (London: Methuen, 1984), 160.

61 Minute of 8 November 1667, Company of Goldsmiths of Dublin, Ms. 1: 3, Dublin, Assay Office.

62 Minute of 9 November 1694, Company of Goldsmiths of Dublin, Ms. 1: 48, Dublin, Assay Office.

63 The oath of a quarter brother, which is included at the back of Minute Book 1, Company of Goldsmiths of Dublin, Ms. 1, Dublin, Assay Office and dated 1680, refers to the fact that at that date they were not to keep journeymen.

64 Minute of 1 May 1738, Company of Goldsmiths of Dublin, Ms. 2: 73, Dublin, Assay Office. Bennett, *Irish Georgian Silver*, 11 reproduces the oath of a quarter brother, stating that individuals were obliged to abide by its rules. In fact, guild evidence suggests that rules in relation to quarter brothers engaging journeymen and apprentices were relaxed as the century progressed. Guild minutes for 1697 register a number of payments of 2s 6d per quarter journeymen. See, for example, Company of Goldsmiths of Dublin, Ms. 1: 10, Dublin, Assay Office.

65 Enrolment of Apprentices, 2 May 1752–7 November 1823, Company of Goldsmiths of Dublin, Ms. 97, Dublin, Assay Office.

66 Jacqueline Hill, 'The Shaping of Dublin Government in the Long Eighteenth Century', in *Two Capitals*, ed. Clark and Gillespie, 163.

67 For information on the concerns of London goldsmiths regarding Huguenots, see John Forbes, 'Search, Immigration and the Goldsmiths' Company', 120–21.

68 Minute of 27 January 1697, Company of Goldsmiths of Dublin, Ms. 1: 70, Dublin, Assay Office. In the same year the Council of Cork ordered that 'no papist quarterer of any society take any covenanted servant or papist quarterer to work journey work for him nor take more than one apprentice' (Wall, 'The Catholics of the Towns and the Quarterage Dispute', 64).

69 The Treaty of Limerick was signed on 3 October 1691, ending the Williamite war in Ireland between the Jacobites and the supporters of William of Orange. It coincided with the first of a new wave of laws against Catholics.

70 Minute of 27 January 1697, Company of Goldsmiths of Dublin, Ms. 1: 70, Dublin, Assay Office.
71 Minute of 2 November 1767, Company of Goldsmiths of Dublin, Ms. 5: 145–56, Dublin, Assay Office. This can be seen as direct guild response to the wider political climate. In the previous year, petitions were presented to parliament on behalf of a number of Irish cities and corporate towns, including Cork and Dublin, seeking legal confirmation of the rights of corporations to demand the payment of quarterage from non-freemen. See Wall, 'The Catholics of the Towns and the Quarterage Dispute', 66–67.
72 Minute of 2 February 1758, Company of Goldsmiths of Dublin, Company of Goldsmiths of Dublin, Ms. 2: 351, Dublin, Assay Office. It seems likely that the woman in question was the widow of Jonathan Hutton, whom Bennett lists as a quarter brother between 1749 and 1755. Bennett, *Irish Georgian Silver*, 311.
73 Maureen Wall, 'The Catholic Merchants, Manufacturers and Traders of Dublin, 1778–1782', *Reportorium Novum* 2 (1960), no. 2: 301.
74 Hill, *From Patriots to Unionists*, 39.
75 Minute of 1 November 1776, Company of Goldsmiths of Dublin, Ms. 5: 334, Dublin, Assay Office.
76 Ibid.
77 A waiter or salver is a flat dish with or without handles.
78 Duty was charged at a rate of 6d per oz. at this stage.
79 Minute of 13 December, 1769, Company of Goldsmiths of Dublin, Ms. 5: 195.
80 Forbes, *Hallmark*, 147–48.
81 *Freeman's Journal* (*FJ*), 9 April 1818.
82 Ibid.
83 Ibid.
84 Minute of 2 March 1833, Company of Goldsmiths of Dublin Ms. 8: 174–75, Dublin, Assay Office.
85 Timothy Breen, 'An Empire of Goods: The Anglicization of Colonial America 1690–1776', *Journal of British Studies* 25 (1986): 467–99; Timothy Breen, 'Baubles of Britain; The American and Consumer Revolution of the Eighteenth Century', *Past and Present* 119 (1988): 73–104; John Styles, 'Manufacturing, Consumption and Design in Eighteenth-Century England', in *Consumption and the World of Goods*, ed. John Brewer and Roy Porter (London: Routledge, 1993), 527–54; John Styles and Amanda Vickery, eds., *Gender, Taste, and Material Culture in Britain and North America, 1700–1830* (New Haven and London: Yale University Press, 2007).
86 Moran, 'Manufacturing Mythology?', 129.
87 On the question of the 'Irishness of Irish silver', see Bennett, *Irish Georgian Silver*, 113 and 122–25; Teahan, *Irish Silver*, 5–6; Ticher, *Irish Silver*, 5–28; Francis Townshend, 'Irish Silver, Decoration and Re-Decoration', *Quarterly Bulletin of the Irish Georgian Society* (*QBIGS*) 8 (1965): 10; M.S.D. Westropp, *National Museum of Ireland, Dublin: General Guide to the Art Collections, Part VI, Metalwork* (Dublin: Stationery Office, 1914), 51; Robert Wyse Jackson, *Irish Silver* (Cork and Dublin: Mercier Press, 1972), 59, 20, 43, and 46.
88 On Irish silver dish rings, see Conor O'Brien, 'The Evolution of Silver Dish Rings', *Collectors' Guide* (January 1977), 71–75; Christopher Monkhouse, 'A Chinoiserie Dish Ring by Charles Townsend', *IADS* 17 (2014): 70–79.
89 *Hibernian Journal*, 20–30 November 1772.
90 Handbill for John Ash, No. 8, Capel Street, Dublin, Ms. EPH A755, Ephemera Collection, Department of Prints and Drawings, National Library of Ireland.
91 *Volunteers Journal; or, Irish Herald*, 20 February 1784. This retailer was selling plated wares, which were certainly imported, and also plate. She claimed to be able to supply 'services of plate made on the best terms, and finished in the best manner'. I am grateful to John Rogers for generously sharing his transcriptions from Irish newspapers.
92 See, for example, *Faulkner's Dublin Journal* (*FDJ*), 28 December–1 January 1757; and the *Cork Evening Post*, 12 April 1781. See also the *Volunteers Journal; or, Irish Herald*, 16 July 1784; and *Cork Evening Post*, 12 April 1781, as cited in Mairead Dunlevy, *Jewellery, 17th to 20th Centuries* (Dublin: National Museum of Ireland, 2001), 10. Some Irish goldsmiths advertised that their work could be had at a more competitive price than imported equivalents.

For more on the question of national identity, see Sarah Foster, 'Going Shopping in Georgian Dublin: Luxury Goods and the Negotiation of National Identity' (MA thesis, Royal College of Art, London, 1995); Sarah Foster, 'Going Shopping in 18th-Century Dublin', *Things* 4 (Summer 1996): 33–61; Moran, 'Manufacturing Mythology?'; Martyn Powell, *The Politics of Consumption in Eighteenth-Century Ireland* (Basingstoke: Palgrave Macmillan, 2004).

93 'Japanning' refers to various Western methods which attempted to imitate Oriental lacquer. There were a number of retailers selling japanned wares in eighteenth-century Dublin.

94 Benjamin Henfrey to Matthew Boulton, 1783, Birmingham City Archives, Microfilm 171; Letter on behalf of Matthew Boulton to Benjamin Henfrey, c.1784, Birmingham City Archives, Ms. 3782/3/14: 223.

95 Letter from Matthew Boulton's representative to Ann Cormick, 18 March 1783, Birmingham City Archives, Matthew Boulton Papers Ms. 3782/2/14, Letter Book 1782–86 [147]: 87.

96 Kenneth Quickenden, 'Samuel Garbett and Early Boulton and Fothergill Assay Silver', in *Matthew Boulton: Enterprising Industrialist of the Enlightenment*, ed. Kenneth Quickenden, Sally Baggott, and Malcolm Dick (Aldershot: Ashgate, 2013), 144.

97 Letter to James Hewitt from Boulton and Fothergill, 22 November 1777, Ms. 3782/1/11:123, Birmingham City Archives. I am grateful to Breda Scott for this reference.

98 For more on this, see Helen Clifford, 'Concepts of Invention, Identity and Imitation in the London and Provincial Metal-working Trades, 1750–1800', *Journal of Design History* 12 (1999): 241–55.

99 Clifford, *Silver in London*, 7–8.

100 For French influence in an Irish context, see Barnard, *Making the Grand Figure*; Foster, 'Going Shopping in Georgian Dublin'; McDonnell, 'Irish Rococo Silver'; and John Turpin, 'French Influence on Eighteenth-Century Art Education in Dublin', *Eighteenth-Century Ireland* 5 (1990): 105–16.

101 Clifford, *Silver in London*, 27.

102 Ibid.

103 Foster, 'Going Shopping in Georgian Dublin', 81; Foster, 'Going Shopping in 18th-Century Dublin', 43.

104 Foster, 'Going Shopping in 18th-Century Dublin', 43.

105 A full run of records survives for this period.

106 Ledgers of Imports and Exports from London and the Outports, 1697 to 1780, CUST 3, National Archives, Kew.

107 *Dublin Spy*, 10 October 1753.

108 David Skinner, *Wallpaper in Ireland 1700–1900* (Tralee: Churchill Press, 2014), 89.

109 Victoria Morgan has noted the same phenomenon in relation to the way in which retailers in provincial England played up London in their advertisements. See Victoria Morgan, 'Beyond the Boundary of the Shop: Retail Advertising Spaces in 18th-Century Provincial England', in *Cultures of Selling: Perspectives on Consumption and Society since 1700*, ed. John Benson and Laura Ugolini (Aldershot: Ashgate, 2006), 59–80.

110 *FDJ*, 30 August–1 September 1791.

111 Robert Day, 'Notes and Queries', *JCHAS* 12 (1906): 149. Ambrose Heal, *The London Goldsmiths, 1200–1800* (Cambridge: Cambridge University Press, 1935), 125 lists a John Christian, jeweller and goldsmith, in Gracechurch Street 1763 to 1765 and in Leadenhall Street in 1766, which tallies with these dates.

112 Joan Evans, 'Huguenot Goldsmiths in England and Ireland', *Huguenot Society's Proceedings* 14 (1933), no. 4: 514; McDonnell, 'The Influence of the French Rococo Print'; John Turpin, 'The School of Ornament of the Dublin Society in the 18th Century', *JRSAI* 116 (1986): 38–50; Turpin, 'French Influence'.

113 Evans, 'Huguenot Goldsmiths'; Jessica Cunningham, 'Dublin's Huguenot Goldsmiths: Assimilation and Divergence, 1690–1750', *IADS* 12 (2009): 158–85.

114 Accounts of Oliver St George, n.d., Ms. C110/46/136, National Archives, Kew.

115 *Sotheby's Irish Sale*, Thursday 21 May 1998, lot 211.

116 Minute of 1 November 1771, Company of Goldsmiths of Dublin, Ms. 5: 226, Dublin, Assay Office; Minute of 1 May 1790, Company of Goldsmiths of Dublin, Ms. 6: 169; Minute of 2 February 1796, Company of Goldsmiths of Dublin, Ms. 6: 238.

117 Hill, *From Patriots to Unionists*, 19–42 deals with the different routes to freedom.

118 On London goldsmith apprentices, see Philippa Glanville, *Silver in England* (London, Unwin Hyman, 1987), 168–69; William Kahl, 'Apprenticeship and the Freedom of the London Livery Companies, 1690–1750', *Guildhall Miscellany* 7 (1956): 17–20. ROLLCO: http://www.londonroll.org provides records of apprentices and freemen in the City of London livery companies between 1400 and 1900.

119 S.R. Epstein and Maarten Prak, eds., *Guilds, Innovation and the European Economy 1400–1800* (Cambridge: Cambridge University Press, 2008).

120 For analysis of goldsmiths' shops in eighteenth-century London, see Packer, 'Refining the Goldsmith'; Claire Walsh, '"Their Shops Are Dens, The Buyer Is Their Prey": Shop Design and Sale Techniques', in *The Complete Tradesman: A Study of Retailing, 1550–1820*, ed. Nancy Cox (Aldershot: Ashgate, 2000), 76–116; Claire Walsh, 'The Design of London Goldsmiths' Shops in the Early Eighteenth Century', in *Goldsmiths, Silversmiths and Bankers*, ed. Mitchell, 96–111; Claire Walsh, 'Shop Design and the Display of Goods in Eighteenth-Century London', *Journal of Design History* 8 (1995): 157–76; Walsh, 'Shop Design and the Display of Goods in the Eighteenth Century'. For further information on eighteenth-century retailing, see Helen Berry, 'Polite Consumption: Shopping in Eighteenth-Century England', *Transactions of the Royal Historical Society* 12 (2002): 375–94; Cox, *The Complete Tradesman*; Hoh-Cheung Mui and L.H. Mui, *Shops and Shopkeeping in Eighteenth-Century England* (Montreal: McGill-Queen's University Press, 1989).

121 Sarah Foster, '"Ornament and Splendour": Shops and Shopping in Georgian Dublin', *IADS 15* (2012): 12–33; Foster, 'Going Shopping in Georgian Dublin'; Foster, 'Going Shopping in 18th-Century Dublin'; Sarah Foster, 'Buying Irish: Consumer Nationalism in 18th-Century Dublin', *History Today* 47 (1997): 44–52; John Montague, 'A Shopping Arcade in Eighteenth-Century Dublin: John Rocque and the Essex Street "Piazzas"', *IADS* 10 (2007): 225–45.

122 Niall McCullough, *A Vision of the City: Dublin and the Wide Streets Commissioners* (Dublin: Dublin Corporation, 1991); Edward McParland, 'The Wide Streets Commissioners: Their Importance for Dublin Architecture in the Late 18th–Early 19th Century', *BIGS* 15 (1972), no. 1: 1–31; Edward McParland, 'Strategy in the Planning of Dublin, 1750–1800', in *Cities and Merchants: French and Irish Perspectives on Urban Development, 1500–1900*, ed. Paul Butel and Louis Cullen (Dublin: Trinity College Dublin, 1986), 97–109; Edel Sheridan, 'Designing the Capital City: Dublin, c.1660–1810', in *Dublin through Space and Time*, ed. Joseph Brady and Anngret Simms (Dublin: Four Courts Press, 2001), 66–136.

123 *FDJ*, 24–28 April 1753. There is little known about the context in which bullion was traded in eighteenth-century Dublin, a subject that merits further investigation.

124 *Dublin Mercury*, 14–16 April 1768.

125 Malcolm Baker, 'A Rage for Exhibitions: The Display and Viewing of Wedgwood's Frog Service', in *The Genius of Wedgwood*, ed. Hilary Young (London: V&A, 1995), 124.

126 Bert De Munck, 'The Agency of Branding and the Location of Value: Hallmarks and Monograms in Early Modern Tableware Industries', *Business History* 54 (2012), no. 7: 1056.

127 Bennett, *Irish Georgian Silver*, 47–48 refers to the fact that in 1783 'a group of goldsmiths, jewellers and some watchmakers from Geneva seeking refuge . . . settled in Waterford' and £30,000 was expended to set them up in business. According to Bennett, this represents 'the only instance of an assay office outside Dublin being granted by public statute' and 'it is doubtful if this community ever carried on business there, or manufactured anything; certainly no plate was ever assayed there.' Westropp, *National Museum of Ireland, Dublin: General Guide*, 72 mentions that in 1783 an assay office was opened at New Geneva, and only remained open for about six years. According to Westropp, watchcases were probably the only things marked there. See also, Material relating to the establishment of an assay office at Cork, Ms. 30/9/147, National Archives, Kew. No piece has yet come to light assayed at 'New Geneva'. Alison FitzGerald, 'Fighting for "A Small Provincial Establishment": The Cork Goldsmiths and Their Quest for a Regional Assay Office', *Provincial Ireland*, ed. Roy Foster and Raymond Gillespie (Dublin: Four Courts Press, 2012), 120–30.

128 For tables of London assay figures, see Forbes, *Hallmark*, 319–20.

129 See, for example, Peter Earle, *The Making of the English Middle Class* (Berkeley: University of California Press, 1989); Carole Shammas, *The Pre-Industrial Consumer in England and America* (Oxford: Oxford University Press, 1990); Lorna Weatherill, *Consumer Behaviour and Material Culture in Britain 1660–1760* (London: Routledge, 1988).
130 The only eighteenth-century ledger containing such exceptional detail is Assay Book 1787–89, Company of Goldsmiths of Dublin, Ms. 21. For an itemisation of objects assayed in these years see FitzGerald and O'Brien, 'The Production of Silver in Late Georgian Dublin'.
131 Barnard, *A New Anatomy of Ireland*, 328.
132 Thorstein Veblen, *The Theory of the Leisure Class* (New York: Dover, 1994). For summaries and critiques of the emulation theory, see Ann Bermingham, 'Introduction', in *The Consumption of Culture 1600–1800: Image, Object, Text*, ed. Ann Bermingham and John Brewer (London: Routledge, 1995), 1–20; Amanda Vickery, *The Gentleman's Daughter: Women's Lives in Georgian England* (New Haven and London: Yale University Press, 1998); Lorna Weatherill, 'The Meaning of Consumer Behaviour in Late Seventeenth- and Early Eighteenth-Century England', in *Consumption and the World of Goods*, ed. John Brewer and Roy Porter (London: Routledge, 1993), 206–28; Weatherill, *Consumer Behaviour*.
133 For a good analysis of this, see the introduction in Bruno Blondé et al., *Fashioning Old and New: Changing Consumer Patterns in Western Europe 1650–1900* (Turnhout: Brepols, 2009).
134 Susan Flavin, *Consumption and Culture in Sixteenth-Century Ireland: Saffron, Stockings and Silk* (Woodbridge: Boydell & Brewer, 2014).
135 On the proliferation of new products during this period see Jan de Vries, *The Industrious Revolution: Consumer Demand and the Household Economy, 1650 to the Present* (Cambridge: Cambridge University Press, 2008); Weatherill, *Consumer Behaviour*.
136 See, for example, Bruno Blondé et al., *Buyers and Sellers: Retail Circuits and Practices in Medieval and Early Modern Europe* (Turnhout: Brepols, 2006); John Benson and Laura Ugolini, eds., *A Nation of Shopkeepers Five Centuries of British Retailing* (London: I.B. Tauris, 2003); Nancy Cox, *Retailing and the Language of Goods* (Aldershot: Ashgate, forthcoming); Ian Mitchell, *Tradition and Innovation in English Retailing 1700 to 1850, Narratives of Consumption* (Aldershot: Ashgate, 2014); Jon Stobart, Andrew Hann, and Victoria Morgan, eds., *Spaces of Consumption: Leisure and Shopping in the English Town* (London: Routledge, 2007).
137 See Blondé et al., *Fashioning Old and New*; also Beverly Lemire, 'Consumerism in Pre-Industrial and Early Industrial England: The Trade in Second-Hand Clothes', *Journal of British Studies* 27 (1988): 1–24; Stana Nenadic, 'Middle-Rank Consumers and Domestic Culture in Edinburgh and Glasgow 1720–1840', *Past and Present* 145 (1994): 122–56.
138 Barnard, *Making the Grand Figure*, 96.
139 Clifford, *Silver in London*, 11.
140 Blondé et al., *Fashioning Old and New*, 9.
141 Neil McKendrick, John Brewer and J. H. Plumb, eds., *The Birth of a Commercial Society: The Commercialisation of Eighteenth-Century England* (London: Europa, 1982).
142 Maxine Berg, 'Product Innovation in Core Consumer Industries in Eighteenth-Century Britain', in *Technological Revolutions in Europe: Historical Perspectives*, ed. Maxine Berg and Kristine Bruland (Cheltenham: Edward Elgar, 1998), 138–57; Maxine Berg, 'New Commodities, Luxuries and Their Consumers in Eighteenth-Century England', in *Consumers and Luxury: Consumer Culture in Europe 1650–1850*, ed. Maxine Berg and Helen Clifford (Manchester: Manchester University Press, 1999), 63–83; John Styles, 'Product Innovation in Early Modern London', *Past and Present*, 168 (2000): 125–69.
143 See, for example, Vickery, *The Gentleman's Daughter*; Amanda Vickery, *Behind Closed Doors: At Home in Georgian England* (New Haven and London: Yale University Press, 2010).
144 Berg, 'Product Innovation in Core Consumer Industries in Eighteenth-Century Britain'; Matthew Craske, 'Plan and Control: Design and the Competitive Spirit in Early and Mid-Eighteenth-Century England', *Journal of Design History* 12 (1999): 187–216; Styles, 'Manufacturing, Consumption and Design in Eighteenth-Century England'.

145 Anon., *Short Reasons Why Our Gold-Money in Ireland Should Not Be Lowered* (Dublin, 1737).
146 Marriage Settlement of James Russell of the City of Dublin Merchant, 1716, Ms. MMIIL1, 229, Quaker Archive, Dublin.
147 Margot Finn, 'Men's Things: Masculine Possession in the Consumer Revolution', *Social History* 25 (2000): 142.
148 Daniel Beaumont, 'The Gentry of the King's and Queen's Counties: Protestant Landed Society, 1690–1760' (PhD thesis, Trinity College Dublin, 1999).
149 Helen Clifford, 'A Commerce with Things: The Value of Precious Metalwork in Early Modern England', in *Consumers and Luxury*, ed. Berg and Clifford, 151.
150 For instance, plate was given in official contexts as tokens of appreciation, not just in the case of freedom boxes, when the freedom of a town or city was being conferred.
151 *Dublin Intelligencer*, 1–22 April 1693.
152 Barnard, *Making the Grand Figure*, 135.

1 The business of becoming a goldsmith in eighteenth-century Dublin

In 1747 R. Campbell, author of *The London Tradesman*, singled out the goldsmiths' profession as 'the most genteel of any in the mechanic way'.[1] The same could have been said of Dublin, where a significant amount of capital was required to enter and follow the trade. This chapter considers the requirements for establishing oneself as a goldsmith in eighteenth-century Dublin, including the training of apprentices, leasing of premises and sourcing of materials and equipment. The most important institution in the professional life of a Dublin goldsmith was the guild (Fig. 1.1). It regulated the trade and its guildhall also housed the assay office, which aimed to ensure the purity of silver and gold used in manufactured goods. For most of the eighteenth century the guildhall was located on Werburgh Street, close to Dublin Castle, with the surrounding streets populated with goldsmiths, jewellers and watchmakers.

There has been considerable debate about the economic value of guilds during the early modern period.[2] Ever since Adam Smith's *Wealth of Nations* (1776), the dominant opinion has been that guilds were a throwback to a medieval past, that they encouraged restrictive and protectionist policies and were agents against progress. However, this viewpoint has been challenged, particularly in the last two decades. Economic historians such as S.R. Epstein have pointed to the positive role played by guilds in transmitting skills through the apprenticeship system, in adapting to and actively promoting technological change and in inspiring consumer confidence through quality control and branding.[3] Revisionist ideas about guilds have not been universally accepted: Sheilagh Ogilvie, for example, believes that they were essentially rent-seeking institutions which looked after the financial interests of their own members at the expense of other sectors of the economy, and had an adverse effect on quality, skills and innovation.[4]

Pursuing a career as a goldsmith, whether in Dublin or London during the eighteenth century, involved confronting a range of competitive markets: for labour, premises, raw materials and most significantly of all, products. In the second city to London, with a more limited labour pool and smaller client base, it could be argued that Dublin goldsmiths faced even more acute challenges to survive in business. They needed to respond to 'the newest and most fashionable taste', which inevitably meant keeping abreast of developments in London.[5] As the century progressed, imports would become an increasingly contentious issue for those who made their principal living as manufacturers. Wholesalers or specialist retailers, on the other hand, could prove singularly ambivalent to patriotism when profits were at stake.

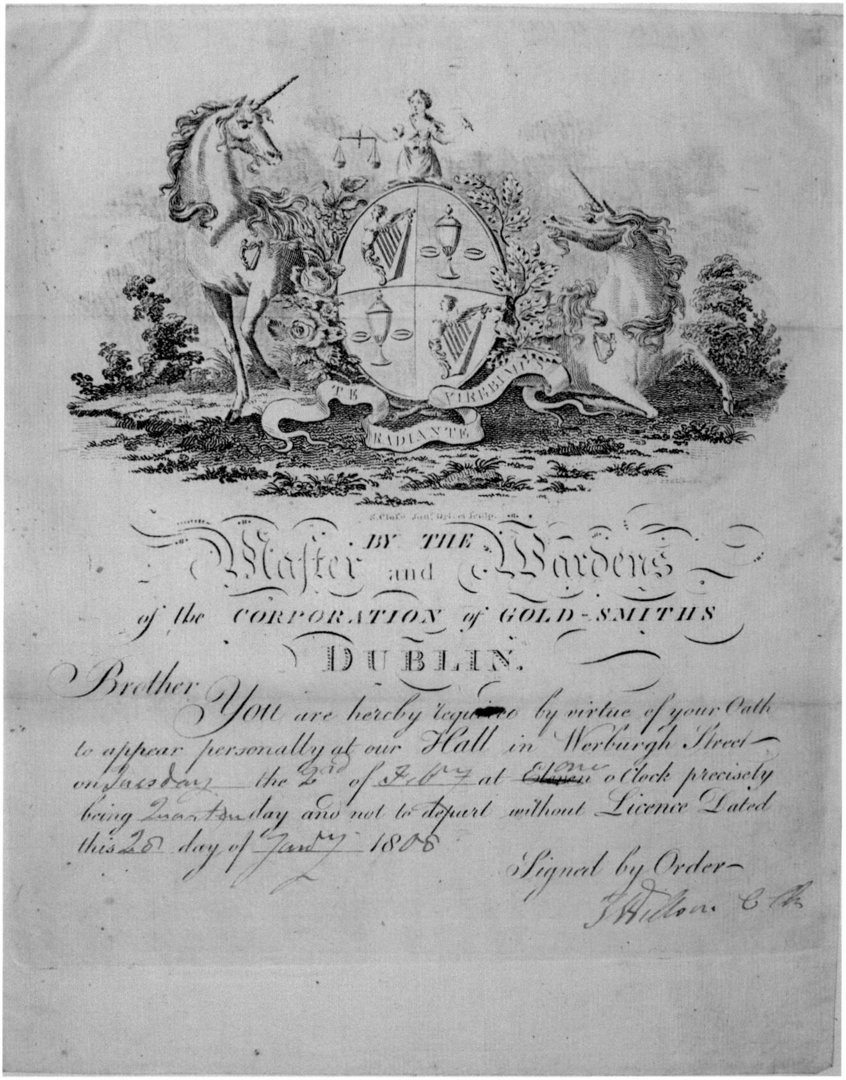

Figure 1.1 Arms of the Dublin goldsmiths' guild on a summons requiring the acquisition of a license to trade (1808), engraving, 25 × 19 cm

Source: Company of Goldsmiths of Dublin, Assay Office, Dublin. Photo credit: © Company of Goldsmiths of Dublin.

The dominance of connoisseurship in Irish silver studies has meant that the business of becoming a goldsmith in eighteenth-century Dublin has received little detailed analysis.[6] How many apprentices enrolled in the trade during the course of the century? What were the occupations of their parents? What were the costs involved in acquiring a city-centre premises and how keen was the competition for essential raw materials? Similarly, the tendency has been to focus almost exclusively on what was happening in Dublin, or provincial Irish cities, without addressing to any significant extent the direct impact of the English trade on Irish goldsmiths during this period, and the potential similarities, as well as differences, between the activities of craftsmen and retailers in the two capital cities.

Training

A goldsmiths' guild had a key role to play in the provision of a skilled labour force. By overseeing the apprenticeship system, mediating in disputes, and regulating the length of time that an apprentice should serve, the guild endeavoured to ensure a competent and competitive workforce.[7] Standard Dublin indentures for the goldsmiths' guild (Fig. 1.2) stipulated that apprentices were to be bound for a period of seven years and that their masters were required to feed, clothe and lodge them.[8] They also required boys to be obedient, faithful, morally upright – even to the extent of shunning visits to 'taverns, alehouses or playhouses' – and remaining unmarried. In professional terms, apprentices were forbidden to reveal the workshop's 'secrets', to buy or sell goods, or lend any of the master's products. Beyond the master promising to impart knowledge of his trade 'by the best means' he could, and teaching 'with due correction', apprenticeship contracts have nothing to say about the nature and structure of the training programme.

In considering the wider issue of apprenticeship, and the guild's central role, a series of questions arise. How large was this nascent labour force in Dublin, and how did it compare in terms of size with London? From what sort of backgrounds did apprentice goldsmiths come and from how far afield? How accurate a profile of the burgeoning labour force is provided by guild apprenticeship ledgers?[9] Were there reasons why individuals might not appear in them? The subject of European guild history has received considerable attention from scholars, many of whom focus on the breakdown of guild control during the course of the eighteenth century.[10] In an Irish context, there remains a wealth of unanswered questions in relation to the practices of individual guilds. A series of articles published in the *Journal of the Royal Society of Antiquaries of Ireland* in the early twentieth century continue to be an authoritative source on the trade practices of individual guilds, and Jacqueline Hill's work has illuminated their political and civic activities.[11] While the pioneering work of Charles Jackson remains an essential source for those interested in the work of Dublin goldsmiths, his principal book is largely a work of reference, incorporating tables of data abstracted from guild records, principally with the collector in mind.[12] Douglas Bennett's important publications reveal much about the goldsmiths' trade, though a connoisseurship methodology underpins them as well, with the result that wider questions remain unanswered. When investigating the market for labour in terms of the Dublin goldsmiths' guild, Mary Pollard's study of the Guild of St Luke, the guild of cutlers, painter-stainers and stationers, offers a useful model for comparison.[13] Pollard's work is primarily an exhaustive guide to members of the Dublin book trade, which also includes broader profiles of the guild's apprentices. In the absence of comparable material for other Dublin craft guilds, this can be usefully employed to contrast with the case of the goldsmiths' guild. Equally, comparative material for the London goldsmiths' guild can be used to demonstrate their apprentice numbers relative to Dublin, to identify the origins of its members and to illustrate the differing character of guild membership

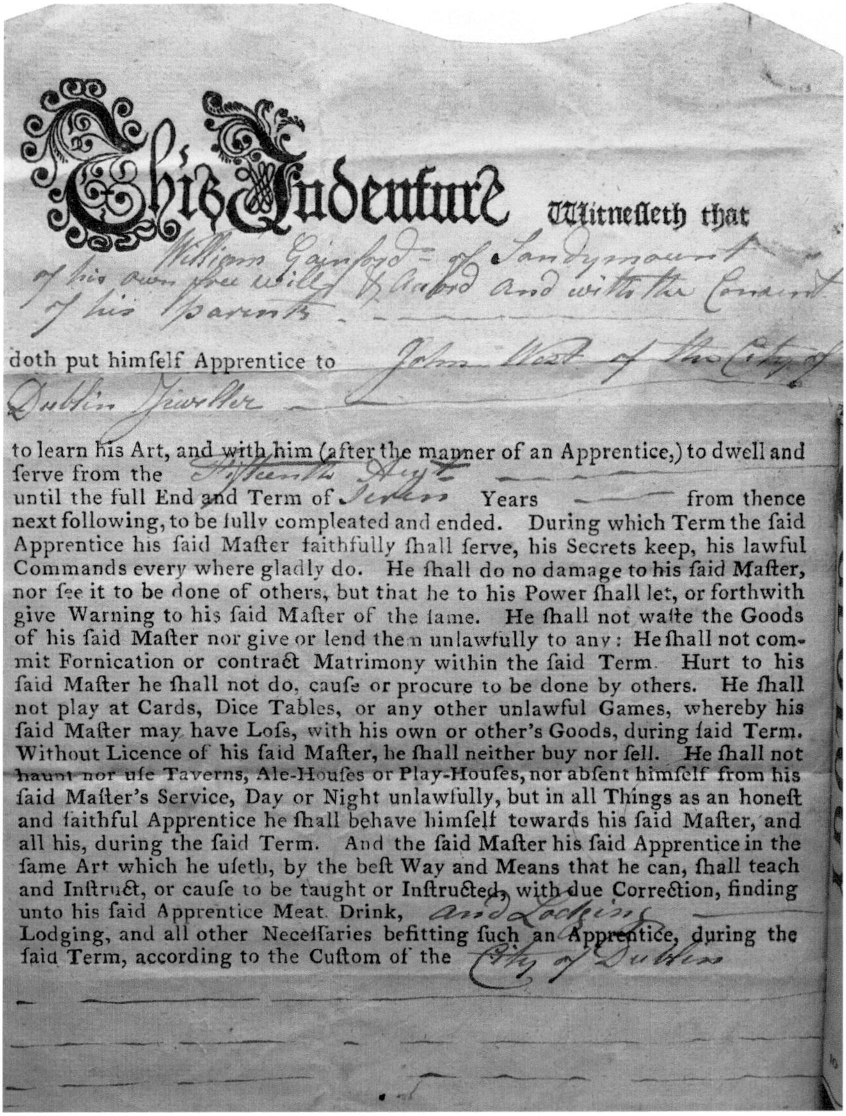

This Indenture Witneſſeth that William Gainsford of Sandymount of his own free Will & Accord and with the Consent of his Parents

doth put himſelf Apprentice to John West of the City of Dublin Jeweller

to learn his Art, and with him (after the manner of an Apprentice,) to dwell and ſerve from the Fifteenth Augt until the full End and Term of Seven Years from thence next following, to be fully compleated and ended. During which Term the ſaid Apprentice his ſaid Maſter faithfully ſhall ſerve, his Secrets keep, his lawful Commands every where gladly do. He ſhall do no damage to his ſaid Maſter, nor ſee it to be done of others, but that he to his Power ſhall let, or forthwith give Warning to his ſaid Maſter of the ſame. He ſhall not waſte the Goods of his ſaid Maſter nor give or lend them unlawfully to any: He ſhall not commit Fornication or contract Matrimony within the ſaid Term. Hurt to his ſaid Maſter he ſhall not do, cauſe or procure to be done by others. He ſhall not play at Cards, Dice Tables, or any other unlawful Games, whereby his ſaid Maſter may have Loſs, with his own or other's Goods, during ſaid Term. Without Licence of his ſaid Maſter, he ſhall neither buy nor ſell. He ſhall not haunt nor uſe Taverns, Ale-Houſes or Play-Houſes, nor abſent himſelf from his ſaid Maſter's Service, Day or Night unlawfully, but in all Things as an honeſt and faithful Apprentice he ſhall behave himſelf towards his ſaid Maſter, and all his, during the ſaid Term. And the ſaid Maſter his ſaid Apprentice in the ſame Art which he uſeth, by the beſt Way and Means that he can, ſhall teach and Inſtruct, or cauſe to be taught or Inſtructed, with due Correction, finding unto his ſaid Apprentice Meat, Drink, and Lodging Lodging, and all other Neceſſaries befitting ſuch an Apprentice, during the ſaid Term, according to the Cuſtom of the City of Dublin

Figure 1.2 Apprentice Indenture of William Gainsfort to the Dublin jeweller John West (1806), engraving

Source: Company of Goldsmiths of Dublin, Assay Office, Dublin. Photo credit: © Company of Goldsmiths of Dublin.

in London. In London, for example, the goldsmith son of a butcher might become free of the butcher's guild, whereas in Dublin it was necessary to be free of the guild whose trade you practised, at least in the first half of the eighteenth century. By the second half of the century, the requirements regarding eligibility for civic freedom were relaxed in Dublin.[14]

When it came to apprenticeship, a range of variables, including the trade in question, the reputation of the master, and the town or city involved, could affect the scale of fees. The cost of training with one Dublin Chancery officer in 1723 was more than three times the fee commanded by an attorney during the same period.[15] The goldsmiths' trade was expensive to pursue, given the range of tools required and the intrinsic value of the materials. Apprentice goldsmiths could expect to pay more than plumbers.

The premiums sought by master goldsmiths are occasionally recorded in guild minute books, generally when disputes arose. In 1695, an apprentice named James Brenan petitioned the guild against his master David Swan, who he alleged had treated him 'barbarously'. Swan was instructed to repay Brenan £10 and furnish him with a new suit of clothes.[16] During the same period, the goldsmith John Cuthbert received £35 for one of his apprentices.[17] In 1728 Thomas Sutton was obliged to return half an apprenticeship premium of 20 guineas when one of his boys died less than two years into his apprenticeship.[18] Sutton's full premium amounted to more than the value of a silver cup and cover, quart cup, chamber pot and snuffers, which he supplied to Thomas Taylor of Headfort, Co. Meath, during the same period.[19]

These sums confirm the level of respectability associated with the trade, and the reality that the cost of apprenticeship placed it out of range for many. Pupils from St John's Charity School in Dublin, which had been established in the 1690s, gravitated towards more modest crafts like shoe making and hosiery, and were apprenticed for premiums in the region of £3 to £4.[20] Premiums could be flexible and depended on a variety of factors, including the reputation of the master, the speed with which relevant skills could be mastered, and the extent to which the master needed extra pairs of hands. In January 1785, the Dublin printer Charles Campbell sought 'a lad of good morals and decent parentage' and specified a fee of £30 in his advertisement. Two months later, and short of takers, he halved the sum.[21]

Evidently, flexible fee structures also applied in England. Writing to her husband in 1762, Emily, Marchioness of Kildare (later Duchess of Leinster) (Fig. 1.3), mused on the cost of financing an apprenticeship in the millinery trade there. Having been quoted a range of fees, she explained to her husband that 'the longer the term the less the sum . . . because they then become useful to their masters.'[22] The master's reputation was also decisive. A Mrs Leprince, who commanded higher sums than others, combined two specialisations, 'being like most of the French, both milliner and mantua maker, besides being the first woman of that sort in London'.[23]

This reference to London raises the question of the Irish who chose to train in England. Doing so offered access to a larger and more sophisticated market, but also involved specific drawbacks like the additional cost of travel and the necessity of having contacts there. The author of *The London Tradesman* reported that London goldsmiths' premiums ranged from £20 to £50, but they could be substantially more.[24] Three Surrey boys bound between 1717 and 1731 paid premiums ranging from £94 to £200, while two Sussex gentlemen each gave £100 to apprentice their sons in the early eighteenth century.[25] A relatively small number of Irish parents opted to send their sons to London for training as goldsmiths. Between 1708 and 1760 just twelve Irish boys from Kildare, Waterford, Cork and Dublin were bound apprentices to London goldsmiths.[26] The guardians of Dubliners William Overand and George Jameson paid £28 and £30 in 1736, while a contemporary, Benjamin Walmsley, was charged double that amount.[27] The higher fee may have reflected experience in retailing as well as manufacturing, offering future potential for a larger income.[28]

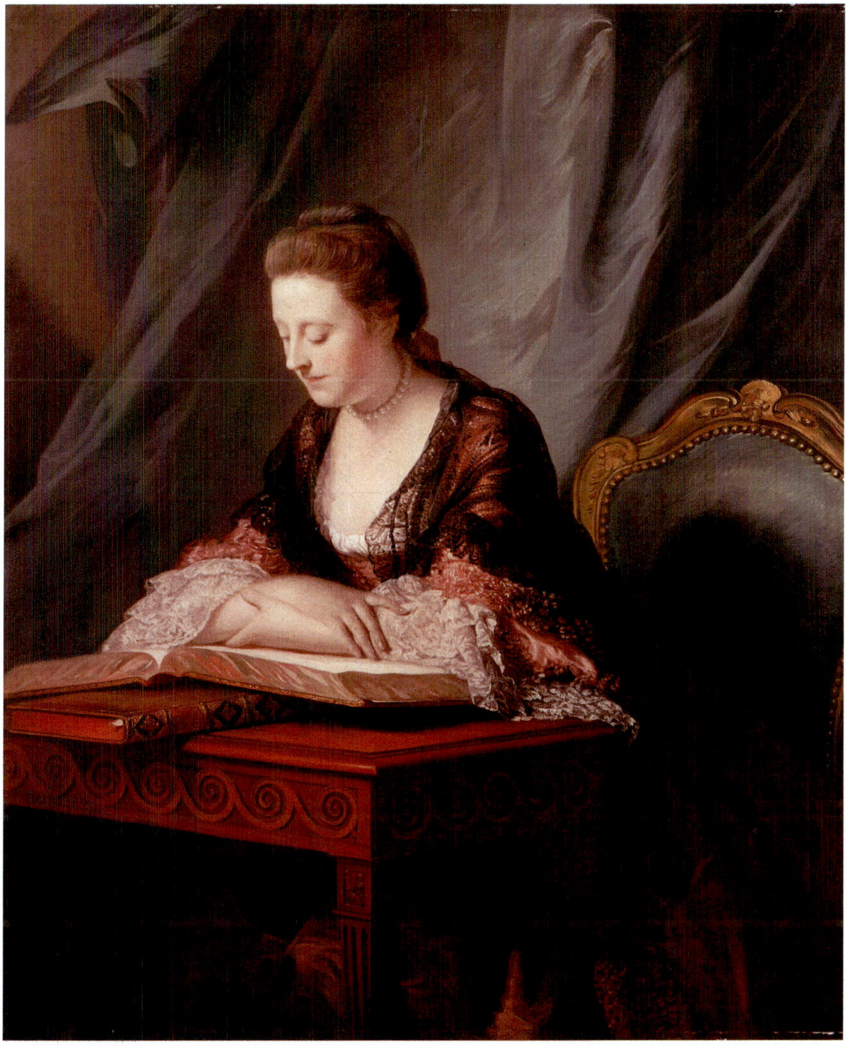

Figure 1.3 Allan Ramsay, *Portrait of Emily, Marchioness of Kildare* (1765–66), oil on canvas, 125.7 × 102 cm

Source: National Museums, Liverpool. Photo credit: © Walker Art Gallery, Liverpool.

In contrast to these exceptional cases, the apprenticeship ledgers of the Dublin goldsmiths' guild reveal that between 1700 and 1800 over 700 apprentices were enrolled (Fig. 1.4).[29] This figure provides an initial indication of the numbers who would ultimately follow the trade, though as will be seen, a comparatively small number advanced to become freemen.

Not surprisingly, given population size in the capital, over half of the apprentice goldsmiths came from Dublin and its hinterland. As Toby Barnard has observed, 'This was the area with an abundance of Protestants able to afford admission.'[30] Even in

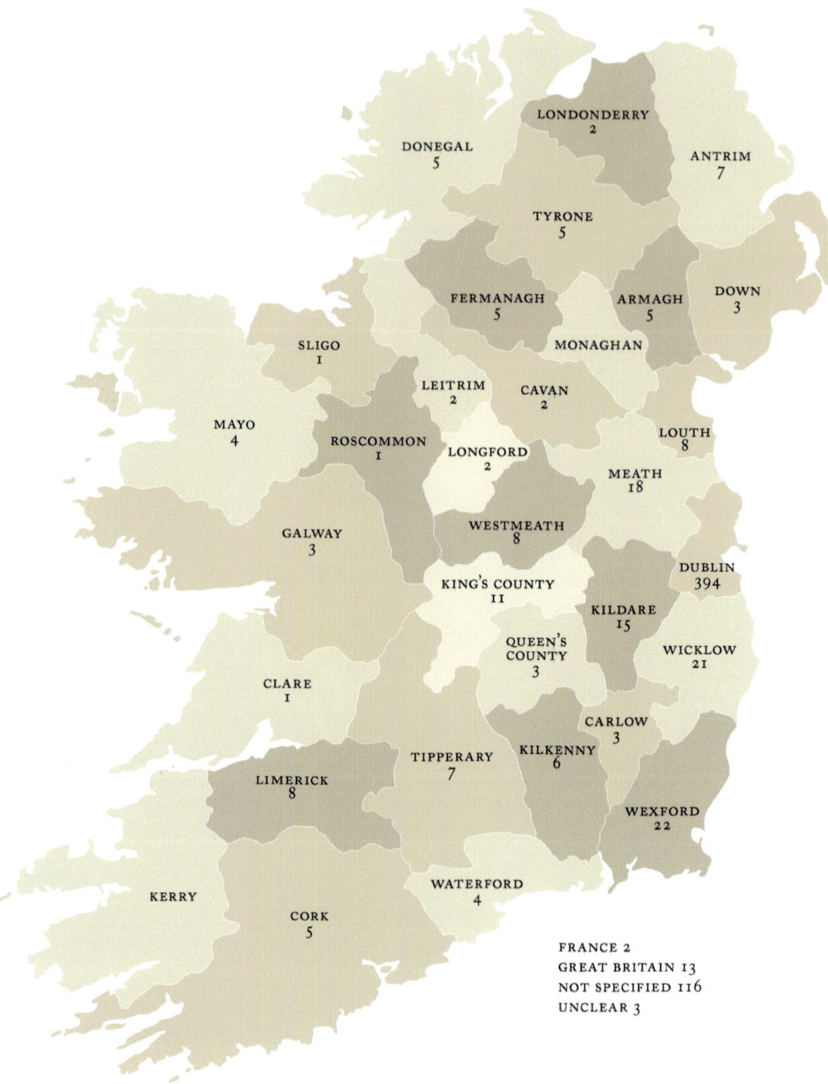

Figure 1.4 Origins of apprentices bound to Dublin goldsmiths between 1700 and 1800
Photo credit: © Author's collection.

London, where religion was less of a decisive factor, the wealth of prosperous members of the urban community, and the concentration of citizens, were apparent in the origins of apprentices to London's livery companies. In 1690, 53 per cent of apprentices who enrolled in the London goldsmiths' guild came from London and its adjacent counties Middlesex, Surrey, Kent and Essex. These also represented the most highly populated counties during the first half of the eighteenth century. This figure increased steadily as the century progressed, so that in the period between 1740 and 1750 it had reached 78 per cent.[31] The greater scale of the London market, relative to Dublin, is patently evident when the numbers of recorded apprentices in the two cities are compared. Between 1700 and 1750, 3,169 apprentices registered with the London goldsmiths' guild (see Table 1.1). In the first two decades of the century these decennial totals exceeded the quota recorded in Dublin for the entire century.

While the origins of apprentices bound to Dublin goldsmiths reveal a metropolitan bias, the prestige of the trade is also borne out by the wider picture. Only two Irish counties, Monaghan and Kerry, were absent from the places of origin of apprentices recorded by the guild between 1700 and 1800.[32] Other distant counties like Armagh, Antrim, Cork, Limerick and Tipperary were included. Predictably, the proximity to Dublin of Meath, Wicklow and Wexford meant that more apprentices were drawn from these counties. The surviving data for the Guild of St Luke mirrors this Dublin-centric bias. More than two-thirds of the apprentices to cutlers, painter-stainers and stationers in the latter half of the eighteenth century hailed from the capital city.[33] As a rival centre for printing, Cork was also important for training apprentices in this field. No boy from any of Munster's five counties appears in apprentice ledgers for the Guild of St Luke. The same pattern applies to the goldsmiths' trade. Only a handful of apprentices from Cork were recorded in the Dublin ledgers during the eighteenth century. Outside Dublin, Cork had the most vibrant silver trade; apprentice enrolments for the city confirm that training locally was convenient.[34] In 1782, Carden Terry, one of Cork's most prolific goldsmiths, advertised his stock in the *Hibernian Chronicle*.[35] He also took the opportunity to state that he was looking for an apprentice.

So, from what sort of backgrounds did apprentice goldsmiths come? The high sums involved might suggest that only the sons of those with a decent income could afford to pay apprenticeship premiums. In fact, the prestigious reputation of the trade lent it an extremely broad appeal (Appendix 1). For a father in a modest occupation the chance to improve his son's prospects must have seemed attractive. Three of those bound to Dublin goldsmiths between 1700 and 1800 gave their fathers' profession as braziers, indicating an ascent of sorts within the field of metalwork. The goldsmiths' trade was consistently associated with status, due to the high cost of raw materials and end products, and the elite clientele it served. In contrast, Stuart surgeons, who often doubled as barbers, lacked the stature and wealth of their nineteenth-century counterparts.[36]

The prevalence of parents described as 'gentlemen' is striking – clearly their credentials varied.[37] As Toby Barnard puts it, 'What constituted gentility proved as mutable as the uses of "quality".'[38] Peter Earle has remarked that 'the temptation to upgrade one's status when beginning a career . . . must have been considerable.'[39] Almost a quarter of those apprentices whose parents' or guardians' occupations were recorded by the Dublin goldsmiths' guild were described as gentlemen. At the very least, this indicates their aspirations.[40] In his analysis of the origins of London apprentices during the late seventeenth and early eighteenth century, Peter Earle comments on the frequency with which the term was used. Over a quarter of his sample of apprentices, drawn from a range of trades, were described as the sons of gentlemen. While he concedes that some may have boosted their own titles, he is confident that, overall, the term was not entirely meaningless.[41] This is supported by evidence from the Dublin ledgers. The children of over two dozen clergymen and esquires joined the sons of 'gentlemen' hoping to learn goldsmiths' skills in eighteenth-century Dublin.

It is somewhat surprising that fewer than 10 per cent of those apprenticed to Dublin goldsmiths during this period were the sons of goldsmiths. Some within the trade enrolled their own sons, while others opted to put them out, presumably seeking specialised skills or experience. A similar number described themselves as 'merchants' – a broad title, but generally implying solid business connections. Among the more modestly represented trades were butchers, felt-makers, hairdressers and stocking-weavers. Two charity school boys received a good start by being apprenticed to the Dublin goldsmiths William Steele and Robert Breading in 1769 and 1787 respectively.[42] Similar occupational diversity is found in the records of the Guild of St Luke. Of the 284 stationer apprentices enrolled between 1740 and 1799, the sons of gentlemen, stationers, parsons, farmers, merchants and esquires were most numerous.[43]

Apart from some newspaper advertisements seeking apprentices, we have little information as to how the parents of potential apprentices came in contact with a master or why they chose one goldsmith over another. The reputation of the master must have played a part and it is hardly surprising that the workshops with the largest

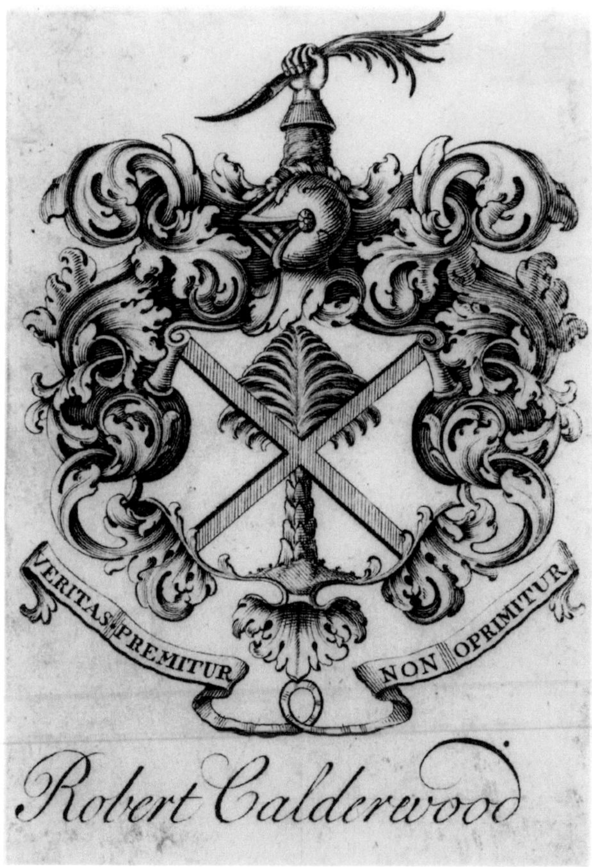

Figure 1.5 Bookplate of the Dublin goldsmith Robert Calderwood (n.d.), engraving, 9 × 6.5 cm
Source: National Library of Ireland, Dublin. Photo credit: © National Library of Ireland.

concentration of apprentices were among the most productive and highly regarded (Appendix 2). It is difficult to determine the extent to which family ties or other social contacts were involved in the choice of master. Robert Calderwood (Fig. 1.5), perhaps exploiting connections through his mother to genteel families in the north of Ireland, took on one apprentice, George Brush, from Down in 1764, while ten years previously he took one who was the son of an Antrim clergyman.[44] However, recent research into the socio-economic background of London apprentices between 1600 and 1749 indicates that the vast majority of apprentices had no identifiable kinship, professional, or geographical ties to their masters.[45] Just as with the London livery companies, the Dublin goldsmiths' guild was relatively open to sons whose parents were in different occupations and resident in almost every part of the country.

When it came to how goldsmith apprentices were distributed in the eighteenth century, more than 200 masters were involved, yet the dispersal was by no means equal. Over half the masters enrolled only one or two apprentices each, yet others were clearly much in demand.[46] Fewer than 10 per cent registered more than three. Collectively, the goldsmiths John Hamilton (Fig. 1.6) and Robert Calderwood (Fig. 1.7)

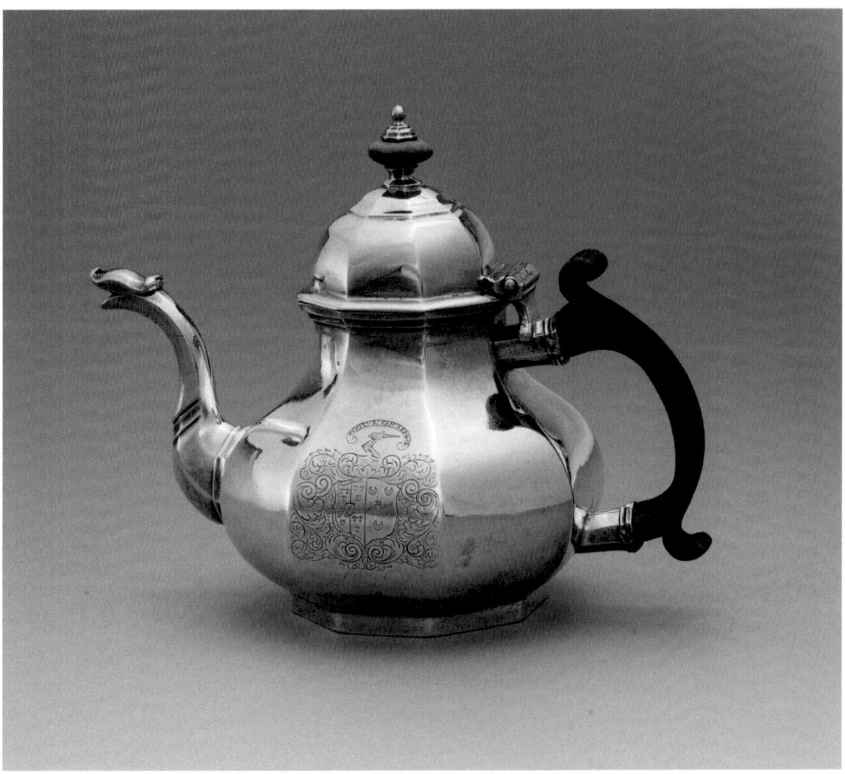

Figure 1.6 John Hamilton, *Teapot* (1720), silver, 17.1 × 12.1 cm

Source: San Antonio Museum of Art, Texas. Bequest of John V. Rowan Jr, 2004.13.130. Photo credit: © Courtesy of the San Antonio Museum of Art. Photography by Peggy Tenison.

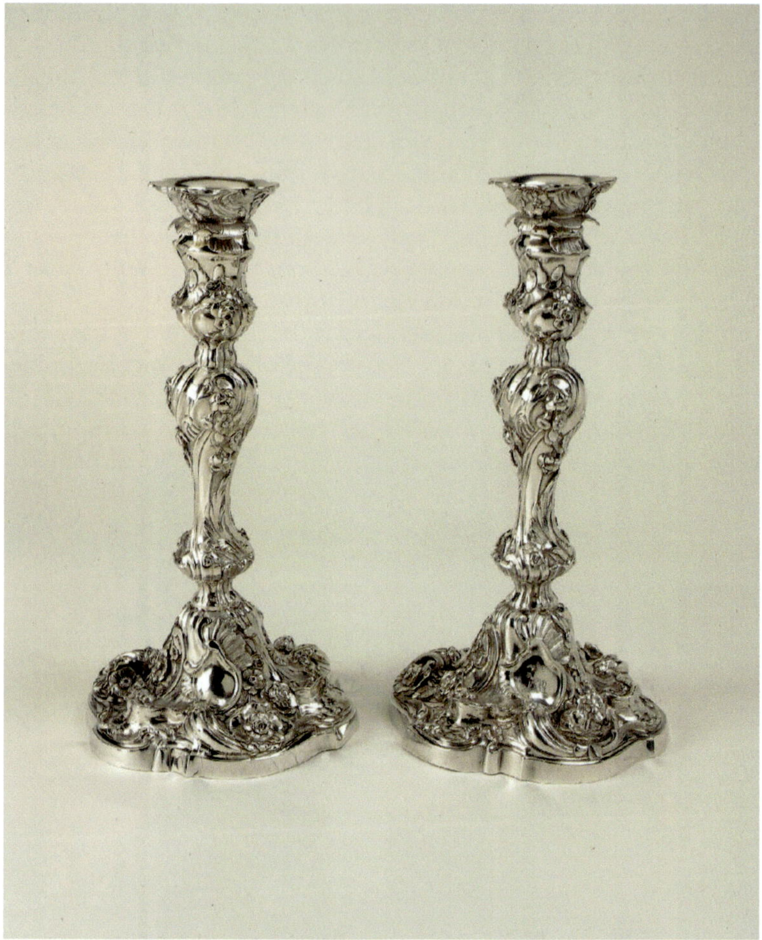

Figure 1.7 Robert Calderwood, *Candlesticks* (c.1745), silver, 28.57 cm (h)
Source: National Museum of Ireland, Dublin. Photo credit: © National Museum of Ireland.

engaged over two dozen apprentices between 1709 and 1764, not including turnovers. Turnovers were boys who faced irreconcilable differences with their masters or whose mentors had retired or, in some cases, died.[47] Calderwood alone registered fourteen apprentices from 1727 to 1764, as well as inheriting more from colleagues.[48] He was one of Dublin's most enterprising goldsmiths, submitting almost one-tenth of the total volume of plate assayed in 1754, and counting the viceroy William Cavendish, Marquess of Hartington (Fig. 1.8) and Lord Bessborough among his clients. Equally desirable as a master was John Hamilton, who served as master and warden of the guild, and along with Calderwood ran one of the most productive workshops during the 1740s, sending a wide range of objects for assaying. Hamilton registered eleven apprentices between 1709 and 1743.

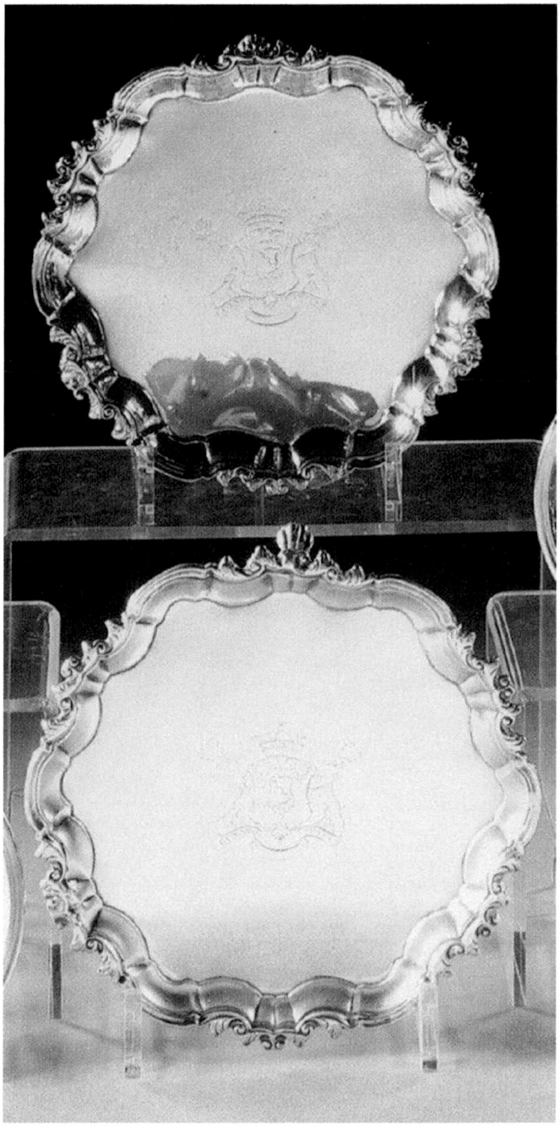

Figure 1.8 Robert Calderwood, *Pair of salvers engraved with the arms of William, Marquess of Hartington* (c.1755), silver, 19 cm diam

Photo credit: © Courtesy of Sotheby's, London.

Apart from those taken on for the full term of seven years, a number of goldsmiths, including Calderwood, also accepted turnovers.[49] Turnover contracts could prove mutually beneficial, as the apprentice completed the required term of training, and the new master gained an assistant already proficient in basic skills. The value of a skilled apprentice is confirmed by the survival of isolated references to the poaching of apprentices, one of the few areas of contract infringement in which the guild interfered in its efforts to police members. In 1739, Francis Smith was fined 10 shillings, when William Currie claimed that Smith had tried to 'seduce his apprentice to work for him'.[50] Seven years later, the goldsmith Christopher Locker made a similar charge against Samuel Walker. The guild ruled that for any person to employ another man's apprentice or generate work for him was 'a very bad practice and ought to be discouraged'.[51]

One of the most remarkable features of the apprenticeship system in the Dublin goldsmiths' guild is the strikingly small number who, having completed their training, went on to become freemen, with the right to establish their own workshops and sell goods. Of more than 700 apprentices who were registered with the guild between 1700 and 1800, just over 20 per cent became independent masters.[52] One explanation for this is that the costs and risks of establishing oneself as an independent master were so high that only a tiny minority could afford to embark on this path. Consequently, many trained goldsmiths were content to work as journeymen, earning a daily wage – some, no doubt, with the intention of saving up for their own equipment and premises, while others were destined to spend their entire careers as journeymen. The Huguenot goldsmith David Bomes (Fig. 1.9) took on at least

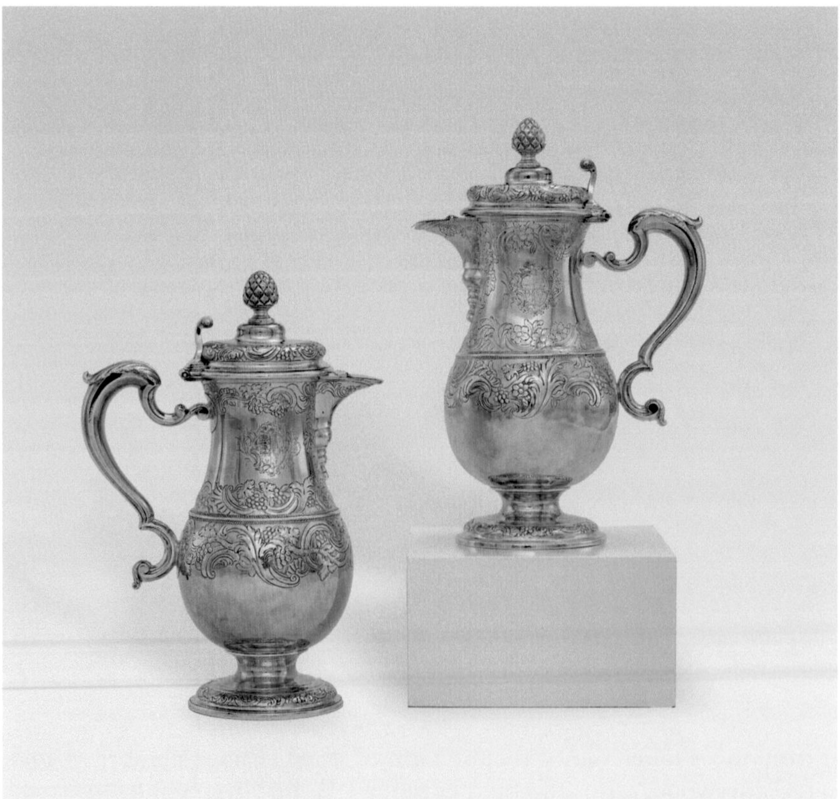

Figure 1.9 David Bomes, *Pair of wine ewers* (c.1740), silver, 30.5 × 12.4 cm

Source: The Art Institute of Chicago. Bequest of Mary Hooker Dole. Photo credit: © The Art Institute of Chicago.

twelve apprentices between 1739 and 1766; none of these seems to have become a freeman, and at least some of them must have remained as journeymen.[53] His compatriot Daniel Pineau, a jeweller, also registered a large number of apprentices, many of them of French origin, but only one, James Vidouze, probably a cousin of his first wife, became a freeman in 1739, a full thirteen years after the start of his apprenticeship.

Patrick Wallis has observed a similar phenomenon for apprenticeships in seventeenth-century England, where fewer than half of apprentices became freemen.[54] Death, illness, and disability would have accounted for some of the fall-off. As Wallis clarifies, freedom rates should not be confused with completion rates; some apprentices completed their training but remained journeymen, while others also served out their time and then migrated. However, a significant number of apprentices quit at various stages before the completion of their term. There were several reasons for these early departures: a breakdown in relations between the master and his apprentice or a slump in the workshop's business. Alternatively, the young man might have left to get married, take up an inheritance, or pursue a more advantageous trade elsewhere. These circumstances also applied for goldsmiths' apprentices in eighteenth-century Dublin. Complaints of ill treatment were common. James Devin, who was apprenticed to Burton Wright, protested in 1751 of 'bad and cruel usage by his master' and his apprenticeship indenture was terminated.[55] Occasionally the apprentice was in the wrong; in 1734, for example, James Maguire left the service of his master, the clockmaker John Crampton, because he had 'greatly misbehaved'.[56] The quality of training was sometimes contentious. In March 1741 the guild decided that James Steele should be discharged from his indenture with Francis Smith because 'the master does seldom work himself [and] neither does he keep anyone at work whereby to learn ye boy his trade.'[57]

The substantial dropout rate among London apprentices also led Wallis to revise the established notion of apprenticeship during the early modern period.[58] Instead of the old notion that apprentices received most of their practical training during the early years before becoming more directly involved in workshop output and repaying the master's initial investment, he suggested an alternative. According to Wallis, apprentices made an important economic contribution from the beginning, even if it involved unskilled tasks such as making deliveries, watching the shop in the master's absence, or cleaning the premises. They gradually acquired skills and knowledge through observation, imitation and practice over the entire apprenticeship and not in distinct modules. Moreover, the size of the premium and the value of unskilled and semi-skilled labour were sufficient to compensate the master for the inevitable early departure of apprentices. There is no reason to doubt that the same was true of the apprenticeship system for goldsmiths in eighteenth-century Dublin.

The analysis so far has relied on the guild's records of apprentice enrolments to profile the emerging labour force, but how accurate is this official picture? The guild required that all apprentices bound in the city should be enrolled in their books, but do these records really offer a reliable gauge of the numbers who would ultimately train in the field? In fact, there were various reasons why apprentices might not appear in them. There were those who had completed their apprenticeship outside Dublin, or even outside Ireland, but wanted to work in the city. In 1698, for example, Thomas Elliot petitioned the guild, stating that he had served his time to a watchmaker in England, and applying for guild freedom.[59] Similarly, in 1703 John Paturle was admitted free, after reporting that he had been apprenticed to a jeweller in France, 'and had exercised that art several years since'.[60] He represents one of the many Huguenots who settled in Dublin during the seventeenth and eighteenth centuries.[61] The guild also agreed to accept John Pennyfather as a member in 1704. He claimed to have served seven years to a goldsmith in Limerick. He was instructed to present the master of the guild with a pair of gloves, in addition to the customary fee.[62]

Fathers who bound their own sons did not always consider it necessary to record such arrangements with the guild; sometimes they simply did not bother to do so, even though it was obligatory. For instance, in 1771 Roger Finch, a freeman, wrote to the guild on behalf of his son John. He claimed that, having served him for almost a decade, John had emigrated to Portugal, and was now running into difficulties there because he did not have proof of his credentials.[63] Despite the fact that Roger Finch had enrolled nine apprentices with the guild between 1725 and 1741, his son John does not appear among them. A second example from later in the century confirms this laissez-faire attitude on the part of some. When Thomas Walsh petitioned for freedom in May 1790, he was obliged to admit that he had no official indenture, despite the fact that he had served a full term to his father. By way of explanation, he simply remarked that 'his father did not think it was necessary.' While the guild accepted his evidence, his father's oversight cost him an additional fine.[64]

There were also retailers who had not been apprenticed within the trade, but who went on to deal in silver wares. According to an Act of Parliament in 1784, it was enacted that:

> From and after September 1784 no person being a merchant, manufacturer or dealer in gold or silver wares should sell or expose to sale, buy or exchange without first registering his name and place of abode with the Company of Goldsmiths of Dublin in a book to be kept by the said Company for that purpose, under a penalty of £100 for every offence.[65]

This suggests that market expansion during the course of the eighteenth century made the task of monitoring the trade increasingly difficult for the guild, particularly when some retailers in the field may not have served an official apprenticeship. The surviving registration book compiled by the goldsmiths' guild serves as a valuable source for the history of the trade.[66]

Richard Singleton was one of those whose names and addresses were entered with the guild in accordance with the 1784 Act. In the records for the Guild of St Luke he is described as a cutler, and he apprenticed his own son William in 1774.[67] He was therefore someone who had trained in a complementary field, and was evidently retailing silver goods, yet had not undergone a goldsmiths' apprenticeship. Retail skills could also be transferable across trades. An advertisement in 1799 bears this out: John Nixon advertised in the *New Cork Evening Post* that he required 'a smart lad of genteel connections' for the linen-drapery and hosiery business. He specified that the boy would 'be taught book-keeping and the principles of commerce' which would 'fit him for any department in the mercantile line'.[68]

An individual with capital and retailing ability, as opposed to craft skills, could be useful, as the examples of London goldsmiths' firms of Rundell and Bridge and Parker and Wakelin testify.[69] It was also possible that enterprising boys could work their way up in the goldsmiths' trade, without having finance or the benefits of official indentures. The London goldsmith Joseph Brasbridge describes exactly this sort of situation in his memoirs, referring to the spoon-maker Richard Crossley:

> He came originally to London as a boy and was employed by Chawner, the spoon-maker in Paternoster-row, to carry charcoal to his men; hence he was known by the name of Charcoal Dick, but being a smart lad and writing a good hand, he was soon promoted to a place in the counting house.[70]

It is also difficult to quantify those individuals who operated on the margins of the trade as journeymen.[71] While the guild noted their names along with quarter brothers in the period c.1670 to 1700, similar records do not survive for the eighteenth century.[72] Their apprenticeships were not necessarily recorded consistently with the guild. Some are revealed in guild accounts when they broke the rules or ran into difficulties, but for these there must have also been others who remain in the shadows. During the 1760s, a goldsmith described simply as 'Makemaid' appears in guild minutes, implicated in a case of substandard work.[73] He is not listed in the apprenticeship ledgers, nor in Jackson's lists of quarter brothers, journeymen, or freemen,[74] and he is described only as 'a workman of Mr. Cormick's'. No mark has been ascribed to him. The date in this instance is significant. As previously noted, warnings had been issued by the guild during the 1760s to Protestant freemen and quarter brothers who were amenable to engaging 'popish apprentices'. Since Cormick himself was a Catholic, it is possible that his workman was too.[75]

Another group who do not show up in records of apprentice enrolments, but could practise the trade, were the widows of former guild members. When the goldsmith Francis Girard died in 1710, his business was continued by his widow Mary, who continued using his mark and had small quantities of plate assayed between 1711 and 1713.[76] The same was true of Edward Barrett's widow Mary, who kept the business going after her husband's death in 1722.[77] Though some widows were left with the quandary of how best to honour indentures, Mary Barrett was successful enough to attract two new apprentices after her husband's death.[78] Her contemporary, Dorothy Manjoy, also had plate assayed after the death of her husband Benjamin, in 1715 (Fig. 1.10). Later in the century, Eleanor Champion, widow of the jeweller James Champion, announced to the nobility and gentry that she intended carrying on business as usual.[79] Michael Cormick's widow Ann, and William Keene's widow Jane, were similarly enterprising, though necessity could prove a spur to continuity. Jane Keene, for example, was left with five children to support when her husband died in 1801, a fact which she mentioned on her newly designed billhead (Fig. 1.11).[80]

There were also illicit reasons for not registering an apprentice with the guild. Three examples from the first half of the eighteenth century illustrate this fact, and they could not have been the only cases.[81] In 1704, the goldsmith Murtagh Dowling applied for guild freedom. It emerged that his master had not become free himself until four years after Dowling was bound. This meant that he had been taken on illegally,

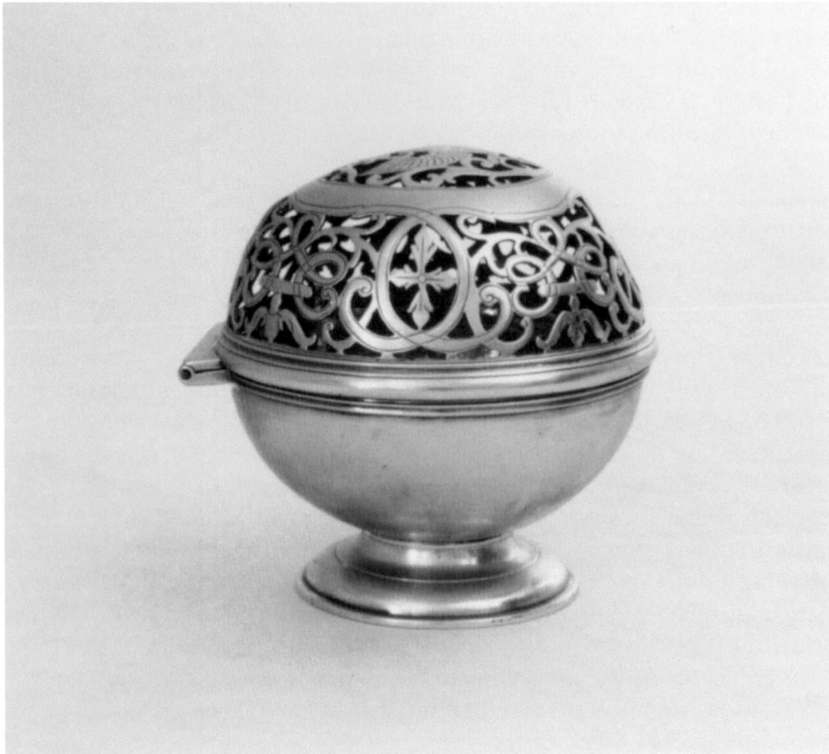

Figure 1.10 Possibly Dorothy Manjoy, *Sponge box* (c.1725), silver, 9.7 cm diam

Source: Metropolitan Museum, New York. Gift of Irwin Untermyer, 1968. Photo credit: © Metropolitan Museum of Art.

during the period when quarter brothers were prohibited from doing so, and it was agreed that he would have to give the guild a piece of plate valued at 20 shillings as a fine.[82] An even more suspect case was recorded in 1738, when the guild intervened in a dispute between the apprentice Arthur Rogers and his master John Low. It emerged that Rogers had been bound purely for a period of three years, which was decreed to be 'contrary to the known laws of the City'.[83] Neither Low nor Rogers appears in the apprentice registers, either as a master or as an apprentice, which makes it difficult to assess their motives. In 1741, in a similar case involving Pierce Jones and his master James St Maurice, the guild ruled that both parties were

> worthless persons and that the Master notwithstanding the Indentures being for seven years entered into an agreement to discharge the apprentice at the end of three years for half a crown contrary to the custom of the City of Dublin.[84]

As the next chapter will explore, a full-term apprenticeship was fundamental from the guild's perspective in ensuring satisfactory levels of competence and craftsmanship in the trade. However, for every rule, there would be those who would flout it.

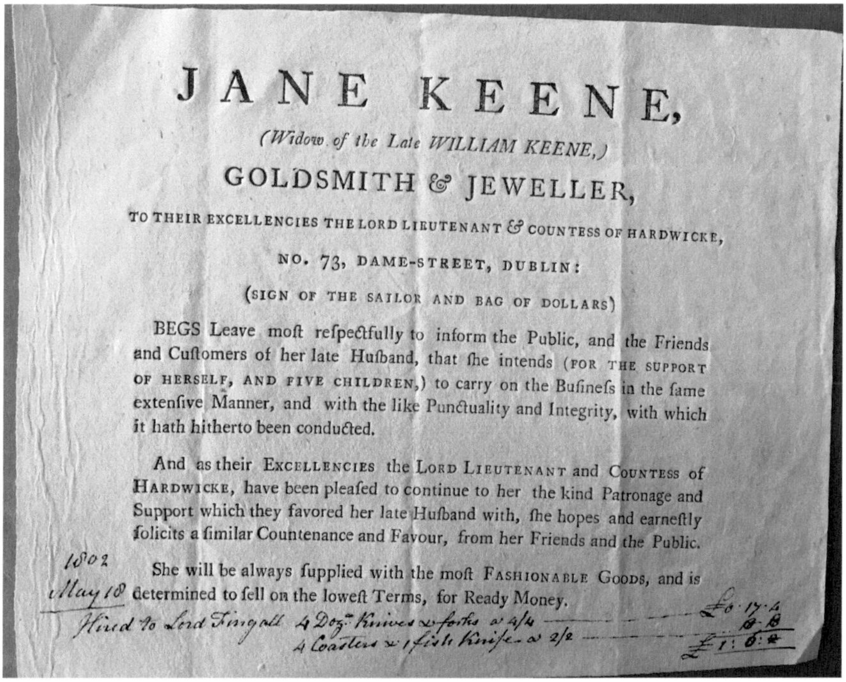
JANE KEENE,

(*Widow of the Late WILLIAM KEENE,*)

GOLDSMITH & JEWELLER,

TO THEIR EXCELLENCIES THE LORD LIEUTENANT & COUNTESS OF HARDWICKE,

NO. 73, DAME-STREET, DUBLIN:

(SIGN OF THE SAILOR AND BAG OF DOLLARS)

BEGS Leave moſt reſpectfully to inform the Public, and the Friends and Cuſtomers of her late Huſband, that ſhe intends (FOR THE SUPPORT OF HERSELF, AND FIVE CHILDREN,) to carry on the Buſineſs in the ſame extenſive Manner, and with the like Punctuality and Integrity, with which it hath hitherto been conducted.

And as their EXCELLENCIES the LORD LIEUTENANT and COUNTESS of HARDWICKE, have been pleaſed to continue to her the kind Patronage and Support which they favored her late Huſband with, ſhe hopes and earneſtly ſolicits a ſimilar Countenance and Favour, from her Friends and the Public.

1802 May 18 She will be always ſupplied with the moſt FASHIONABLE GOODS, and is determined to ſell on the loweſt Terms, for Ready Money.

Hired to Lord Fingall 4 Dozⁿ Knives & forks @ 4/4 — £0:17:4

4 Coasters & 1 fish Knife @ 2/2 — 8:8

£1:6:0

Figure 1.11 Billhead of Jane Keene (handwritten receipt dated 1802), 18.5 × 14.5 cm

Source: National Library of Ireland, Dublin. Photo credit: © National Library of Ireland.

When it came to guild freedom, practices differed in London and Dublin. While London craftsmen working within the city limits were obliged to be members of one of the City Companies, it was not necessary for craftsmen to be free of the guild whose trade they practised. Over 300 goldsmiths have been recorded for the period between 1697 and 1837 as members of such disparate London guilds as the butchers, girdlers and longbowstring makers.[85] As Arthur Grimwade has observed, there were various reasons why this happened. There were cases of freedom by patrimony, facilitated by fathers who were not goldsmiths themselves. Also, those who had completed an apprenticeship to a working goldsmith who was free of another guild automatically became eligible to apply for freedom through the guild with which their master was affiliated.[86] The London goldsmith, Peter Archambo I, represents a case in point. Archambo was apprenticed to Joseph Margas, 'Citizen and Butcher', in 1710.[87] The fact that he was in a position to enter a mark as a practising goldsmith just a year after completing an apprenticeship to a 'butcher' seems confusing. However, Margas was a goldsmith. He had, in his turn, been apprenticed to Thomas Jenkins of the Butcher's Company in 1699.[88]

In Dublin, on the other hand, while it was possible to apply for freedom of a guild by birth (Fig. 1.12), one of the requirements of admission to freedom of the city was a promise not to intrude upon the trades of any other guild.[89] This meant that, at least in the first half of the eighteenth century, the members of the Dublin goldsmiths' guild

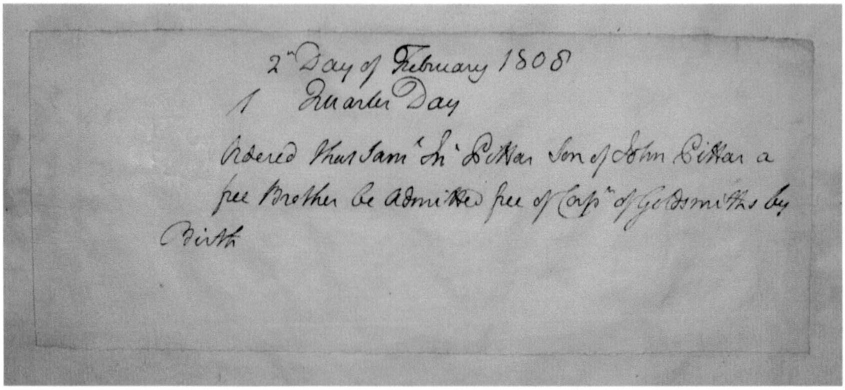
2nd Day of February 1808
1 Quarter Day
Ordered That Sam' Jn' Pittar Son of John Pittar a
free Brother be admitted free of Corpn of Goldsmiths by
Birth

Figure 1.12 Certificate of admission to the goldsmiths' guild for John Pittar Jr, son of John Pittar Sr (1808), 10 × 24 cm

Source: Company of Goldsmiths of Dublin, Assay Office Dublin. Photo credit: © Company of Goldsmiths of Dublin.

followed that specific trade almost exclusively.[90] However, as Hill has noted, in the latter half of the eighteenth century, Dublin Corporation ceased insisting that freedom should only be granted to individuals following their guild's trades.[91] With a final reminder issued in 1772, the way was eased for sons who did not follow their father's trades to secure freedom of the city and acquire a parliamentary vote. Interestingly, the decline in apprenticeship numbers within the Dublin goldsmiths' guild comes in this period (Table 1.1).[92] Kahl has proposed of London that

> the traditions of London . . . were against the survival of apprenticeship . . . According to the custom of the City many freemen carried on a trade which had neither

Table 1.1 Number of apprentices registered with the Dublin and London Goldsmiths' Companies, 1700–1800[93]

Date	*Dublin*	*London*
1700–09	56	790
1710–19	80	743
1720–29	113	564
1730–39	91	562
1740–49	94	510
1750–59	123	–
1760–69	95	
1770–79	39	–
1780–89	18	–
1790–1800	6	–

Source: Apprentices 1637–1703, Company of Goldsmiths of Dublin, Ms. 95, Dublin, Assay Office; Apprentices September 1704–1 March 1752, Company of Goldsmiths of Dublin, Ms. 96, Dublin, Assay Office; Apprentices 2 May 1752–7 November 1823, Company of Goldsmiths of Dublin, Ms. 97, Dublin, Assay Office.

> any relation to the craft in which they had served their time nor any connection with the trade of the company of which they were members.[94]

In London, a marked fall-off in apprentice goldsmiths was already evident by the 1720s. In Dublin, this did not happen until the latter decades of the century.

Premises

The ability to attract an adequate labour force was just one of the competitive markets which eighteenth-century goldsmiths needed to negotiate. The perception of the trade as genteel is reflected in Campbell's estimated costs for setting up as a master in mid-eighteenth-century London. He reckoned that the capital required by a cutler was in the region of £50 to £200, and a coppersmith roughly £100 to £1,000, while goldsmiths' estimated costs were significantly higher, ranging from £500 to as much as £3,000.[95] Securing premises, shop fittings and tools could involve a considerable outlay of capital and the raw material itself was expensive.[96]

Claire Walsh and Emma Packer have employed Orphan's Court inventories to reconstruct the physical worlds of eighteenth-century London goldsmiths.[97] A considerable number of trade cards also survive for London goldsmiths from this period.[98] Although it was quite rare for these to include interior or exterior views of goldsmiths' shops (Fig. 1.13), a reasonable number incorporate shop signs as part of their design.[99] While many fewer trade cards survive for eighteenth-century Dublin, the minutes of the Wide Streets Commission of Dublin offer rich material regarding the rental costs of goldsmiths' premises in Dublin's city centre.[100] The Commissioners for making Wide and Convenient Ways, Streets, and Passages were established by Act of Parliament in 1757 and were active until 1851.[101] As Edel Sheridan has observed:

> The importance of the Wide Streets Commission for Dublin's evolution as a capital in a European context is unique. The Commissioners regulated spatially extensive and significant developments for nearly a hundred years and represent an important shift from independent municipal control to State involvement in planning the capital city.[102]

These records are useful for a number of reasons. First, they detail valuations for the many buildings that were purchased at the behest of the Commissioners in order to accommodate their ambitious programmes of urban development. Included among these were properties leased by goldsmiths, jewellers, watchmakers and allied traders. As well as indicating the scale of rental costs for city centre outlets, and the terms of individual leases, these minutes also include accounts from, and on behalf of, the tenants themselves. Although the minutes of the Wide Streets Commission have been used by historians to measure Dublin's physical expansion, they merit further investigation, beyond the scope of this book, expressly from the standpoint of the wider population of Dublin craftsmen and retailers.

According to evidence compiled on behalf of the Commissioners, Dublin goldsmiths were paying average rents of between £20 and £35 per annum for premises in

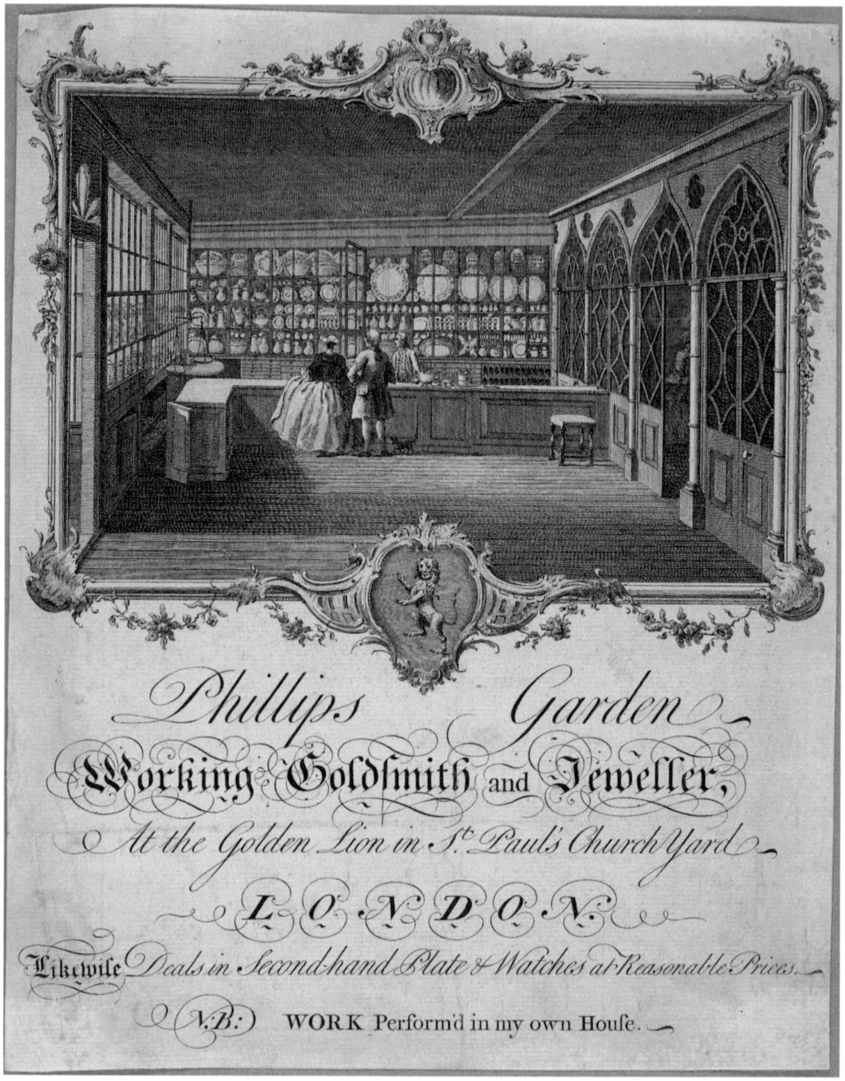

Figure 1.13 Trade card of Phillips Garden (1750s), engraving

Source: British Museum, London, Heal Collection. Photo credit: © The Trustees of the British Museum.

areas like Cork Hill close to Dublin Castle (Table 1.2). With their guildhall located on Werburgh Street from 1709, goldsmiths found adjacent streets like Skinner Row, Hoey's Court and East Cole Alley to be convenient locations, close to the assay office and the fashionable hub of the viceregal court (Fig. 1.14). Economic historians have emphasised the importance of clustering for producers and consumers. Apart from proximity to patrons and markets, geographical clusters of goldsmiths meant that knowledge and expertise could be more easily exchanged and that innovation could occur through rivalry and innovation. There were also benefits for customers in terms of accessibility and the potential to make immediate product and price comparisons.[103]

Table 1.2 Annual rents for buildings leased by goldsmiths and allied traders in the streets surrounding Dublin Castle, 1742–80

Date	*Lessee*	*Trade*	*Rent per annum*
1742	Christopher Clarke	Watchmaker	£22
1744	William Wilson	Goldsmith	£50
1746	Robert Calderwood	Goldsmith	£40
1750	William Currie	Goldsmith	£33
1758	Isaac D'Olier	Goldsmith	£35
1764	George Hill	Silversmith	£12
1773	Robert Deane	Watchmaker	£20
1774	Joseph Nixon	Jeweller	£34 2s 6d
1776	John O'Neill	Gold-beater	£22 15s 0d
1780	Joseph Blackmore	Engraver	£9

Source: Wide Streets Commission of Dublin. Minutes, 1758–1780, Ms. WSC/Mins/1-3, Dublin City Archives. Where the dates of the beginning of leases are known, these dates have been used.

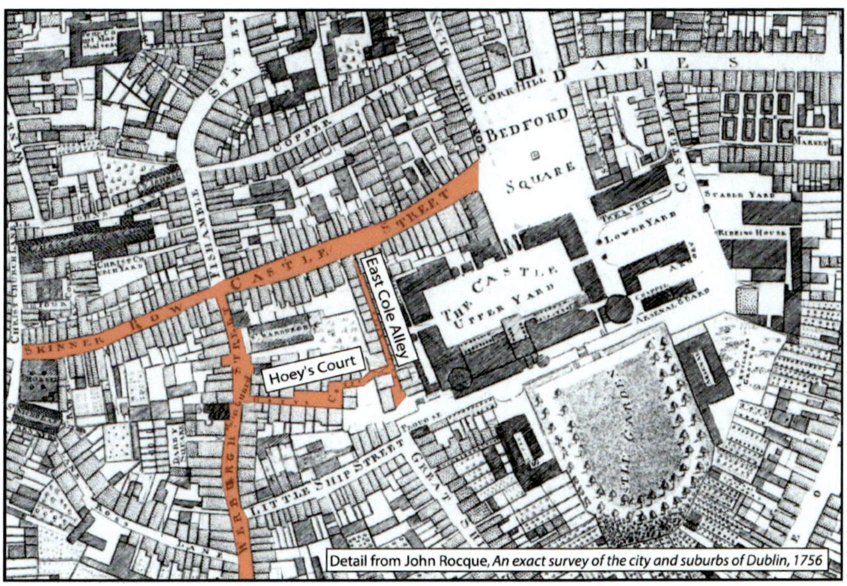

Figure 1.14 Detail of John Rocque's Map of Dublin (1756), showing the area around Werburgh Street where goldsmiths' shops were clustered

Photo credit: Frank Cullen.

After the newly laid out Parliament Street was completed by 1762, a visitor to the city remarked that 'for regularity, excellence of architecture, and grandeur of shops, this street is in no way inferior to the best trading streets in London.'[104] Parliament Street quickly attracted jewellers and goldsmiths to its fashionable address.[105] Rents in the environs of the Dublin Castle could be as low as 9 pounds, but this usually indicated a limited degree of space. In 1780, the engraver Joseph Blackmore paid 9 pounds for rooms on the east side of Georges Lane, which comprised simply 'a room in said house up one pair of stairs backwards . . . and a workshop'.[106]

The length of leases taken on by Dublin goldsmiths varied, but those who were in a position to commit to extended terms could benefit as rental values increased. For instance, Robert Calderwood, already mentioned for his success in attracting apprentices, signed a forty-year lease for premises on Cork Hill in 1746, with an annual rent of £40.[107] Twenty years later, his associate Samuel Epwell reckoned that the building could potentially yield a rent of £190 per annum.[108] In 1761, the goldsmith Isaac D'Olier confirmed that he would still accept £200 compensation for the remainder of his lease on a Cork Hill premises from the Wide Streets Commissioners. This was despite the fact that he thought it 'severe', because house prices had 'risen greatly' since he had suggested the sum three years earlier.[109] D'Olier was paying annual rent of £35 for his shop, but said that he 'would give £50 with all his heart for it', if he had the option of an extended lease.[110] Aside from the fact that rising property values could favour those with long-term leases, securing the lease on an entire building offered potential for rental income. The watch- and clockmaking partnership of Eccleston and Ruxton, for example, offered a first-floor apartment to let above their shop in Nicholas Street in 1763. They specified its suitability 'for a lawyer'.[111] During the same period, the goldsmith and jeweller Richard Tudor advertised 'a commodious first and second floor, furnished and unfurnished, suitable for a lawyer or attorney, to be let' above his shop at the 'Pelican and Ring' in Skinner Row.[112]

Adam Smith explained in 1776 that 'a tradesman in London' was obliged to take 'a whole house in that part of town where his customers live. His shop is upon the ground floor, and he and his family sleep in the garret'.[113] Certainly, newspaper advertisements for the period provide examples of goldsmiths in Dublin who lived and worked at the same address, with retail shops at street-front level and upper floors leased.[114] When the goldsmith and jeweller Robert Holmes retired in 1769, his stock, household furniture and the lease on his premises in Castle Street were auctioned. The lease had twelve years remaining at a rent of £44 per annum and the premises was described as a remarkably good 'situation for any kind of business; the house is upwards of fifty feet deep, and in thorough repair'.[115]

Goldsmiths like D'Olier, Calderwood and Tudor, who made and retailed high-quality large wares, needed spacious and relatively well-appointed premises. However, small, portable commodities like jewellery were sold in some cases from rented outdoor stalls. As well as leasing part of a house on Dame Street from 1774, the jeweller Joseph Nixon also rented a 'bulk and stall at the entrance to Castlemarket for £9 2s 0d a year at will'.[116] Nixon had become a freeman of the goldsmiths' guild in 1759 and represented his guild on the Common Council of the City in 1769 and 1774.[117] Carolyn Sargentson has identified similar patterns of retailing among the population of Parisian *marchands merciers* who operated out of the fashionable rue St Honoré during the eighteenth century. According to Sargentson's findings:

> Some sold from shops at street level, others traded from rooms on the upper stories and others traded from stalls (*échoppes*) set up on the street, some on a relatively long-term basis . . . The shopkeepers and stall holders on the rue St Honoré . . . constituted collectively a luxury market place within which traders both competed with and complemented each other.[118]

The minutes of the Wide Streets Commission also suggest that a good location was perceived as an important asset, particularly when it came to securing the business of country customers. In the early 1760s, the goldsmith William Wilson had to be compensated for his Cork Hill premises, when it was subject to a compulsory purchase order by the Wide Streets Commissioners. Fellow goldsmith and neighbour Isaac D'Olier estimated that Wilson 'could not remove for less than £300, besides the loss of his trade'.[119] Just a few years earlier, the goldsmith Edward Raper (Fig. 1.15) had advertised the sale of his lease in the same general area as 'a

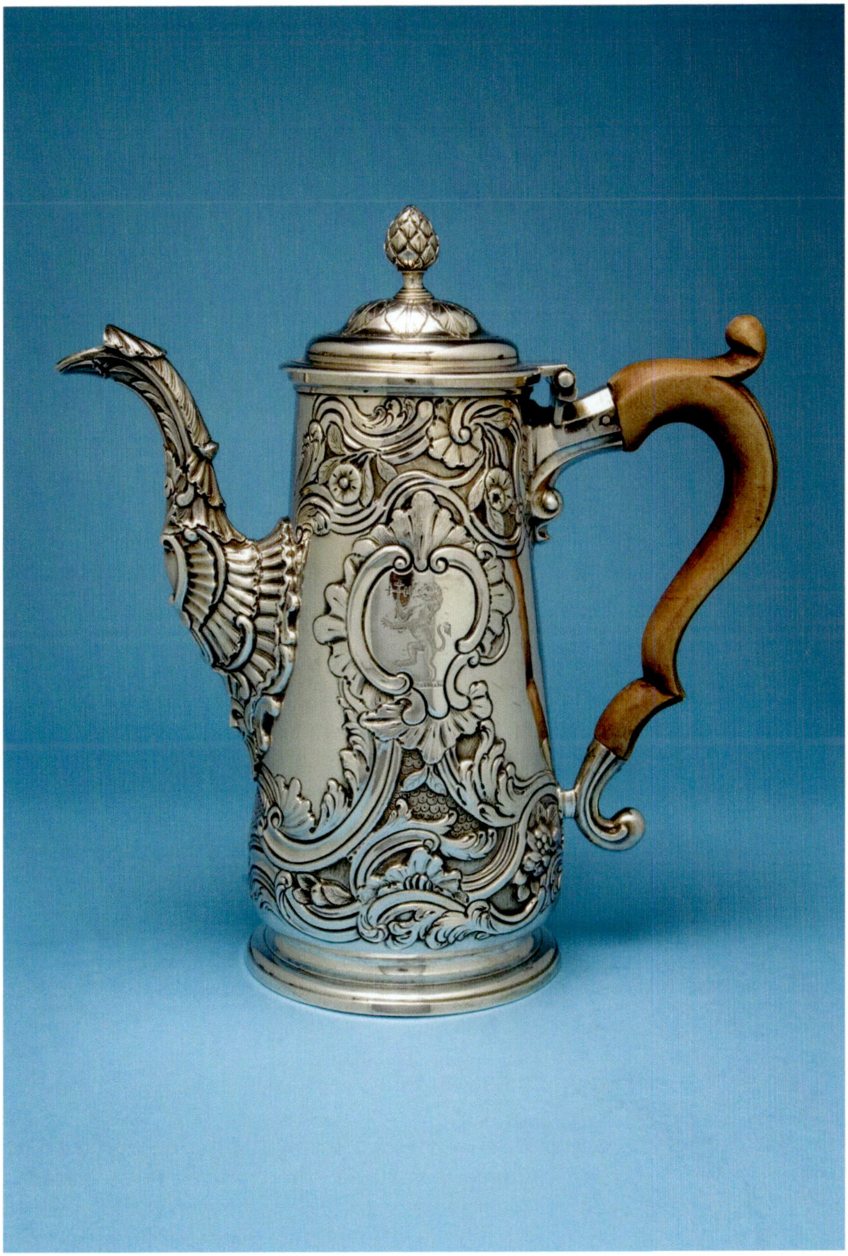

Figure 1.15 Edward Raper, *Coffee pot* (1752–53 or 1753–54), silver, 24.7 cm (h)

Source: Red McCombs Collection, San Antonio, Texas. Photo credit: © Al Renton.

remarkably good standing for goldsmith's, toyman's, or any other kinds of business'.[120] Claire Walsh has argued, in relation to London, that 'in the eighteenth century, it was the shop which was branded rather than the goods sold.'[121] A well-located shop helped to establish a solid client base and in eighteenth-century London, at least, the client list could be purchased with a lease. The London goldsmith Joseph Brasbridge was understandably aggrieved when the new owner of his shop implied this kind of agreement in his advertising, despite the fact that he had not purchased the 'good will' of the shop, including the addresses of close to a thousand 'principal customers'.[122]

In Dublin, an apprentice to the watchmaker Christopher Clarke gave evidence before the Commissioners in 1761, reiterating the drawbacks of moving from well-established premises. Clarke was operating from a former alehouse on Crane Lane. According to the testimony of his apprentice, it would represent 'a great loss to Mr Clarke to remove, as his country customers would not readily find him'.[123] This was a genuine cause for concern. In 1766, a fellow watchmaker exhorted those customers 'who live in the country' to 'be more particular in directing the persons they send with their watches, as by mistake they have often left them in other shops'.[124]

It seems likely that the cost involved in renting retail space was a factor which encouraged some Dublin goldsmiths and jewellers to sell products which were unrelated to the goldsmiths' trade. The goldsmith John Tuite found a niche making and selling 'all sort of old fashioned ornaments for coffins . . . as cheap as the worst work . . . done in the town by tin men'.[125] In *Wilson's Dublin Street Directory* for 1789, Henry Wilme of Dame Street was listed as a 'goldsmith and hatter' and in 1792, the jeweller James Brush advertised the sale of the choicest 'real Madeira wine' from his shop (Fig. 1.16).[126] It made economic sense for those renting shops to try to maximise their selling opportunities. While this was not unique to Dublin, it seems likely that in an exclusive and highly competitive field like the goldsmiths' trade it may have been a more prevalent phenomenon in smaller markets like Dublin, Cork or Limerick than, for example, London. In the second half of the eighteenth century, one Limerick retailer operated a dual trade in stationery and bookbinding. He advertised his demand for 'old books and broken gold and silver'.[127] His colleague George Moore, trading as a silversmith and haberdasher on Quay Lane in Limerick, offered 'fine Carolina hats, sold as cheap as by the maker'.[128] Visiting Ireland in the late eighteenth century, the irascible traveller Richard Twiss commented that:

> The indigence of the middle class of people is visible even in Dublin, where there are many shops, which serve at once for two different trades; such as silversmiths and booksellers; saddlers and milliners, & c.[129]

Materials

Compared with craftsmen working in other branches of the luxury goods trade, goldsmiths enjoyed a somewhat advantageous position when it came to the supply of raw material, since their customers frequently provided them with silver when they wished to cash in foreign coin or old, unwanted plate, or reduce the cost of a bill.[130] While little is known about the way in which the bullion trade operated in eighteenth-century Dublin, it is clear that goldsmiths depended heavily on used plate, coin and silver lace

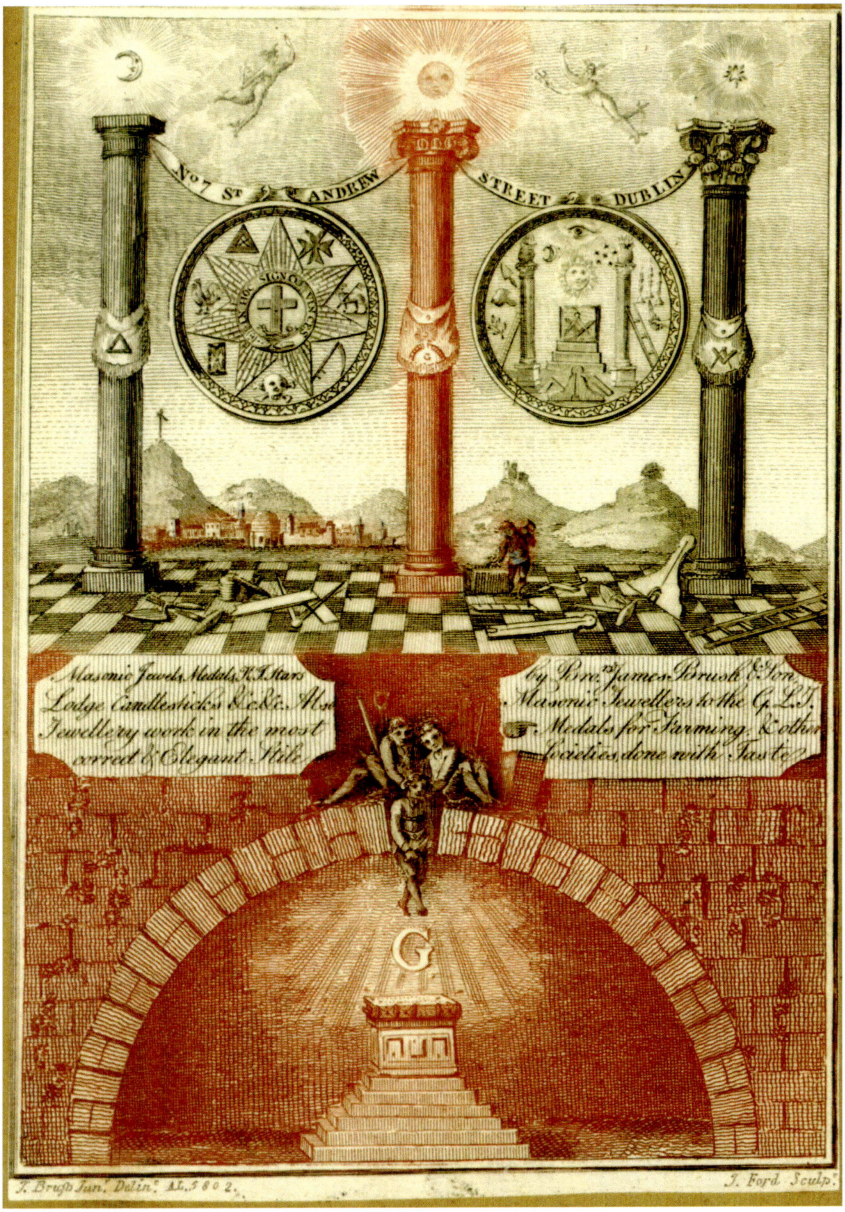

Figure 1.16 Trade card of James Brush (late eighteenth century), engraving, 14 × 10 cm

Source: Masonic Hall, Dublin. Photo credit: © By permission of the Grand Lodge of Freemasons of Ireland.

as raw material and that these were all being constantly recycled. In 1710, a notice in the *Flying Post* advised those who wanted 'lead ores, copper ores, tin ores or any other ores, or materials, tried and assayed for lead, copper, silver' to enquire of Mr Percy at the 'Silver Cat' in Castle Street.[131] In London, silver refining was a separate branch of trade by the mid-eighteenth century, although many goldsmiths were able to refine their own silver.[132] Mortimer, in his *Universal Director* (1763), listed eight specialist refiners in London but there were many more.[133] Clearly, independent refiners were slower to emerge in Dublin than in London. One is listed in the *Universal Advertiser* for 1753–55.[134] In 1768, the gold-beater Samuel Guinness advertised his intention to set up a refinery in the city 'after the manner of those in London'.[135] He claimed that in the English capital refiners were an established and distinct trade, and he evidently perceived what he regarded as a niche in the market.

As well as providing goldsmiths with a supply of raw material, the existence of a market for second-hand plate (which will be explored in chapter 3) also presented opportunities for selling stolen silver wares and, as a result, the Dublin guild aimed to limit the activities of hawkers and itinerant tradesmen.[136] In 1700, the mayor of Dublin responded to a complaint by wardens of the guild about individuals believed to be 'intruding' on their trade. These included hawkers and criers who bought up broken gold, silver and silver lace.[137] Undoubtedly, the guild was concerned about protecting the public interest, but a less philanthropic and more monopolistic motive must also have prompted the protest. Ensuring a ready supply of raw material was essential to their livelihoods and, as Kahl has remarked in relation to London, 'the desire of craftsmen like the goldsmiths to serve the consumer was secondary.'[138] First on their agenda was securing the market for themselves and protecting the interests of their members.

As well as general advertisements offering customers good prices for used plate, some goldsmiths and jewellers were more specific and highlighted their demand for specific types of coin. As chapter 4 explores, the particular economic circumstances in eighteenth-century Ireland were such that putting money into plate must have seemed attractive to those who could afford it, at least during the late seventeenth and early eighteenth century, when banking was in its infancy. With no mint and frequent currency crises, foreign coin was validated in Ireland as legal tender, and the shortage of specie excited considerable contemporary debate. In 1739, the jeweller Thomas Isack advertised a rate of 5s 11d an ounce for burnt silver, indicating that silver lace also had a value on the second-hand market (Fig. 1.17).[139] In 1751, the goldsmith and jeweller John Moore in Christchurch-yard offered 'four pounds and one shilling and six pence per ounce for diminished guineas, and the highest prices for Spanish and other bullion'.[140]

Later in the century, a Cork jeweller who was trading in a 'rich assortment' of silver, plated ware and jewellery advertised his interest in light guineas, port pieces and dollars.[141] For reasons that will be investigated in chapter 3, London goldsmiths did not make much use of newspaper advertising. When silver was referred to in London newspapers, it was often in the case of stolen goods. One exception was the enterprising goldsmith Stafford Briscoe, who had a shop at the corner of Friday Street and Cheapside, in the heart of London's silver district.[142] His advertisements in the *General Evening Post* of 1751 include his commitment to 'give the most money for any quantities of old plate, watches, &c'. Not only was his use of the press distinctive, he also emphasised his specialisation as a dealer in used plate.[143] In a trade associated with such exclusivity, this was unusual for London. While his contemporaries facilitated trade-ins, they generally referred to this practice in a more understated way, often in the closing lines of printed trade cards.[144] In contrast, North American goldsmiths mirrored the practices of their Irish counterparts, and actively highlighted their demand for used silver and gold in the press. Two who did so during the 1780s were in fact

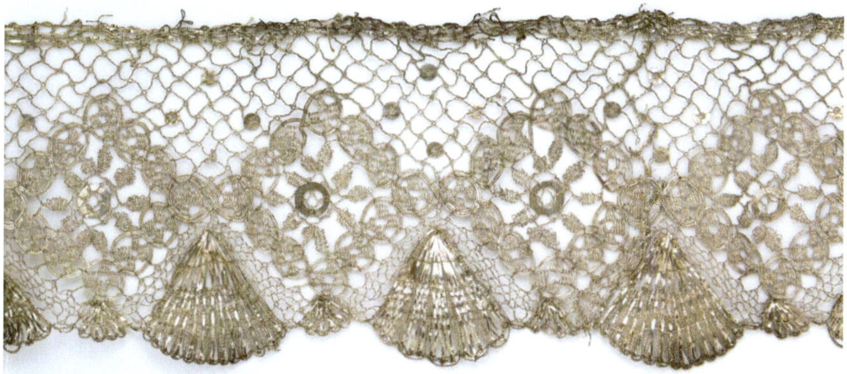

Figure 1.17 Lace (1725–75), silver, 89 × 13.5 cm
Source: V&A, London. Photo credit: © V&A.

Dublin émigrés. William Hughes offered goods for sale in Baltimore 'on moderate terms for ready money, or in exchange for old gold, gold-clippings, old silver, or lace'. His contemporary Thomas Reynolds advertised as a stonecutter and jeweller from Dublin who, as well as executing orders from across the continent, offered the 'highest prices for old gold'.[145]

A report in the *Belfast News Letter* indicates that some foreign coins that might not have been in widespread use gravitated naturally towards goldsmiths. In July 1765, the *Earl of Sandwich* ship sailed from London to South America.[146] On the return trip, having picked up a cargo that included Madeira wine, silver and a large quantity of Spanish dollars, four of the mariners staged a coup and rerouted the ship to Wexford. On arrival, they buried part of their loot, and headed forth on foot with a cache of dollars, gold, ingots, jewels and gold dust. When two of the men were caught, they informed on their cohorts who, they claimed, had sold to a Dublin goldsmith a significant haul of Spanish dollars.

A later notice in the same newspaper confirms that certain foreign coins, of a kind not readily exchangeable in the course of trade, were actually useful to goldsmiths. A contributor to the *Belfast News Letter* in 1787 (a period when there was a 'scarcity of good silver') pointed out that French crowns and dollars should be more widely accepted.[147] The correspondent suggested that since a French crown was 'fully worth, by weight, and in sterling bullion five shillings English', and that dollars were worth 'four and sixpence Irish to a silversmith', they should be more acceptable.[148] This, it was argued, would be greatly convenient, and would anticipate a general prevalence of French currency in Ireland, when proposed commercial treaties were ratified.

As well as the regular exchange of plate and coin between craftsmen and clients in eighteenth-century Dublin, there was also a degree to which raw materials were exchanged within the trade. As Carolyn Sargentson has shown, it was not unusual for suppliers of luxury goods in eighteenth-century Paris to provide one another with goods and component parts.[149] In 1778, the goldsmith 'Mr Connor' was summoned before the Dublin goldsmiths' guild over a pair of substandard spurs. He claimed that the fraud was an innocent error on his part since he had used silver acquired from the goldsmith 'Mr Delandre'.[150] This highlights the problems of working with recycled metal, if it was not properly refined.

Raw materials also changed hands in subcontracting, or private agreements. A series of recent studies investigating the business of subcontracting in eighteenth-century London confirm that it was a defining characteristic of the market there during that period.[151] Rather than infringing on guild control, subcontracting and outsourcing is now seen as a vital part of the corporate system which allowed small-scale makers, some of whom never became freemen, to maintain workshops, to specialise in a narrow range of skills and to share the financial risks involved in production.[152] As already indicated, the London goldsmiths Parker and Wakelin subcontracted work to a network of seventy-five different specialists between 1760 and 1776.[153] The situation regarding subcontracting in the Dublin goldsmiths' trade during the eighteenth century is less clear. No comparable business archive for an Irish goldsmith or firm survives from this period. The smaller scale of the Dublin domestic market, and the absence of a significant export demand in this sector, make it less likely that it could have sustained the same sophisticated webs of outworkers who made a living from piecework in eighteenth-century London.[154] There are, however, cases at intervals across the eighteenth century detailing dual-party agreements around the supply of raw materials. In 1765, the goldsmith William Cordner was exposed by the guild for fraudulent practice.[155] It emerged that he had been commissioned by other makers to produce objects for them and was supplied with the silver as part of the arrangement. He had tried to increase his profits by using base metal in place of silver in a tactically fraudulent way. For instance, when he made a two-handled cup for the goldsmith Richard Tudor in 1765, he used base metal within the handles.[156] Presumably he thought that when the piece was assayed, a sample would be taken from the base, or from another part of the object, which was actually sterling, and he would get away with it. One of the most interesting aspects of this case is the fact that when the guild realised what was happening, they asked their members to deliver any work by Cordner that they had in stock. A number of prominent goldsmiths came forward. While their maker's marks have been recorded, Cordner's has not.[157] He was one of those semi-invisible goldsmiths, for whom no mark has been attributed, yet he appears to have made objects as an outworker for other craftsmen.[158]

Since the commerce in second-hand goods was essential to the trade, a final point should be made in regard to the supply of raw materials: the option of buying plate at auction for subsequent resale or recycling. The lure of auctions from a consumer's perspective will be examined in chapter 3, but there is evidence to suggest that goldsmiths also purchased plate at auction. It is impossible to verify how frequently Dublin goldsmiths sold, as opposed to melted, what they bought; many factors, including the condition of the piece and how fashionable it was, must have entered the equation. In 1727, the goldsmiths' guild sold off some of their silver cups and three of their members bought pieces. William Barry and Roger Finch paid 5s 11½ d per oz. for their cups, while Edward Slicer paid 6s per oz. for his. Either Slicer's cup was slightly more decorative or accomplished in its execution, or the bidding more competitive by that stage.[159]

As previously indicated, goldsmiths' need of numerous tools, components, and fittings required a larger capital outlay than many other branches of trade. Newspaper notices suggest that some of these could be acquired second-hand. After Thomas Sutton's tragic death in 1745 from a horse fall, the goods from his goldsmith's shop were auctioned, along with all his working tools and a variety of lead patterns.[160] Inventory analysis for British and North American goldsmiths has uncovered the minutiae of working tools owned by eighteenth-century craftsmen.[161] An early probate inventory for the Boston goldsmith Richard Conyers itemises countless anvils, weights, punches, hammers, vices, tongs and bellows.[162] Goldsmiths in the melting, refining, and assaying of precious metals also used melting pots, or crucibles. They could be made in various materials including charcoal or bisque clay and were usually recorded in 'nests' or 'sets'.[163] Customs records indicate that large numbers of melting pots were imported into Ireland during this period.[164] Over 30,000 were imported during the first half of the century. While it is unlikely that all of these were used in the precious metals trade, they were specifically referred to in some cases as 'melting pots for goldsmiths'.[165] Although the 7,200 pots imported in the 1730 to 1731 season were rated at less than £33, this still represented a commodity that was being bought in, when it could have been manufactured locally. When Joseph Bracken later petitioned the Dublin Society seeking support for a business in Irish-made crucibles, he was successful.[166] The adjudicators of his application judged that he had 'made crucibles of equal goodness with those imported', that the required materials were indigenous to Ireland and that, since he did not have sufficient funds to underwrite the costs of setting up himself, he should be encouraged.[167]

Manufacturing goldsmiths also required charcoal. They used it to support small metal objects during the soldering process, where its heat-retentive properties were useful.[168] In February 1718, the Dublin goldsmiths' guild opened their own charcoal yard in Chancery Lane and went on to supply it to their members. Shortly afterwards, a guild reference indicates that advance subscribers were offered preferential terms. If they paid half their bill at the time of subscription, and the balance on receipt, a rate of 1s 7d per barrel was being quoted. Non-subscribers faced an inflated rate of 2s for the same goods.[169] More preferential terms were offered to freemen than to quarter brothers and foreigners, indicating the guild's hierarchical and partisan tendencies.

For those involved in retailing, specialist shop fittings were also required. Eighteenth-century goldsmiths used glass cases, or 'show glasses', to display their wares.[170] According to Claire Walsh, goldsmiths' wares in London were not placed on open shelves. In Dublin, in some cases, they evidently were. *Saunders' News-Letter* reported how, in October 1776, thieves had broken a small window above the entrance to a goldsmith's shop in Skinner Row. Operating in the dead of night, they had made off with 'a large plate cup'. With the aid of 'a stick with an iron hook at the end' they had been able to lift the cup right off the shelf.[171]

Other contemporary sources confirm that Dublin goldsmiths, like their London counterparts, used glass display cases. The average yearly value for glass cases imported into Ireland between 1734 and 1736 was almost £2,000.[172] In 1743, a portable glass case was stolen from the counter of a goldsmiths' shop in Skinner Row.[173] Later in the century, Jacob West, son of the goldsmith Matthew West, recounted how a thief had 'strained the sash' of a glass case in his father's shop, in an attempt 'to get in her hand'.[174] The case had been 'locked in the middle, and hasped at one end'.[175] On this occasion the thief had been trying to steal a buckle. Small items like jewellery and buckles could be conveniently stored in nests of drawers, so these were also useful.[176] An early nineteenth-century auction notice in the *Star and Fashionable World* outlined the stock of a perfumer, jeweller and haberdasher, which consisted of 350 lots, including 'a large counter glass case, with brass rod' and 'a round table, adapted for a museum or a fancy shop-keeper'.[177] The appearance of a Dublin silversmiths' shop is vividly conveyed by an auction notice of 1830, which describes shop fixtures, 'chiefly adapted to Jewellers and Silversmiths':

> The Entire Valuable Shop Fixtures – Comprising one Mahogany Topped Counter with seven Drawers, Falling Leaf, and Brass Guard; one Smaller Counter; one Counter Glass Case with twelve Drawers, one small ditto; one Single two-fall Office Desk with Mahogany Top and Inner Drawers; six Reflecting Glasses in Frames for Shop Windows; forty-four Upright Slide Sashes of various Sizes in Mahogany Frames; one Pier Glass; large Wareroom table; a Cast Iron Spiral Stair Case, various Lots of Shelving; Door Labels, Outside Blinds and Lattice Work, Gas Branches &c.[178]

Though large numbers of aspiring goldsmiths signed up for apprenticeships, only about two in every ten who registered with the guild actually went on to establish themselves as full independent masters. Even taking into consideration obvious reasons for attrition (death or illness, decline in business, a breakdown in relations between master and apprentice) and the fact that some worked as journeymen, it is an extraordinarily small number. Considerable numbers of trainees must have completed their education in the goldsmiths' trade but never became free of the guild and set out on their own. The only reasonable explanation for this pattern is that the capital risks involved were too great and that the Dublin market in luxury goods was too small to allow much competition or to make it attractive for newcomers to become freemen or full members of the guild. The guild system (particularly in cases where masters took on multiple apprentices) facilitated the rise of select individuals, goldsmiths like Thomas Bolton and Robert Calderwood, who created monopolies at the expense of emerging or less successful goldsmiths.[179]

The fundamental differences between the London and Dublin guild system had interesting consequences. Dublin's quarter-brother system, though contentious, seems to have facilitated a greater degree of control over the trade, and the decline in apprenticeship numbers, and guild regulation of the trade, came considerably later in Dublin than in London. This seems to have been directly linked to the fact that London traditions militated against the survival of the apprenticeship system. Prior to 1600, freedom of a London livery company had 'represented legal recognition of a man's right to carry on a craft or trade', whereas 'during the seventeenth and eighteenth centuries the freedom became a mark of prestige' which was increasingly acquired by right of inheritance or purchased.[180] Equally, London's more relaxed legislation did not oblige craftsmen to be free of the guild whose specific trade they practised. By contrast, as clarified for Dublin, it was the late eighteenth century before the Corporation ceased insisting that freedom of the city should only be granted to individuals following their guild's trades.[181]

The Dublin guild monitored the apprenticeship system by insisting on the registration of all apprentices, thus controlling numbers and competition between masters and by playing a mediating role if later disputes involving apprentices emerged. However, it adopted a surprisingly backseat role when it came to other aspects of the training process. It did not prescribe a curriculum, or even ensure that adequate instruction took place. The seventeenth-century charter of the Dublin goldsmiths' guild stipulated that freedom was only bestowed on those apprentices who, after they had completed seven years of training, could prove that they had achieved a standard of workmanship by submitting an example of their best work – the so-called masterpiece – to the wardens for adjudication. As the next chapter explores, there is no evidence that this provision was consistently enforced in the Georgian era – the guild in all its activities was more concerned about the quality of metal used rather than any skill requirements. Economic historians have recently challenged the long-held notion that guilds assiduously regulated and enforced apprenticeship contracts and have gone so far as to suggest the master-apprenticeship system occurred in spite of and not because of the guilds.

Notes

1 R. Campbell, *The London Tradesman* (London: Printed by T. Gardner, 1747), 142.
2 For a summary of the issues involved in this debate, see S.R. Epstein and Maarten Prak, eds., *Guilds, Innovation and the European Economy 1400–1800* (Cambridge: Cambridge University Press, 2008), 1–24.
3 S.R. Epstein, 'Craft Guilds, Apprenticeship, and Technological Change in Preindustrial Europe', *Journal of Economic History* (*JEH*) 58 (1998): 684–713; and S.R. Epstein, 'Craft Guilds in the Pre-Modern Economy: A Discussion', *Economic History Review* (*EHR*) 61 (2008): 155–74.
4 Sheilagh Ogilvie, 'Guilds, Efficiency, and Social Capital: Evidence from German Proto-Industry', *EHR* 57 (2004): 286–333; and Sheilagh Ogilvie, 'Rehabilitating the Guilds: A Reply', *EHR* 61 (2008): 175–82.
5 These were common puffs used in the newspapers advertisements placed by goldsmiths and jewellers in eighteenth-century Ireland and referred in many cases to the sale of imported wares. See for instance *Volunteers Journal, or Irish Herald*, 20 February 1784; *Belfast News Letter*, 4–7 March 1788; and *Cork Courier*, 1 April 1795. For discussions of the persuasive advertising used by craftsmen in eighteenth-century London and Paris, see Julia Muir, 'Printing Persuasion: Advertising Goods in Eighteenth-Century England' (MA thesis, Royal College of Art, London, 2000); Natasha Coquery, 'Consumption, Credit, Diffusion; Semi-Luxury Shops in Eighteenth-Century Paris', unpublished research paper, presented at the University of Warwick, November 2002 (TS in author's possession).
6 Douglas Bennett, *Irish Georgian Silver* (London: Cassell, 1972), 3–38 provides a short history of the goldsmiths' guild. See also Alison FitzGerald, 'The Business of Being a Goldsmith in Eighteenth-Century Dublin', in *Georgian Dublin*, ed. Gillian O'Brien and Finola O'Kane (Dublin: Four Courts Press, 2008), 127–35.
7 For more on the historical role of guilds see, Anthony Black, *Guilds and Civil Society in European Political Thought* (London: Methuen, 1984); M.J. Walker, 'The Extent of the Guild Control of Trades in England, c.1660–1820' (PhD thesis, University of Cambridge, 1985); John J. Webb, *The Guilds of Dublin* (Dublin: Three Candles, 1929). The rules and regulations of the Company of Goldsmiths of Dublin in 1667 record that seven years should be the minimum period of apprenticeship. Company of Goldsmiths of Dublin, Ms. 1: 2–4, Dublin, Assay Office.
8 Bennett, *Irish Georgian Silver*, 13–14.
9 Although the Dublin goldsmiths' guild required all apprentices bound in the city to register with the guild, this did not always happen, for reasons that will be shown. Unpublished research by Christopher Challis has revealed that, in late sixteenth-century London, of

fifty-two 'servants' employed by alien goldsmiths in the city only 4 per cent were actually described as apprentices. See Christopher Challis, 'Training and Workshop Practice in England in the Seventeenth Century', unpublished paper given at the V&A/RCA study day, London, November 1993 (TS in author's possession).

10 See, for instance, Black, *Guilds and Civil Society*; Ian Anders Gadd and Patrick Wallis, eds., *Guilds, Society and Economy in London 1450–1800* (London: Centre for Metropolitan History, 2002); William Kahl, *The Development of London Livery Companies* (Cambridge, MA: Harvard University Press, 1960); J. R. Kellett, 'The Breakdown of Guild and Corporation Control over the Handicraft and Retail Trades of London', *EHR*, 2nd ser., 10 (1958): 381–94; Walker, 'The Extent of the Guild Control of Trades in England'; and Webb, *The Guilds of Dublin*.

11 Henry F. Berry, 'The Records of the Dublin Gild of Merchants, Known as the Gild of Holy Trinity, 1438–1671', *Journal of the Royal Society of Antiquaries of Ireland* (*JRSAI*) 30 (1900): 44–68; H. F. Berry, 'The Goldsmiths' Company of Dublin', *JRSAI* 31 (1901): 119–33; H. F. Berry, 'The Ancient Company of Barber Surgeons, or Gild of St. Mary Magdalene, Dublin', *JRSAI* 33 (1903): 217–38; H. F. Berry, 'The Records of the Feltmakers' Company of Dublin, 1787–1841: Their Loss and Recovery', *JRSAI* 41 (1911): 26–45; H. F. Berry, 'The Merchant Tailors' Gild – That of St. John the Baptist, Dublin, 1418–1841', *JRSAI* 48 (1918): 19–64; W. C. Stubbs, 'The Weavers' Guild, the Guild of the Blessed Virgin Mary, Dublin, 1446–1840', *JRSAI* 49 (1919): 60–88; and Henry S. Guinness, 'Dublin Trade Gilds', *JRSAI* 52 (1922): 143–63. See also Webb, *The Guilds of Dublin* and Jacqueline Hill, *From Patriots to Unionists* (Oxford: Oxford University Press, 1997).

12 Charles J. Jackson, *English Goldsmiths and Their Marks* (2nd ed., London: Macmillan, 1921). These include the Dublin goldsmiths' marks, chronological lists of the names of Dublin goldsmiths and freemen of the guild from 1637 to 1905.

13 Mary Pollard, *A Dictionary of Members of the Dublin Book Trade, 1550–1800* (London: Bibliographical Society, 2000). There is no comparable analysis available for the apprenticeship figures of another Dublin guild.

14 See Hill, *From Patriots to Unionists*, 204.

15 Toby Barnard, *Making the Grand Figure: Lives and Possessions in Ireland 1641–1770* (New Haven and London: Yale University Press, 2004), 30.

16 Minute of 15 April 1695, Company of Goldsmiths of Dublin, Ms. 1: 53, Dublin, Assay Office. Precisely a century later, the Incorporated Society for Promoting Protestant Schools paid the premium of £5 13s 9d to place its pupils in the less prestigious jobs of binding and papermaking. See Pollard, *A Dictionary of Members of the Dublin Book Trade*, xxix.

17 Minute of 1 May 1696, Company of Goldsmiths of Dublin, Ms. 1: 57, Dublin, Assay Office.

18 Minute of 16 July 1728, Company of Goldsmiths of Dublin, Ms. 1: 261, Dublin, Assay Office. An apprenticeship fee of 20 guineas equated to £21.

19 Accounts of Thomas Taylor, 25 March 1728, Ms. 25, 386: 160, National Library of Ireland.

20 Toby Barnard, *A New Anatomy of Ireland: The Irish Protestants, 1649–1770* (New Haven and London: Yale University Press), 310.

21 Pollard, *A Dictionary of Members of the Dublin Book Trade*, xxix. Interestingly, a decade later Campbell requested 50 guineas (£52 10s).

22 Brian FitzGerald, ed., *Correspondence of Emily, Duchess of Leinster*, vol. 1 (Dublin Stationery Office, 1949), 147–48. The duchess was considering financing an apprentice in England at that time.

23 Ibid.

24 Campbell, *The London Tradesman*. For more on apprenticeship in the London goldsmiths' trade, see Philippa Glanville, *Silver in England* (London: Unwin Hyman, 1987), 168–69.

25 Joan Lane, *Apprenticeship in England, 1600–1914* (London: Routledge, 1996), 163.

26 Registration of Apprentices from 1708 to 1722, Worshipful Company of Goldsmiths of London, Apprenticeship Book No. 5, London, Goldsmiths' Hall; Registration of Apprentices from 1722 to 1740, Worshipful Company of Goldsmiths of London, Apprenticeship Book No. 6, London, Goldsmiths' Hall; Registration of Apprentices 1740 to 1763, Worshipful Company of Goldsmiths of London, Apprenticeship Book No. 7, London, Goldsmiths' Hall.

27 Apprentice indentures for William Overand, George Jameson, and Benjamin Walmsley, Registration of Apprentices from 1722 to 1740, Worshipful Company of Goldsmiths of London, Apprenticeship Book No. 6: 216, 231.

28 G. Fox, *Memoirs of the Late Philip Rundell Esq. Goldsmith and Jeweller to His Majesty and the Royal Family* (London: J. Fairburn, 1827).
29 Jackson, *English Goldsmiths*, provides a list of those bound between 1632 and 1823. However, particularly in the latter half of the century, Jackson is not consistent in registering the professional background from which the apprentices came. Consequently, this information has been confirmed by a systematic search of the eighteenth-century ledgers covering apprentice enrolment and registration: Company of Goldsmiths of Dublin, Mss. 95, 96 and 97, which record the registration of apprentices with the guild between 1637 and 1823.
30 Barnard, *A New Anatomy of Ireland*, 308.
31 William Kahl, 'Apprenticeship and the Freedom of the London Livery Companies, 1690–1750' Guildhall Miscellany 7 (1956): 17–20.
32 These counties may have been represented but simply not recorded, as Fig. 1.4 indicates that the place of origin of a number of the apprentices was unspecified.
33 Four hundred and thirty apprentices were enrolled in the Guild of St Luke during this period. See Pollard, *A Dictionary of Members of the Dublin Book Trade*, xxx–xxxii. Figures are not available for the earlier period.
34 Caulfield Indenture Transcripts, 1881, Ms. U225, Cork City Archives.
35 *Hibernian Chronicle* (Cork), 30 September 1782.
36 Joan Lane, *Apprenticeship in England 1600–1914* (London: University College London Press, 1996), 12.
37 Barnard, *A New Anatomy of Ireland*, 41–80. According to James Whitshaw, a gentleman is 'one who can live idly, and without manual labour, and will bear the part, charge and countenance of a gentleman, he shall be called master, and taken for a gentleman'. James Whitshaw, *A New Law Dictionary* (London: J. & T. W. Clarke, 1829), 124. I am grateful to W. E. Vaughan for this reference.
38 Barnard, *A New Anatomy*, 42.
39 Peter Earle, *The Making of the English Middle Class* (Berkeley: University of California Press, 1989), 87. Earle was essentially referring to out-of-town apprentices, but a fluid use of the term 'gentleman' was also more broadly applied.
40 I am not aware of any female apprentice officially enrolled with the guild during this period.
41 Earle, *The Making of the English Middle Class*, 86–89.
42 Indenture of Michael Graham with William Steele, 14 September 1769; and indenture of Thomas Townsend with Robert Breading, 10 April 1787, Company of Goldsmiths of Dublin, Ms. 97: 61, 91, Dublin, Assay Office. The entrepreneurial earthenware manufacturer Henry Delamain magnanimously offered employment for a host of 'parish or distressed tradesman's children'. Boys and girls who elected to undergo a seven-year apprenticeship were promised a wage which would rise from 2s to 4s 6d as their training progressed; *Faulkner's Dublin Journal*, 17–20 September 1754. See also Peter Francis, *Irish Delftware* (London: Jonathan Horne, 2000).
43 Pollard, *A Dictionary of Members of the Dublin Book Trade*, xxxi.
44 Alison FitzGerald, 'Cosmopolitan Commerce: The Dublin Goldsmith Robert Calderwood', *Apollo* (September 2005): 47.
45 Tim Leunig, Chris Minns, and Patrick Wallis, 'Networks in the Premodern Economy: The Market for London Apprenticeships, 1600–1749', *Journal of Economic History* (*JEH*) 71 (2011): 413–43.
46 Unless otherwise specified, the discussion refers to apprentices who were officially enrolled with the guild.
47 Indenture of Joseph Jackson with John West, 14 July 1782, Company of Goldsmiths of Dublin, Ms. 97: 35, Dublin, Assay Office.
48 FitzGerald, 'Cosmopolitan Commerce', 47.
49 This would have been a common practice in other places too.
50 Minute of 1 August 1739, Company of Goldsmiths of Dublin, Ms. 2: 105, Dublin, Assay Office.
51 Ibid., 229.
52 This figure is based on individuals whose apprenticeships were registered with the guild and those who later became free of the guild. As has been shown, not all apprentices were registered.
53 This is based on Jackson's 'List of Freemen' in Jackson, *English Goldsmiths*, 634–40 and Dublin City Council's database of the Ancient Freemen of Dublin: http://databases.dublincity.ie/freemen/about.php.

54 Patrick Wallis, 'Apprenticeships and Training in Premodern England', *JEH* 68 (2008): 832–61.
55 Minute of 15 October 1751, Company of Goldsmiths of Dublin, Ms. 2: 285, Dublin, Assay Office.
56 Minute of 20 November 1734, Company of Goldsmiths of Dublin, Ms. 2: 31, Dublin, Assay Office.
57 Minute of 17 March 1741, Company of Goldsmiths of Dublin, Ms. 2: 135, Dublin, Assay Office. This must be Francis Smith Sr who, according to Bennett, *Irish Georgian Silver*, 329 was a quarter brother between 1738 and 1753.
58 Wallis, 'Apprenticeships and Training in Premodern England'.
59 Minute of 3 May 1698, Ms. 1: 72, Company of Goldsmiths of Dublin, Dublin, Assay Office.
60 Minute of 4 July 1703, Company of Goldsmiths of Dublin Ms 1: 115, Dublin, Assay Office.
61 Joan Evans, 'Huguenot Goldsmiths in England and Ireland', *Proceedings of the Huguenot Society* 14, no. 4 (1933): 496–554. See also David Dickson, 'Huguenots in the Urban Economy of Eighteenth-Century Dublin and Cork', in *The Huguenots and Ireland: Anatomy of an Emigration*, ed. C. E. Caldicott, Hugh Gough, and Jean-Paul Pittion (Dun Laoghaire: Glendale Press, 1987), 321–32; R. P. Hylton, 'Dublin's Huguenot Communities: Trials, Development, and Triumph, 1662–1701', *Huguenot Society Proceedings* 24 (1985): 221–31.
62 Minute of 25 September 1704, Company of Goldsmiths of Dublin, Ms. 41: 123, Dublin, Assay Office.
63 Minute of 1 November 1771, Company of Goldsmiths of Dublin, Ms. 5: 226, Dublin, Assay Office. This laxity was not unique to 'in-house' or parental apprenticeships.
64 Minute of 1 May 1790, Company of Goldsmiths of Dublin, Ms. 6: 169, Dublin, Assay Office. Six years later John Teare, son of Samuel Teare, goldsmith, petitioned the guild for freedom, and explained that he had not been enrolled and his indentures had been mislaid. The guild concurred that he could be admitted if his father supplied a sworn affidavit to the effect that he had served his apprenticeship; Minute of 2 February 1796, Company of Goldsmiths of Dublin, Ms. 6: 238.
65 23 and 24 George III Chapter 23, 1784, quoted in Bennett, *Irish Georgian Silver*, 43–47.
66 Registration Book of Silversmiths under the 1784 Act: 1784–1838, Company of Goldsmiths of Dublin, Ms. 99, Dublin, Assay Office.
67 Register of Apprentices for the Guild of St Luke, Ms. 12131, National Library of Ireland (NLI).
68 *New Cork Evening Post*, 13 May 1799.
69 See Shirley Bury, 'The Lengthening Shadow of Rundell's, Part I: Rundell's and Their Silversmiths', *Connoisseur* 161 (1966): 78–85; Helen Clifford, *Silver in London: The Parker and Wakelin Partnership 1760–1776*; Fox, *Memoirs of the Late Philip Rundell Esq.*
70 Joseph Brasbridge, *The Fruits of Experience* (2nd ed., London, 1824), 142–43.
71 See Enrolment of Apprentices 1637–June 1703, Freeman and Journeymen 1656–1702, Company of Goldsmiths of Dublin, Ms. 95. There are also isolated references to journeymen in the guild minute books. See, for example, Minute of 2 May 1687, 1 Aug. 1687, Company of Goldsmiths of Dublin, Ms. 1: 10, Dublin, Assay Office.
72 I am grateful for Jessica Cunningham for this information.
73 Minute of 1 October 1769, Company of Goldsmiths of Dublin. Ms. 5: 185, Dublin, Assay Office.
74 Jackson, *English Goldsmiths*, 636–40, 656–66. The list of quarter brothers and journeymen referred to covers the period between 1750 and 1784.
75 Cormick may even have been subcontracting work to Makemaid, as the evidence also refers to the latter's journeyman. In a Minute of 7 October 1768, Company of Goldsmiths of Dublin, Ms. 5: 166, Dublin, Assay Office, another similar instance is recorded where Makemaid was involved. On this occasion Makemaid had made a piece on behalf of James Holmes which had a duty mark fraudulently let in. For more on the practice of duty dodging, see Bennett, *Irish Georgian Silver*, 216–17, 219–22; Glanville, *Silver in England*, 161–62.
76 See Tessa Murdoch, ed., *Beyond the Border: Huguenot Goldsmiths in Northern Europe and North America* (Brighton: Sussex Academic Press, 2008), 152–53.
77 See Bennett, Irish Georgian Silver, 295.
78 Other widows either turned their husband's charges over to new masters or instructed journeymen to see out the terms. See also Philippa Glanville and Jennifer Faulds Goldsborough,

Women Silversmiths 1685–1845: Works from the Collection of the National Museum of Women in the Arts (London: Thames and Hudson, 1990).

79 *Faulkner's Dublin Journal* (*FDJ*), 14–17 July 1764.

80 This surname was also spelt Keen. See Fig. 4.2.

81 These cases often came to light when individuals sought freedom of the guild.

82 Minute of 14 October 1704, Company of Goldsmiths of Dublin, Ms. 1: 117, Dublin, Assay Office.

83 Minute of 22 September 1738, Company of Goldsmiths of Dublin, Ms. 2: 78, Dublin, Assay Office.

84 Minute of 15 December 1741, Company of Goldsmiths of Dublin, Ms. 2: 153, Dublin, Assay Office.

85 J.P. Fallon, *Marks of London Goldsmiths and Silversmiths, 1837–1914* (London: Barne and Jenkins, 1992), 10; and Arthur Grimwade, *London Goldsmiths: Their Marks and Lives* (3rd ed., London: Faber & Faber, 1990), 729–31.

86 Grimwade, *London Goldsmiths*, 8.

87 Ibid.

88 Ibid., 424, 590.

89 Hill, *From Patriots to Unionists*, 30. This recalls the continental model. See for instance Carolyn Sargentson, *Merchants and Luxury Markets, The Marchands Merciers of Eighteenth-Century Paris* (London: Victoria and Albert Museum with the J. Paul Getty Museum, 1996), 13.

90 There were obvious exceptions, including members of the gentry or nobility who had been granted freedom of a particular trade guild by 'grace especial'.

91 Hill, *From Patriots to Unionists*, 204.

92 By August 1802, the members of the goldsmiths' guild were moved to resolve 'unanimously that the freedom of this Corporation shall not be given by Grace Especial to any person who shall not at the time of his petitioning for such freedom, carry on or follow some branch of the Goldsmiths' trade'; Minute of 2 August 1802, Company of Goldsmiths of Dublin, Ms. 6: 321, Dublin, Assay Office.

93 The date of commencement has been used in each case.

94 Kahl, 'Apprenticeship and the Freedom of the London Livery Companies, 1690–1750', 17.

95 Campbell, *The London Tradesman*, 331–40.

96 The price of gold and silver fluctuated during the course of the eighteenth century. See John J. McCusker, *Money and Exchange in Europe and America 1660–1775* (Chapel Hill: University of North Carolina Press, 1978). In 1773, the guild agreed to appoint a committee to meet 'as often as occasion may require in order to raise or lower the Price of Bullion agreeable to the London Market' and it was agreed that members would then 'strictly adhere to the different prices of Bullion from time to time as shall be stated regulated and furnished by the said Committee', Minute of 2 August 1773, Company of Goldsmiths of Dublin, Ms. 5: 257, Dublin, Assay Office.

97 Emma Packer, 'Refining the Goldsmith' (MA thesis, Royal College of Art, London, 1992); Claire Walsh, 'Shop Design and the Display of Goods' (MA thesis, Royal College of Art, London, 1993).

98 See, for example, the Banks and Heal collections in the British Museum.

99 See Muir, 'Printing Persuasion', 190. Of fifty-nine eighteenth-century goldsmiths' trade cards in the Guildhall archive, London, 34 per cent included illustrations of shop signs in their design.

100 The difference between the advertising strategies adopted by London and Dublin goldsmiths will be discussed later in this book. The minutes of the Wide Streets Commission of Dublin are held in Dublin City Archive.

101 Niall McCullough, *A Vision of the City: Dublin and the Wide Streets Commissioners* (Dublin: Dublin Corporation, 1991); Edward McParland, 'The Wide Streets Commissioners', *Bulletin of the Irish Georgian Society* (*BIGS*) 15, no. 1 (1972): 1–31; Edel Sheridan, 'Designing the Capital City', in *Dublin through Space and Time*, ed. Joseph Brady and Anngret Simms (Dublin: Four Courts Press, 2001), 66–136.

102 Sheridan, 'Designing the Capital City', 110.

103 S.P. Epstein, 'Craft Guilds, Apprenticeship, and Technological Change in Pre-Industrial Europe', 686.

104 *Walker's Hibernian Magazine*, February 1783, quoted in Sarah Foster, 'Going Shopping in Georgian Dublin' (MA thesis, Royal College of Art, London, 1995), 34.
105 See, for example, *FDJ*, 18–22 June 1765; 14–17 October 1769; and 7–10 January 1775.
106 Minutes of the Wide Streets Commission of Dublin, 1780, vol. 3: 194, Dublin City Archives.
107 Minutes of the Wide Streets Commission of Dublin, 21 July 1766, vol. 2: 39, Dublin City Archives. He also appears to have committed a sum of £150 in addition to the annual fee for the lease.
108 Ibid.
109 Minutes of the Wide Streets Commission of Dublin, 8 August 1761, vol. 1: 91, Dublin City Archives.
110 Ibid.
111 *Pue's Occurrences*, 29 October–1 November 1763.
112 *FDJ*, 17–20 October 1761.
113 Quoted in Clifford, *Silver in London*, 23.
114 *FDJ*, 11–14 February 1769.
115 Ibid.
116 Minutes of the Wide Streets Commission of Dublin, 6 May 1779, Ms., vol. 2: 220, Dublin City Archives.
117 Bennett, *Irish Georgian Silver*, 321.
118 Sargentson, *Merchants and Luxury Markets*, 20.
119 Minutes of the Wide Streets Commission of Dublin, 24 July 1761, vol. 1: 89, Dublin City Archives.
120 *Universal Advertiser*, 16 March 1756.
121 Walsh, 'Shop Design and the Display of Goods', 135.
122 Brasbridge, *Fruits*, cited in Walsh, 'Shop Design and the Display of Goods', 64. The new owner altered the shop sign to imply 'an amicable union of interests'.
123 Minutes of the Wide Streets Commission of Dublin, 31 July 1761, vol. 1: 122. Dublin City Archives.
124 *Dublin Mercury*, 18–22 March 1766.
125 *FDJ*, 26 April 1729. Tuite later moved to London. He was a patentee for hydraulics there and a well-known goldsmith. See Helen Clifford, 'Goldsmiths of Invention: Hidden Connections and Alternative Occupations', *Silver Society Journal* 9 (1997): 574.
126 *Hibernian Journal*, 2 January 1792.
127 *Munster Journal*, 15 December 1766.
128 *Limerick Chronicle*, 23 February 1769.
129 Richard Twiss, *A Tour in Ireland in 1775* (2nd ed., Dublin: Printed for Messrs Shephard et al., 1776), 31.
130 They would not necessarily receive the goods which were to be traded in before the new ones were made.
131 *Flying Post*, 2 January 1710.
132 Clifford, *Silver in London*, 76.
133 Ibid.
134 Colm Lennon, ed., *Dublin Part 2, 1610–1756*. No. 19 of *Irish Historic Towns* Atlas (Dublin: Royal Irish Academy, 2008), 38.
135 *Freeman's Journal*, 22–26 March 1768.
136 Since silver was regarded as bullion, it was naturally linked to debates on money flow and the economy. The connections between plate and 'ready money' in eighteenth-century Ireland will be examined in chapter 4.
137 Minute of 4 May 1700, Company of Goldsmiths of Dublin Ms. 1: 8, Dublin, Assay Office.
138 Kahl, *The Development of London Livery Companies*, 13.
139 *FDJ*, 27 February–5 March 1739.
140 *Pue's Occurrences*, 9–13 July 1751.
141 *Volunteer Journal, or Independent Gazetteer*, 18 November 1782.
142 Geoffrey Wills, 'Stafford Briscoe: A London Silversmith', *Apollo* 117 (January 1983): 50–54.
143 Ibid.

144 For examples, see Ambrose Heal, *London Tradesmen's Cards of the XIII Century* (London: B.T. Batsford, 1925); Ambrose Heal, *The London Goldsmiths, 1200–1800* (Cambridge: Cambridge University Press, 1935).

145 Alfred Cox Prime, ed., *The Arts and Crafts in Philadelphia, Maryland and South Carolina, 1721–1785* (Philadelphia: Walpole Society, 1929), 71–72, 105. The advertisements referred to appeared in the *Maryland Journal* and *Pennsylvania Packet*, respectively.

146 *Belfast News Letter*, 3 January 1766.

147 *Belfast News Letter*, 8–11 May 1787.

148 Ibid.

149 Sargentson, *Merchants and Luxury Markets*, 30–31 notes of the *marchands merciers* that 'the number of instances recorded in the inventories of mercers exchanging goods with each other is notable. By no means did the mercers act as the only intermediary between manufacturer and private customer. Their customers were also sometimes artisans (buying raw materials and tools), and frequently other mercers.'

150 Minute of 7 July 1778, Company of Goldsmiths of Dublin, Ms. 5: 364, Dublin, Assay Office. The goldsmith in question was most probably Bartholomew Delandre, a freeman of the Goldsmiths' Company.

151 Clifford, *Silver in London*; Giorgio Riello, *A Foot in the Past* (Oxford: Oxford University Press, 2005; Werner Freundel, 'The Production and Commissioning of London-Made Private Carriages: 1740–1800' (MA thesis, Royal College of Art, London, 1999); John Styles, 'The Goldsmiths and the London Luxury Trades, 1550–1750', in *Goldsmiths, Silversmiths and Bankers*, ed. David Mitchell (London: Sutton, 1995), 112–20; Pat Kirkham, *The London Furniture Trade, 1700–1870* (London: Furniture History Society, 1988).

152 On subcontracting and outsourcing, see S.R. Epstein and M. Prak, 'Introduction: Guilds, Innovation, and the European Economy, 1400–1800', in *Guilds, Innovation, and the European Economy, 1400–1800*, ed. Epstein and Prak, 12; and Catharina Lis and Hugo Soly, 'Subcontracting in Guild-Based Export Trades, Thirteenth to Eighteenth Centuries', in *Guilds, Innovation, and the European Economy, 1400–1800*, ed. Epstein and Prak, 81–113.

153 Clifford, *Silver in London*.

154 Piecework usually paid at a higher rate but craftsmen working in this way nonetheless depended on a ready flow of work.

155 Minutes of 31 January 1765, and 1 May 1765, Company of Goldsmiths of Dublin, Ms. 5: 101, 103, Dublin, Assay Office.

156 Silver is too soft to be used in its pure form for making durable objects. However, this fraudulent and excessive use of base metal, which seems to have been knowingly concealed by the maker was a serious matter.

157 In modern silver scholarship the term 'sponsor's mark' is sometimes used in place of 'maker's mark' to acknowledge that a piece was not necessarily made by the person or firm whose initials appeared on it. Jackson, *English Goldsmiths*, 638, notes that Cordner became free of the guild in 1764.

158 The reason that this case came to light in the first place is not made explicit in the minute book. However, it is clear that Tudor was made aware of Cordner's dubious reputation. Contemporaneously, the goldsmith Benjamin Stokes pursued a prosecution against Cordner for the same type of deception, which described how the latter ' knowingly, wilfully, craftily, deceitfully, & Injuriously' defrauded him, (Prosecution by Benjamin Stokes of William Cordner, 11 February 1765, Company of Goldsmiths of Dublin, Box File I Miscellaneous loose documents, unpaginated).

159 Minute of 6 September 1727, Company of Goldsmiths of Dublin Ms. 1: 258, Dublin, Assay Office.

160 *FDJ*, 19–21 May 1745.

161 Packer, 'Refining the Goldsmith'; Edgard Moreno, 'Glossary of Tools, Supplies and Processes Used by Silversmiths and Jewellers', in *Colonial Massachusetts Silversmiths and Jewelers*, ed. Patricia Kane (New Haven: Yale University Art Gallery, 1998).

162 Packer, 'Refining the Goldsmith', 124–25. The inventory dates from 1709.

163 Moreno, 'Glossary of Tools, Supplies and Processes'.

164 Ledgers of Imports and Exports from London and Outports 1697 to 1780, CUST 3, National Archives, Kew.

165 This figure was achieved by abstracting the data for individual years during the period 1700 to 1750 from CUST 3, National Archives, Kew.
166 *Proceedings of the Dublin Society*, 27 October 1768, vol. 5: 229–30.
167 Ibid.
168 Moreno, 'Glossary of Tools, Supplies and Processes', 1059.
169 Minute of 25 August 1721, Company of Goldsmiths of Dublin, Ms. 1: 221, Dublin Assay Office.
170 Walsh, 'Shop Design and the Display of Goods', 72.
171 *Saunders' News-Letter*, 9–11 October 1776.
172 'A list of commodities imported yearly into Ireland, being such as may be either raised or manufactured therein, together with their yearly value taken at a medium for the years 1734,1735,1736', Commerce Folder 1A, John Johnston Collection, Bodleian Library, Oxford. The individual weight of these cases is not given.
173 *FDJ*, 2–5 April 1743.
174 Vincent Dowling, *Trials at Large* (Dublin, 1792).
175 Ibid. The sentence in this case was transportation.
176 *Dublin Courier*, 5–7 November 1764. See also Foster, 'Going Shopping in Georgian Dublin', 35.
177 *The Star and Fashionable World*, 17 May 1824.
178 *FDJ*, 9 September 1830. I grateful to Breda Scott for this reference.
179 I am grateful to Jessica Cunningham for insights on this question.
180 Kahl, *The Development of London Livery Companies*, 17.
181 Ibid., 204.

2 Goldsmiths and market forces in eighteenth-century Ireland

In 1751 the *Dublin Courant* announced the death of the goldsmith John Hamilton. Described as 'a dealer of the most unblemished character', Hamilton was acknowledged for his assiduity 'in improving the several branches of his business'. He ran one of the busiest workshops in the city and served as master warden of the guild on two separate occasions (Fig. 2.1).[1] His contemporary, Thomas Isaacs, had died the previous year and had been described in the same newspaper as 'a dealer of fair character'.[2] A reputation for honesty and integrity was essential in the goldsmiths' trade and the guild took its regulatory responsibility seriously, but how was its role as guardian of quality actually implemented? Was the regulation of intrinsic value (the value of the raw materials) consistently prioritised over design and technical proficiency? How much work did they test for metal purity as an integral part of the hallmarking process, and what can eighteenth-century assay records indicate about the scale and composition of the market?[3] Were Dublin goldsmiths quick to employ new labour-saving equipment, and what was their response to competition from Sheffield plate in the second half of the century?

'Tried and tested': the guild and the issue of quality control

The decline of guild authority in eighteenth-century Europe is a well-documented phenomenon. Anthony Black has observed that English guilds were in decline well before 1750, 'under the twin pressures of legal liberalism and parliamentary aristocracy', while 'in France the still intact guild system was abolished by law in 1791, as part of a revolutionary republican attack on corporations and separate jurisdictions.'[4] Yet despite an ideological shift away from the restrictive practices of guilds towards a more open market, goldsmiths' guilds in Dublin, and in London, actively continued to regulate the quality, or at least the intrinsic value of work produced by their members. W. F. Kahl has noted of the London livery companies that 'only the goldsmiths' company and the gun-makers' company would ultimately continue to inspect work produced by craftsmen,'[5] contending:

> These two companies have been able to retain more of their traditional privileges of craft supervision because their crafts have survived the factory system to serve a small luxury market. Also, the interest of the industrial branch of these trades in maintaining a high standard of quality, has contributed to the retention of a system of regulation, which other industries overthrew in the eighteenth century because it hampered the expansion of production.[6]

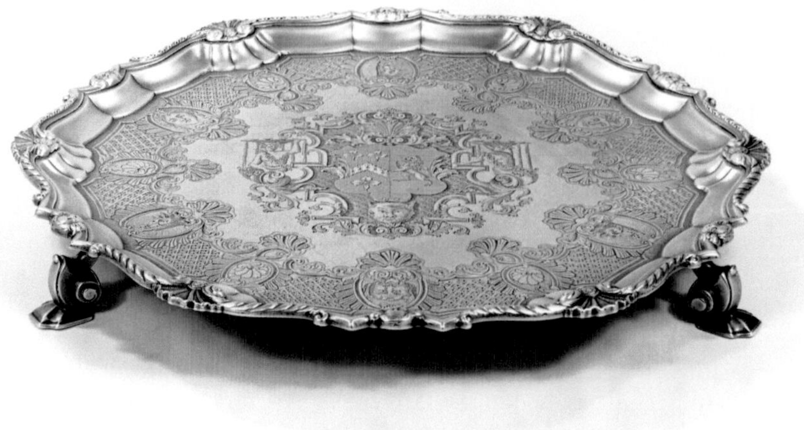

Figure 2.1 John Hamilton, *Salver* (1735–37), silver, 30.2 cm diam

Source: Ashmolean Museum Oxford, Farrer Bequest. Photo credit © Ashmolean Museum, University of Oxford.

It is interesting that Kahl refers to goldsmiths' 'small luxury market'. Inevitably, their exclusivity would leave them vulnerable as old luxuries were challenged by new, particularly in the second half of the eighteenth century. Increasingly, perceptions of value would shift, 'from a situation in which the value of a product derived from the value/quality of the raw materials used to one in which invention, newness and fashion played a more prominent role'.[7]

So how did guilds assess quality? De Munck has argued that ' "intrinsic value" (the value of the raw material used) was a broadly shared and very important convention in the urban and guild-based context of the late medieval and early modern period,' but that 'from an economic perspective, the seventeenth and eighteenth centuries witnessed a shift from intrinsic value to design and decoration as important ingredients of product quality.'[8] In Dublin, there seems to have been a decline in emphasis on the production of masterpieces by the beginning of the eighteenth century. Earlier writers on Irish silver refer to the importance of the masterpiece as test and proof of craftsmanship, without factoring in the likelihood of changes in corporate practice over time. Charles Jackson cites the Dublin guild charter of 1637:

> That no man shall be admitted to be privileged, or made free of such company of the mystery aforesaid, until he be approved by men of the said mystery to have served seven years an apprentice in said mystery, and from thenceforth to be a sufficient workman or craftsman; also to have made and framed with his hands a certain work or vessel of gold, in English called his masterpiece, tried and approved by the Wardens aforesaid.[9]

Similarly, in *Irish Georgian Silver* Douglas Bennett states that on completion of their training apprentices were customarily required to make and submit their masterpieces 'without the help of any other hand'.[10]

It should not be assumed that the modus operandi outlined in the guild's seventeenth-century charter was consistently observed in the eighteenth century. In fact, this was unlikely. The seventeenth-century minutes of the Dublin goldsmiths' guild indicate that the presentation of a masterpiece was required on completion of an apprenticeship. Abel Ram was clearly hoping to endear himself to guild authorities when, shortly after having been sworn a free brother in 1665, 'he brought in his Master peece and bestowed it upon the Corporacion being a peece of plate weighing eleaven ounces or thereabouts and thereupon engraven: The Gift of Abell Ram to the Corporavion [*sic*] of Goldsmiths.'[11]

Nevertheless, there is insufficient evidence to claim that the practice of requiring, submitting and registering masterpieces was consistently regulated in eighteenth-century Dublin. A minute of 1667 states that no apprentice should be granted freedom without first producing a masterpiece.[12] Certainly, when the goldsmith John Garrard applied for guild freedom after completing his apprenticeship during the 1690s he was required to present a masterpiece to the guild.[13] Christian Waggoner's application for freedom in 1697 was accepted on different grounds. He was married to the widow of a former freeman and had a number of dependent children. His application was accepted but he was required to deliver a masterpiece to the guild.[14]

Clearly, other Dublin guilds required masterpieces during the late seventeenth century. The painter-stainer Edward Stretton was allowed a month to bring his 'proof piece' before the master and wardens of the guild of Saint Luke.[15] Another applicant was refused admission to the same guild in 1699, on the grounds that he was 'no painter stainer nor ever produced a proof piece'.[16] Yet by the early eighteenth century references to masterpieces or 'proof pieces' are conspicuously absent in the minutes of the Dublin goldsmiths' guild. If masterpieces were routinely required, received and inspected, some craftsmen must have failed to deliver them, and one would expect to find these cases noted. In fact, the copious entries in guild minutes relating to apprenticeships suggest that the requirement of a fixed term of training was perceived by the guild as a means to an end in ensuring levels of competence.[17]

This correlation of experience with proficiency is confirmed by a comment made by guild officials in a letter to the Chancellor of the Exchequer in 1807. It refers to the trust invested in those 'who from serving an apprenticeship to the trade of a goldsmith must have acquired sufficient experience to discover such deceits and frauds as might be attempted'.[18] In other words, by the Georgian period, proof of apprenticeship seems to have satisfied adequately as proof of expertise. Similarly, in eighteenth-century London, it would seem that the production of masterpieces was neither consistently required nor regulated, with the result that the practice appears to have effectively petered out.[19] The fact that subdivision of labour and subcontracting of work was such a distinctive feature of the London market during this period may have contributed to the decline in emphasis on such a traditional craft practice. In *The London Tradesman*, the author drew particular attention to the distinctive character and composition of the London market:

> The goldsmith employs several distinct workmen, almost as many as there are different articles in his shop; for in this great city there are hands that excel in

every branch, and are constantly employed but in that one of which they are masters. This gives us an advantage over many foreign nations in this article, impossible to expect that a man employed in such an infinite variety can finish his work to any perfection, at least, not so much as he who is constantly employed in one thing.[20]

Other continental models differed from the examples of Dublin and London. In order to become a fully qualified artisan in Barcelona during the eighteenth century a practical demonstration of skill was expected and a mandatory *passantia* or masterpiece was required. Craftsmen were obliged to make drawings of their pieces when approved, and these designs were then retained by the guild. In a trade dependent on the recycling of metal, these *Llibres de Passantia* offer an invaluable profile of evolving taste in eighteenth-century Spain.[21]

The guild as guardian of 'the standard'[22]

The example of the Dublin goldsmiths' guild certainly supports De Munck's thesis in respect of early modern guilds that 'what guilds guaranteed with their trademarks was typically the nature and characteristics of the raw materials used – in other words intrinsic value.'[23] In Dublin, the harp crowned served as the hallmark of the Dublin assay office, and was accompanied variously by maker's marks, retailer's marks, duty marks and date letters depending on the type of object and the period in which it was produced (Fig. 2.2).[24] Numerous guild minutes describe cases involving substandard materials, and robust language is used in cases of perceived fraud. In contrast, there are few references in the same sources to poorly manufactured work. Since the public could not easily judge metal quality, it was reasonable that the guild should function in this way; indeed, they were empowered by royal charter to do so.[25] Nevertheless, it is interesting that quality was consistently defined by the guild in terms of metal purity (Fig. 2.3) rather than technical competence. Two cases from 1742 and 1761 document guild arbitration on standards of execution and craftsmanship, but these were the exceptions rather than the rule.[26] One of these concerned Thomas Shephard and his apprentice Gregory McCannon. McCannon claimed that his master was not teaching him requisite skills, while Shephard claimed that his charge was 'idle, kept bad hours and left his service without cause'.[27] The proof was in the work – Shephard produced metal hilts partly executed by McCannon; they were found to be well executed and so the apprentice was judged to have no cause of complaint against his master. How Shephard was able to prove McCannon's input can only be conjectured – arguably the master had the upper hand unless compelling evidence proved otherwise.

The role of the Dublin Society

While the guild saw apprenticeship as a tacit route to acquiring technical knowledge, the Dublin Society was active in trying to raise standards of Irish design and draughtsmanship. From the mid-eighteenth century its drawing schools offered tuition as well as premiums.[28] Some of the pupils from these schools went on to pursue careers in branches of the Dublin goldsmiths' trade, but accurate numbers are difficult to estimate, largely because of the ubiquity of certain surnames.[29] One of the earliest formal announcements from the Dublin Society's School of Ornament certainly confirms that

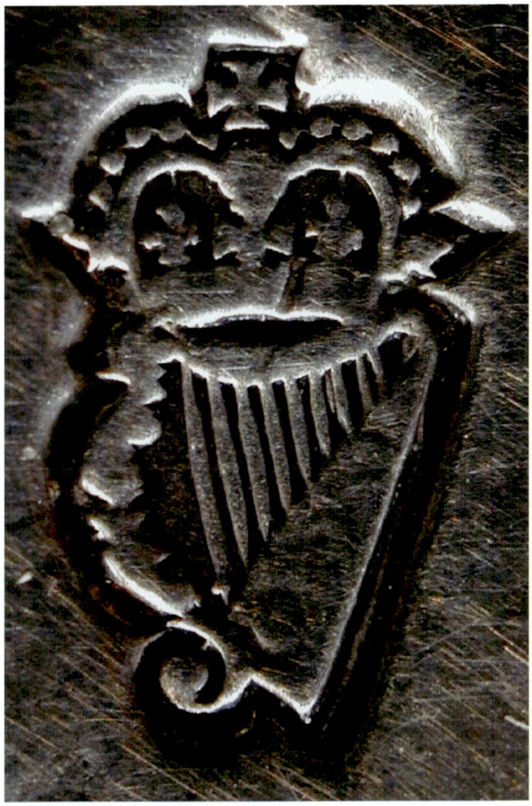

Figure 2.2 Harp crowned, hallmark of the Dublin goldsmiths' guild

Photo credit: © Thomas Sinsteden.

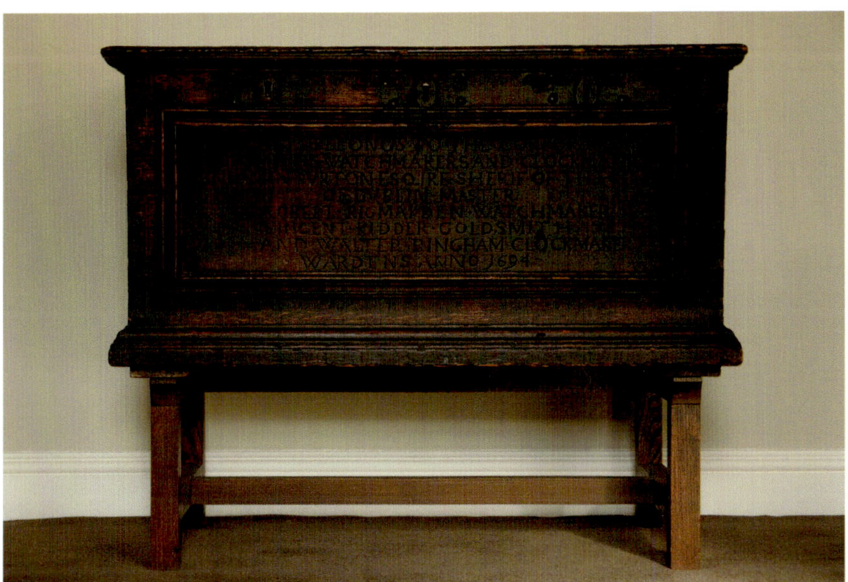

Figure 2.3 Chest used for securing the touch money (fee for assaying), collected by the Dublin goldsmiths' guild (seventeenth century), wood, 51 × 100 cm

Source: Company of Goldsmiths of Dublin, Assay Office, Dublin. Photo credit: © Company of Goldsmiths of Dublin.

it intended to attract goldsmiths and allied traders. In March 1764, *Faulkner's Dublin Journal* ran the following notice:

> The Dublin Society, having established schools for figure and ornamental drawing, all painters, carvers, chasers, goldsmiths, carpet-weavers, linen and paper stainers, damask and diaper weavers, their journeymen and apprentices, and others whose profession depends upon design, may have free admission to view the drawing of said schools in Shaw's Court, Dame Street, having first obtained tickets from the Society.[30]

Proficiency in two-dimensional patterns was essential for those involved in the surface decoration of plate. A student called Edward Percy joined two of the Society's drawing schools in 1778.[31] This was most likely the same Edward Percy who advertised as a 'gold and silver chaser' in 1789.[32] His namesake, Edward Lorenzo Percy, joined the drawing schools in 1810, before being awarded a premium in 1819.[33] He was responsible for the chasing on a large silver salver which was exhibited by the Society in 1835. Unusually, Percy's input was acknowledged in the catalogue, independently of the goldsmith who had actually made the piece.[34] Chasers and their oeuvres frequently elude identification, yet there is clear evidence that Dublin chasers benefited from the programmes offered by the Dublin Society schools.[35] A surviving silver coffee pot bearing the mark of William Nowlan apparently incorporates the 'signature' of Henry Teare, inscribed as H. TEARE in a detail of the elaborate chasing (Fig. 2.4).[36]

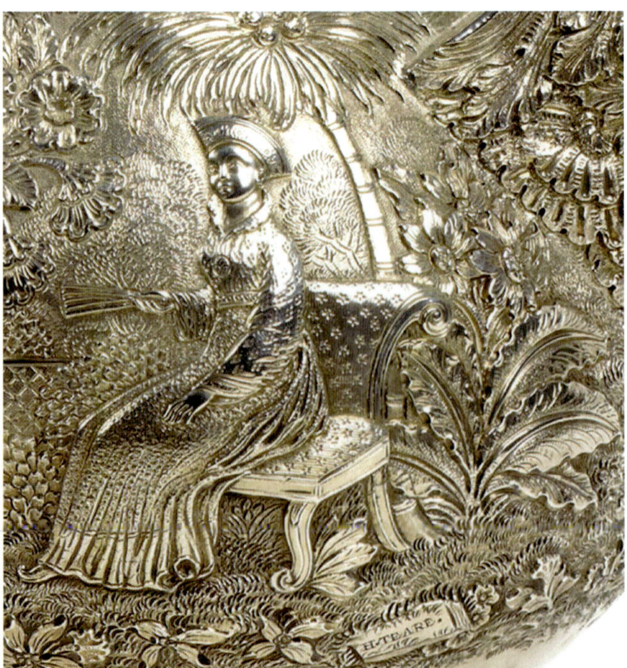

Figure 2.4 William Nowlan, *Coffee pot*, detail of the chasing, silver

Source: Ulster Museum Belfast. Photo credit: © Ulster Museum.

The role of the assay office

Undoubtedly, when it came to regulating the market, the process of assaying plate offered a unique form of customer assurance, and one of the oldest. Hallmarks, the outcome of having passed the assay, offered buyers a visual guarantee of an object's intrinsic value, which was unparalleled in its consistency and control to other sectors of the luxury goods trade. Other manufacturers employed marks, but none offered the assurance of an official hallmark. In 1725, the cutler Alexander McCarty opted to mark his wares with a hammer and heart, 'to do justice to the public' and 'for fear of counterfeiters'.[37]

During the long eighteenth century, goldsmiths in Cork, Birmingham and Pennsylvania campaigning for the establishment of local assay offices identified a direct correlation between them and the expansion of trade.[38] Clearly for some, assayed goods were perceived to be superior, and convenient access to an assay office was considered by goldsmiths to be a factor in generating, or at least facilitating, increased demand for goods. In Ireland, under the terms of the royal charter granted to the Dublin goldsmiths' guild in 1637, the Dublin guild was responsible for supervising the assaying and hallmarking of all gold and silverwares produced throughout Ireland (Fig. 2.5).[39] In theory,

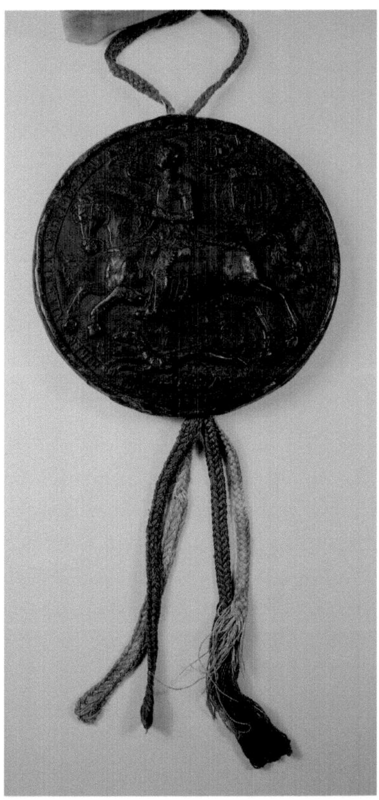

Figure 2.5 Seal affixed to the Charter of the Dublin goldsmiths' guild (seventeenth century), 16.5 cm diam

Source: Company of Goldsmiths of Dublin, Assay Office, Dublin. Photo credit: © Company of Goldsmiths of Dublin.

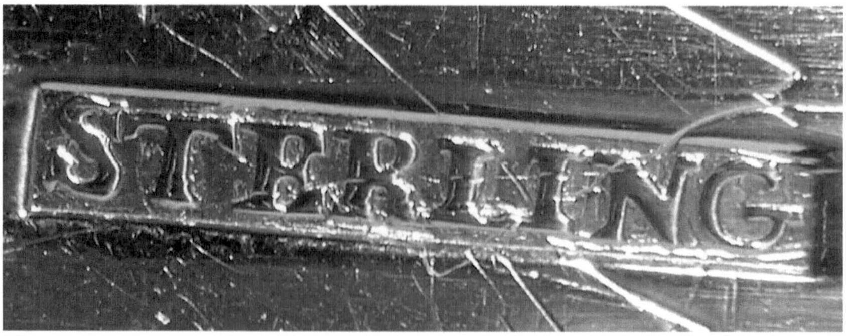

Figure 2.6 Carden Terry and Jane Williams, *Detail of 'sterling' mark on skewer* (Cork, c.1790)
Photo credit: © Thomas Sinsteden.

this meant that all craftsmen engaged in the manufacture of plate were obliged to have their goods tested and hallmarked at the assay office. In reality, this was impractical. The delays and expenses of sending goods on a round trip to Dublin placed craftsmen in cities like Cork and Limerick at a distinct disadvantage and exposed them to delays, transport costs and even highwaymen. While some did send their work to the capital to be assayed, provincial goldsmiths also relied on a series of locally recognised town marks to secure consumer confidence (Fig. 2.6).[40] Examples include Cork goldsmiths stamping their wares with a ship between two castles (derived from the city's coat of arms), Galway pieces marked with a ship and Limerick silverware stamped with a castellated gateway.[41] However, as the eighteenth century progressed it seems to become more common for provincial goldsmiths to stamp variants of the word 'sterling' on their wares, along with the maker's name or initials.

The campaign for a Cork assay office

From at least the early eighteenth to the early nineteenth century, Cork goldsmiths made intermittent attempts to win support for a regional assay office. Their arguments are paralleled by those of their English and North American counterparts, but ultimately the various Cork campaigns proved unsuccessful. It would seem that opposition from the Dublin guild was not purely motivated by public interest, but also by a desire to safeguard their monopoly.[42] According to some of the Cork lobbyists, Dublin would oppose any proposal for a new assay office, 'being interested in the monopoly of assaying and vending the goods of the whole kingdom'.[43]

In 1801 a delegation of Cork goldsmiths wrote to Mountifort Longfield, MP, Commissioner of the Revenue, seeking his support (Fig. 2.7).[44] Explaining that they had sought consumer confidence up to this point, 'by marking on each article their name and the word sterling', they claimed that they had recently been made aware that their goods were liable to confiscation if they were not officially assayed and hallmarked.[45] This argument is hard to accept. Since 1730, a duty had been payable on all wrought plate manufactured in Ireland, indicated by the duty mark of a figure of Hibernia punched on pieces at the time of assay. This tax was collected at the time of assay, and

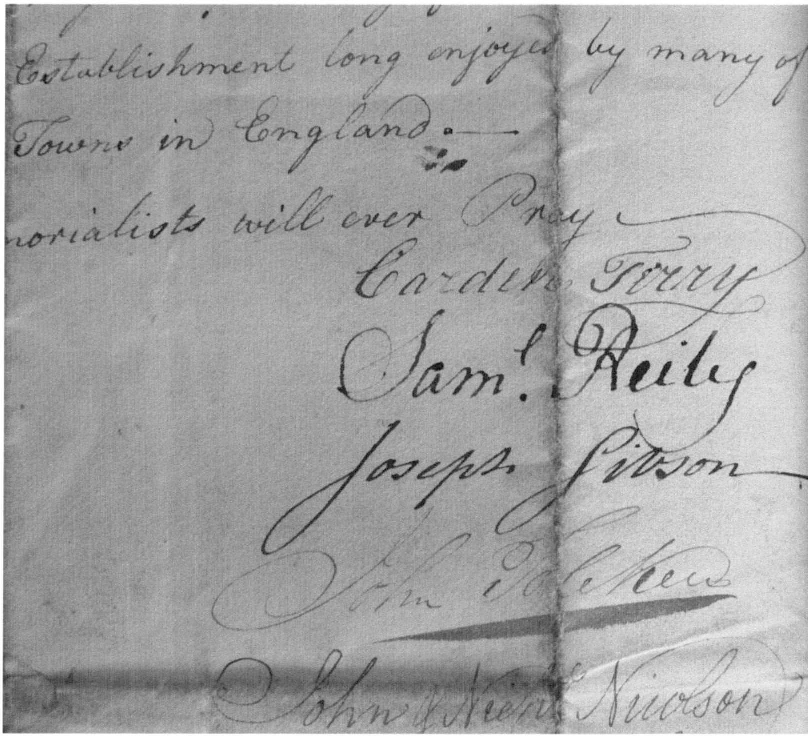
Establishment long enjoyed by many of
Towns in England:—
norialists will ever Pray
Carden Terry
Saml. Reily
Joseph Gibson

Figure 2.7 Signatures of Cork goldsmiths, on a draft petition to the Commissioner of the Revenue seeking the establishment of a local assay office (1801)

Source: Company of Goldsmiths of Dublin, Assay Office, Dublin. Photo credit: © Company of Goldsmiths of Dublin.

was additional to the 'touch money', the charge levied for having goods tested.[46] Some of the goldsmiths campaigning on this occasion certainly had sent work to the capital for assaying. They therefore understood the financial implications, and the duties for which they were liable.

The case was quickly referred to the secretary of state, who in turn consulted the advice of Jeremiah D'Olier.[47] D'Olier was an interesting figure with a number of commercial and political connections. He had served as lord mayor of Dublin and had also been a pivotal figure within the Dublin goldsmiths' guild, having been elected master in 1781.[48] Evidently, his comments revealed some fraternal bias, since one of his objections was subsequently annotated with the words 'impertinent' and 'savours too much of the Dublin silver trade'.[49]

D'Olier expressed reservations about the professional integrity of a second assay office, and specifically its ability to uphold standards. He predicted that 'the preservation' of 'chastity' (an interesting choice of language) would be a problematic task.[50] The London goldsmiths' guild had raised similar objections when they unsuccessfully opposed the establishment of assay offices in Sheffield and Birmingham in 1773. They had argued 'that if the goldsmiths' manufactory in the towns of Sheffield and Birmingham should be increased, that of London must suffer a proportional decrease'.[51] Goldsmiths in Cork, Dublin, London and Philadelphia were unanimous in identifying that assaying could positively influence the demand for their goods, so it is not surprising that the Dublin guild wished to protect its advantage, even if Cork manufactures did not pose them a real threat.[52] The Cork goldsmiths claimed that they were producing annual quantities in the region of 20,000 oz. by the end of the eighteenth century.[53] This was substantially more than Newcastle, which had its own assay office.[54] The accuracy of their estimates is hard to verify, and no doubt they were aiming to make their case as compelling as possible. Between 1709 and 1733, just 4,518 oz. in total were assayed for Cork goldsmiths in Dublin.[55] In 1788, of over 80,000 oz. assayed in Dublin, there were no parcels submitted by Cork or indeed from any provincial goldsmiths.[56]

Not surprisingly, their figures were questioned by Jeremiah D'Olier, in particular their estimate that, with the establishment of a local assay office, '150 people would benefit from the encouragement to the silver industry in Cork.'[57] According to D'Olier, the capital's manufacturing goldsmiths totalled fewer than half that number, yet produced 'all the silver and gold made in Dublin for all Ireland and hallmarked'.[58]

Clearly, the decision makers believed that Cork should be granted 'the privilege of assay in the same condition' as provincial English cities.[59] Yet, despite the fact that the Dublin guild was repeatedly pressed to appoint an assay master for the city, they resisted doing so. Why Birmingham and Sheffield succeeded where Cork failed is not entirely clear, but Matthew Boulton's persuasive lobbying and influential network of contacts was certainly critical to Birmingham's success. There was also a stronger precedent in England for allowing assay offices with modest turnovers to remain open, like that of York.[60] Evidently, some practices within the goldsmiths' trade in eighteenth-century Ireland, such as the regulation of masterpieces, did change over time, while other traditions and privileges, like the monopoly on assaying and hallmarking, were staunchly maintained by the guild.

Demand and supply

As already noted, remarkably good records survive for the Dublin goldsmiths' guild.[61] Though the assay books are by no means intact, they offer a rich perspective on the volume of work manufactured in Georgian Dublin.[62] Many ledgers simply log goldsmiths' names beside the date and weight of their parcels of goods. However, in certain years the contents of their parcels are also itemised (Fig. 2.8). Nothing of comparable specificity exists for eighteenth-century London. The much larger scale of production there meant that this sort of detail would have been unmanageable. Even in a Dublin context, it was more usual to find clerks recording the weights of goods submitted rather than their type or number.[63] In the absence of goldsmiths' business ledgers, which have been used so effectively by historians of English silver, guild assay records offer an opportunity to analyse the quantities (Table 2.1) of goldsmiths' work being produced in Dublin, the demand for particular types of goods, the individuals who were dominating the market and the way in objects were described in a contemporary context.

Between 1638 and 1649, a total of 10,393 oz. of silver was submitted to the Dublin assay office.[64] By 1706 the annual total was almost 40,000 oz., and the volume

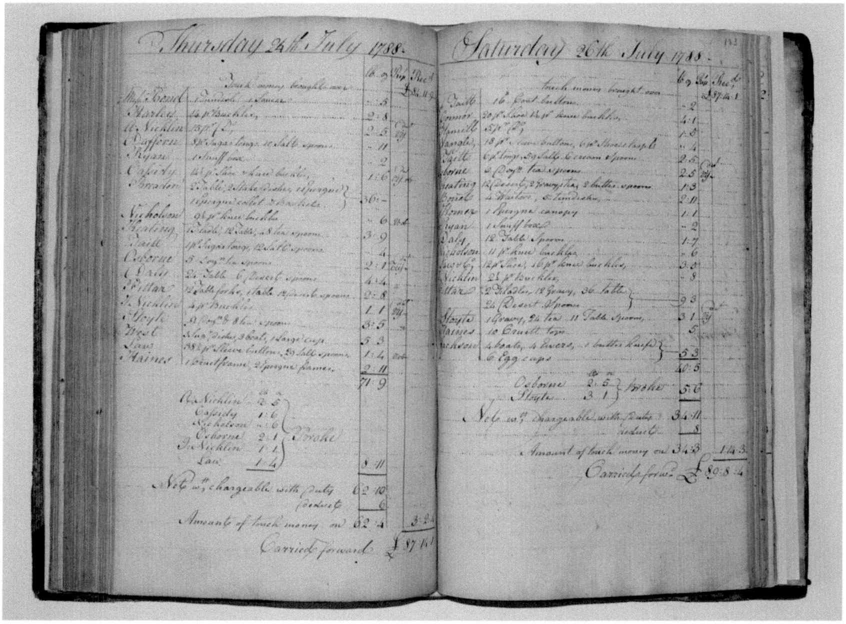

Figure 2.8 Detail of a Dublin assay book showing parcels of goods submitted for assaying (1788)

Source: Company of Goldsmiths of Dublin, Assay Office, Dublin. Photo credit: © Company of Goldsmiths of Dublin.

Table 2.1 Annual totals for plate assayed in Dublin during the long eighteenth century

Year	*Volume (troy oz.)*	*Year*	*Volume (troy oz.)*	*Year*	*Volume (troy oz.)*
1706	39,556	1712	49,675	1732	46,139
1707	42,428	1726	70,051	1746	39,314
1708	43,975	1727	52,908	1747	37,420
1709	45,211	1728	61,255	1748	50,470
1710	47,745	1730	65,529	1788	80,784
1711	48,700	1731	33,030	1810	113,686

Source: Thomas Sinsteden, 'Surviving Dublin Assay Records, part 2, 1708–48', *Silver Studies* 16 (2004), and 'Four Selected Assay Records', *Silver Society Journal* 11 (1999). The figures in each case refer to twelve-month periods, ending in the year specified. Totals are given for the years currently available.

continued to rise over the next six years, reaching almost 55,000 oz. for the assay year 1712.[65] The introduction in 1730 of a duty of 6d per ounce on all manufactured plate wrought in Ireland dealt the industry a blow from which it was slow to recover, and encouraged a spate of deliberate tax evasion or 'duty dodging'.[66] In the immediate lead up to the introduction of this duty, there was a rush to assay goods, leading to a peak of over 65,000 oz. submitted in the assay year 1729–30. Robert Calderwood, the goldsmith mentioned in chapter 1 for his prodigious number of apprentices, was establishing his workshop during this period. Ultimately, it would come to be regarded as one of the most productive and fashionable in the city.[67] In 1727, when Calderwood accepted his first apprentice, he had just been admitted free of the guild. He was at the outset of his career and was submitting a relatively modest quantity of plate to the assay office. Only a few hundred ounces of plate were recorded for him in the assay ledgers between November 1726 and October 1727. By the following assay year, his output was almost seven times greater and he soon registered a second apprentice with the guild.[68] Assessing individual levels of productivity for eighteenth-century goldsmiths is problematic, especially given that some had several journeymen working for them and others subcontracted work out. Determining what a single goldsmith could or should have been able to produce must be somewhat speculative. However, it is possible to draw some conclusions about what prominent goldsmiths were capable of. Margaret Gill's work on the goldsmiths of Newcastle has revealed that the four principal workshops submitting goods for assaying between 1747 and 1755 were those of Isaac Cookson, Robert Makepeace I, James Kirkup and William Partis.[69] By comparing Gill's evidence for the output of these prominent men with the data on their apprentices and journeymen, Robert Barker has concluded that a reasonable estimate for the output of a well organised master silversmith lay in the region of between 1,000 and 1,350 oz. per annum per skilled craftsman.[70] This tallies with the correspondence about the proposals for a Cork assay office, where average productivity totals per individual craftsman were estimated in the region of 1,000 oz. per annum.[71] Inevitably, an estimate of this kind is tentative, since certain types of objects were more time-consuming than others to make.[72] However, in the assay year 1727–28, Calderwood submitted almost 3,500 oz. of plate to the Dublin assay office, at a time when he had just two apprentices in the very early stages of their training. It seems very likely that he would have needed to engage some additional help in order to meet that output. In the same year, Thomas Sutton submitted a fine and extant silver wine cooler for assaying, a rare example in terms of Irish silver of this period (Fig. 2.9). It was made for Robert FitzGerald, nineteenth Earl of Kildare.[73] Sutton's workshop was the most productive in Dublin during the 1720s.[74] He took on at least six apprentices during his career and sold, by his own account, 'all kinds of goldsmiths' and jewellers' work in the newest and most fashionable manner'.[75]

The accounts of Thomas Taylor of Headfort, Co. Meath, offer fascinating detail on the costs involved in buying different items of domestic plate.[76] A silver chamber pot bought from Sutton in 1723 weighed 24 ounces and cost 6s 10d per oz., while a large silver dish purchased from John Hamilton in the same year weighed 150 ounces and was charged at 6s per oz. In the case of the goldsmith Robert Calderwood, there were a number of assay years where his quota reached or exceeded 4,000 oz.[77] In terms of his impact on the market, guild assay books allow his productivity relative to his peers to be profiled. For instance, between January and December 1754, 32,000 oz. of goods were submitted for assaying.[78] Calderwood sent in almost 10 per cent of this total. While he was one of approximately eighty different names recorded in the ledger, he registered parcels on sixty-two out of ninety-two potential assay days that year. This clearly suggests a busy workshop. From 1736 onwards, he had been steadily taking on more apprentices, so that there were periods during the 1740s and 1750s where he had up to four apprentices in his workshop. That did not include

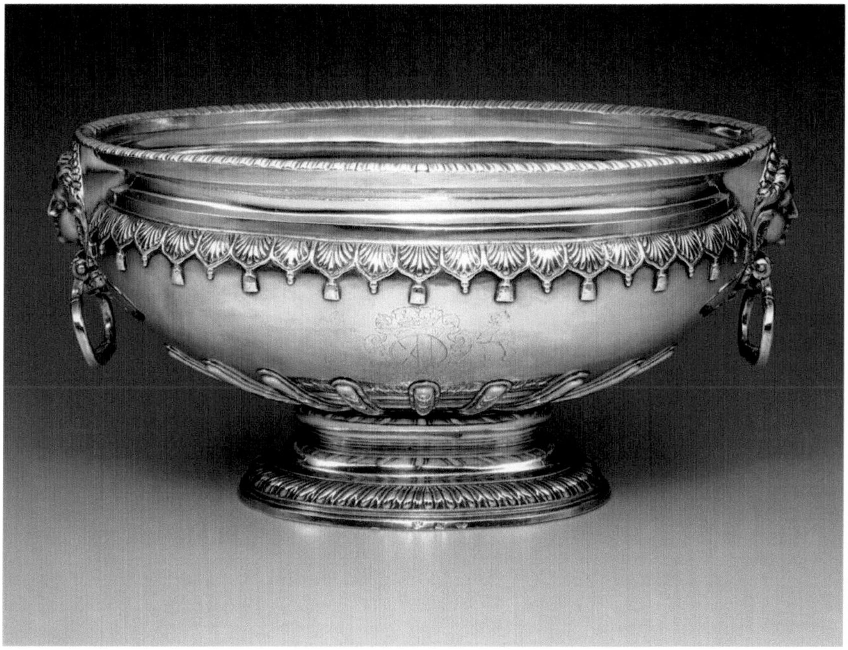

Figure 2.9 Thomas Sutton, *Wine cooler* (1727), silver, 24.13 × 48.26 cm

Source: Dallas Museum of Art, the Karl and Esther Hoblitzelle Collection, gift of the Hoblitzelle Foundation. Photo credit: © Dallas Museum of Art.

the various hammermen, journeymen, chasers, engravers and other specialists that he would have employed.

This pattern of a small number of goldsmiths dominating the market at any one time is consistent over the course of the eighteenth century, despite the fact that hundreds were employed in the industry. At the outset of the period, workshops like those run by Thomas Bolton, Joseph Walker and David King were the most prolific (Figs. 2.10–2.12).[79] Between 1693 and 1699, Thomas Bolton was responsible for almost a quarter of all silver assayed.[80] Thomas Sinsteden has noted that 'even by the late 1740s, the total ounces hallmarked had not recovered to the levels of the 1720s,' a factor due in no small measure to the 6d per ounce tax introduced in 1730.[81] The most productive workshops during the 1740s were those run by Robert Calderwood (Fig. 2.13), John Hamilton and William Townsend.[82]

In 1788, the leading manufacturer in terms of assay output was the flatware specialist John Pittar, who submitted close to 10,000 oz. for assaying that year (Fig. 2.14). By 1810, this position was held by the goldsmith Richard Sawyer, whose workshop was on Fishamble Street (Fig. 2.15).[83] Sawyer, unlike Pittar, produced an extensive range of both large and small wares, from cutlery to teapots and domestic to ecclesiastical plate. He was responsible for 17,000 items that year, from chalices to teapots, and could not possibly have produced them singlehandedly.[84]

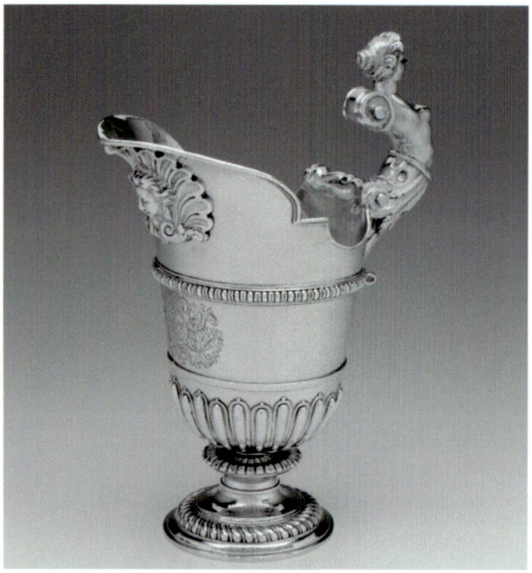

Figure 2.10 Thomas Bolton, *Ewer* (1699–1700), silver, 33 × 24.7 cm

Source: Museum of Fine Arts, Boston, Theodora Wilbour Fund in memory of Charlotte Beebe Wilbour. Photo credit: © Museum of Fine Arts Boston.

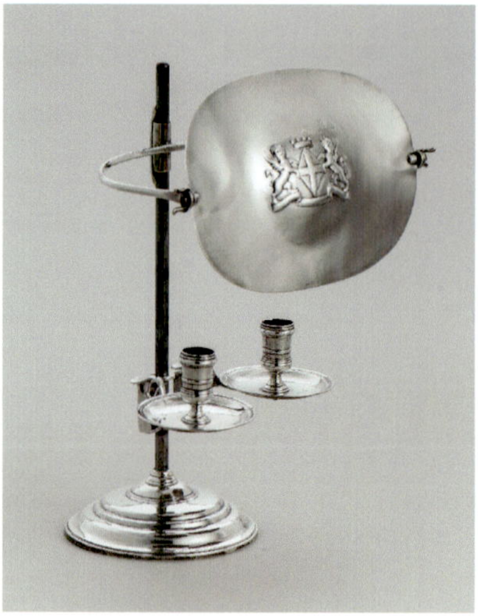

Figure 2.11 Joseph Walker, *Reading lamp* (1719–20), silver, 41.9 × 41 cm

Source: San Antonio Museum, Texas. Bequest of John V. Rowan Jr, 2004.13224.a-d. Photo credit: © Courtesy of the San Antonio Museum of Art. Photography by Peggy Tenison.

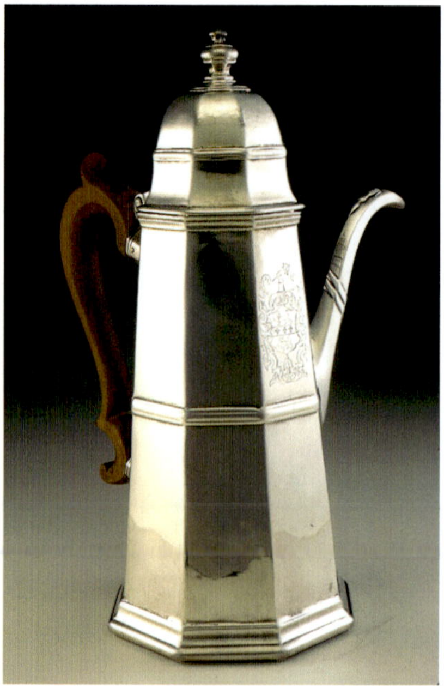

Figure 2.12 David King, *Coffee pot* (1708–9 to 1709–10), silver, 27 × 17.1 cm

Source: Sterling and Francine Clark Institute, Williamstown, Massachusetts. Photo credit: © Sterling and Francine Clark Institute.

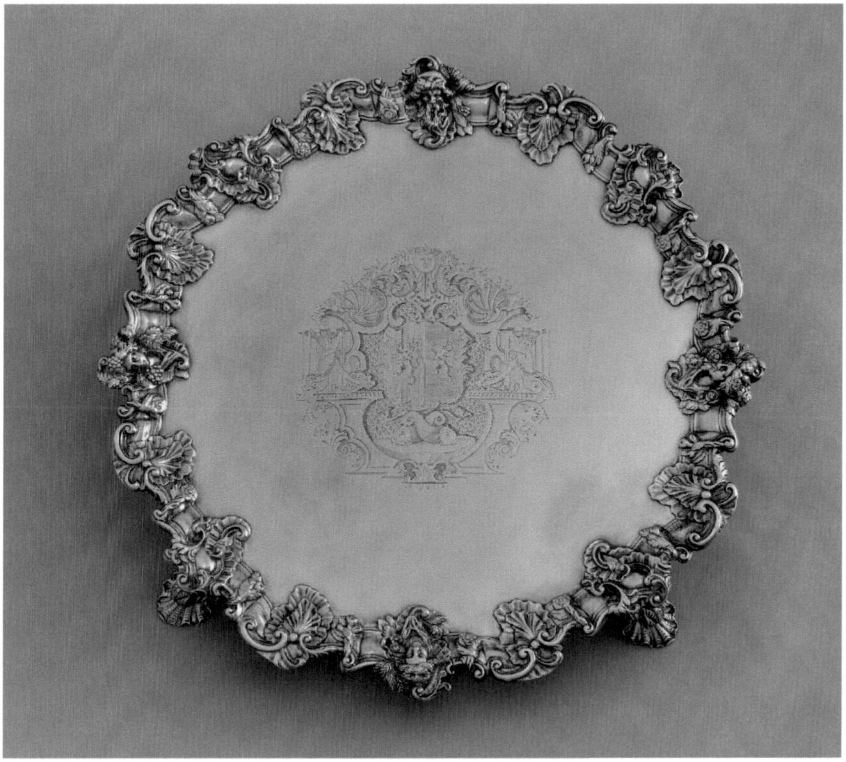

Figure 2.13 Robert Calderwood, *Salver* (1745–46), silver, 54.6 cm diam

Source: San Antonio Museum of Art, Texas. Bequest of John V. Rowan Jr, 2004.12.46. Photo credit: © Courtesy of the San Antonio Museum of Art. Photography by Peggy Tenison.

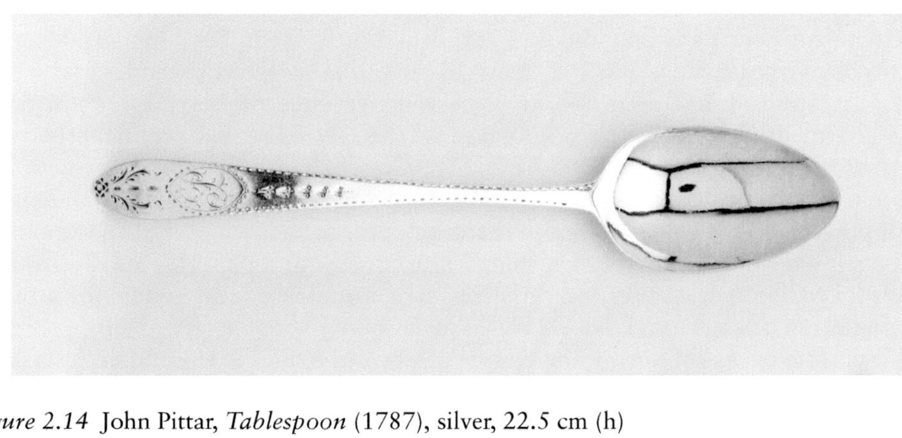

Figure 2.14 John Pittar, *Tablespoon* (1787), silver, 22.5 cm (h)

Source: Indianapolis Museum of Art. Gift of A. Ian Fraser (2010.111). Photo credit: © Indianapolis Museum of Art.

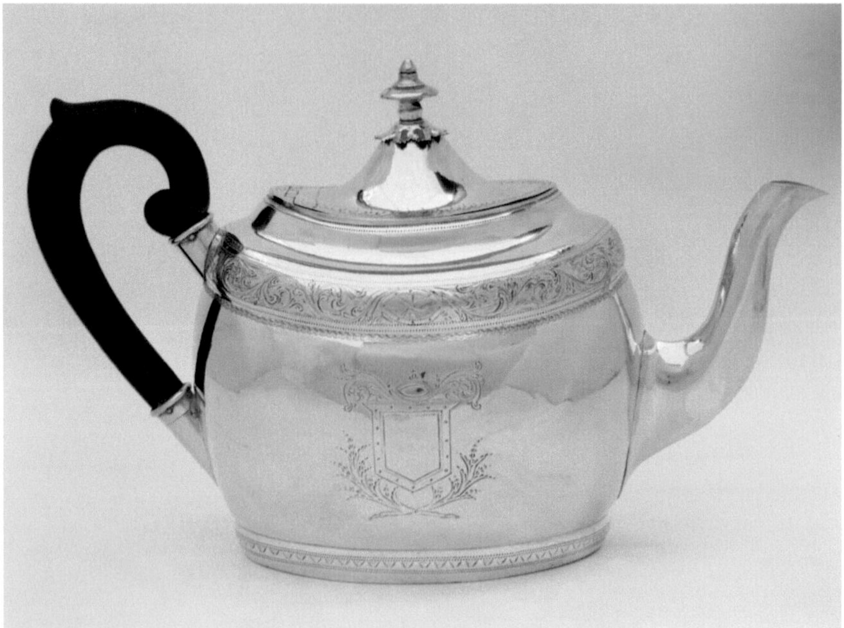

Figure 2.15 Richard Sawyer, *Teapot* (1801–2), silver, 18.1 × 12.4 cm

Source: Metropolitan Museum, New York. Bequest of Alphonso T. Clearwater, 1933. Photo credit: © Metropolitan Museum of Art.

The expansion of Dublin

Irish population growth was rapid by European standards during the period between 1700 and 1845.[85] David Dickson has pointed out that no other European region comparable in terms of size quadrupled its inhabitants between the late seventeenth and mid-nineteenth centuries.[86] The economy witnessed a transformation from the 'technologically archaic, economically un-integrated and almost autarkic' system of the seventeenth century to an industrialised rural economy equipped to meet demands in terms of overseas trade.[87] As the viceregal and administrative capital – and a port city – generating almost 40 per cent of customs revenue of Ireland, Dublin occupied a charmed position.[88] The population of the city increased significantly, from 60,000 in 1700 to around 224,000 by 1821.[89] Coupled with population growth and economic expansion, the landed classes were seeking increasingly 'an urban expression of power'.[90] This was reflected in the development of town houses in the capital and the related expenditure on furnishings, stuccowork and plate. Commissions also came from individuals, professional bodies, civic authorities and guilds, for a range of presentation plate (Figs. 2.16–2.17).[91] The Dublin Society awarded silver palettes on at least one occasion during the eighteenth century (Fig. 2.18) and ecclesiastical plate was required by religious orders and parish churches.[92]

In the context of confessionalism, plate played a significant practical and symbolic role within the rituals of both Protestant and Catholic congregations. The

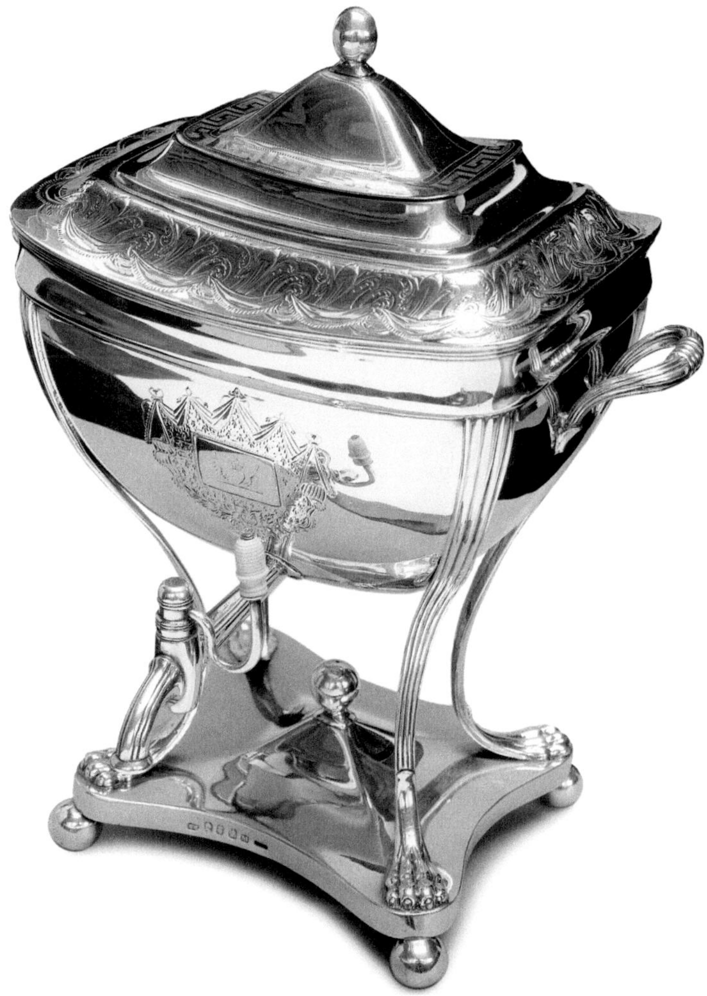

Figure 2.16 Robert Breading, *Hot water or tea urn* (1808), silver, 35.56 cm (h)

Engraved inscription: *'Presented by the officers of the Tipperary Militia to John C. Douglas M.D. as a memorial of the high estimation, in which they uniformly held both his professional and general conduct; during the period of seven years, that he filled the situation of surgeon in their regiment, ANNO DOMINI 1808'.*

Source: National Museum of Ireland, Dublin. Photo credit: © National Museum of Ireland.

former administered bread and wine to the laity and needed flagons (Fig. 2.19). As Barnard has noted, these 'have no counterpart among Catholic liturgical vessels' but 'are frequently the showiest items of Church of Ireland (and of Church of England) Communion plate'.[93] William Bond, Ambrose Boxwell and Joseph Jackson were among the Dublin silversmiths who supplied chalices in the 1780s, and by 1810 Richard Sawyer was the leading producer of these, according to the guild's assay records.[94]

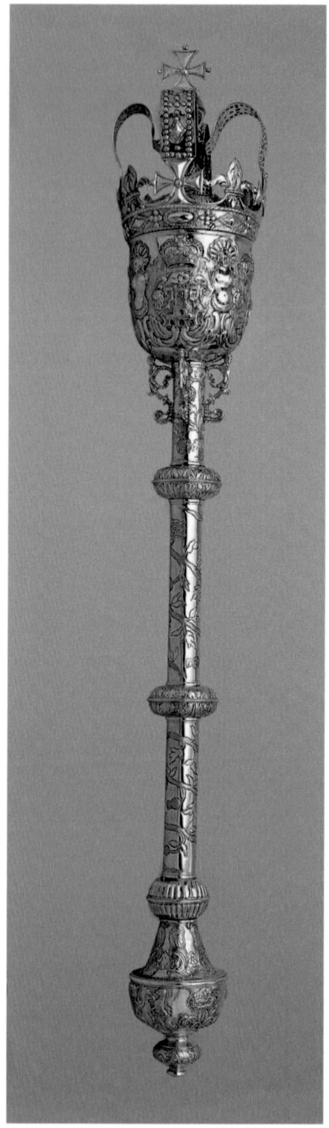

Figure 2.17 John Wilme, *Mace of the borough of Athy, County Kildare* (1746–47), silver, 117.5 × 17.8 cm

Source: San Antonio Museum of Art, Texas. Bequest of John V. Rowan Jr, 2004.13.274. Photo credit: © Courtesy of the San Antonio Museum of Art. Photography by Peggy Tenison.

Aside from the canonical requirements of church plate, it also offered the pious and the privileged opportunities for munificence. Several extant items are engraved with the name of the donor. An unmarked monstrance, thought to have been made in Dublin in 1772, is inscribed on the back with the name of John O'Connor, O.P., who

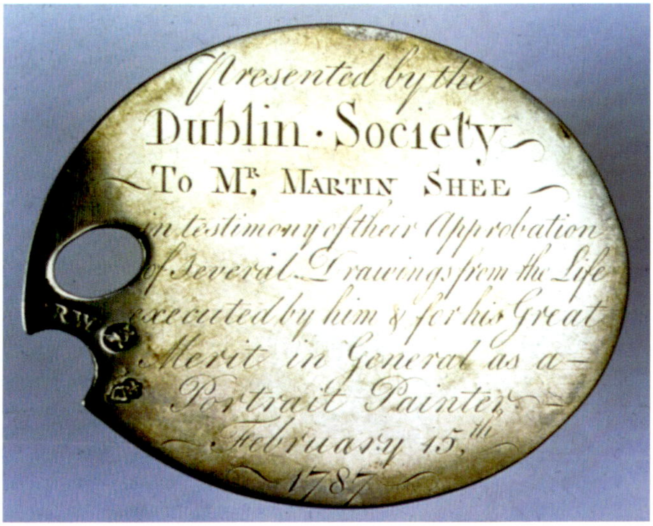

Figure 2.18 Palette presented by the Dublin Society to the artist Martin Shee in 1787 (c.1787), silver, 4.9 × 6.6 cm

Source: National Museum of Ireland, Dublin. Photo credit: © National Museum of Ireland.

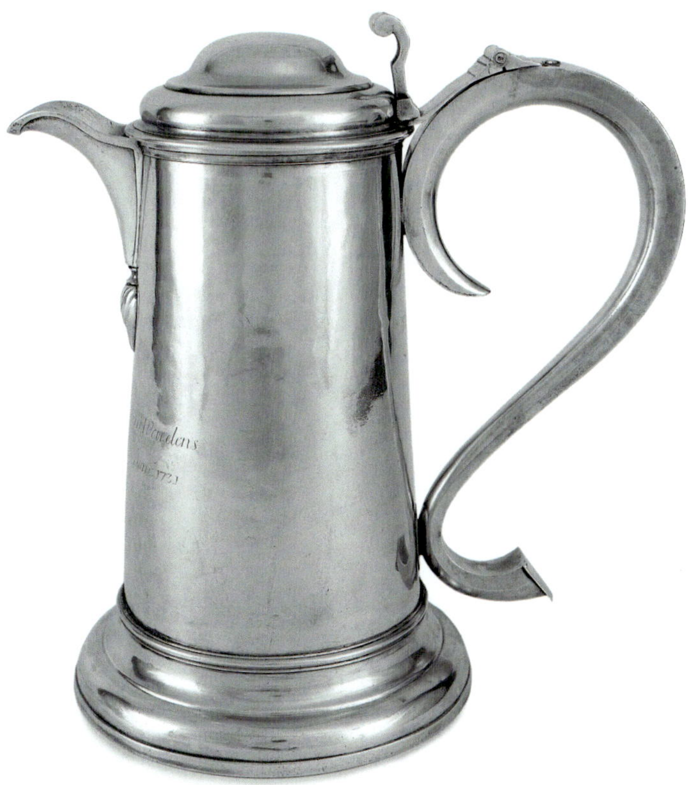

Figure 2.19 Thomas Walker, *Communion flagon* (1730–31), silver, 27.9 cm diam

Source: National Museum of Ireland, Dublin. Photo credit: © National Museum of Ireland.

was attached to the Dominican Chapel on Bridge Street in Dublin and donated it on the occasion of its refurbishment.[95]

Goldsmiths' networks

A particularly detailed assay ledger covering the period 1787 to 1789 illustrates the growing range of silver goods available in Dublin by the late eighteenth century and dates to a period of relative economic prosperity.[96] However, the climate of the 1780s had not been consistently favourable. A fluctuating economy during the early part of the decade had resulted in one of the most acute economic crises of the eighteenth century. A combination of falling demand for Irish linen in Britain, poor harvests and rising food prices placed a strain on the country, from which it was only beginning to recover by the end of 1784. The total of over 80,000 oz. assayed in 1788 implies a sound and confident market. How many workshops contributed to this total? Whose workshops were particularly dominant in terms of productivity and what sorts of objects were most in demand?

Forty-nine goldsmiths are listed in the ledger for 1788.[97] The volume of work entered for these individuals varies considerably. For instance, while John Pittar was the most productive at 10,000 oz., his contemporary John Bolland entered just 61 oz. during the same period.[98] But how representative of the trade are the names logged in these assay books? What do they reveal about its structure? For instance, *Wilson's Dublin Street Directory* for 1789 lists more than one hundred individuals directly or indirectly associated with the trade, over double the number logged in the assay book.[99] This is before legions of journeymen are factored in. Unquestionably, those named in the assay records for 1788, and in other, less detailed ledgers, formed the core of a much wider professional body.

When items submitted for assaying proved to be below sterling standard, they were routinely broken by the guild (Fig. 2.20).[100] A pattern can be seen in the types of goods that regularly failed the test. Not surprisingly, the majority of specialists in large wares rarely had their work broken. The manufacture and decoration of large items of plate was a time-consuming and costly business. Makers were understandably slow to take chances on expensive objects failing the assay. For instance, the surface decoration on a fine tureen could involve several weeks' work by a chaser, a considerable investment of time (Fig. 2.21).[101]

Smaller, less valuable items like buckles and flatware much more frequently failed the assay. They were quicker to make and individually less profitable, which may explain in part why more of them tested substandard.[102] It must also be acknowledged that the challenge of working under pressure, using a range of recycled metal as standard practice, made genuine error inevitable. It is hard to accept that Jonas Osborne, a small-scale worker who had more than 25 per cent of his output broken by the guild in that year, intentionally entered substandard goods so consistently.[103]

Infringements of the sterling standard were often presented as 'accidental' by those responsible. As already noted, while the goldsmith John Kavanagh was in England in 1790, twelve pairs of 'tea tongs' made from recycled silver were submitted for assaying from his workshop. They were all deficient in fineness, three pairs in particular. Kavanagh pleaded that since he had been out of the country, 'it would be a great hardship' for him 'to suffer on account of the carelessness or inattention of his workman'. As he was ultimately responsible for goods bearing his mark, his argument was a little

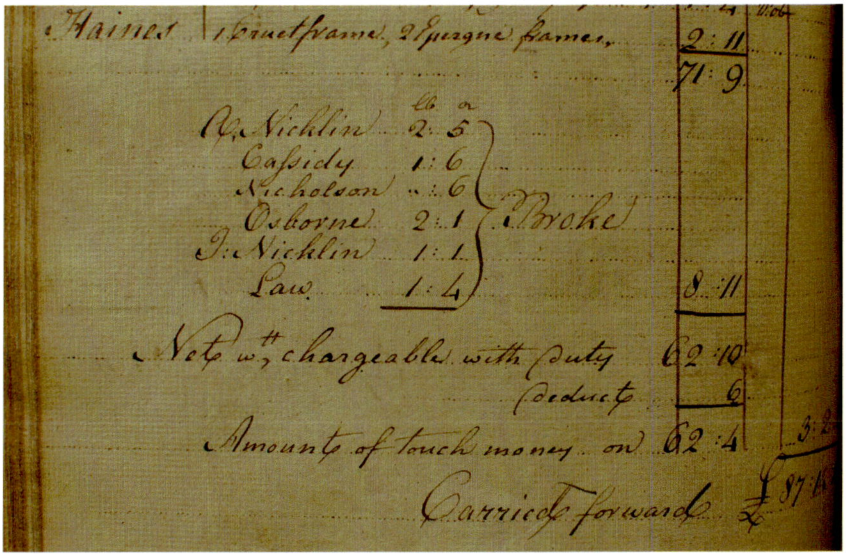

Figure 2.20 Detail of a late eighteenth-century Dublin assay book showing items broken by the guild for failing to pass the assay

Source: Company of Goldsmiths of Dublin, Assay Office, Dublin. Photo credit: © Company of Goldsmiths of Dublin.

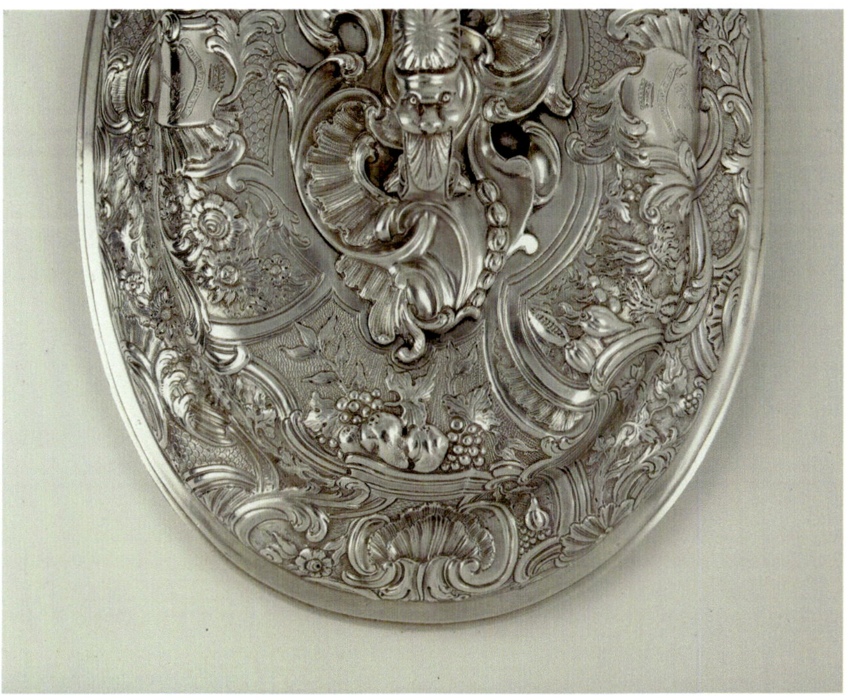

Figure 2.21 Thomas Walker, *Soup tureen and cover* (detail) (1751), silver, 26.67 × 50.8 cm

Source: National Museum of Ireland, Dublin. Photo credit: © National Museum of Ireland.

thin.[104] It also reiterates the fact that many Irish goldsmiths and jewellers had occasion to travel to England in the regular course of business.

Objects in demand in late eighteenth-century Dublin

The 1787 to 1789 assay ledger shows that the principal demand during this period was for items of domestic tableware and, in particular, for small objects like cutlery. By far the most popular items assayed in Dublin in 1788 were silver teaspoons. Almost 28,000 of them were recorded in that year, compared to a mere 27 silver teapots.[105] This certainly implies that ceramic teapots of various sorts were in much more widespread use (Fig. 2.22).[106] In May 1784, an auction of 'the largest assortment of foreign china' ever exposed to the city was advertised. This included a range of 'complete tea sets of the best Nanking Blue'.[107] Suppliers of high quality ceramics actively competed with those of plate. A notice in *Faulkner's Dublin Journal* in 1789 remarked that 'the finer kinds of Queensware . . . are to be found in every genteel house throughout Ireland.'[108] Ceramics were usually less expensive than silver and, even at the top end of the market, imported continental and Asian porcelain could be more affordable than plate.[109] In the same year, the Irish nabob James Alexander spent almost £9 on 'a strong silver teapot', while a retailer in Clonmel was selling full earthenware dinner services, with over 150 separate pieces, during the same period, for less than a third of that price.[110]

As the price of tea fell during the course of the eighteenth century, the demand for tea wares inevitably increased.[111] The average annual consumption of tea in Ireland, by the

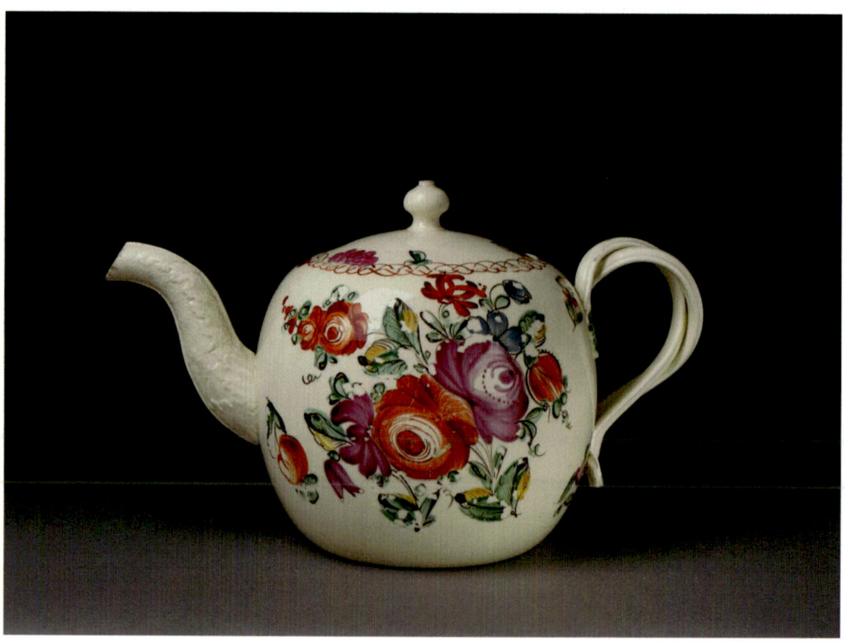

Figure 2.22 Josiah Wedgwood, *Teapot* (c.1770), lead-glazed earthenware, 23.2 × 13.3 cm
Source: V&A, London. Gift of Mr Arthur Myers Smith through the Art Fund. Photo credit: © V&A.

late eighteenth century, has been estimated at roughly two to three pounds per person (Fig. 2.23).[112] In contrast, the Conollys of Castletown in Co. Kildare were untypical. Their household consumed roughly 2,000 lbs. of sugar and 50 lbs. of tea annually during the 1780s. Even their maids received monthly allocations of sugar, on top of their regular wages.[113] According to the assay records, vessels for sugar were produced in considerable quantities in late eighteenth-century Ireland, an inevitable consequence of the fashionable hot drinks (Fig. 2.24). They were more frequently described as 'sugar dishes' than as 'sugar basins', or bowls, though the reason for this distinction, if deliberate, is not entirely clear.[114] While a 'chased, pierced, polished, sugar basin' cost over £4 in 1772,[115] sugar tongs were available for a modest 12s. Metal was much more practical than ceramic for use in the manufacture of tongs. This, combined with the fact that tongs were less expensive to acquire than silver dishes, milk jugs or caddies, accounts for their comparative prominence in the Dublin assay records.

Only five items called butter coolers were specified in the assay ledger in 1788.[116] They may have included the object illustrated in Fig. 2.25, which bears the mark of Robert Williams. The design is reminiscent of coopers' work and evokes the kind of *faux* rusticity which was fashionable in an eighteenth-century context.[117] The Dublin goldsmith Richard D'Olier supplied a 'chased pierced butter cooler' to a client in 1784. It had a cover and cost £8 4s 6d.[118] Irish silver piggins of the period can also reflect this sort of self-conscious naivety (Fig. 2.26).[119] They were originally made from wood and used as vessels for porridge, milk and water, before being fashioned in silver in the late eighteenth century and transposed to the tables of the fashionable elite.[120]

Assay books also reveal much about etiquette. The number of tablespoons recorded in 1788 was more than five times the quantity of table forks, and the number of

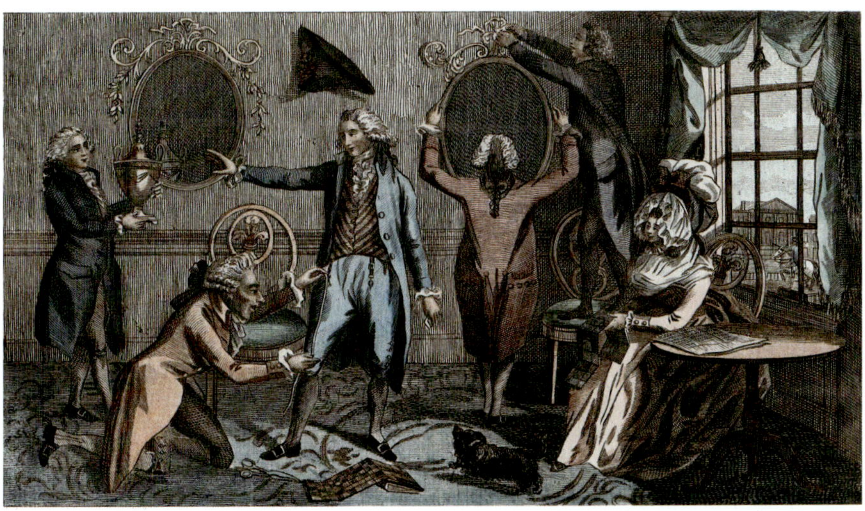

Figure 2.23 Frederick elegantly furnishing a large house (1786?), hand-coloured etching and engraving, 22.5 × 32.3 cm. The form of the metal urn being carried in on the left is similar to the forms of tea urns made from silver and Sheffield plate retailed in Dublin during the second half of the eighteenth century.

Source: Lewis Walpole Library, Yale University, New Haven. Photo credit: © Courtesy of the Lewis Walpole Library, Yale University.

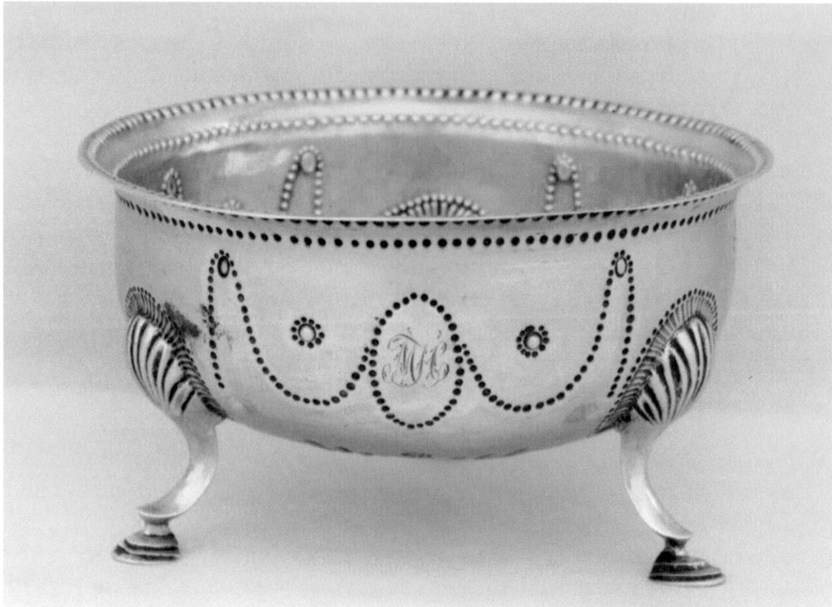

Figure 2.24 Matthew West, *Sugar bowl* (1784–85), silver, 7.6 × 13.7 cm
Source: Metropolitan Museum, New York. Rogers Fund, 1911. Photo credit: © Metropolitan Museum of Art.

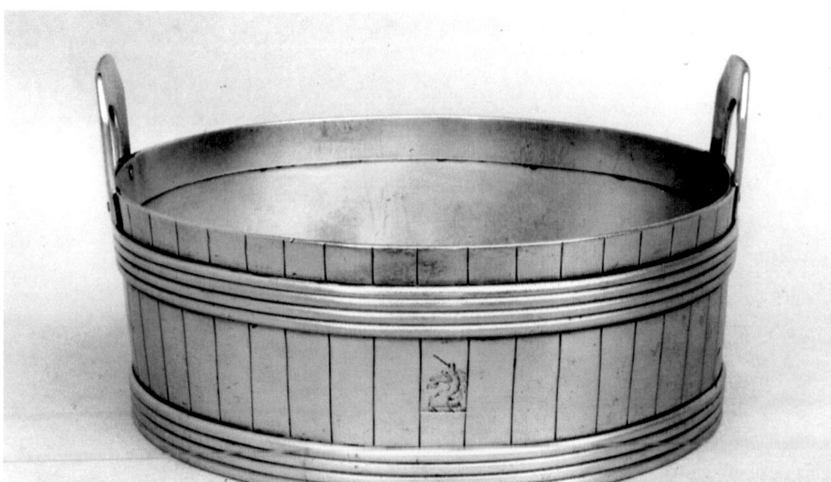

Figure 2.25 Robert Williams, *Butter cooler* (1810), silver
Source: Whereabouts unknown. Photo credit: Author's collection.

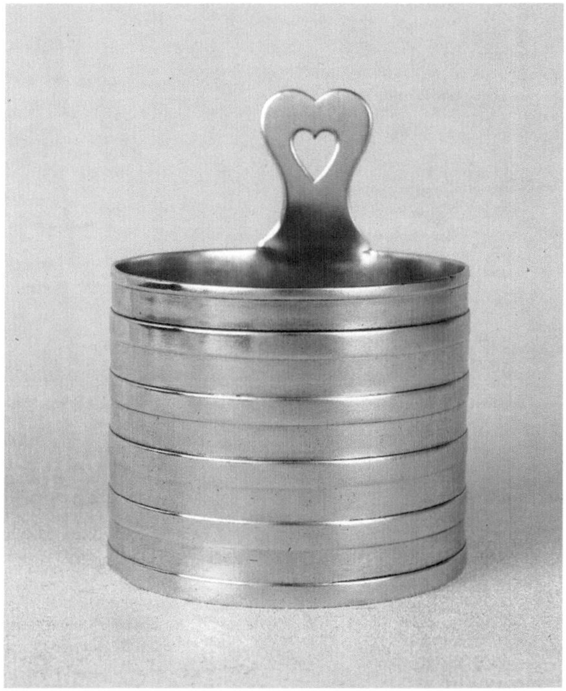

Figure 2.26 Unmarked, *Piggin* (c.1775), silver

Source: National Museum of Ireland, Dublin. Photo credit: © National Museum of Ireland.

dessert spoons exceeded dessert forks almost sixteen-fold.[121] While this preference for spoons reflected their usefulness and adaptability, it also reflects, to some extent, trends in contemporary cuisine. Tablespoons were practical utensils for the preparation and serving of dishes like casseroles and ragouts. *The Lady's Companion: Or Accomplish'd Director in the Whole Art of Cookery*, published in Dublin in 1767, includes a recipe for a ragout of cockscombs, which specifies the use of a 'plate spoon' in its preparation.[122]

Close to 40,000 teaspoons, tablespoons and dessert spoons were assayed in Dublin in 1788, indicating that, unlike a lot of silver objects, they represented a comparatively affordable luxury. Earlier in the century, Jonathan Swift had facetiously advised sensible cooks to use their hands in place of silver spoons, 'for fear of wearing out' their master's plate, and a range of contemporary sources allude to the prestige value of plate, a theme explored in chapter 4.[123] It was not only Ireland's elite who enjoyed these small luxuries. Contemporaneously with the ledger, a Dublin tanner and a Cork shopkeeper both possessed various silver spoons. As Parisian inventories have shown, the market for comparatively inexpensive versions of aristocratic luxury items gained in momentum in the second half of the eighteenth century, with silver featuring in over 50 per cent of lower-class household inventories there in 1785.[124]

Apart from readily identifiable objects, some things are registered in the assay books in curiously unfamiliar terms. For instance, in 1787 two objects intriguingly described as 'fecques' were entered (Fig. 2.27). These items could not have weighed more than a couple of ounces which, added to the fact that the supplier was a flatware specialist, suggests that they were probably small items of domestic tableware. As *feice* is an Irish word for spade it seems possible that the two pieces in question were butter spades.[125] The next year a single 'bushiea' was recorded, which was conceivably a phonetic spelling of the word 'bougie'. Bougie boxes, as taper stands or wax jacks, were a practical bureau component, and were used when sealing correspondence.[126]

Equally, out of thousands of things submitted for assaying between February and December 1787, just one 'mether' was specified.[127] Methers were traditional wooden drinking cups made in Ireland from the medieval period to the nineteenth century. Claudia Kinmonth cites an Irish proverbial expression for a stormy night – 'the wind ris, and the rain fell as if it came out of methers' – implying that their usage was familiar in the vernacular at one time.[128] Nevertheless, Irish silver methers are rare for the Georgian period, and two-handled cylindrical cups were infinitely more popular in late eighteenth-century Dublin. The Metropolitan Museum in New York holds a silver mether marked by the Dublin goldsmith Richard Williams (Fig. 2.28), and the National Museum of Ireland has a silver-gilt version by John Sherwin.

Among the larger items of silverware produced in Dublin during this period, cups were strongly represented. The goldsmith Matthew West (Fig. 2.29) was a leading supplier of these, and they were manufactured in a variety of sizes. West submitted 280 cups for assaying in 1788 alone.[129] They also featured in goldsmiths' shop signs, newspaper advertisements and trade cards. An advertisement for the Limerick goldsmith Collins Brehon in 1766 refers repeatedly to links with Dublin and includes an illustration of a two-handled cup (Fig. 2.30). Dublin's burgeoning fraternal societies

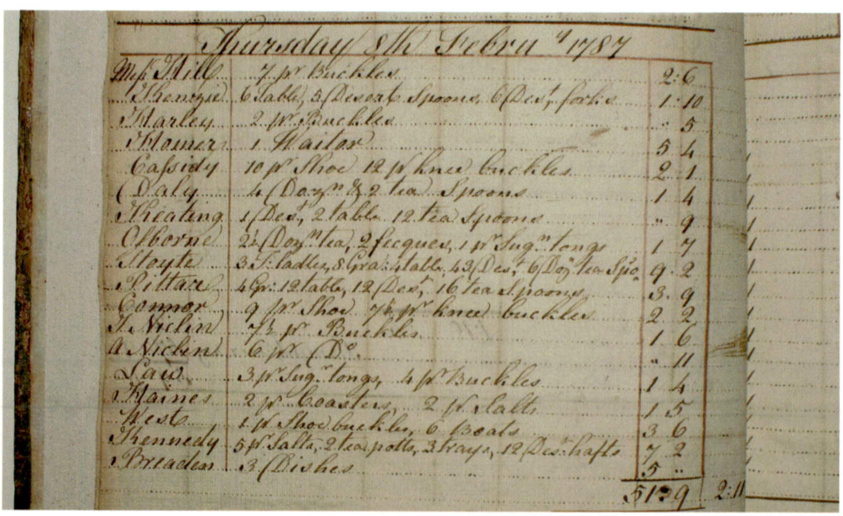

Thursday 8th Febru.y 1787

Mess. Hill	7 pr Buckles	2:6
Kenzie	6 Table, 5 Dessert Spoons, 6 Des.t forks	1:10
Harley	2 pr Buckles	": 5
Homer	1 Waiter	5 4
Cassidy	10 pr Shoe 12 pr knee buckles	2 1
Daly	4 Dozn & 2 tea Spoons	1 4
Keating	1 Des.t, 2 table 12 tea Spoons	" 9
Osborne	2½ Dozn tea, 2 fecques, 1 pr Sugr tongs	1 7
Stoyte	3 S. ladles, 8 Gra. 4 table, 43 Des.t, 6 Dozn tea Spo.	9 2
Pittar	4 Gr. 12 table, 12 Des.t, 16 tea Spoons	3 9
Connor	9 pr Shoe 7½ pr knee buckles	2 2
J. Nicklin	7½ pr Buckles	1 6
A. Nicklin	6 pr Do	" 11
Law	3 pr Sugr tongs, 4 pr Buckles	1 4
Haines	2 pr Coasters, 2 pr Salts	1 5
West	1 pr Shoe buckles, 6 Boats	3 6
Kennedy	5 pr Salts, 2 tea potts, 3 trays, 12 Des.t hafts	7 2
Breaden	3 Dishes	5 ..
		51:9

2:11

Figure 2.27 Detail from a late eighteenth-century Dublin assay book showing an entry for 'fecques'

Source: Company of Goldsmiths of Dublin, Assay Office, Dublin. Photo credit: © Company of Goldsmiths of Dublin.

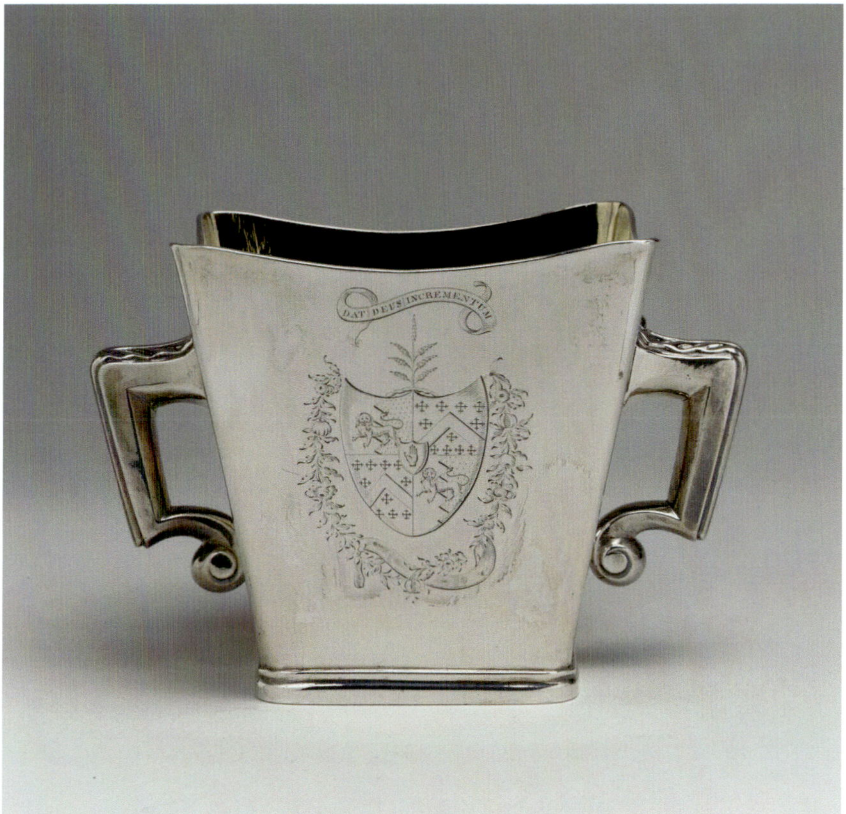

Figure 2.28 Richard Williams, *Mether* (1772), silver, silver gilt, 12.7 cm (h)

Source: Metropolitan Museum, New York. Gift of Irwin Untermyer, 1968. Photo credit: © Metropolitan Museum of Art.

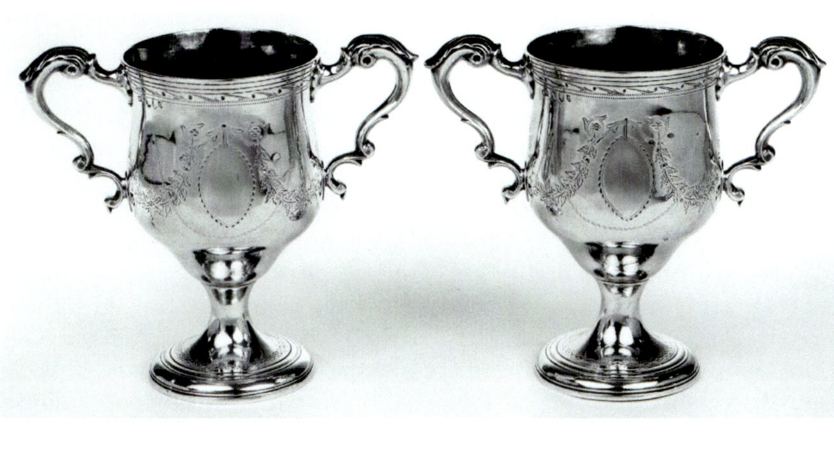

Figure 2.29 Matthew West, *Pair of two-handled cups* (1792), silver, 16.5 cm (h)

Photo credit: © Christie's Images.

COLLINS BREHON,
AT THE TWO BLUE-
POSTS, op- poſite the
Exchange, LIMERICK,

HAS enlarged his Shop in a ſpacious Manner, in order to carry on the Watch-making and mending Buſineſs, together with the Goldſmith's Trade, all to the higheſt Perfection; and has, for that Purpoſe hired and brought to this City the beſt Watch-maker that could b had in Dublin. He alſo makes all kinds of repeating Watches, and mend them, in the beſt and ſafeſt Manner, and is recommended by the mo eminent Watch-makers in Dublin, which makes me the ſaid Collins Brehoſt certain, that I ſhall have it in my power to give the Public Satisfaction and, particularly, all thoſe who are pleaſed to favour me with their Cu ſtom.

Said Brehon has a large Aſſortment of touch'd Plate; Butter-boats large and ſmall, ditto; large and ſmall Cups; Variety of touch'd Shoe and Knee-Buckles. and a large Aſſortment of Jewelling work from the ... in Dublin, ſuch as Paſte and Stone Shoe and Knee-Buckles, ... Gold Set Lockets, Rings of different Kinds, Pebble Rings ſet round with Garnets, Watches, & which he will engage; alſo plain and chaſed Coffee pots, and Plate-handled Knives and Forks with Caſes, with ſeveral other Articles too tedious to inſert. N. B. He will give the higheſt Price for oild Gold and Silver, and for Silver and Gold Lace.—— N. B. An Appren tice is wanting to the above Buſineſs.

Figure 2.30 Newspaper advertisement for Collins Brehon, *Munster Journal* (31 March 1766)
Photo credit: Author's collection.

and clubs may also have encouraged the use of these objects. These gentlemen's clubs generally met for dinner in the late afternoon before proceeding to endless leisurely toasts.[130] For instance, the 'Sportsman's Club', which met at the Rose Tavern in Dame Street, organised prizes for race meets at the Curragh in Co. Kildare.

Silver cups made ideal racing trophies. A fine hunt trophy supplied by Robert Calderwood survives from 1757 and records both the date of the race and the name of the victor (Fig. 2.31). An engraved horse led by his jockey accompanies the inscription: 'Given by the Kildare-Hunt on Tuesday the 13th September 1757 and won by Sir Ralph Gore's grey horse Spot'.[131] By all accounts, Gore was a man who took his sport very seriously. A punch bowl in the Museum of Fine Arts at Boston commemorates the triumph of another of his horses, in a race held at Kildare six years previously (Fig. 2.32).[132] When his opponent, Lord March, was foolish enough to cheat, Gore challenged him to a duel. In a dramatic gesture, he arrived for the showdown with a coffin

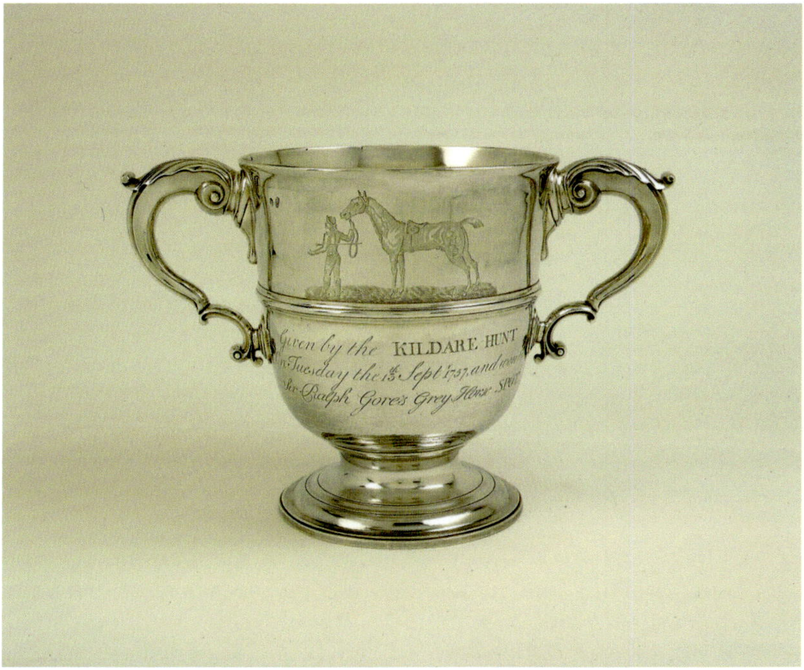

Figure 2.31 Robert Calderwood, *Race trophy* (1757), silver, 21.3 cm (h)

Source: National Museum of Ireland, Dublin. Photo credit: © National Museum of Ireland.

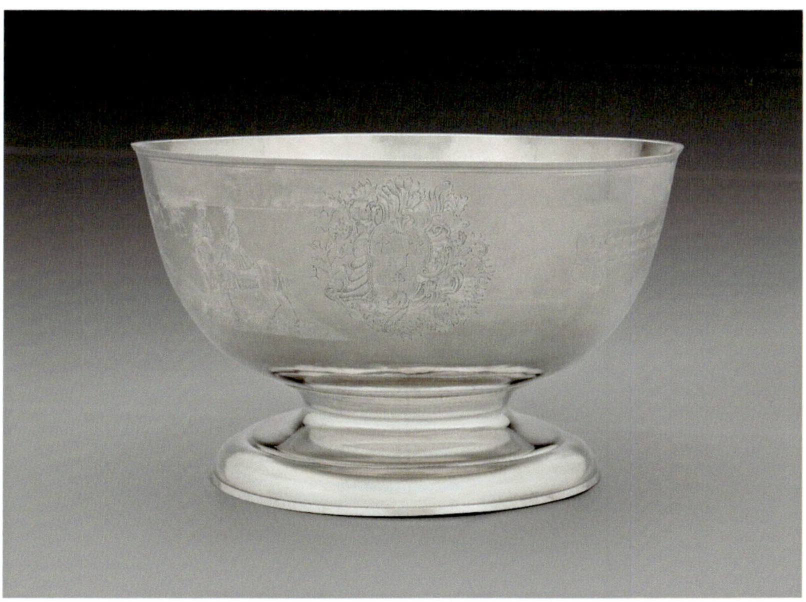

Figure 2.32 William Williamson II, *Punch bowl* (racing trophy), engraved by Daniel Pomerade (1751), silver, 36.2 cm diam

Source: Museum of Fine Arts, Boston. Theodora Wilbour Fund in memory of Charlotte Beebe Wilbour. Photo credit: © Museum of Fine Arts, Boston.

bearing March's name.[133] For merchants, ownership of a fine silver cup might indicate solid professional standing and signify the fruits of industry. As will be explored in chapter 4, this can help to explain their prevalence in Irish Quaker inventories.

Less sober urges also contributed to the demand for a wide range of alcohol-related silverware. Visitors to the country and indigenous commentators harped on the theme of Irish hospitality. In 1745, the fourth Earl of Chesterfield vigorously criticised the excesses of the Irish gentry, observing:

> Drinking is a most beastly vice in every country, but it really is a ruinous one in Ireland; nine gentlemen out of every ten are impoverished by the great quantity of claret which, from the mistaken notions of hospitality and dignity, they think it necessary should be drunk in their houses; this expense leaves them no room to improve their estates by proper indulgence upon proper conditions to their tenants, who pay them to the full, and upon the very day, that they may pay their wine-merchants.[134]

In 1788, *Finn's Leinster Journal* declared that 'what is called hospitality swallows up everything: eating, drinking and rural sports fills up the whole of our Irish country gentlemen. The principal point of ambition is to outdo his neighbours in hospitable profusion.'[135] Wine imports, which had totalled 12.4 million gallons annually in the 1720s, had actually eased relative to population growth by the late eighteenth century, but there is evidence that they were supplemented by an increased consumption of locally distilled spirits. This stimulated the market for silver 'tundishs' or wine funnels, wine labels and coasters, goblets and tankards, and cups of various sorts (Fig. 2.33) as

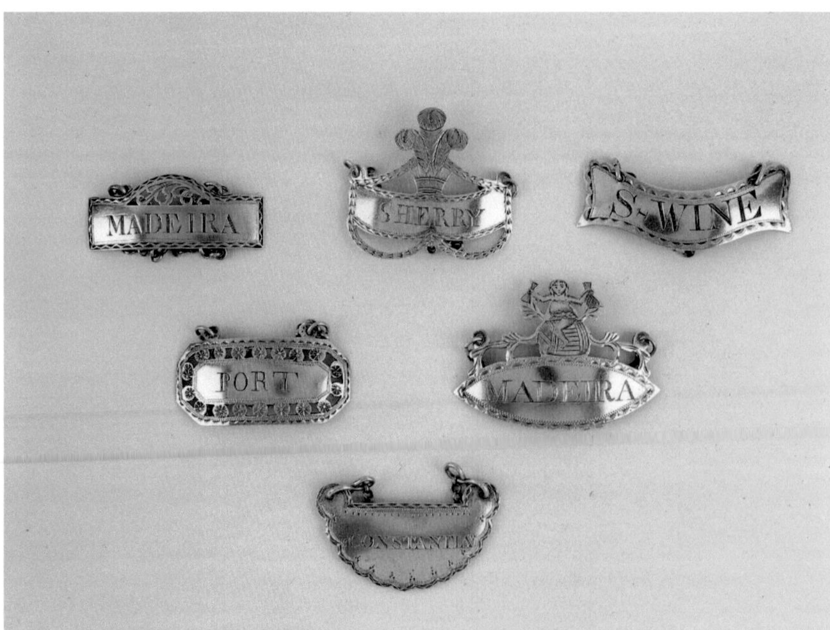

Figure 2.33 Wine labels (late eighteenth/early nineteenth century), silver

Source: National Museum of Ireland, Dublin. Photo credit: © National Museum of Ireland.

well as items made from glass (Fig. 2.34). In 1789, *Faulkner's Dublin Journal* reported with more than a hint of patriotic pride:

> White glass of Irish manufacture is at present in very good demand at the American market and a considerable quantity of wine glasses, goblets, and decanters have been exported with these few days for Philadelphia. These articles of manufacture are superior to what they are in England and we are able to undersell the English in this branch of manufacture at a foreign market, from ten to fifteen per cent.[136]

The leading wine label specialist in Dublin in 1788 was John Sherwin Jr, who submitted over 300 for assaying that year. For those who favoured cheaper alternatives to silver, paper bottle tickets offered a more ephemeral but less expensive option and were advertised in Dublin almanacks and newspapers.[137]

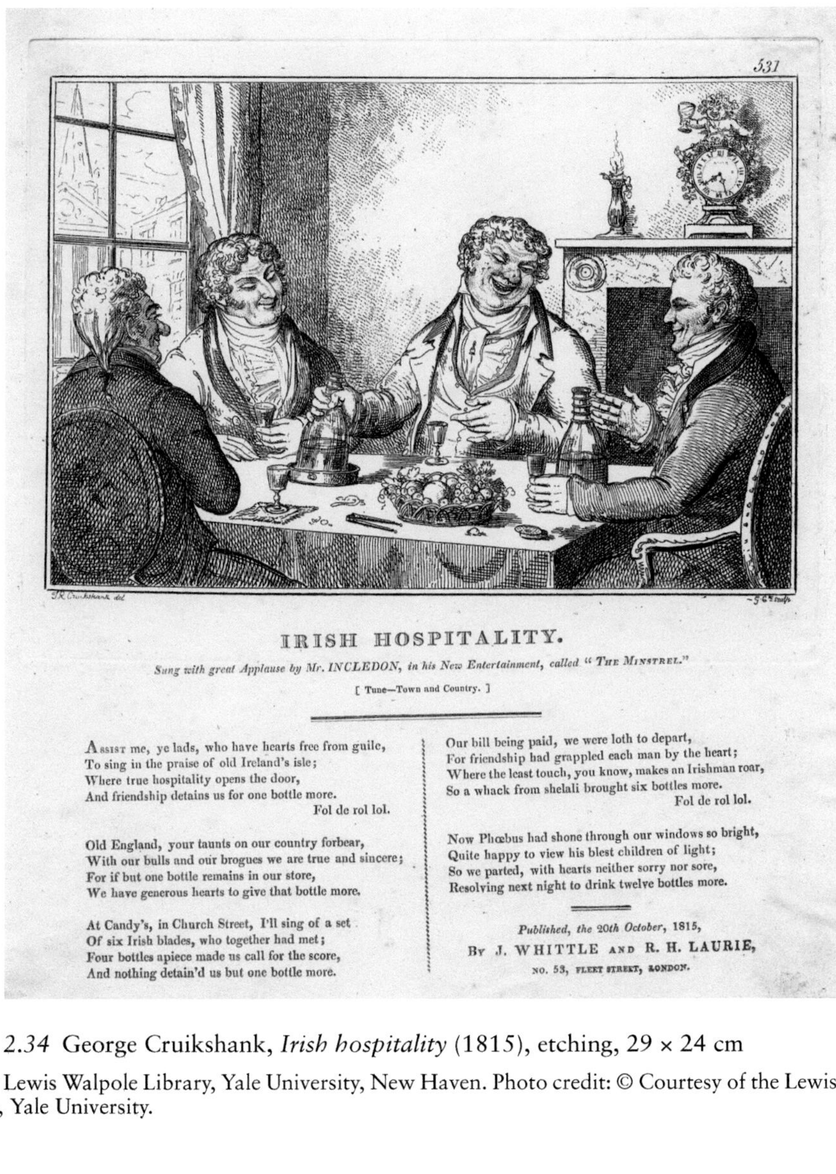

Figure 2.34 George Cruikshank, *Irish hospitality* (1815), etching, 29 × 24 cm

Source: Lewis Walpole Library, Yale University, New Haven. Photo credit: © Courtesy of the Lewis Walpole Library, Yale University.

When it came to impressive tableware, large items like silver tureens and épergnes (elaborate centrepieces) were the ultimate luxuries.[138] However, in an Irish context, and specifically based on the assay records for 1787 to 1789, they were not produced in large numbers (Fig. 2.35). They were expensive to buy, could be substituted by alternatives in less costly materials and customers with ample resources frequently bought in London. The new viceroy, Lord Temple, was lauded for electing to order his plate in Dublin rather than in London in 1782. His dinner service, which included four épergnes, was purchased from 'an eminent goldsmith in Parliament Street'.[139] In 1789, William Digges La Touche paid more than £100 for a silver épergne purchased from the Dublin goldsmith Jeremiah D'Olier.[140] Only three were submitted for assaying in Dublin 1788 at a time when London's silver trade could support specialist

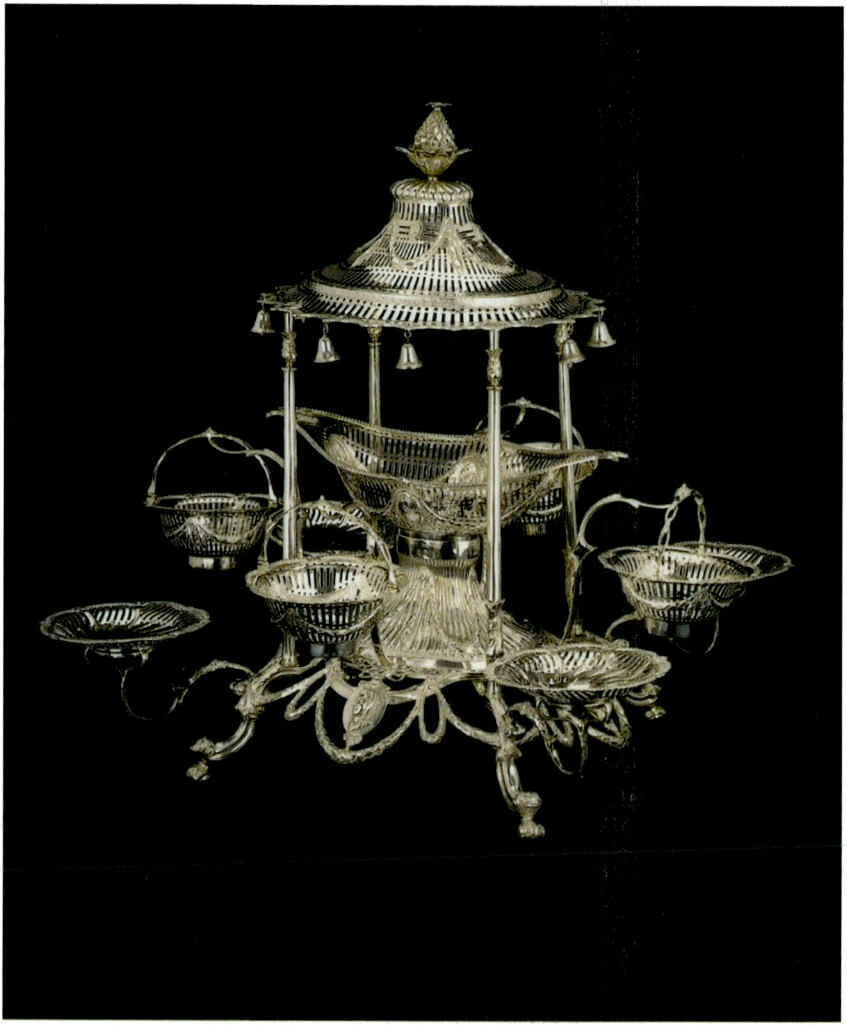

Figure 2.35 Attributed to Robert Breading, *Épergne* (1787), silver, 61 cm (h)
Photo credit: © Christie's Images.

suppliers.[141] Christopher Haines, Joseph Jackson and Robert Breading were among the Dublin goldsmiths making them during this period.

As they are elaborate and impressive items of silver, it is not surprising that épergnes are often centralised in museum displays.[142] One could be forgiven for assuming that they were far more plentiful in the shops of Dublin goldsmiths during this period and far more ubiquitous in affluent Irish homes. Silver buckles, on the other hand, attract much less attention, and comparatively few survive (Fig. 2.36), yet buckle making was a vital branch of the goldsmiths' trade in late eighteenth-century Dublin. More than 24,000 buckles were sent for in assaying Dublin in 1788: knee buckles, shoe buckles and, much more rarely, stock buckles.[143] By 1810, when shoe ribbons had eclipsed them, a mere eighteen buckles were assayed in Dublin.[144] Newspaper advertisements indicate the range of prices and varieties which were on offer in eighteenth-century Ireland, but other, less obvious sources can be similarly revealing. A contemporary poem by the Ulster poet John Anketell describes a young woman's pride in new buckles, which were clearly not silver or gold, pointing once more to the availability of cheaper copies of luxury goods:

> Here *Oonagh* stands; her pumps, you see are new,
> Her gown stripp'd linen, and her stockings blue;
> Last week in *Glasslough* were her buckles bought,
> How bright they shine, tho' purchased for a groat![145]

Evidently, an extensive network of goldsmiths and allied traders operated in eighteenth-century Dublin, supplying an ever-growing range of specialised and luxury commodities, yet only a small number of workshops dominated production. There was an inevitable demand for prestigious costly wares, but the market also depended on the regular purchases of smaller, more modest, pieces which kept the wheels of

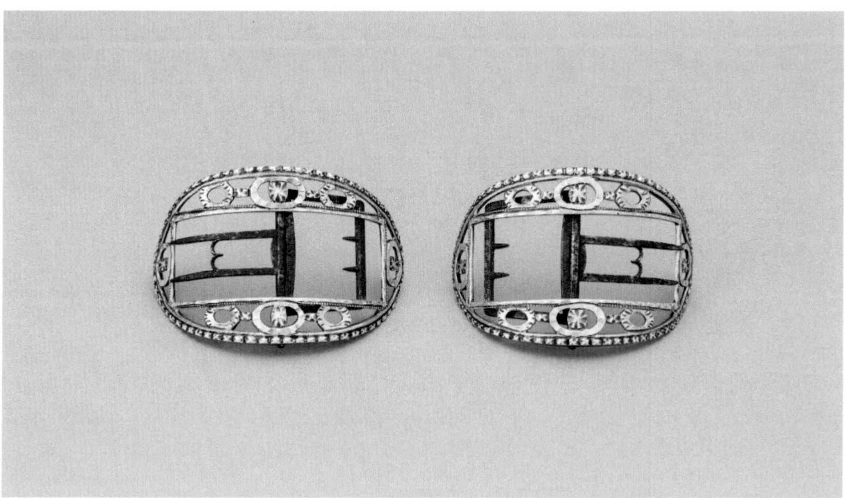

Figure 2.36 Joseph Jackson, *Pair of shoe buckles* (c.1790), silver, each 5.4 × 7.6 cm

Source: San Antonio Museum of Art, Texas. Bequest of John V. Rowan Jr, 2004.13.156.a–b. Photo credit: © Courtesy of the San Antonio Museum of Art. Photography by Peggy Tenison.

commerce turning. This is borne out by the fact that the two goldsmiths who produced the most plate numerically and by weight in 1788 were both flatware specialists. Undoubtedly, Dublin's proximity to London had a bearing on this pattern. Some of Ireland's most affluent patrons clearly favoured London for substantial orders for plate and, in terms of scale and fashion, London clearly had the advantage. Where Dublin goldsmiths were producing over 80,000 oz. of plate in 1788, their London counterparts were manufacturing close to 1,000,000 oz. during the same period.[146] While responsibility for the Dublin total was credited to 49 individuals, an average of close to 2,000 names were recorded during a single month in London.[147] The findings from the 1787 to 1789 assay book, which reveal the large numbers of fairly modest pieces of domestic plate being produced, also suggest the importance to Dublin goldsmiths of middle-class consumers. Given the small size of Ireland's landed elite, and the reality of competition from London, the patronage of middle-class consumers must have been increasingly significant. One Dublin surgeon had amassed 'upwards of 400 ounces of fashionable plate' by 1778.[148] The house contents of the city surveyor in 1782 included a silver sugar dish, cream ewer, quart cup and pint cup, as well as tongs and a variety of spoons.[149] During the same period, the dwelling house of a Kinsale shopkeeper was relieved of 'a large quantity of plate'.[150] The large demand for silver cutlery, relative to hollowware, is also explained by the fact that metal was ideally suited to making things like knives and forks; centrepieces, on the other hand, could be fashioned from silver, ceramic or glass.

The Dublin goldsmiths and technology

So, having considered the question of quality control and levels of demand and supply in the market, it remains to consider the impact of technology. The technological advances of the eighteenth century, like improved steel for metal dies and the application of new machines like rolling mills which allowed silver to be produced more cheaply and in larger quantities, were slower to make their impact in Ireland than in London.[151] By 1747, the author of *The London Tradesman* was in a position to note how the introduction of 'flatting-mills' had greatly assisted London goldsmiths:

> Their business required much more time and labour formerly than at present: they were obliged to beat their metal from the ingot into what thinness they required; but now there are invented flatting-mills, which reduce their metal to what thinness they require, at a very small expense.[152]

According to Helen Clifford,

> the introduction of flatting mills in the 1720s, and their widespread use by the 1760s, meant that for the first time standard gauge sheet metal could be produced, using a fraction of the time and labour compared with hand hammering from the ingot.[153]

This fact, coupled with the development of a stamping machine, patented in London in 1769, and fly presses, collectively enabled the efficient production of lightweight forms and standardised ornament, leading to a dramatic increase in the volume of silverware going through the London assay office between the 1750s and 1770s.[154]

Evidence from both the Dublin goldsmiths' guild and the Dublin Society highlights the slower pace at which Irish craftsmen engaged with this sort of technology.[155] This was an inevitable symptom of 'second city syndrome'. Dublin's smaller scale relative to London could not accommodate the same level of specialisation. It was 1779 before the Dublin guild concurred that the best measure it could adopt 'to encourage the manufacture of plate' was the erection of a flatting mill in or near the city.[156] Five years later, two Dublin goldsmiths were awarded premiums by the Dublin Society for the manufacture of 'light plate' with 'rollers'.[157] By this stage, rolling mills had been in general use in London for roughly four decades, yet the Society evidently felt that some encouragement was required in an Irish context.[158] The benefits of embracing new technology are clearly spelt out in an advertisement of 1796. Offering gorgets and breastplates for Volunteers' Corps, the Dublin goldsmith John Ash Rainey specified that since he had 'the different dies and flatting mills', he could afford to sell these goods by the dozen, at 20 per cent less than 'any other person in Dublin'.[159]

Undoubtedly, the quicker onset of technology for serial production in England placed Irish goldsmiths at a commercial disadvantage. The use of dies for duplicating patterns was standard in the London goldsmiths' trade during the latter half of the eighteenth century, yet as chapter 5 will explore, Irish goldsmiths were importing die-stamped components for cost effectiveness in the early nineteenth century. Much of their jewellery was also apparently handmade, 'rather than with dies, or by engine turning, due to the lack of available equipment'.[160] Specialised equipment could be expensive, often depending on high production levels to ensure viability – Ireland could not rival England in this regard, either in technological innovation or economies of scale.

The commercial availability of Sheffield plate from the second half of the eighteenth century represented a mixed blessing for the Dublin goldsmiths' trade. For those who were exclusively manufacturers this new commodity was a clear blow, yet for those with retail concerns it offered attractive potential for profit.[161] As previously explained, plated wares (as distinct from plate) were a fraction of the cost of silver, but had the same reflective qualities.[162] The additional cachet of novelty, the agency of which cannot be underestimated in an eighteenth-century context, enhanced the appeal of Sheffield plate to eighteenth-century consumers.[163] In 1773, the Dublin goldsmiths' guild prepared a petition to their parliamentary representatives aimed at quashing a proposed additional duty on gold and silver plate. The following plea was central to their defence:

> That lately, very large quantities of plated ware has been imported into this kingdom, which has greatly injured the manufacture of plate; and which, they humbly conceive, will be considerably increased by the proposed duty on plate; which will not only prejudice your petitioners, but the public in general, as they, in said ware have scarce any real value for their money, which goes out of the kingdom in large sums for that article.[164]

The allusion to the intrinsic value of silver and its correlation with 'ready money' or silver coin is a theme that will be examined in chapter 4. As already mentioned, modern scholarship identifies a clear decline throughout the seventeenth and eighteenth centuries in the value accorded to high quality or expensive raw materials as opposed to new and fashionable goods which depreciated more quickly, particularly on second-hand markets. It is telling that the Dublin goldsmiths' guild was more vocal on the subject of the English market in the second half of the eighteenth century, when techniques for serial production and plating technology were transforming the English trade.[165] In the three years preceding March 1779, the annual value of plated ware imported from Britain was assessed at £9,794. The value of imported wrought plate, by contrast, was just £4,648.[166] It has already been noted that the Dublin Society was active in encouraging native design skills through their drawing schools, and the manufacture of light plate through their premiums. It also encouraged the manufacture of plated wares during the 1780s, at least two decades after they had become widely commercially available in England. In 1782, the Society publicised a premium for 'Irish plated goods'.[167] Two years later, the goldsmith John Lloyd was awarded a modest award on that basis.[168]

It was clearly a reality that, while Irish goldsmiths campaigned for the encouragement of their manufactures, whether during periods of heightened economic nationalism, or when increased duties were proposed, some of their counterparts were actively benefiting from the sale of imported plate and plated wares, an issue further explored in chapter 5.[169] Just as certain guild practices changed over time, so the gap between makers and sellers widened. The availability of English plate in eighteenth-century Ireland will be examined in chapter 3, in an analysis of the choices available to Irish consumers. However, the ledgers of English retailers of plated wares, like Joseph Wilson and Matthew Boulton, indicate the alacrity with which some Irish goldsmiths responded to the commercial potential of Sheffield plate, the ease with which goods could be had from England and the way in which agents facilitated this commerce.[170]

The entrepreneur Joseph Wilson established a plated manufactory in Sheffield in 1771 after experimenting with a variety of different enterprises.[171] He was in business until 1775, when he went bankrupt, leaving plated goods and hardware in America and Ireland. Over forty Irish clients were listed among his debtors, including a number of Irish goldsmiths and jewellers, one of whom, Robert Wogan, went bankrupt at the same time.[172] William Moore of Crampton Court, whose trade card describes him as a working jeweller (Fig. 2.37), appears twice on the list of debtors, once for items described as 'his own', and the second for 'goods on sale'.[173] The Dublin jeweller William Stafford and goldsmith Michael Cormick were also on Wilson's books. The items on hand in Ireland at the time of his bankruptcy included plated candlesticks, goblets, coffee pots, waiters, breadbaskets, tankards and tureens. The detailed Dublin assay ledger for the late 1780s indicates that a modest number of candlesticks were assayed in Dublin during that period. The fact that English manufacturers collectively produced large numbers of plated versions must have had an impact on this sector of the Dublin goldsmiths' trade.[174] In 1795 the goldsmith Edward Egerton advertised that he had just got in his 'Winter assortment' of plated goods, which included 'above 350 pairs of candle-sticks and 150 pairs of Branches'.[175]

Joseph Wilson also supplied Irish clients with a small number of silver goods. Sheffield Assay Office records for 1773 to 1774 itemise a modest number of objects submitted by Wilson for hallmarking. Some of these seem to have found their way to

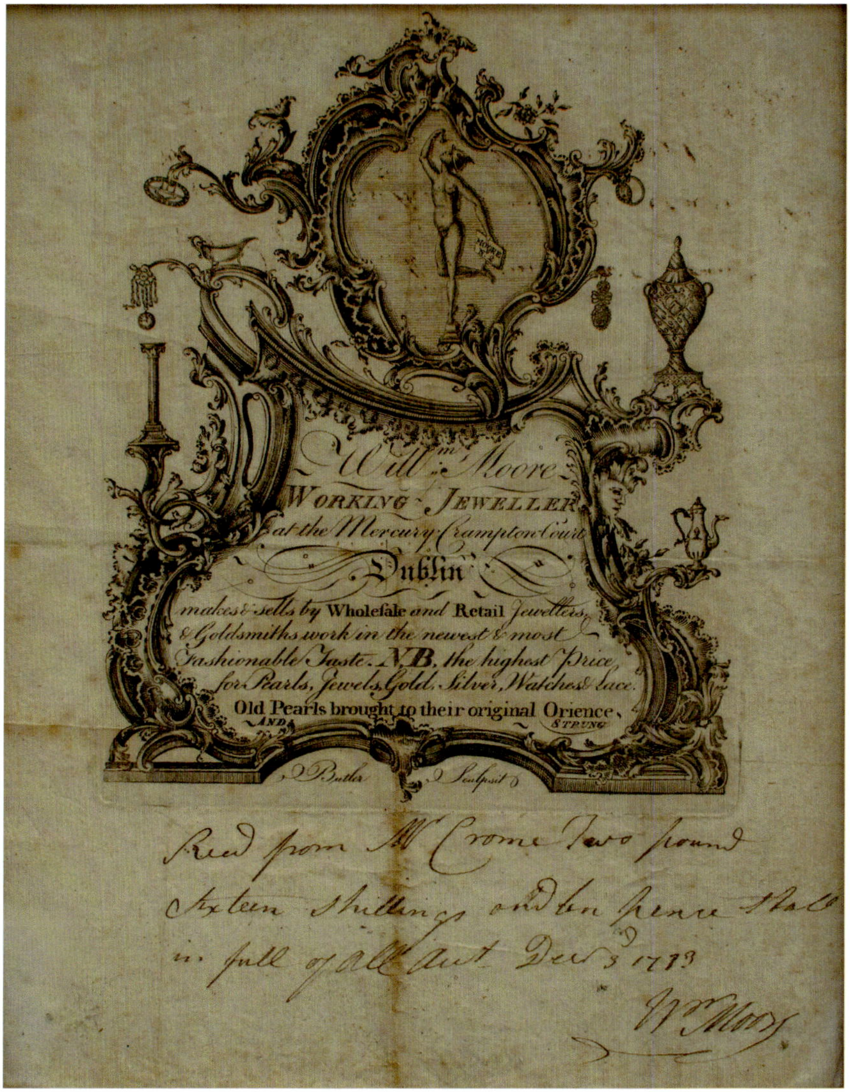

Figure 2.37 Trade card of William Moore (handwritten receipt for 1773), 26 × 21 cm
Photo credit: Author's collection.

Ireland.[176] Four candlesticks and three dish rings assayed during those years appear to correspond with orders placed by the Dublin retailer William Moore (Fig. 2.38). The dish ring, as a distinctive item of eighteenth-century tableware, has come to be particularly associated with Irish Georgian silver.[177] This lends some irony to the fact that an English merchant, specialising in plated wares, supplied an Irish goldsmith with silver dish rings during this period.

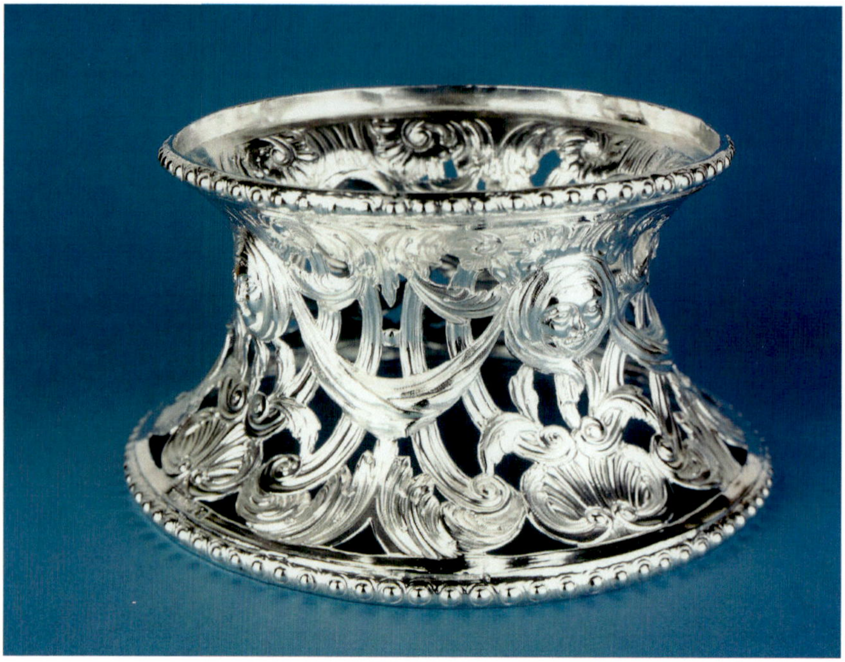

Figure 2.38 Joseph Wilson, *Dish ring* (Sheffield, 1774), silver, 10.2 × 19.6 cm
Source: City Museum, Sheffield. L1928.4. Photo credit: © Museums Sheffield.

Surviving letter books from Matthew Boulton's Birmingham manufactory are similarly revealing about the Dublin goldsmiths' trade. Dublin goldsmiths and jewellers like William Moore, Edward Rice and Jeremiah D'Olier all bought goods from Boulton's Soho emporium.[178] When the retailer Ann Cormick returned samples of candlesticks to Boulton in 1783, his clerk concluded from her actions that 'the cheapest vendors' would ultimately 'have the lead'.[179] While some Dublin retailers travelled to Soho (and indeed it was a popular destination for industrial tourism), Boulton also employed an agent, both to assist him in gauging the Irish market and to expand his sales networks in Dublin. This was Benjamin Henfrey, who had previous experience in the 'Japan business',[180] and also claimed limited experience as an agent for Sheffield plated wares in Dublin.[181] Henfrey approached Boulton in 1783 with a mutually beneficial sales proposal. Boulton was persuaded to entrust him with patterns with which to solicit orders from the 'principal houses' of Dublin.[182] Undoubtedly, there were benefits to having a contact on the spot. In one letter Henfrey was advised that he could adjust at his discretion the prices of certain objects 'deemed too high'.[183] By 1784 he had established himself as a 'wholesale silver plated and hardware merchant' in the city, and in 1788 he submitted more than 700 silver buckles to the Dublin assay office.[184]

Clearly, there were conflicts of interest between makers and sellers of plate in Dublin during this period. In August 1780, the guild noted that several goldsmiths who had entered into a non-importation agreement had gone to England to buy goods 'by which means several workmen would be totally unemployed'.[185] The following month it was agreed that an advertisement highlighting the fact that members of the public were buying imported silver instead of Irish goods would be placed in *Saunders' News-Letter* and the *Dublin Evening Post*.[186]

For those in the retail sector, anticipating public demand meant keeping abreast of developments in England. Variously, novelty, fashion and (in the case of Sheffield plate) price lent imported plate and plated wares appeal in eighteenth-century Dublin. The slower development of plating technology in Ireland contributed to the impetus for the commercially opportunistic to stock imported wares. But then, just as now, multiple factors informed what people bought, where they shopped for goods and why. So, before considering the fate of the goldsmiths' trade in post-Union Dublin, it is worth considering the consumers' perspective.

Notes

1 *Dublin Courant*, 12 October–16 November 1751.
2 *Dublin Courant*, 1–4 December 1750.
3 Assaying was the process by which the purity of precious metal objects was tested. See Douglas Bennett, *Irish Georgian Silver* (London: Cassell, 1972), 21–24; Susan Hare, ed., *Touching Gold and Silver: 500 Years of Hallmarks* (London: Goldsmiths' Hall, 1978); *Report from the Committee Appointed to Enquire into the Manner of Conducting the Several Assay Offices in London, York, Exeter, Bristol, Chester, Norwich, and Newcastle upon Tyne* (London, 1773).
4 Anthony Black, *Guilds and Civil Society in European Political Thought* (London: Methuen, 1984), 167.
5 William Kahl, *The Development of London Livery Companies* (Cambridge, MA: Harvard University Press, 1960), 6.
6 Ibid.
7 Bert De Munck, 'Guilds, Product Quality and Intrinsic Value. Towards a History of Conventions?', *Historical Social Research/Historische Sozialforschung* 36 (2011): 4, 112.
8 Ibid., 105, 112.
9 Charles J. Jackson, *English Goldsmiths and Their Marks* (2nd ed., London: Macmillan, 1921), 573. Jackson also refers to the fact that a similar practice was followed in Scotland. In the Aberdeen hammermen's guild and tailors' guild the masterpiece seems to have remained important into the eighteenth century. Personal communication from Helen Clifford.
10 Bennett, *Irish Georgian Silver*, 14.
11 Company of Goldsmiths of Dublin, Ms. 95: 88, Dublin, Assay Office. Ram was sworn free in April 1665 and presented his piece on 1 August that year. I am grateful to Jessica Cunningham for this reference.
12 Minute of 8 November 1667, Company of Goldsmiths of Dublin, Ms. 1: 2, Dublin, Assay Office.
13 Minute of 13 January 1696, Company of Goldsmiths of Dublin, Ms. 1: 55, Dublin, Assay Office. It was also specified that it should not weigh less than 10s sterling, which implies that it may have been more of an entry fine than a proof of ability. This goldsmith is listed as John Garrett in Douglas Bennett, *Collecting Irish Silver* (London: Souvenir Press, 1984), 144.
14 Minute of 29 September 1697, Company of Goldsmiths of Dublin, Ms. 1: 67, Dublin, Assay Office.
15 Proceedings of the Guild of St Luke, 1677–1728, Ms. 12123: 14, National Library of Ireland.
16 Ibid., 26. A by-law made by the feltmakers' guild in 1668 required 'proof pieces to be made; in default a fine', and 'every apprentice when admitted to pay a spoon'; Henry F. Berry, 'The Records of the Feltmakers' Company of Dublin, 1787–1841', *Journal of the Royal Society of Antiquaries of Ireland (JRSAI)* 41 (1911): 30.

17 The guild certainly intervened in cases where masters were charged with being inattentive to their apprentices' welfare. See, for instance, Minutes of 3 November 1742 and 21 February 1755, Company of Goldsmiths of Dublin, Ms. 2: 181, 320, Dublin, Assay Office; Minute of 21 September 1762, Company of Goldsmiths of Dublin, Ms. 5: 56.

18 Minute of 10 June 1807, Company of Goldsmiths of Dublin, Ms. 6: 424, Dublin, Assay Office.

19 Philippa Glanville, *Silver in England* (London: Unwin Hyman, 1987), 169, identifies sporadic attempts from the fifteenth century onwards to restore this practice in an English context. In a discussion of seventeenth-century practice she asserts that 'there is no equivalent in England to the collection of masterpieces presented to their guilds by the Nuremberg or Augsburg goldsmiths, although sometimes London goldsmiths followed this procedure.'

20 R. Campbell, *The London Tradesman* (London, 1747), 142.

21 Margarita Tinto, 'The "Llibres de Passantia" of the Silversmiths of Barcelona (16th–19th Centuries)', *Jewellery Studies* 6 (1993): 29–37. It is not inconceivable that records pertaining to the adjudication of masterpieces in Dublin once existed, but this does not explain why references to them occur in the seventeenth- but not the eighteenth-century minutes of the guild.

22 This term was repeatedly used by the guild to denote the sterling standard of 92.5 per cent pure silver, as opposed to a level of technical proficiency or design skills. See, for example, Minute of 18 November 1773, Company of Goldsmiths of Dublin, Ms. 5: 270, Dublin, Assay Office.

23 De Munck, 'Guilds, Product Quality and Intrinsic Value', 110.

24 For tables of these see Jackson, *English Goldsmiths*, 606–24.

25 The Company of Goldsmiths of Dublin was incorporated by Royal Charter in 1637 and given the responsibility for assaying and hallmarking all gold and silver wares produced in Ireland. The full text of the charter is given in Jackson, *English Goldsmiths*, 565–74. The charter and Jackson's essays on Irish silver are omitted from the revised, third edition of this work, published in 1989.

26 Minute of 12 October 1742, Company of Goldsmiths of Dublin, Ms. 3: 163, Dublin Assay Office; Minute of 12 March 1761, Company of Goldsmiths of Dublin, Ms. 5: 37, Dublin, Assay Office. However, in May 1812, the Corporation 'Resolved unanimously that the freedom of the Corporation of Goldsmiths be presented to Mr. John Sherwin Jr, in testimony of the sense they entertain of his distinguished talents as an artist by which he has successfully improved the manufacture of chased plate in this country'; Minute of 1 May 1812, Company of Goldsmiths of Dublin, Ms. 7: 160, Dublin, Assay Office.

27 Minute of 12 March 1761, Company of Goldsmiths of Dublin, Ms. 5: 37.

28 Gitta Willemson, *The Dublin Society Drawing Schools: Students and Award Winners, 1746–1876* (Dublin: Royal Dublin Society, 2000); Henry F. Berry, *A History of the Royal Dublin Society* (London: Longmans Green, 1915); John Turpin, 'The School of Ornament of the Dublin Society in the Eighteenth Century', *JRSAI*, 116 (1986): 38–50.

29 Willemson, *The Dublin Society Drawing Schools*.

30 Turpin, 'The School of Ornament of the Dublin Society', 43.

31 Willemson, *The Dublin Society Drawing Schools*, 78.

32 *Faulkner's Dublin Journal* (*FDJ*), 5–7 February 1789.

33 Willemson, *The Dublin Society Drawing Schools*, 78.

34 *Second Annual Exhibition of Articles of Irish Manufacture, Produce and Invention at the Royal Dublin Society's House, May 1835* (Dublin: R. Graisberry, 1835), 4. For more on Percy, see also Walter Strickland, *A Dictionary of Irish Artists*, vol. 1 (Shannon: Irish University Press, 1969), 225–26; *The Proceedings of the Dublin Society* for 1812, vol. 48: 149 record that books to the value of two guineas were to be presented to Lorenzo Percy in acknowledgement of the merit of his pen drawings.

35 Minute of 25 June 1813, Company of Goldsmiths of Dublin, Ms. 7: 198, Dublin, Assay Office, refers to ornament chased by John Macklin on behalf of the goldsmith James Le Bas. A John Macklin entered the Dublin Society's School of Landscape and Ornament in 1785. See Willemson, *The Dublin Society Drawing Schools*, 60.

36 Teare was a student at the Dublin Society School of Ornament. See also chapter 5.

37 *Dublin Weekly Journal*, 17 April 1725.

38 Alison FitzGerald, 'Fighting for "A Small Provincial Establishment": The Cork Goldsmiths and Their Quest for a Regional Assay Office', in *Provincial Ireland*, ed. Roy Foster and Raymond Gillespie (Dublin: Four Courts Press, 2012), 120–30.
39 The charter stipulated that for silver this should be 'his Majesty's standard, otherwise called eleven ounces two pennyweights', it being understood that this referred to the proportion of pure silver in one pound troy of the alloy. At 20 pennyweights to the ounce and 12 ounces to the pound, this translates in modern terminology to 92.5 per cent purity, commonly called sterling standard. Goods that met the required sterling standard of 92.5 per cent pure silver were marked with a series of punches. The harp crowned indicated that the silver was the correct fineness, the maker's or sponsor's mark denoted the craftsman who was asserting his or her responsibility for the piece and, from 1730, a figure of Hibernia was used to indicate the payment of 6 pence per ounce duty, in accordance with an Act of Parliament. Throughout the eighteenth century, date letters were also used, but with much more irregularity and selectivity. See Kurt Ticher, Ida Delamer, and William O'Sullivan, *Hall-marks on Dublin Silver, 1730–1772* (Dublin: National Museum of Ireland, 1968); Thomas Sinsteden, 'Four Selected Assay Records of the Dublin Goldsmiths Company', *Silver Society Journal* 11 (1999): 143–58; and Ida Delamer and Conor O'Brien, 'Dublin Hallmarks: A Reappraisal', *Silver Society Journal* 11 (1999): 158–67.
40 Bennett, *Irish Georgian Silver*, 168. Thomas Sinsteden, 'A Sterling Relationship: The Cork Goldsmiths and the Company of Goldsmiths of Dublin', in *Cork Silver and Gold*, ed. John Bowen and Conor O'Brien (Cork: Collins Press, 2005), 20 gives totals for the volume of Cork silver recorded as hallmarked in Dublin between 1700 and 1750: 4,418 oz. in total. For more on Cork, see Bowen and O'Brien, eds., *Cork Silver and Gold*; M.S.D. Westropp, 'The Cork Goldsmiths, Silversmiths, Jewellers, Watchmakers and Apprentices', *Cork Historical and Archaeological Society Journal* (*JCHAS*) 31 (1926): 8–13.
41 Ida Delamer and Conor O'Brien, *500 Years of Irish Silver* (Bray, Co. Wicklow: Wordwell/National Museum of Ireland, 2005), 18–19.
42 Miscellaneous Correspondence Relating to the Establishment of an Assay Office in Cork, Ms. 30/9/147, National Archives, Kew. I am grateful to Robert Barker for drawing my attention to this material.
43 Cork goldsmiths to John Foster, n.d., Company of Goldsmiths of Dublin, Ms. 131, 45.
44 Cork goldsmiths to Mountifort Longfield, 17 August 1801, Ms. 30/9/147, National Archives, Kew. For a biographical entry on Longfield, see Edith Mary Johnston-Liik, *History of the Irish Parliament 1692–1800*, vol. 5 (Belfast: Ulster Historical Foundation, 2002), 116–17.
45 Cork goldsmiths to Mountifort Longfield, 17 August 1801, Ms. 30/9/147, National Archives, Kew.
46 See Bennett, *Irish Georgian Silver*, 22.
47 T.W. Moody, F.X. Martin, and F.J. Byrne, *A New History of Ireland*, vol. 9 (Oxford: Oxford University Press, 1984), 527.
48 See Bennett, *Irish Georgian Silver*, 304. It is likely that D'Olier was not active in the trade at this point, or that he was winding up his business. For further information on D'Olier, see Paul Butel and Louis Cullen eds., *Cities and Merchants: French and Irish Perspectives on Urban Development, 1500–1900* (Dublin: Trinity College Dublin, 1986), 207.
49 Notes on the proposed assay office for Cork, n.d., Ms. 30/9/147, National Archives, Kew.
50 Jeremiah D'Olier to unknown, 28 September 1801, Ms. 30/9/147, National Archives, Kew.
51 *Case of the Wardens and Assistant of the Company or Mystery of Goldsmiths of the City of London* (London, 1773).
52 As well as the aforementioned texts, see Robert Barker, 'Proposals for an Assaying System in Pennsylvania 1753–1770', *Silver Society Journal* 2 (1991): 75–79.
53 Cork goldsmiths to Mountifort Longfield, 20 October 1801, Ms. 30/9/147, National Archives, Kew.
54 In 1788, only seven individual makers or firms were recorded in the assay records for Newcastle. Between them they submitted a modest 6,913 oz. See Margaret Gill, *A Directory of Newcastle Goldsmiths* (Newcastle: Margaret A.V. Gill, 1980), 336.

55 Sinsteden, 'A Sterling Relationship', 20.
56 Alison FitzGerald and Conor O'Brien, 'The Production of Silver in Late Georgian Dublin', *Irish Architectural and Decorative Studies* (*IADS*) 4 (2001): 8–48.
57 Memorial of the Cork goldsmiths in support of their petition for a Cork assay office, 27 August 1801, Ms. 30/9/147, National Archives, Kew.
58 Jeremiah D'Olier to unknown, 28 September 1801, Ms. 30/9/147, National Archives, Kew. The Cork goldsmiths subsequently clarified that their estimate included all affected parties, including families of goldsmiths and their journeymen rather than solely individual manufacturers.
59 For instance, apart from London, the English cities of Chester, Exeter, Newcastle, Sheffield, York and Birmingham had their own assay offices. By 1811, the population of Co. Cork, including Cork City, was estimated at 675,364. See David Dickson, *Old World Colony: Cork and South Munster, 1630–1830* (Cork: Cork University Press, 2005), 306.
60 FitzGerald, 'Fighting For 'a Small Provincial Establishment', 120–30.
61 A complete list of surviving eighteenth-century assay records, apprenticeship ledgers, and minute books has been provided in the bibliography along with other relevant manuscripts from the archive of the Company of Goldsmith of Dublin. For the comparative paucity of records for many other Dublin guilds, see Mary Clark and Raymond Refaussé, *Directory of Historic Dublin Guilds* (Dublin: Dublin Public Libraries, 1993).
62 Naturally there were those, even in Dublin, who contravened legislation and did not have their work assayed, usually to avoid the payment of duties. See, for instance, Minutes of 26 April 1762 and 7 October 1768, Company of Goldsmiths of Dublin, Ms. 5: 50, 166); Minute of 2 February 1792, Ms. 6: 192, Dublin, Assay Office.
63 Just to emphasise this fact, the number of boys officially recorded as being apprenticed to London goldsmiths between 1700 and 1709 alone was more than the total officially recorded in Dublin for the whole century. See Table 1.1, and William Kahl, 'Apprenticeship and the Freedom of the London Livery Companies, 1690–1750', *Guildhall Miscellany* 7 (1956): 17–20. J.S. Forbes, *Hallmark: A History of the London Assay Office* (London: Goldsmiths Company and Unicorn Press, 1999), 219–20 reproduces graphs of the annual weights and numbers of articles handled at the London Assay Office.
64 Sinsteden, 'Four Selected Assay Records', 145–46.
65 Ibid., 153 for 1706; Thomas Sinsteden, 'Surviving Dublin Assay Records, part 2. 1708–48', *Silver Studies* 16 (2004): 90. These figures refer to assay years, so the total for 1709 for example refers to the assay year 1708–9.
66 Sinsteden, 'Four Selected Assay Records' and 'Surviving Dublin Assay Records'. As indicated in the previous footnote, Sinsteden's figures refer to the Dublin Assay Office accounting year, 1 November to 31 October. See also M.S.D. Westropp, *National Museum of Ireland, Dublin: General Guide to the Art Collections* (Dublin: Stationery Office, 1914), 49–50. On 'duty dodging', see Bennett, *Irish Georgian Silver*, 213–44.
67 Alison FitzGerald, 'Cosmopolitan Commerce: The Dublin Goldsmith Robert Calderwood', *Apollo* (September 2005), 47.
68 Sinsteden, 'Surviving Dublin Assay Records', 94. A silver bowl in the Museum of Fine Arts, Boston, dates to this period. See Ellenor Alcorn, *English Silver in the Museum of Fine Arts, Boston. Volume II: Silver from 1697 Including Irish and Scottish Silver* (Boston: Museum of Fine Arts, 2000), 346.
69 Gill, *A Directory of Newcastle Goldsmiths*.
70 Communication from Robert Barker to the author, 4 August 2004.
71 Anonymous notes on the proposed assay office for Cork, n.d., Ms. 30/9/147, National Archives, Kew.
72 Box making, for example, was a highly specialised task.
73 Alison FitzGerald, 'A Sterling Trade: Making and Selling Silver in Ireland', in *Ireland: Crossroads of Art and Design, 1690–1840*, ed. William Laffan and Christopher Monkhouse (New Haven and London: Yale University Press, 2015), 175–76.
74 Sinsteden, 'Surviving Dublin Assay Records', 96.
75 *FDJ*, 5–8 January 1740.
76 An Acct. of my plate, when boght [*sic*] & from whom. NLI Ms. 25, 386, National Library of Ireland, 159–60.

77 Sinsteden, 'Surviving Dublin Assay Records'.
78 Assay Book, 27 March 1752–1 August 1755, Company of Goldsmiths of Dublin, Ms. 17, Dublin, Assay Office. The observations that follow were achieved by transcribing all the assay entries records for that twelve-month period and analysing the results.
79 Sinsteden, 'Surviving Dublin Assay Records', 89.
80 Sinsteden, 'Four Selected Assay Records', 151.
81 Sinsteden, 'Surviving Dublin Assay Records', 98.
82 Ibid., 100.
83 According to Bennett, *Irish Georgian Silver*, 328, Sawyer became free of the guild in 1807 and died in 1812.
84 This came to a combined total in excess of 20,000 oz.
85 David Dickson, 'The Demographic Implications of Dublin's Growth 1650–1850', in *Urban Population Development in Western Europe*, eds. Richard Lawton and Robert Lee (Liverpool: Liverpool University Press, 1989), 178–89.
86 Ibid., 178.
87 Ibid.
88 Jacqueline Hill, *From Patriots to Unionists* (Oxford: Oxford University Press, 1997), 19.
89 David Dickson, ed., *The Gorgeous Mask: Dublin 1700–1800* (Dublin: Trinity College Dublin Press, 1987), vii.
90 Hill, *From Patriots to Unionists*, 22.
91 Dublin Corporation appears to have been an instigator of this practice, presenting three pieces to the Lord Deputy Henry Cromwell on the occasion of his son's baptism in 1656. Later, in July 1662, when it was decided to confer the freedom of the city on the Duke of Ormond, the Corporation decided that the freedom should 'be presented to him in a golden box to be made for that purpose'. Thereafter the presentation of certificates of corporate freedom or laudatory addresses in gold or silver boxes became a regular practice throughout the country. See Sir John T. and Lady Gilbert, eds., *Calendar of Ancient Records of Dublin*, vol. 4 (Dublin, 1892), 243.
92 *FDJ*, 1–3 April 1788. A silver basket in the collection of the National Museum of Ireland, presented by the Dublin Society, commemorates Lancelot Sandes' achievement in reclaiming bog in the Queen's County. Illustrated in John Teahan, *Irish Silver* (Dublin: Stationery Office, 1979), 42.
93 Toby Barnard, 'Fabrics of Faith: The Material Worlds of Catholic Ireland and Protestant Ireland, 1500–1800', in *Franciscan Faith: Sacred Art in Ireland, AD 1600–1750*, ed. Raghnall Ó Floinn (Dublin: Wordwell, 2011), 25–26.
94 Alison FitzGerald and Conor O'Brien, 'The Production of Silver in Late Georgian Dublin', *IADS* 4 (2001): 35, 41.
95 Joseph McDonnell, ed., *Maynooth Bicentenary Art Exhibitions: Ecclesiastical Art of the Penal Era* (Maynooth: Saint Patrick's College, 1995), 37.
96 Assay Book, 3 February 1787–2 February 1789, Company of Goldsmiths of Dublin, Ms. 21, Dublin, Assay Office.
97 This included two partnerships or firms: Law and Co. and Peter and Co. The full name and accurate identity of the maker can generally be determined from references in other contemporary sources such as street directories and lists of freeman and quarter brothers. The year 1788 has been chosen for analysis, since the ledger is incomplete for 1787 and 1789. Unless otherwise specified, the figures cited refer to silver assayed between January and December 1788. This is the only full calendar year covered in the ledger.
98 It would not have been possible for Bolland to make a living purely on the basis of such a modest output.
99 For example, this figure includes persons describing themselves as goldsmiths and silversmiths, watchmakers and jewellers, gold-beaters, etc. The information provided in the directory for 1789 provides a profile of what was happening in 1788.
100 This was to prevent them from coming on the market.
101 Jennifer Tann, *Birmingham Assay Office, 1773–1993* (Birmingham: Assay Office, 1993), 16. Tann was commenting on Matthew Boulton's underestimate of the time involved in making 'a fine article for a noble table'.

102 For example, in 1794, the Irish patron James Alexander bought a variety of items including eight tureens and eighteen dessert spoons from the London goldsmith firm of Rundell and Bridge. The fashioning cost for the former was 3s 3d per oz. while the fashioning costs of the latter were essentially the same. However, comparatively speaking, the manufacture of the larger object represented a greater investment of time. Accounts of Lord Caledon, May 1794, Ms. D2433/B/1/1/30, Public Record Office of Northern Ireland (PRONI). *Report from the Committee Appointed to Enquire into the Manner of Conducting the Several Assay Offices in London, York, Exeter, Bristol, Chester, Norwich, and Newcastle upon Tyne* (London, 1773), also confirms that a large percentage of the goods broken by guilds in England were made by workers of small wares.

103 Osborne's contemporary, the buckle maker Ambrose Nicklin, had roughly 16 per cent of his items rejected in the same year. Clearly, many goldsmiths bought scrap, yet it is unknown how many of them were competent when it came to assaying metal. I am grateful to Thomas Sinsteden for the latter comment.

104 Minute of 8 November 1790, Company of Goldsmiths of Dublin, Ms. 6, 178, Dublin Assay Office.

105 For the consumption of tea in an eighteenth-century context, see L. A. Clarkson and E. M. Crawford, *Feast and Famine: Food and Nutrition in Ireland 1500–1920* (Oxford: Oxford University Press, 2001) and Carole Shammas, *The Pre-Industrial Consumer in England and America* (Oxford: Oxford University Press, 1990).

106 Some Irish patrons also acquired silver teapots in England. See, for example, George Wickes' Gentleman's Ledger 1740–48: 12, Garrard Ledgers, V&A, and Accounts of James Alexander, 19 September 1772, Ms. D2433/B/1/1/1, PRONI.

107 *FDJ*, 13–15 May 1784.

108 *FDJ*, 12–15 December 1789.

109 For more on eighteenth-century ceramics, in particular porcelain, see Sarah Richards, *Eighteenth-Century Ceramics: Products for a Civilised Society* (Manchester: Manchester University Press, 1999); Hilary Young, *English Porcelain 1745–95: Its Makers, Design, Marketing and Consumption* (London: V&A, 1999).

110 Accounts of James Alexander, 12 June 1789, Ms. D2433/B/1/1/23, PRONI. James Alexander later acquired thirty-six 'india' cups and saucers for less than half that price from a Dublin retailer. See Accounts of James Alexander, 6 June 1796, Ms. D/2433/B/1/7, PRONI. The *Clonmel Gazette; or, Hibernian Advertiser*, 19–22 December 1792 advertised dinner services for two guineas.

111 Toby Barnard, 'Integration or Separation? Hospitality and Display in Protestant Ireland 1660–1800', in *A Union of Multiple Identities*, ed. Laurence Brockliss and David Eastwood (Manchester: Manchester University Press, 1997), 139.

112 This statistic refers to the 1780s. See L. A. Clarkson, 'Hospitality, Housekeeping and High Living in Eighteenth-Century Ireland', in *Luxury and Austerity*, ed. Jacqueline Hill and Colm Lennon (Dublin: University College Dublin, 1999), 98.

113 Clarkson, 'Hospitality, Housekeeping and High Living', 87.

114 Perhaps 'dish' implied a lidded container. One contemporary inventory itemised 'a sugar dish and cover'; Inventory of household furniture in Cavendish Street House, 1 January, 1763, Ms. 48,314, British Library.

115 Account of James Alexander with Courtauld and Cowles, London, 19 September 1772, Ms. D2433/B/1/1/1, PRONI.

116 One was recorded in the assay records for 1810. However, it is likely that more were made and simply entered in another way.

117 The effect of *faux* wood construction is also seen in English eighteenth-century silver.

118 Accounts of Richard Johnston, 1783, Ms. D/1594/185, PRONI.

119 For further information on piggins, see Bennett, *Irish Georgian Silver*, 127, 132, 134. Piggins were also made in glass. See Mary Boydell, 'The Origin of the Glass Piggin', *Irish Arts Review* (*IAR*) 3, no. 3 (1986): 22.

120 The comparative rarity of silver piggins is suggested by the absence of the term in 1788 and 1810, respectively.

121 This disparity had been resolved considerably by 1810 when the margin had narrowed.

122 Anon., *The Lady's Companion: Or, Accomplish'd Director in the Whole Art of Cookery* (Dublin: Printed for John Mitchell, 1767), 29. This was possibly because it was thought that silver as opposed to base metal would not affect the taste of the dish. In the dinner book of Robert Jocelyn, 1740–51, Ms. 219, Henry Francis du Pont Museum, Winterthur, a ragout of coxcombs is among the dishes specified.

123 Jonathan Swift, *Directions to Servants* (Dublin: George Faulkner, 1745), 28.

124 Cissie Fairchilds, 'The Production and Marketing of Populuxe Goods in Eighteenth-Century Paris', in *Consumption and the World of Goods*, ed. John Brewer and Roy Porter (London: Routledge, 1993), 230. Interestingly, the figure had been higher (almost 75 per cent) in 1725, illustrating the competition that silver faced from new luxuries in the second half of the eighteenth century.

125 Butter knives and butter spades were submitted for assaying during this period, making it difficult to identify the shape of 'fecques'. I am grateful to Thomas Sinsteden for this comment.

126 I am grateful to Peter Kaellgren and the late Conor O'Brien for their suggestions in this regard.

127 There were no methers recorded between January and December 1788.

128 Claudia Kinmonth, *Irish Country Furniture, 1700–1950* (New Haven and London: Yale University Press, 1993), 198–20. Methers were carved out of wood and were round at the bottom and quadrangular at the top. They usually had four handles, though sometimes two are found. Travelling in the south of Ireland in 1788, Daniel Beaufort observed 'wooden mugs of all sizes neatly turned, with handles of the same piece, a difficult work'. Daniel Beaufort, 'Journal of a Tour throughout Ireland', 1788, Ms. 4030: 19, Trinity College Dublin.

129 This figure refers to items specifically described as cups. West also submitted one tankard and eleven tumblers in addition to a range of other items.

130 See Tighernan Mooney and Fiona White, 'The Gentry's Winter Season', in *The Gorgeous Mask*, ed. Dickson, 13–14. They also note that in June 1784 the 'Funny Club' of Kildare Street, a gentleman's club, organised two balls to support Irish manufactures.

131 Philippa Glanville has observed that while 'cups had always been a staple of the goldsmiths' trade,' elaborately decorated rococo cups 'did not lend themselves to the addition of inscriptions', which 'accounts for the continued popularity of the earlier simple form for sporting prizes'; Glanville, *Silver in England*, 92.

132 Ellenor Alcorn, *English Silver in the Museum of Fine Arts, Boston*, vol. 2 (Boston: Museum of Fine Arts, 2000), 347–49. The piece bears the mark of the Dublin goldsmith William Williamson. See also Thomas Sinsteden, 'Victory Bowl', *Magazine Antiques* (March/April 2015), 94–97.

133 Ibid.

134 Clarkson, 'Hospitality, Housekeeping and High Living', 84.

135 Quoted in Barnard, 'Integration or Separation?', 129.

136 *FDJ*, 4–6 August 1789.

137 They were also made in ceramics.

138 An épergne was an elaborate centrepiece for the dining table. They were heavy and could incorporate extravagant ornament. See Michael Clayton, *The Collector's Dictionary of the Silver and Gold of Great Britain and North America* (New York and Cleveland: World, 1985), 122; and Toby Barnard, *Making the Grand Figure: Lives and Possessions in Ireland, 1641–1770* (New Haven and London: Yale University Press, 2004), 142.

139 *Belfast News Letter*, 17–20 September 1782.

140 Accounts of William George Digges La Touche, January 1789, Ms. 19.898: 17, National Library of Ireland.

141 Some Irish patrons certainly ordered épergnes from England. See, for example, Account of the Right Reverend, The Lord Bishop of Elphin, 7 November 1759, George Wickes' Gentleman's Ledger 1756–60: 221, Garrard Ledgers, V&A.

142 See, for example, the silver galleries in the National Museum of Ireland, Collins Barracks.

143 The latter was used to secure a neckcloth in place. Goldsmiths like William Law and Ambrose Nicklin were prominent suppliers of buckles. They alone submitted more than 5,000 buckles in 1788.
144 This figure refers to individual buckles rather than pairs.
145 Andrew Carpenter, ed., *Verse in English From Eighteenth-Century Ireland* (Cork: Cork University Press, 1998), 493. The demand for buckles had had fallen off sharply by the early nineteenth century.
146 Total Book, 1782–1791, Worshipful Company of Goldsmiths, London.
147 Ibid. This figure is based on an average made by combining the following specified categories: large workers, workers under four pounds, small workers, watch-case makers. Gold parcels are also recorded in this ledger but have not been used for the purposes of these calculations since gold objects are not specified in the Dublin ledger. For a history of the London assay office, see Forbes, *Hallmark*.
148 *Dublin Evening Post*, 14 July 1778.
149 *Saunders' News-Letter*, 8 July 1782.
150 *Hibernian Chronicle*, 10 May 1781.
151 London was also slower to mechanise relative to cities like Birmingham and Sheffield.
152 Campbell, *The London Tradesman*, 141–42.
153 Helen Clifford, *Silver in London: The Parker and Wakelin Partnership* (New Haven and London: Yale University Press, 2004), 6.
154 Ibid. Clifford notes that the increase in production was also associated with the removal of a duty on silver in 1757.
155 For more on this technology, see John Culme, 'Beauty and the Beast: The Growth of Mechanisation in the Trade', *Proceedings of the Silver Society* 9/10 (1980): 158–65; Susan La Niece and Paul Craddock, *Metal Plating and Patination: Cultural, Technical & Historical Developments* (Oxford: Butterworth-Heinemann, 1993); Glanville, *Silver in England*, 166.
156 Minutes of 12–19 May 1779, Company of Goldsmiths of Dublin, Ms. 5: 379, Dublin, Assay Office.
157 *Proceedings of the Dublin Society*, vol. 21: 21. This was clearly a reference to flatted plate. As Glanville, *Silver in England*, 166 explains, the rolling mill, which produced silver sheet of a uniform thickness without the effort and monotony of hammering it out, had come into general use in London by 1747.
158 The Society had offered premiums for light plate in 1782 but there does not appear to have been any applicants in that year.
159 The Volunteers were a part-time military force raised in 1778–79 to guard against invasion and to preserve law and order. They also played a pivotal role in the campaign for free trade. The objects advertised must have been decorative rather than functional. *FDJ*, 3 December 1796. In this advertisement, Ash Rainey gives his profession as 'goldsmith' though surviving handbills describe his business at 10 Capel Street as 'the established Jewellery and Military Ware-House'.
160 Appendix to *Third Report of the Commissioners of Inquiry into the Collection and Management of the Revenue Arising in Ireland*, xiii (1822), 19–23.
161 For the advertising of imported plated wares see, *FDJ*, 13 February 1796. The Dublin ironmonger John Binns, whose trade card gives an address of 'almost opposite Crow Street', was importing a range of goods, including plated candlesticks, coffee pots, cups, inkstands, cruet frames, tankards and salts; see John Johnson collection, Album III, Bodleian Library, Oxford.
162 See Helen Clifford, 'Concepts of Invention: Identity and Imitation in the London and Provincial Metal-Working Trades 1750–1800', *Journal of Design History* 12 (1999): 241–55.
163 On the value accorded to novelty in an eighteenth-century context, see Grant McCracken, *Culture and Consumption: New Approaches to the Symbolic Character of Consumer Goods and Activities* (Bloomington: Indiana University Press, 1990).
164 Minute of 18 November 1773, Company of Goldsmiths of Dublin, Ms.5: 269, Dublin, Assay Office.

165 They pointed out that that English goldsmiths were at an advantage, since they paid a modest annual licence, rather than a duty of 6d per oz. on manufactured plate. The Dublin goldsmiths complained that they were required to pay the said duty 'although the said Plate often remains long unsold; and frequently, by the Alteration of Fashions, is obliged to be melted again'.
166 *Journal of the House of Commons*, vol. 130: 49.
167 *Premiums Offered by the Dublin Society 1782*, Dublin, 1782.
168 *Proceedings of the Dublin Society*, vol. 21: 18, 21. The premium had been advertised as a percentage of the value of goods manufactured. Lloyd received a modest £2 2s 11d for the manufacture of £35 worth of goods. No information is given in relation to the technique he was using.
169 For examples of retailers within the precious metals trade appealing to patriotic patronage, see *Volunteers Journal; or, Irish Herald*, 3 May 1784 and 25 June 1784. The second of these references refers to an advertisement placed by William Moore who, as will be seen, imported plated wares and silver from England. This demonstrates that economic nationalism was not always incompatible with the sale of imported wares.
170 The Boulton correspondence includes a significant number of references to Irish clients, both in terms of retailers and private individuals.
171 Gordon Crosskey, 'The Early Development of the Plated Trade', *Silver Society Journal* 12 (2000): 27–38.
172 *Saunders' News-Letter*, 3–6 February 1775. I am grateful to Breda Scott for drawing my attention to this connection.
173 Moore was a member of the Dublin goldsmiths' guild. Since the former debt amounted to over £116, it seems unlikely that it reflected his personal consumption. It is more likely that a distinction was being made between plated wares, which he was acquiring for sale himself, and those which he may have been selling on commission for Wilson.
174 Boulton used illustrated catalogues to sell his wares, and the catalogue numbers of some of his wares are specifically referred to in correspondence with Irish clients. See, for example, On Behalf of Matthew Boulton to Benjamin Henfrey, 25 March 1783, Ms. 3782/3/14: 94, Birmingham City Archives. Boulton also sent silver candlesticks to Irish clients. See Kenneth Quickenden, 'Samuel Garbett and Early Boulton and Fothergill Assay Silver', in *Matthew Boulton*, ed. Kenneth Quickenden, Sally Baggott, and Malcolm Dick (Aldershot: Ashgate, 2013), 134–35.
175 *FDJ*, 13 February 1796.
176 I am grateful to Gordon Crosskey for sending me copies of entries from the Wilson ledgers and for his generosity in sharing his knowledge of the English plated trade. Unless otherwise specified, all the references to Wilson's trade are from these documents, which are presently held by Wilson and Co., Sharrow.
177 Although it is acknowledged that they were not unique to Ireland. For more on Irish dish rings, see Conor O'Brien, 'The Evolution of Silver Dish Rings' (Antique Dealer and Collector's Guide, 1977).
178 See, for example, On Behalf of Matthew Boulton to Jeremiah D'Olier, 12 March 1783; Matthew Boulton to Rice and Clark, 1783, Ms. 3782/3/14: 86, 125, Birmingham City Archives.
179 On Behalf of Matthew Boulton to Benjamin Henfrey, 29 May 1783, Ms. 3782/3/14: 115, Birmingham City Archives.
180 As previously indicated, 'japanning' referred to Western imitations of Oriental lacquer, and dealers in the Japan business sold all sorts of household goods. In 1762, the jeweller and goldsmith John Karr advertised the sale of 'all manner of Japanned waiters and bread baskets' among his imported stock. See *Pue's Occurrences*, 26–30 October 1762.
181 Benjamin Henfrey to Matthew Boulton, 1783, Microfilm 171, Birmingham City Archives. Henfrey said of Dublin: 'I have in two journeys sold plated goods for the house I do business for.' He expressed confidence in the superiority of Boulton's patterns, and his belief that they would be successful in Ireland. The reference to 'the Japan business' must have referred to japanned goods.

182 Ibid. If this initiative proved successful, Henfrey was prepared to come up with his own capital 'not exceeding the sum of £700 sterling', which would 'be equal to any stock necessary to be kept on hand'.

183 On Behalf of Matthew Boulton to Benjamin Henfrey, n.d., Ms. 3782/3/14: 223, Birmingham City Archives. This letter is not dated, but based on preceding and subsequent letters appears to date to June 1784.

184 Bennett, *Irish Georgian Silver*, 309 lists Henfrey's professional title in this way.

185 Minute of 9 August 1780, Company of Goldsmiths of Dublin, Ms. 6: 19, Dublin, Assay Office.

186 Minute of 6 September 1780, Company of Goldsmiths of Dublin, Ms. 6: 20, Dublin Assay Office. It was also agreed that the notice should be amended to include jewellers.

3 Shopping for plate in Dublin and London

In 1764, Lady Holland wrote from England to her sister Emily, Marchioness of Kildare, in Ireland offering to help her with some shopping: 'Let me have any orders you may have,' she urged, for as she put it, 'jaunting to town' was no chore.[1] Emily was an enthusiastic shopper, at times to her husband's despair, and as chatelaine of Carton in Co. Kildare and Kildare House in Dublin she had many rooms to fill. But what sort of options did Irish patrons have when it came to buying silver during this period? How did the attraction of buying new from London compare to buying locally, or indeed buying second-hand? What were the advantages of buying new goods from a goldsmith's shop, relative to the excitement of bidding at auction, and were there contexts in which second-hand plate might have been considered to be 'as good as new'?

Goldsmiths' shops

Modern research has extended our knowledge of shopping in an eighteenth-century context.[2] Claire Walsh has refuted the assumption that 'eighteenth-century shops made no attempt to make goods attractive, to make shopping a pleasant experience or to draw the customer's attention to unintended purchases.'[3] She argues instead, in relation to eighteenth-century London, that 'all of these features were very much a part of shop design from the very beginning of the century.'[4] Sarah Foster has shown how in Dublin in the latter half of the century, the newly laid out thoroughfares of Dame Street and Parliament Street 'attracted a mix of goldsmiths, mercers, drapers, haberdashers, cutlers, tailors and hatters', while 'Grafton Street was established as 'a sort of London Bond Street'.[5] Clearly, shopping was a significant social and cultural activity, and when it came to buying silverware a goldsmith's shop or 'warehouse' was the most obvious port of call.[6] Yet, in their efforts to attract customers, goldsmiths in Dublin and in London appear to have differed in their advertising strategies.

Strikingly few London goldsmiths or jewellers advertised their goods in the newspapers, clearly regarding it as an inappropriate way to attract those of what Wedgwood called 'superior spirit'.[7] Stafford Briscoe, the first London goldsmith to do so, gave up after a series of advertisements in the *General Advertiser* for 1751.[8] Yet in eighteenth-century Dublin, for a variety of reasons, goldsmiths and jewellers seem to have made wider use of newspaper advertising. The smaller scale of the Dublin market, and the more limited pool of clients, encouraged forthright competition for business, and newspaper advertisements offered greater potential for visibility than the more expensive medium of trade cards.[9] Irish retailers who dealt in imported plate, plated wares and jewellery were keen to advertise the arrival of consignments of English goods rather than see profits lost if Irish patrons ordered directly from England. Goldsmiths in Cork, Limerick and Dublin shared with their North American counterparts a desire to connect themselves with wider metropolitan developments and, specifically, London fashions.[10] Retailers in both countries used the newspapers in a similar way, to advertise their connections with London (and the English provinces) or to claim that their own goods were on par with those imported. For instance, in 1782, the Cork goldsmith Carden Terry advertised that he had 'lately returned from London and different parts of England' with 'the largest and most elegant assortment' of plate and plated ware ever imported to the city.[11] In the previous decade, an American goldsmith had advertised in the *South Carolina & American General Gazette* that his goods were as competitively priced as those imported from London and Birmingham, and that he was also prepared to insure his work 'to last double the time'.[12]

There were clear advantages to buying in a goldsmith's shop as opposed to at auction. Shops offered access to bespoke wares, services like maintenance and repair work, and the possibility of good terms of credit. Buyers could specify their exact requirements relative to the design, the weight, and the surface appearance of their goods. Surviving accounts confirm that the maintenance of plate was an important service offered by Dublin goldsmiths' shops. In 1747 Richard Edgeworth (Fig. 3.1) paid a Dublin goldsmith for fixing a handle to a silver mustard pot.[13] Over the next few years he noted further payments for similar tasks like 'mending a silver candlestick', repairing 'the silver saucepan' and fixing a pair of tea tongs.[14] Later in the century, James Stewart of Killymoon, Co. Tyrone, paid the Dublin goldsmith Richard Williams for 'repairing a gold pencil case', as well as a silver salt and waiter.[15] In the same year, Sir Richard Johnston paid Richard D'Olier for 'boiling and burnishing a chased tureen ladle'.[16] Some of the orders placed by Irish clients with London goldsmiths also include references to small repairs and maintenance work. Some customers even added cleaning products to their orders. In 1781, Robert Fowler, Archbishop of Dublin's account with John Wakelin and William Taylor included an impressive array of 'wood brushes', 'bone brushes', 'leather skins', 'plate powder' and 'crocus'.[17] As Helen Clifford has shown, it was rare for individuals to buy large quantities of plate in a single order, which goes some way to explaining why businesses were prepared to accommodate modest repairs and maintenance.[18] It was vital to nurture relationships in this sector of the market. Small jobs could also be settled in ready money, an advantage to any shop.

Buyers of luxury goods expected to enjoy favourable terms of credit, a fundamental advantage to buying from a shop. The business ledgers of the London goldsmiths Parker and Wakelin show that between 1760 and 1776 over half of their clients settled accounts between one to six months, a quarter between six months and a year and a further thirty took up to two years.[19] The ability to judge creditworthiness, to balance the prestige of having elite clients against the possibility of having to deal with slow payment, and to gauge the extent to which clients should be 'rubbed up' – to settle their bills – was also a challenge for retailers in Dublin.[20] In 1729, the economic commentator Arthur Dobbs condemned the practice of some Irish traders abusing their access to credit.[21] He reckoned that the dishonest acquisition of goods from 'industrious traders, without any view or design of payment' was a dreadful ploy to create 'a show of business . . . and blaze a little with a borrowed light'.[22]

Such dishonourable behaviour among merchants may not have been as prevalent in a trade as well respected as the goldsmiths'.[23] Nonetheless, Irish goldsmiths and

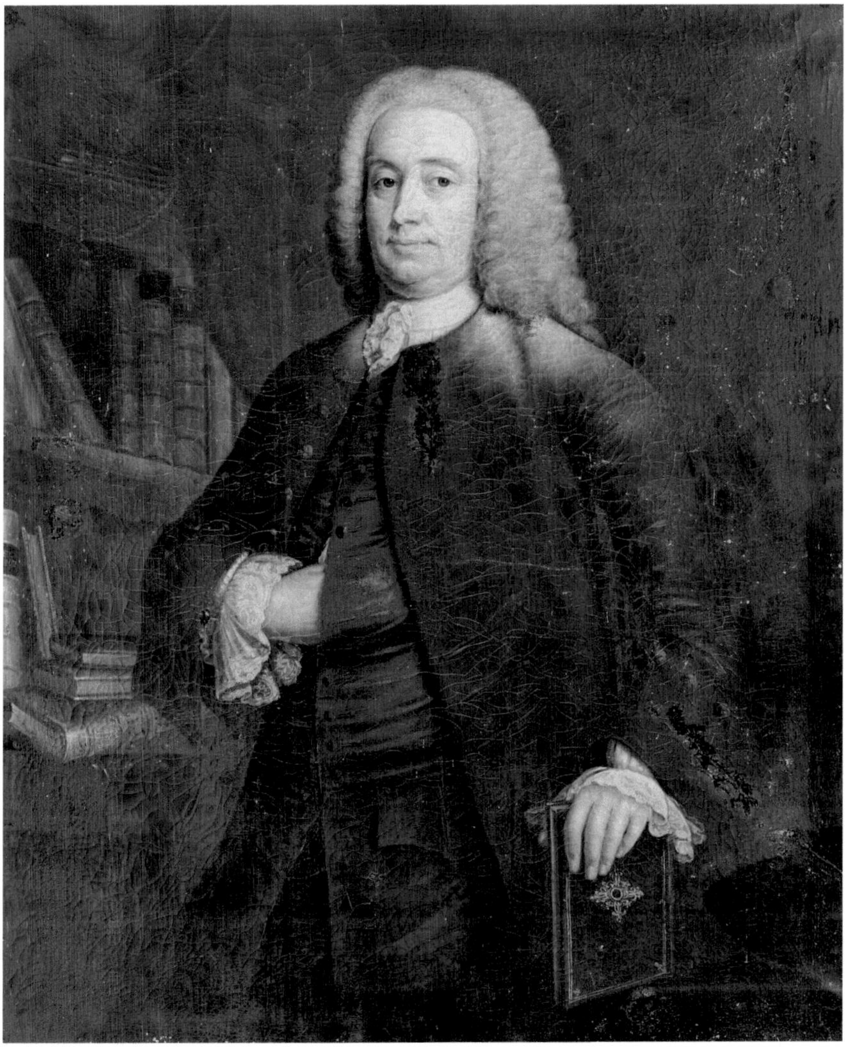

Figure 3.1 Philip Hussey, *Portrait of Richard Edgeworth* (c.1756), oil on canvas, 127 × 102 cm
Source: National Gallery of Ireland, Dublin. Photo credit: © National Gallery of Ireland.

jewellers frequently encountered difficulties when it came to extracting payment. In December 1767 the retired Dublin goldsmith and jeweller Isaac D'Olier placed a notice in *Saunders' News-Letter* requesting that all accounts owing to him should be settled immediately and in full.[24] His business had passed to his sons, Richard and Jeremiah, and he was keen that they should be able to operate with outstanding debts cleared (Fig. 3.2). A year later, he found himself 'under the disagreeable necessity' of having to place a more strongly worded notice, this time threatening to sue those who had not complied or would not do so.[25] D'Olier had made other appeals prior to and after retiring. For him the threat of litigation was a last resort. During the same period,

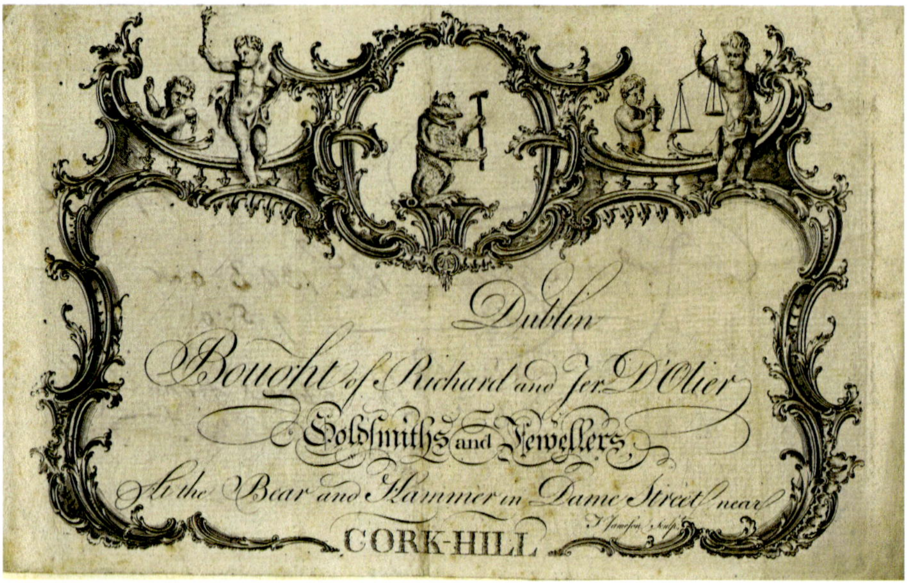

Figure 3.2 Billhead of the goldsmiths Richard and Jeremiah D'Olier (n.d.), engraving
Source: British Museum, London. Photo credit: © The Trustees of the British Museum.

the jeweller Jacob Wile announced his retirement from business. He requested that 'all those indebted to him' settle their accounts immediately, but evidently did not assume that this would be straightforward.[26]

While flexible credit arrangements were expected in goldsmiths' shops, the terms of sale could vary. In 1775, the goldsmith Michael Cormick advertised his intention to sell 'all sorts of jewellers' and goldsmiths' work' at reduced prices 'for ready money'.[27] This may have reflected his personal circumstances, financial standing or the need to realise efficient returns on the sale of imported goods. However, it illustrates a pattern in the second half of the eighteenth century, particularly in the case of goldsmiths' stock that was imported, and not in the most expensive range.[28] In 1763, the jeweller James Holmes had advertised the sale of goods recently imported from London and Birmingham.[29] They included 'a variety of light English plate', including candlesticks, coffee pots, bread and sugar baskets. His stock was on sale 'on the very lowest terms for ready money only'.[30] Matthew Boulton's Soho emporium was prepared to offer Irish clients six months' credit or a 5 per cent reduction on their net order if they paid in ready money.[31] Nevertheless, as his letters make plain, his Dublin agent was charged with reassuring him in relation to his client's character and property. One of the reasons why Boulton ultimately closed the branch of his business that specialised in making silver as opposed to plated goods was the lengthy period of credit that customers expected. As one of his clients put it, 'at least a year's credit was all part of the metropolitan way of doing business.'[32]

Apart from offering a bespoke service, good customer care and variable access to credit, there was a much more obvious reason for visiting goldsmiths' shops. Shopping at this level was a pleasurable and diverting leisure activity. The attentive service in luxury shops was gratifying, and there were close parallels between shopping and the similarly fashionable pursuit of exhibition viewing.[33] A late eighteenth-century English visitor to Dublin described, in a tone of some surprise, his impression of one Dublin glass shop:

> The glass manufacture is also a rising trade in Ireland. Mr Kennedy of Stephen Street is by far the most eminent in this line in Dublin. He is most ingenious as to his business. I was astonished to see his lustres, and could not help remarking the similitude of some shapes to the elegancies in the King of Spain's Museum in Madrid, which were dug from the ruins of Herculaneum. In London, I never saw a happier display of fancy. In short, Mr Kennedy's shop entertained me for an hour – it afforded a treat; and I will confess, I did not expect to meet in this island such models of refined taste and accurate execution.[34]

The reference to being 'entertained' recalls the manner in which a descendant of the goldsmith Robert Calderwood described his shop. His great-grand-niece Sarah Darley recalled how she had heard her father say that 'Calderwood's shop was like White's Coffee House in London, the people would go and sit for an hour and meet' (Fig. 3.3).[35] Towards the end of the eighteenth century, the goldsmith and jeweller William Law responded to the contemporary vogue for exhibition viewing (Fig. 3.4), mirroring the practices of retailers in London and Paris. Alongside his regular stock he advertised the display of 'some of the greatest curiosities from a celebrated museum', one of which was a diamond beetle from the East Indies 'well worth the attention of the curious'.[36]

Auctions

Apart from shops, there was also a lively auction trade in eighteenth-century Ireland, some of which offered opportunities for buying plate.[37] They were held for all sorts of reasons: bankruptcy, a retailer's own decision to quit trade or clear stock, or more usually, death. For the vendor or executor they offered the benefits of a quick sale, exoneration from binding periods of credit and the potential to attract a large and willing audience of prospective buyers. Buyers were seduced by the lure of a bargain, the chance to enjoy a fashionable leisure pursuit and the opportunity to buy objects imbued with additional value, through connections to past owners. As Toby Barnard has shown, 'a willingness to buy what other grandees had discarded' united several Irish patrons with ample means.[38]

In her analysis of English auctions, Cynthia Wall has concluded that auctions could present an ambivalent experience for the fashionable world during this period, by virtue of the broad social milieu to which they appealed.[39] Iain Pears has also indicated that auctions of paintings were popular, not simply on account of the demand for works of art, but because they were part of the social round.[40] They offered, he argues, 'a way in which aristocrats, commoners, traders and even occasionally artisans were brought together in the same room . . . with interest temporarily but significantly erasing social boundaries'.[41] This chance to enjoy what Wall refers to as 'imaginary social mobility' clearly applied in an Irish context too. Lord Charlemont noted an outbreak

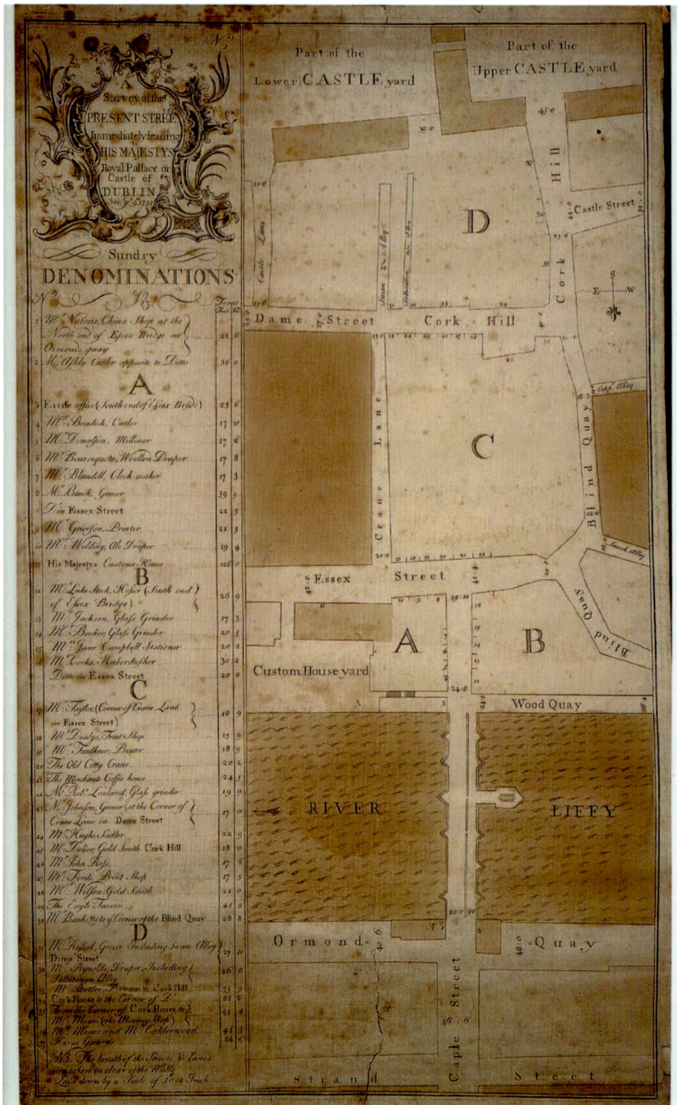

Figure 3.3 A survey of the present streets leading from the Liffey to Dublin Castle, Dublin 1751 (1751), engraving, 63 × 37 cm (Calderwood's shop was located in Zone D)

Source: National Gallery of Ireland, Dublin. Photo credit: © National Gallery of Ireland.

of 'book madness' at the auction of a private library in Dublin in 1792. He wryly observed that 'all men bought, they who could and they who could not read.'[42]

Unquestionably, with auctions, it was a case of 'buyers beware'. Prices could become inflated as bidders vied with one another, and the quality assurances that came with patronising shopkeepers did not usually apply.[43] One Dublin jeweller played on this strategically in his newspaper advertisement. In 1774, Laurence Fowler claimed that

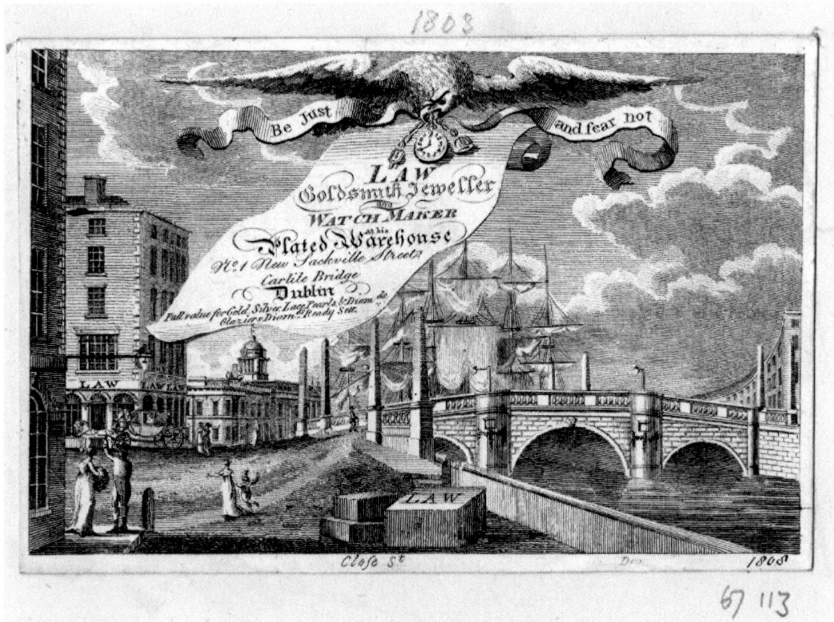

Figure 3.4 Trade card of William Law (late eighteenth/early nineteenth century)

Source: British Museum, London. Photo credit: © The Trustees of the British Museum.

his prices were so good that they could not be surpassed at auction, where, according to him, 'the unwarranted [were] liable to the greatest imposition.'[44] Auctions were not popular with most shopkeepers. Large one-off sales of new goods undermined their trade. Auction houses avoided the provision of credit and were also potential clearing houses for fraudulently acquired goods. In January 1787, the *Hibernian Magazine* warned against 'one of the evils arising from auction-rooms', advising that that gentlemen 'in the mercantile line' could be swindled out of their property 'through the medium of auction rooms', which was 'destructive of that credit so necessary in trade'.[45] The following month, a delegation of Dublin shopkeepers petitioned parliament to express their concern over the increasing number of auctions selling new goods in the city.[46] They claimed that these compromised fair traders, promoted and abetted fraud, and offered outlets for the sale of smuggled goods, while fixed traders, 'lying under heavy duties, rents and taxes', were 'deprived of the ready money sale of their goods and merchandises'.[47]

Unlike other branches of trade, such as the textile industry, or even the ceramic industry, there is no evidence of large consignments of new, imported plate being sold in one-off public sales from Dublin auction rooms.[48] There were, however, plenty of opportunities to buy new and second-hand plate at auctions in the city. In April 1746, the shop goods of the late Susanna Manjoy were auctioned, including 'a large quantity of fashionable plate and jewels, a very curious gold chased snuff box with agate top' and a quantity of toys.[49] An auction in 1759, of the effects of Dublin retailer Charles Leslie (Fig. 3.5), advertised the sale of his household furniture and stock-in-trade from

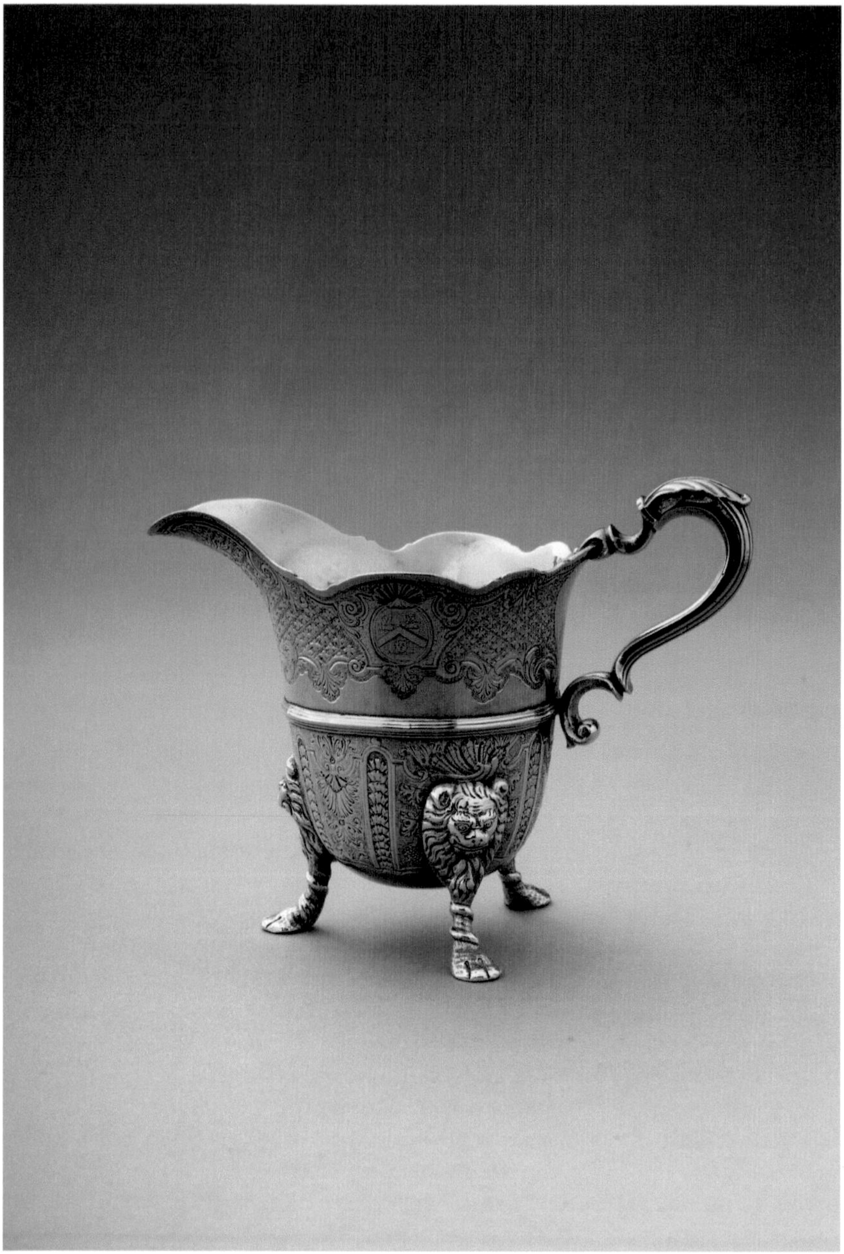

Figure 3.5 Charles Leslie, *Cream jug* (c.1740), silver, 12.1 × 15.2 cm

Source: San Antonio Museum of Art, Texas. Bequest of John V. Rowan Jr, 2004.12.233. Photo credit: © Courtesy of the San Antonio Museum of Art. Photography by Peggy Tenison.

his Castle Street shop.[50] Leslie is believed to have trained in Scotland before settling in Ireland and becoming a freeman, warden, and eventually master of the Dublin goldsmiths' guild.[51] Described as 'a lace man and goldsmith', he had a shop at the heart of the trade's activities, close to the goldsmiths' guildhall and parish church of St Werburgh.

Clearly, the location of an auction had a bearing on its success. When the stock of jeweller Robert Forster was auctioned in the mid-eighteenth century, the sale was held at the guildhall.[52] As the site of the assay office and a central meeting point for goldsmiths, it was an excellent location where his goods were likely to be viewed and bought not just by private patrons, but also by contemporaries within the trade.[53]

For merchants who wanted to quit trade or clear stock, an auction was an efficient way to facilitate the process. In 1769, Henry Dobson organised a sale of the stock-in-trade of goldsmith and jeweller Robert Holmes.[54] Holmes, who was 'determined to retire from business', also offered for sale his household furniture and lease.[55] Six years later, Thomas Atkinson signalled his intention 'to quit the goldsmith, jeweller and toy business for the greater convenience of carrying on the watch- and clock-making trade more extensively'.[56] The apprenticeship records of the Dublin goldsmiths' guild reveal that Atkinson, the son of a Limerick merchant, had been bound to the watchmaker Thomas Johnston in 1753.[57] Evidently he had been acting as a more wide-ranging retailer prior to 1775.[58]

In other cases, non-payment of debts or, at worst, bankruptcy, forced retailers to sell up. The shopkeeper Joel Woolf, who was active in the second half of the century, had his goods auctioned in 1784 when he failed to meet his rent bill.[59] The items auctioned from his shop came mainly under the category of small-scale fancy goods and included watches, jewellery and canes. Woolf also responded to topical fashions. In 1784, when his stock was advertised for sale, it included 'balloon pins'.[60] The first recorded balloon ascent in Ireland was attempted just a few months later.[61]

As previously observed, their efficacy as a medium of sale, and the possibility of wooing a crowd, were two of the most appealing attractions of auctions to any potential vendor. A number of advertisements for them refer not only to the great variety of goods on sale, but also stratify them, to suggest a range of different price categories, and appeal to as wide an audience as possible. When the assignees of Hugh Henry Mitchell auctioned the contents of his Dublin home in 1778, plate was clearly a core part of the sale.[62] Described as 'highly chased and in the present taste', it comprised 2,000 oz. in total.[63] While items like the épergne, tea and coffee pots and salvers would have been expensive even second-hand, a selection of spoons and some silver-plated cutlery were also mentioned in the notice. Mitchell had been involved in the remittance business, acting as a receiver for landlords.[64] His clients included wealthy absentees and this form of banking activity had enabled him to assemble a handsome collection of luxury goods. The failure of his business in 1778 resulted in the dispersal of his plate at auction. The reference to 'highly chased' plate also suggests the rococo rather than neoclassical style, so that the auctioneers' claim that it was 'in the present taste' could be taken with a grain of salt.[65]

Lotteries

Occasionally, lotteries offered chances for acquiring plate and jewellery. The sale of goods in precious metals and other luxuries by lottery was well established in London by the 1730s; the London goldsmith Henry Jernegan offered a magnificent silver wine cooler as a lottery prize in 1737 after he had been spectacularly let down by the client who commissioned it.[66] Like auctions, lotteries vexed shopkeepers. In September 1767, the minutes of the Dublin goldsmiths' guild recorded its members' concern regarding a scheme for carrying on a lottery in the city.[67] Many of the prizes were 'to be paid in various goods in the jewellers' and goldsmiths' way'.[68] According to the guild, members of the public would be 'greatly imposed upon' and 'those of the trade injured' if the scheme were to go ahead.[69] This incident was not unique. In 1771, a similar case was noted in guild minutes.[70] This time 'a lottery for the disposal of jewellery, hardware and other valuable goods grafted on the English scheme' was debated. Similar reservations were articulated, and the master warden was asked to put a stop to it. Apparently, he was successful; the organiser agreed that the scheme would not proceed.[71] Three years later, a lottery again raised problems for the guild.[72] On this occasion the prizes included plate.[73]

Also in 1774, the British entrepreneur and jeweller James Cox brought his celebrated 'museum' of automata and jewellers' work to Dublin (Fig. 3.6).[74] Although he had already mounted a display in London, Cox produced a separate catalogue for the Dublin viewing, which was a scaled-down version of the London show. Not only did he state (rather pointedly) in the catalogue that he had encouraged 'the genius of capital workmen from Ireland' over thirty decades in trade, but also that several of those Irishmen had been directly employed in the manufacture of the items on display.[75] Clearly, he was sensitive to the local climate, and the potential for local opposition. For a British crown one could enjoy 'the sight only', while a lottery ticket, offering the chance to win some of the pieces on view, could be bought for a guinea and a half.[76] The objects in the Dublin show represented a triumph of the jeweller's art. They included 'a chariot made of gold and enamelled', 'a buffalo made of molten copper' with an internal mechanism and 'a richly caparisoned elephant'.[77]

Evidently, the lottery format appealed to some Irish retailers. Though cash prizes were the staple of most lotteries, items as diverse as books, looking glasses and even negligees were occasionally sold in this way in eighteenth-century Ireland.[78] Two schemes for the sale of plate by lottery were organised in the southeast of Ireland in 1774.[79] Henry Hatchell, a Wexford goldsmith, was responsible for 'The Wexford Scheme for the Sale of Plate by Lottery'. The value of prizes offered in his scheme was £510. The odds of securing a prize were roughly five to one; 1,057 prizes were on offer with ticket sales in the region of 5,100. While the prize money in eighteenth-century lotteries could run to thousands of pounds, the top prize on this occasion was valued at £25.[80] An itemised prize list dwindled in value, from candlesticks and quart cups to buttons and hairpins for the final tickets drawn.[81] A second plate lottery, organised in Co. Kilkenny in 1774, cost 2s 2d to enter.[82] While multiple prizes were on offer, in reality, a 'plain gold brooch' or a pair of plated spurs was a much more likely prospect than the candlesticks, or coffee pot which acted as a lure.[83]

Contemporary tales satirised the lure of the lottery.[84] In Maria Edgeworth's *Popular Tales*, a former servant with upwardly mobile aspirations squanders a share in lottery profits in a hopeless attempt to acquire gentility.[85] In typical Hogarthian manner, her downfall is inevitable and the things that she had coveted become symbols of her ruin. Having run up debts and squandered her money, she laments towards the end of the story that her broken china teapot and silver spoons (symbols of the lifestyle she aspired to) have not yet been paid for.[86] The lottery format had sufficiently entered the

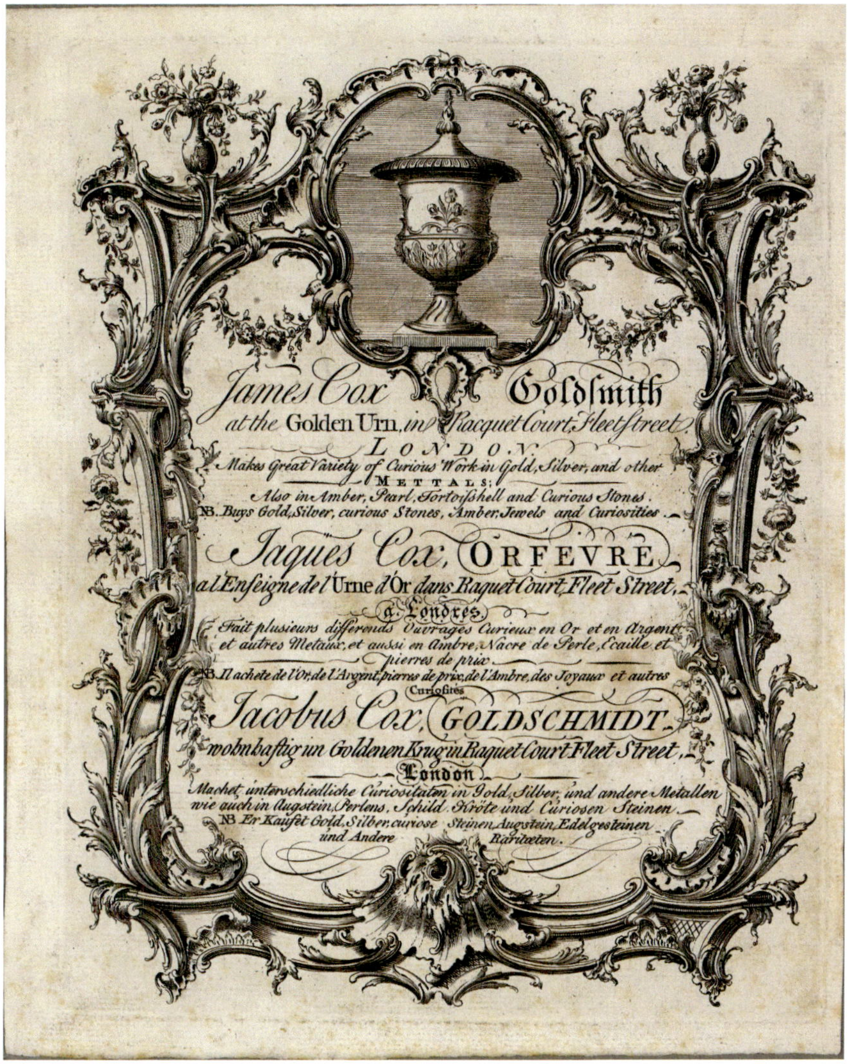

Figure 3.6 Trade card of James Cox (c.1750), engraving

Source: British Museum, London. Photo credit: © The Trustees of the British Museum.

cultural imagination by the late eighteenth century for a farce entitled *Lottery Prize* to be performed at the Theatres Royal in London and in Dublin.[87]

The demand for imported plate

From the early decades of the century, writers like Jonathan Swift and Thomas Prior decried the Irish appetite for English luxury goods, particularly the economic repercussion of such an appetite.[88] Eighteenth-century Dublin was far from anti-metropolitan in outlook; its elite was more predisposed to imitate London rather than challenge it in matters of taste and fashion. Dublin, it appears, was a deeply divided capital. David Dickson identifies a marked split between what he characterises in London terms as 'the West End culture of the gentry and parliament, and the mercantile/artisanal world of the majority of the city'.[89] In 1748, Laetitia Pilkington wrote, 'London has very attractive charms for most people, as our Irish nobility and gentry sufficiently evidence, by spending the greatest part of their time and fortune there.'[90] Just over two decades later Josiah Wedgwood (Fig. 3.7) asked the question, 'Will not the people of Ireland like these things better that come from London? A certain degree of difficulty in coming at fine things may excite, increase and keep up the attention to, and appetite

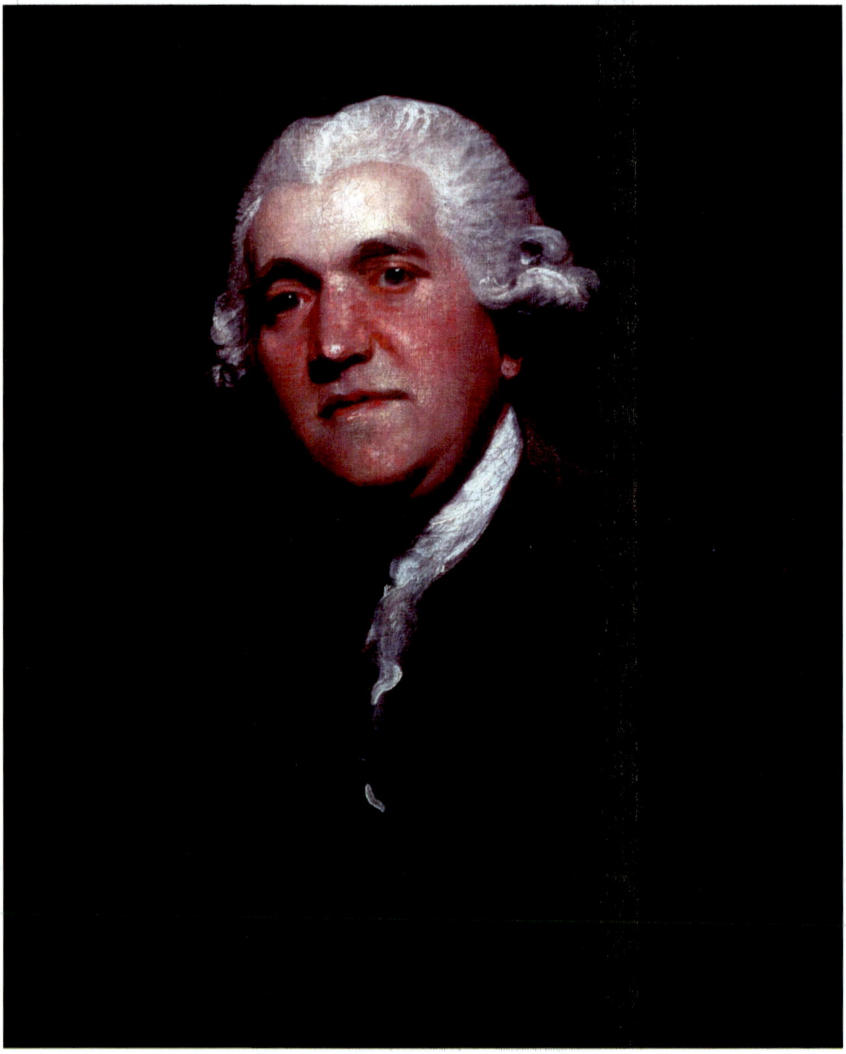

Figure 3.7 Joshua Reynolds, *Portrait of Josiah Wedgwood* (1782), oil on canvas, 108.5 × 96 cm

Source: Wedgwood Museum, Stoke-on-Trent. Wedgwood Collection. Presented by the Art Fund with major support from the Heritage Lottery Fund, private donations and a public appeal. Photo credit: © WWRD.

for them.'[91] Clearly, he, like Boulton and other British entrepreneurs, saw the potential Ireland offered for expanding the market for their products.

Irish clients wishing to buy English goods had a number of options. They could order from Britain directly, use contacts on the ground, or patronise Irish retailers who sold imported wares. In 1759, the beleaguered Earl of Kildare wrote from England to his wife in Ireland about an extravagant order that she had placed for 150 yards of India taffeta. He protested, 'I really am so loaded with things, not only for you but others, that I don't know what to do, or how I shall get them ashore in Ireland.'[92] His own silver dinner service had been ordered in London during the previous decade at a cost in excess of £4,000 (Fig. 3.8).[93]

For Irish patrons adding to existing family plate, it could prove easier and possibly less expensive to commission local goldsmiths to make copies of items already

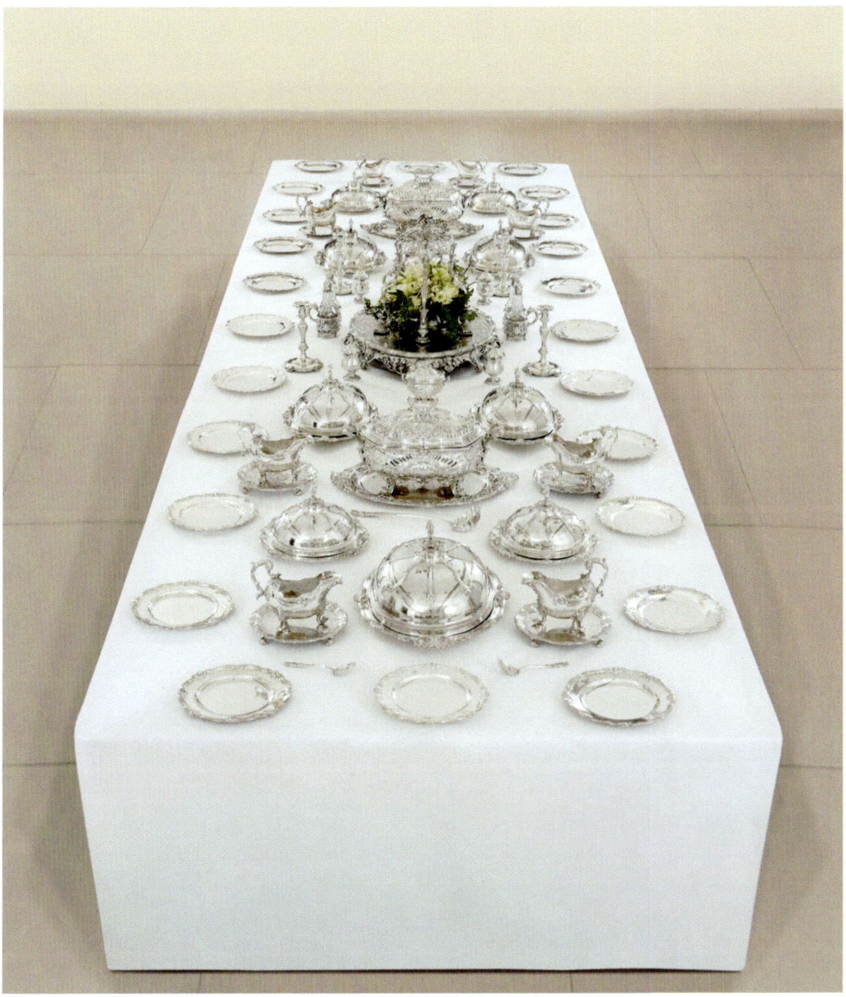

Figure 3.8 George Wickes, *Part of the Leinster dinner service* (London, 1745–47)
Source: Private collection. Photo credit: © Christie's Images.

owned. A set of candlesticks in the Ashmolean Museum Oxford, marked by Robert Calderwood and engraved with the arms of Bishop Henry Maxwell, are virtually indistinguishable from a pair in the same collection, marked by the London goldsmith George Wickes and engraved with the arms of Maxwell's father John Maxwell, later Baron Farnham (Fig. 3.9).[94]

Customs records reveal the profile of plate exports from England to Ireland (Fig. 3.10). During the first decade of the century, demand for British plate was negligible. Louis Cullen has observed that high transport costs during this period acted as a restrictive influence on Europe's trade in manufactured goods, and encouraged self-sufficiency even in the sector of industrial goods.[95] However, plate was such a valuable commodity that patrons could generally absorb transport costs. More significant is the fact that

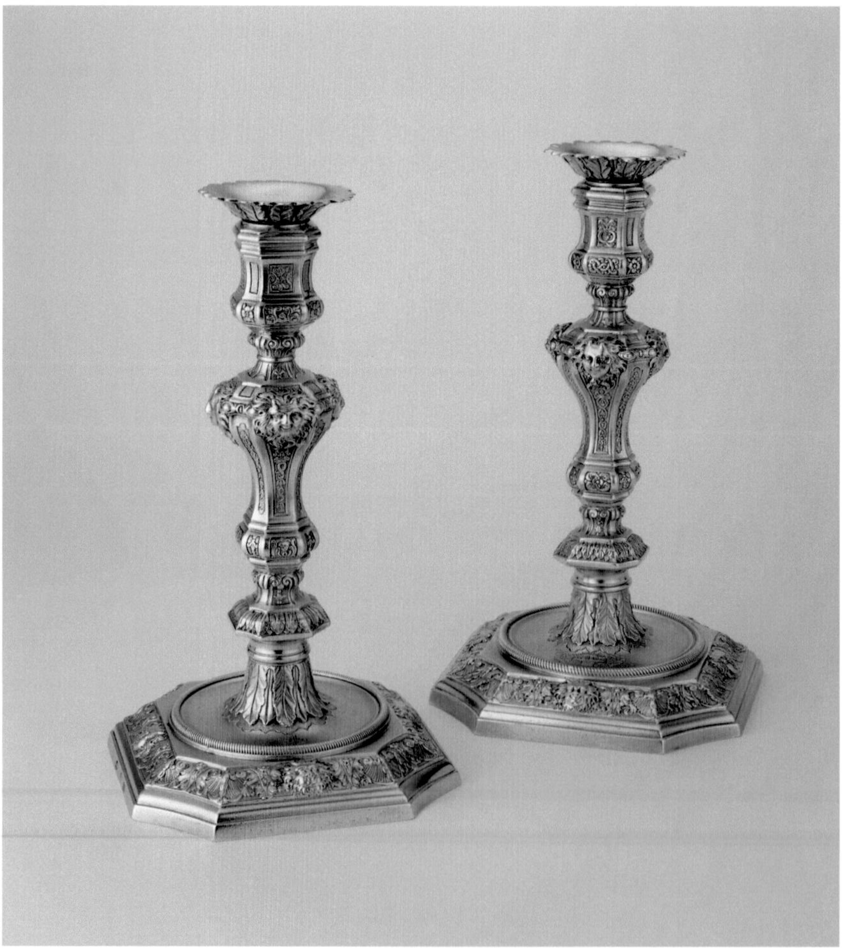

Figure 3.9 Left: George Wickes, *Candlestick* (London, 1742–43), silver, one of a pair, 24.4 and 25.8 cm (h). Right: Robert Calderwood, *Candlestick* (Dublin, c.1759), silver, one of eight measuring 23.8–25.4 cm (h)

Photo credit: © Ashmolean Museum, University of Oxford.

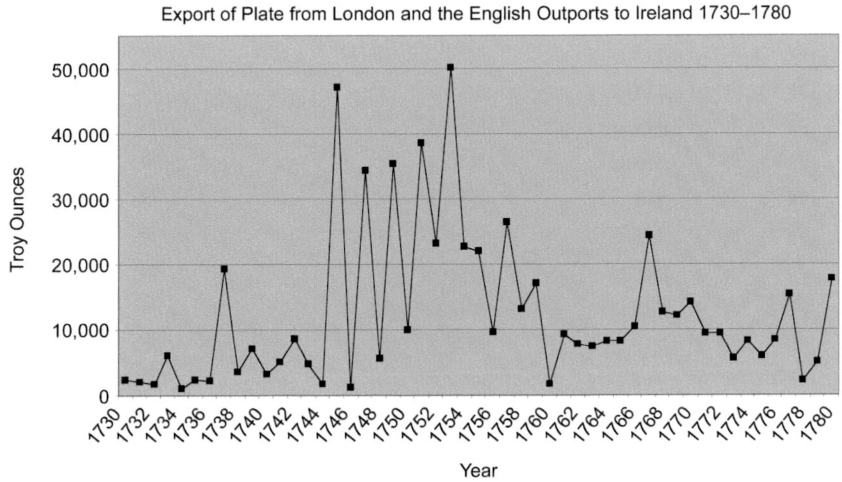

Figure 3.10 Statistics for the export of plate from London and the Outports to Ireland, 1730–1780

Source: Ledgers of Imports and Exports from London and the Outports, 1697 to 1780, CUST3, National Archives, Kew.

Ireland experienced a period of economic depression during the opening decade of the century, with an acute decline in domestic income from 1702. This inevitably lessened the demand for manufactured goods.[96] Nonetheless, Irish goldsmiths still managed to produce combined yearly averages often in excess of 40,000 oz. during this period.[97]

In keeping with the previous two decades, the quantity of plate imported during the 1720s was still very modest. Ironically, the highest annual total by a considerable margin was recorded for 1728 to 1729, a period of harvest devastation leading to famine in Ireland. In this year the cumulative total was 8,522 oz., 9 dwt. At any time, the movement of a large dinner service could boost the figures substantially, and this needs to be taken into consideration when interpreting the data. For example, in 1729 *Faulkner's Dublin Journal* announced that Sir Gustavus Hume had 'entered 7,000 ounces of silver plate for Ireland'.[98] The writer hoped that other members of Ireland's nobility and gentry, who spent 'so much money abroad', would emulate Hume's good example.[99] This was in a period when the economic climate in Ireland had prompted the publication of Thomas Prior's *List of Absentees*.[100]

The first really substantial figure for imported plate was recorded for 1736–37. A total of close to 20,000 oz. in that year coincided with a period of remarkable expansion in the linen industry. Cullen has observed that the growth in the linen trade between 1730 to 1731 and 1733 to 1735 was, with the exception of the late 1780s and early 1790s, the most rapid in its history.[101] From an assessment of the customs data, it appears that the boom period for English plate exports to Ireland was during the years between the mid-1740s to c.1760.[102] A particularly striking statistic is provided by the quantity for 1744–45, which was, at over 47,000 oz., a vastly higher total than any of the preceding years. Over the course of the eighteenth century there were certainly many years when plate imports were not particularly significant,

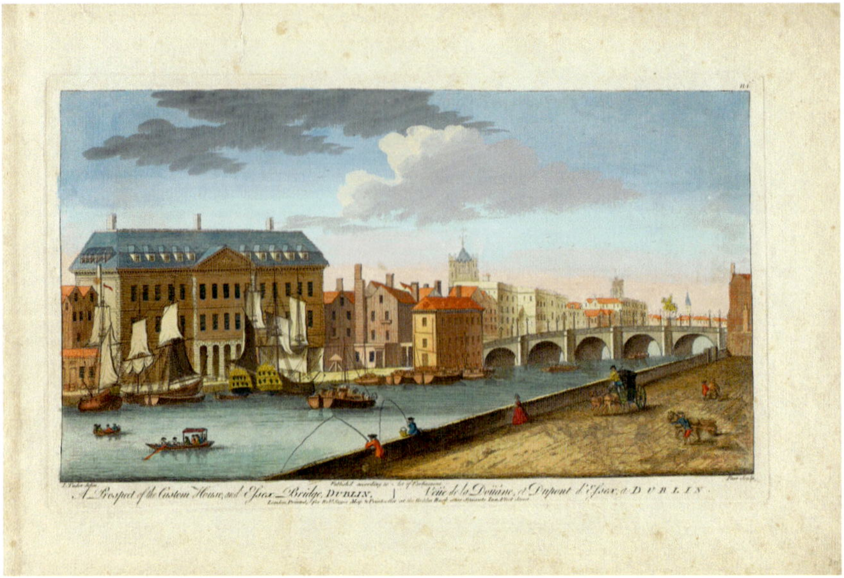

Figure 3.11 After Joseph Tudor, *A prospect of the Custom House, and Essex Bridge, Dublin* (c.1750), engraving

Source: Lewis Walpole Library, Yale University, New Haven. Photo credit: © Courtesy of the Lewis Walpole Library, Yale University.

and there were clear fluctuations, but this period yields a series of remarkable statistics. For example, the peak of over 50,000 oz. in 1752 to 1753 corresponds with approximately 80 per cent of the total volume of plate going through the Dublin assay office that year.[103] This demonstrates unequivocally the impact which British imports could have upon the Dublin goldsmiths' trade (Fig. 3.11).

But how can these statistics be understood in terms of individual consumption? In an assessment of the role of the Royal Jewel House in the eighteenth century, James Lomax has noted that its principal expense during this period was the traditional practice of supplying plate to the King's ambassadors, envoys and principal officials. The largest allocation was given to ambassadors, who were entitled to 5,893 oz. of white plate and 1,066 oz. of gilt each.[104] If roughly 7,000 oz. was considered an appropriate allocation for the King's leading ambassadors abroad, then the significance of these mid-century import totals for Ireland becomes clearer. A variety of economic and stylistic factors help to account for the weighty volumes of plate imported into Ireland during this period.

During the late 1740s and early 1750s, the economy experienced a period of remarkable growth, accompanied by expansion in banking and credit facilities.[105] This must have facilitated those wishing to order from England. Louis Cullen also notes higher levels of expenditure at this time, which he links with an improvement in living standards, a factor certainly consistent with the evidence from the customs ledgers. Apart from economic determinants, prevailing fashions may also help to explain why the volumes of plate exported to Ireland were higher in the middle than in the later part of the century. The rococo style, with its emphasis on highly decorated, elaborately chased, weighty silver, was fashionable mid-century when the largest quotas were recorded. The fine rococo dinner service ordered by the Earl of Kildare from George Wickes in 1745 was the height of fashion and certainly made a stir in Irish circles. The memoirs of the English dramatist, Samuel Foote, for example, describe the experience of a gala dinner there as like dining 'in a silversmith's shop'.[106]

As chapter 2 confirmed, the technology for flatting plate was well established in England by the mid-eighteenth century. By the time that neoclassicism was widespread in the second half of the century, techniques like die stamping and mechanised flatting were not only available but also ideally suited to the more regular, symmetrical forms of a revived antique style. The fact that neoclassical forms lent themselves to translation in lighter gauge silver is significant in the light of the customs data.[107] While plate export volumes declined in the second half of the century, this does not necessarily mean that the number of objects imported immediately declined too, simply that their combined weights were lighter, a factor which likely reflects evolving technology and taste. Even after 1780, exports of plate from England to Ireland in individual years could be quite significant: 22,850 oz. of plate were recorded in 1783. Nevertheless, there is no doubt that plated wares brought a new dimension to the competition in the latter decades of the century, which unquestionably had a bearing on the reduced volumes of plate exported from London and the English outports.[108]

While customs records show broad trends, the ledgers of London retailers like George Wickes and Samuel Netherton, or their successors John Parker and Edward Wakelin, reveal a significant amount regarding the identity of Irish clients, the nature of the objects they were buying, and the amounts that they were prepared to spend. Although the Leinster dinner service has been quite well documented, other noteworthy Irish names appear in the Garrard ledgers over the course of the eighteenth century.[109] These include nouveau riche clients with mercantile or political interests like Joseph Leeson and Nathaniel Clements; prosperous Church of Ireland clergymen like Edward Synge, Bishop of Elphin; and members of the aristocracy like Sir Thomas Prendergast.[110] In 1742, as previously mentioned, Joseph Leeson (Fig. 3.12) placed a significant order with George Wickes, which he supplemented in the following year.[111]

The plate that Leeson ordered from Wickes in 1742 certainly constituted the makings of an impressive silver dinner service.[112] Two weighty tureens and covers, a cistern, and smaller items like salts and cruets, complemented six dozen silver plates.[113] An épergne (Fig. 3.13) costing over £350 represented a lavish centrepiece and a focal point for the dessert course. Wickes also supplied some glass items, including 'cut cruets' and 'mustard glasses'.[114] Leeson's lordly manner of living is further confirmed by his purchase of a chased tea table in 1743.[115] The fact that he settled his accounts in cash on both occasions, rather than trading in old plate, confirms his ample resources. It is also indicative of his comparative youth.[116] The design of Leeson's tureen was copied a decade later by the Dublin goldsmith Thomas Walker (Fig. 3.14), reminding one of how three-dimensional objects as well as print sources assisted the dissemination of designs.[117]

Between 1752 and 1758, the Irish baronet Sir Thomas Prendergast ordered a series of silver items from Wickes. From 1733 until his death in 1760, Prendergast served as MP for Clonmel. His decision to order plate from London is not surprising, given his early aspirations to forge a political career in England. The Duchess of Richmond, a niece of his wife, had returned him for Chichester in 1733, but his career in the British

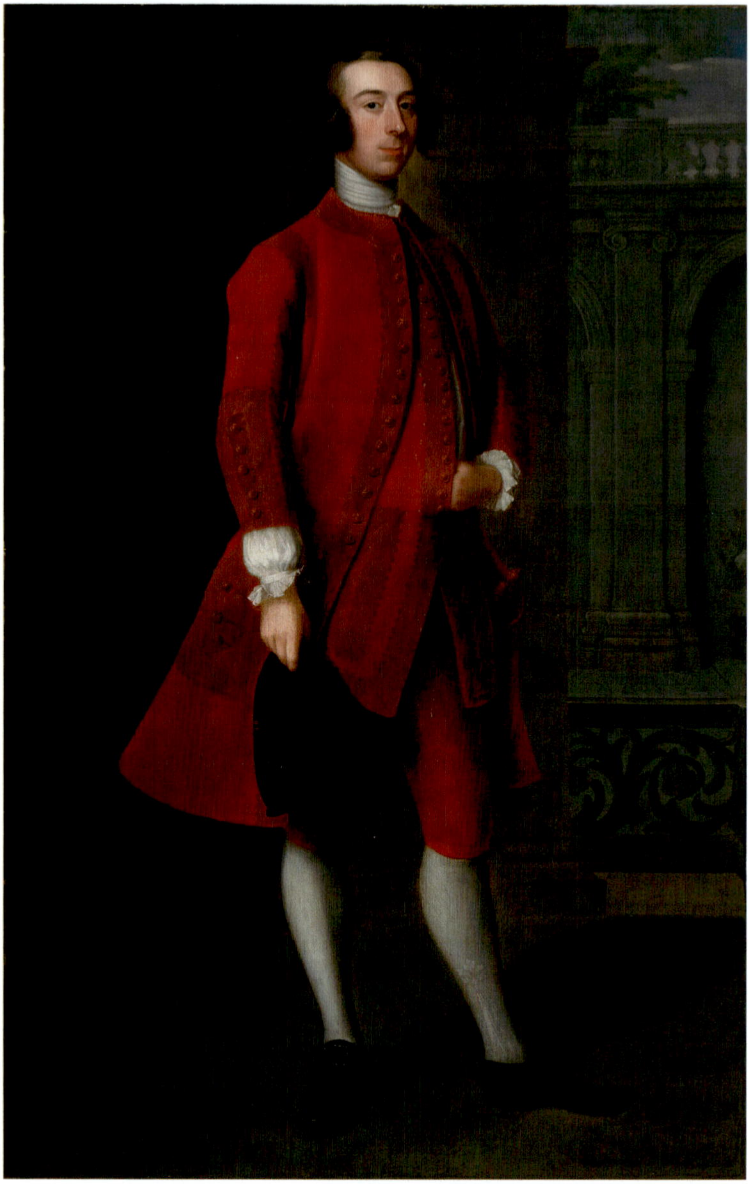

Figure 3.12 Anthony Lee, *Portrait of Joseph Leeson, later first Earl of Milltown* (1735), oil on canvas, 197 × 122 cm

Source: National Gallery of Ireland, Dublin. Photo credit: © National Gallery of Ireland.

parliament was short-lived, and he was not returned the following year.[118] Rather than ordering an extensive dinner service in a single order as Leeson had done, Prendergast was somewhat more typical in ordering plate piecemeal. He added to his plate as his circumstances and finances allowed.[119] In 1754, the year he was appointed Governor

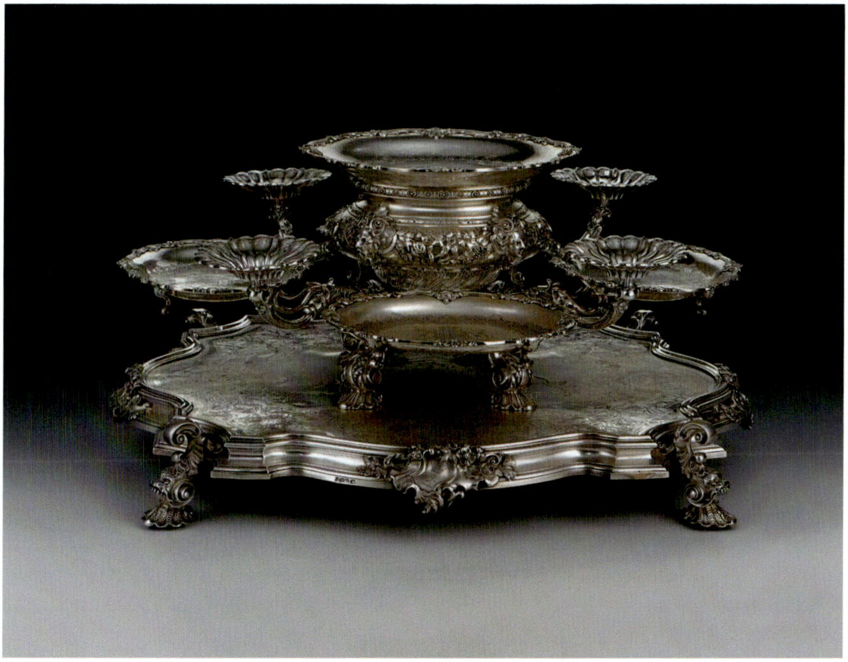

Figure 3.13 George Wickes, *Épergne and stand* (London, 1742–43), silver, 36.8 × 69.9 cm. This impressive centrepiece formed part of the plate ordered by Joseph Leeson from Wickes.

Source: Colonial Williamsburg, Virginia. The Mary Stewart Gaiser Collection. Photo credit: © Courtesy of the Colonial Williamsburg Foundation.

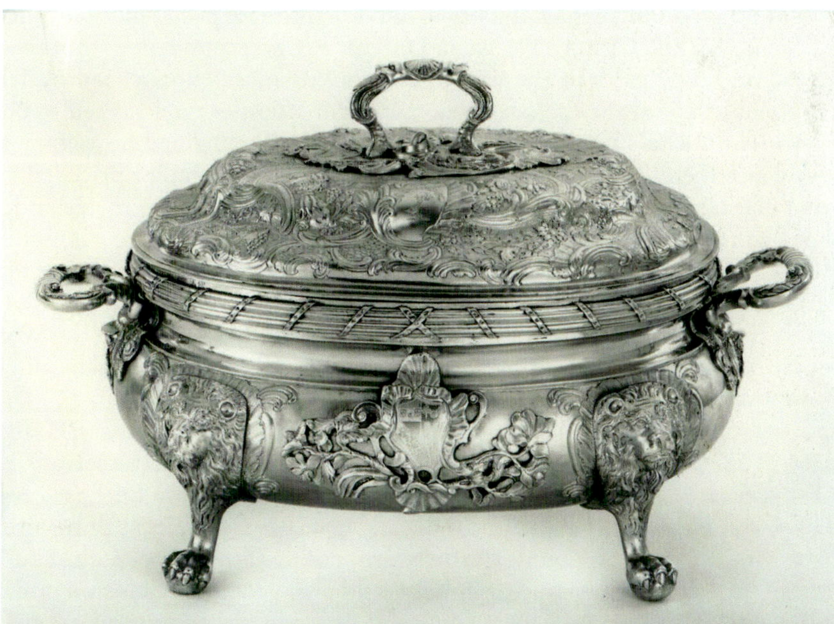

Figure 3.14 Thomas Walker, *Soup tureen and cover* (1751), silver, 26.67 × 50.8 cm

Source: National Museum of Ireland, Dublin. Photo credit: © National Museum of Ireland.

of Galway, he ordered a series of items, including nine dishes and forty-eight plates.[120] His dining plate was supplemented in 1759.[121] The posthumous auction of his possessions included upwards of '4,000 ounces of curious wrought and plain plate', at least some of which must have come from Wickes.[122] Unlike Leeson, Prendergast did trade in used plate on occasion.[123] He was also obliged to pay interest on an outstanding account. There is some irony in the fact that he was a founder member of the Dublin Society, established in 1731 to promote native industry and manufactures, but he was not unique in promoting Irish industry while favouring English goldsmiths with substantial orders. Earlier in the century, Thomas Prior had emphasised the nation's obligation to 'those lords and gentlemen, who constantly live and spend their fortunes among us'.[124] Singled out for particular praise was the Earl of Kildare who, as shown, was one of Wickes' most significant Irish clients.

When the Bishop of Elphin ordered silver from George Wickes in 1759, clerical modesty was clearly not his guiding principle.[125] An épergne with a basin, four saucers, four baskets and eight branches cost him over £100 and were accompanied by two tureens and dishes, bringing his total account to over £200.[126] By the time that Robert Fowler, Archbishop of Dublin, came to order plate in 1781, John Wakelin and William Taylor were managing the firm. He ordered items for a dinner service at a cost of almost £1,000, and settled his account in cash.[127]

Regardless of the appetite for English goods like silverware and Sheffield plate in eighteenth-century Ireland, those who did choose to order from London faced a number of difficulties. This was a factor which evidently influenced Wedgwood in his decision to open a Dublin outlet for his ceramics. He was aware of the 'difficulties, risks, and disagreeable circumstances' which 'a gentleman in Dublin must submit to' in procuring a set of his vases.[128] These included troubling a friend in London, trusting the taste of another, doubts regarding price, and the ultimate possibility that the goods could be forfeited at the Custom House in Dublin.[129] Correspondence from the Derby porcelain factory also refers to the cost and inconveniences experienced by Irish clients. In September 1786, the factory owner William Duesbury was asked to consider offering two Irish dealers preferential terms.[130] His clerk explained how 'they always site very low and there is no doing business with them at the regular price.'[131] He also argued that they faced 'great expenses in getting the goods over' to Ireland, citing customs duties and related costs as validation for the discount.[132] The suggestion that Irish ceramic dealers were trying to cut costs is emphasised by a second letter from the same year. Referring to an Irish dealer who had visited the factory, offered low prices, and then left empty-handed, the clerk explained, 'they all of them go to the Worcester and Salopian Warehouses and buy goods unfinished and then have them gilt, which makes it impossible to do any business with them.'[133]

Inevitably, goods were smuggled, queried at customs and, in some cases, confiscated. In February 1758, the minutes of the Irish Customs Board recorded the seizure of china cups and saucers in Castletownshend, Co. Cork. They were from an East India ship and had been concealed in a basket of candles.[134] In 1782, eight pieces of furniture, the property of Mrs Butler of Kilkenny Castle, were seized, because a captain had landed them without invoices.[135] The issue of duties could also generate confusion and delays. In 1780, the case of a Mr Donovan of Cork was noted in the minutes of the Irish Customs Board.[136] He had left the city four years previously and claimed to have brought with him some old family plate. On his return, his silver was detained, and the customs officers insisted that he should pay duty 'as if he [had] imported it from England'.[137]

As good as new? Demand for second-hand silverware[138]

A final subject worth considering is the significance of the trade in second-hand plate. It is generally understood that goldsmiths in Dublin and in London relied on the flow of used plate through their businesses. The fact that this branch of commercial activity cannot be definitively quantified partly explains why it has received so little attention in the literature. The significance of second-hand markets in the consumer culture of early modern Europe generally is increasingly being acknowledged.[139] David Mitchell has suggested that the modest growth in plate assayed in late seventeenth-century London may indicate that 'wider ownership of plate was linked to an enlarged second-hand market.'[140] The trade in used silverware was sufficiently extensive in mid-eighteenth century London for an appraiser to be published as a pocket guide for brokers.[141] A magnificent silver cistern and fountain (Fig. 3.15) marked by the London goldsmith David Willaume (I), and believed to have been supplied in 1707 to Chambre Brabazon, fifth Earl of Meath, was later bought by George Augustus, Prince of Wales (crowned George II in 1727).[142] In an analysis of middle-rank consumers and domestic culture in Scotland between 1720 and 1840, Stana Nenadic concludes that, even in large prosperous cities like Edinburgh and Glasgow, second-hand markets and recycling operated on a vast scale, and impacted on both rich and poor.[143] However, the goldsmiths' trade represents a unique case, not simply because there was a clear and calculable value placed on their raw materials, but also because, paradoxically, it was a trade that ultimately depended on connotations of exclusivity. As already mentioned, Stafford Briscoe was unusual among London goldsmiths of this period, for boldly advertising a specialisation in used goods (Fig. 3.16).[144] He succeeded in attracting some Irish clients to his shop in London's Cheapside.[145]

The commerce in used plate benefited buyers and sellers in Dublin too. Dublin goldsmiths used the sale of second-hand plate to profit on items that had been traded in in the course of business but were too good to melt.[146] Contemporary correspondence and accounts indicate that some customers were prepared to prioritise economy over fashion, and that others bought second-hand at auction for reasons of sentiment as much as for cost. When plate was traded in, it was reasonable that goldsmiths would compensate the client for its melt value.[147] Nevertheless, *The Compleat Appraiser*, published in London in 1757, advised brokers that if objects were 'wrought after an uncommon neat fashion, and not very much abused', they might be worth more.[148] When Sir Thomas Prendergast ordered plate in London in 1754, one of the items that he purchased was 'an old embossed cup'.[149] Prendergast was charged 6s 2d per oz. for this piece, in a year when the market price for sterling bars was just above 5s 6d per oz.[150] Two years earlier, he had traded in some of his old plate with the same firm, but had received significantly lower rates.[151] Retailers were obliged to estimate how much above the bullion price they could offer, whether the goods should be melted or resold, and what professional markups were viable. The fact that tiered price structures were also the norm in Dublin is borne out by an advertisement from 1777. James Manly, at the Golden Eagle in Dame Street, offered prices of between 5s 8d and 6s 6d per oz. 'for second-hand touched plate, in proportion to the fashion and usage of each article' (Fig. 3.17).[152]

There is no doubt that competitive pricing encouraged the trade in second-hand goods. At the beginning of the eighteenth century, William King, Archbishop of Dublin (Fig. 3.18), wrote to his friend Lady Beresford in London regarding the acquisition of

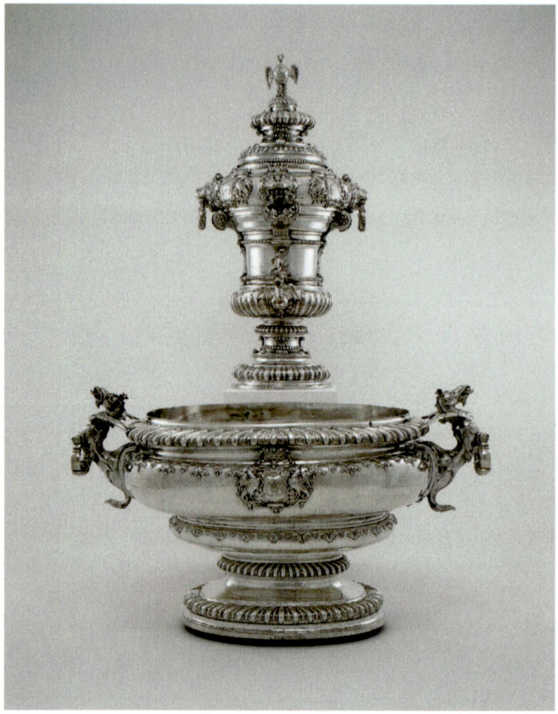

Figure 3.15 David Willaume I, *Cistern and fountain* (1708–9), silver, 66.04 × 114.3 cm (cistern)

Source: Museum of Fine Arts, Boston. Museum purchase with funds donated anonymously, Theodora Wilbour Fund in memory of Charlotte Beebe Wilbour, Harriet J. Bradbury Fund, and other funds by exchange 1999.98.1 & 1999.98.2a–b. Photo credit: © Museum of Fine Arts, Boston.

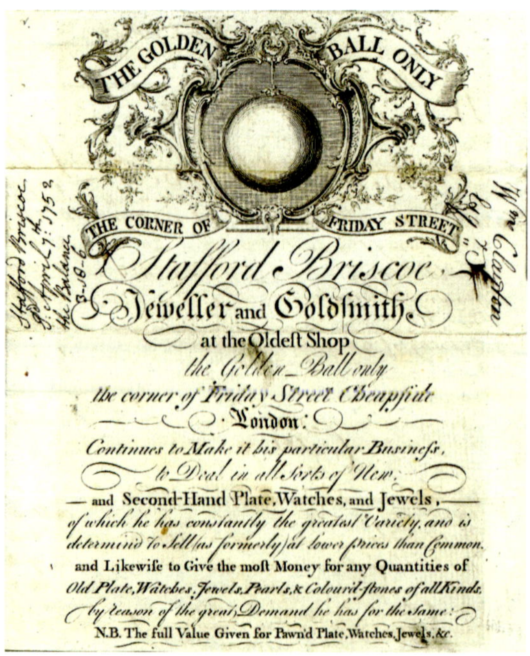

Figure 3.16 Billhead of Stafford Briscoe (mid-eighteenth century), engraving

Source: British Museum, London. Photo credit: © The Trustees of the British Museum.

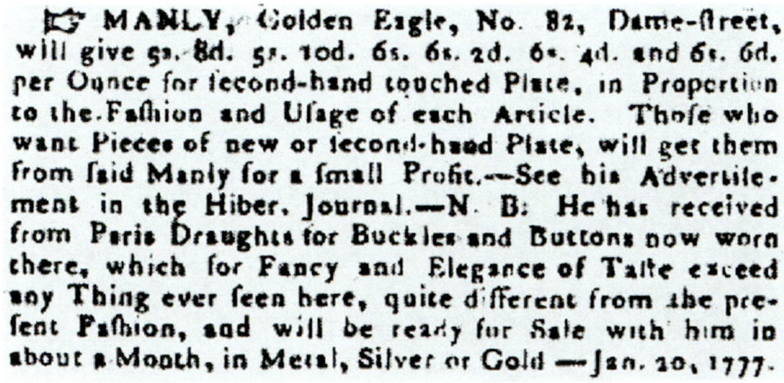

☞ MANLY, Golden Eagle, No. 82, Dame-ſtreet, will give 5s. 8d. 5s. 10d. 6s. 6s. 2d. 6s. 4d. and 6s. 6d. per Ounce for ſecond-hand touched Plate, in Proportion to the Faſhion and Uſage of each Article. Thoſe who want Pieces of new or ſecond-hand Plate, will get them from ſaid Manly for a ſmall Profit.—See his Advertiſement in the Hiber. Journal.—N. B. He has received from Paris Draughts for Buckles and Buttons now worn there, which for Fancy and Elegance of Taſte exceed any Thing ever ſeen here, quite different from the preſent Faſhion, and will be ready for Sale with him in about a Month, in Metal, Silver or Gold.—Jan. 20, 1777.

Figure 3.17 Advertisement for James Manly (Manley) (21 March 1777), *Saunders' News-Letter*

Source: National Library of Ireland. Photo credit: © National Library of Ireland.

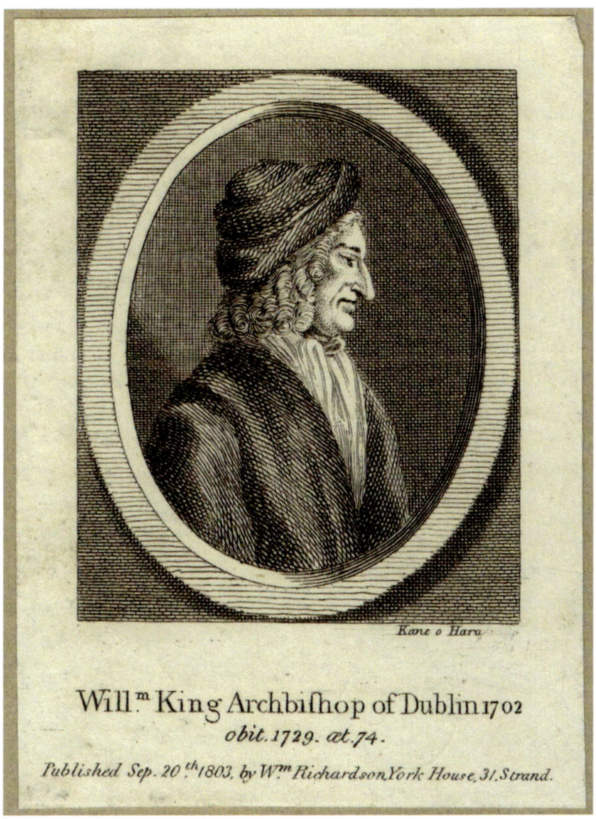

Figure 3.18 Kane O'Hara, after R. Tighe, *Portrait of William King* (1803), etching, 10.1 × 7.2 cm

Source: National Portrait Gallery, London. Photo credit: © National Portrait Gallery, London.

plate on his behalf. His priority was to spend his money wisely and he was not interested in paying a premium for fashion. By avoiding current fashions he thought that he could secure a better deal. King explained:

> I imagine when vanity hath prevailed with many of the nobility of Great Britain to fall into the French mode, that they will part with their present plate, and then I may have choice without paying for the fashion.[153]

Instead of being manipulated by the market, he was prepared to bide his time to secure the best terms. Later in the century, one Dublin retailer offered a small service of second-hand plate for sale. The dishes, plates and candlesticks were declared 'as good as new'.[154] As already mentioned, even the wealthiest clients could opt to buy second-hand from a goldsmiths' shop. For instance, John Duke of Bedford, who was appointed Lord Lieutenant of Ireland in 1757, had amassed more than 20,000 oz. of plate at the time of his death.[155] Nevertheless, as Philippa Glanville has demonstrated, his estate correspondence reveals that 'a policy was consistently followed of acquiring silver as reasonably as possible.'[156] When silver cups were required in 1753, the Duke's steward was sent to the London shop of Stafford Briscoe, well known for its trade in second-hand goods.[157]

Ultimately, what people bought and why was determined by a number of different things. While auctions offered the promise of bargains, sometimes the attraction of second-hand goods was as much about sentiment as cost. The account book of Charles Cobbe (Fig. 3.19), who became Archbishop of Dublin in the 1740s, notes the purchase of plate on two separate occasions from individuals with whom he had been personally associated.[158] One entry records the purchase of goods bought at the sale of Dean Swift's effects. Cobbe had been on friendly terms with Swift before the latter's death in 1745.[159] A second account notes Cobbe's purchase of plate at Sir Richard Levinge's sale. These included items from a toilet set, candlesticks, flatware, two small square waiters and other miscellaneous objects. Cobbe had married the widowed Dorothea, Lady Rawdon in 1730. She was the daughter of Sir Richard Levinge, who had served as Lord Chief Justice of Ireland and had died in 1724. While the circumstances surrounding his purchase of his father-in-law's goods are not entirely clear, it seems highly likely that their value in sentimental terms equalled if not surpassed their value in material terms. He clearly enjoyed buying silver, new and second-hand, and built up a good collection, including a fine silver basket by John Hamilton.[160]

Of course there were circumstances in which individuals and institutions needed extra items for a limited period, for instance, when accommodating large groups. Some Dublin retailers offered hired-out goods. In 1786, Jackson and Co. of Essex Street were offering to hire out china dishes, plates and glasses,[161] while a few years later a retailer on Ormond Quay offered wide range of ceramic table services for hire at 'the shortest notice'.[162]

When it came to 'making the grand figure', Irish patrons enjoyed excellent choice in terms of goods and services. Acknowledging the attractiveness of London wares, some Dublin goldsmiths (like their North American counterparts) used newspaper advertisements to highlight their London connections and ally themselves with fashionable developments there. The small survival rate of trade cards for Dublin goldsmiths may be indicative of particular biases in collecting, but it is also likely that they were in wider usage in the London goldsmiths' trade. Goldsmiths' shops in both cities offered

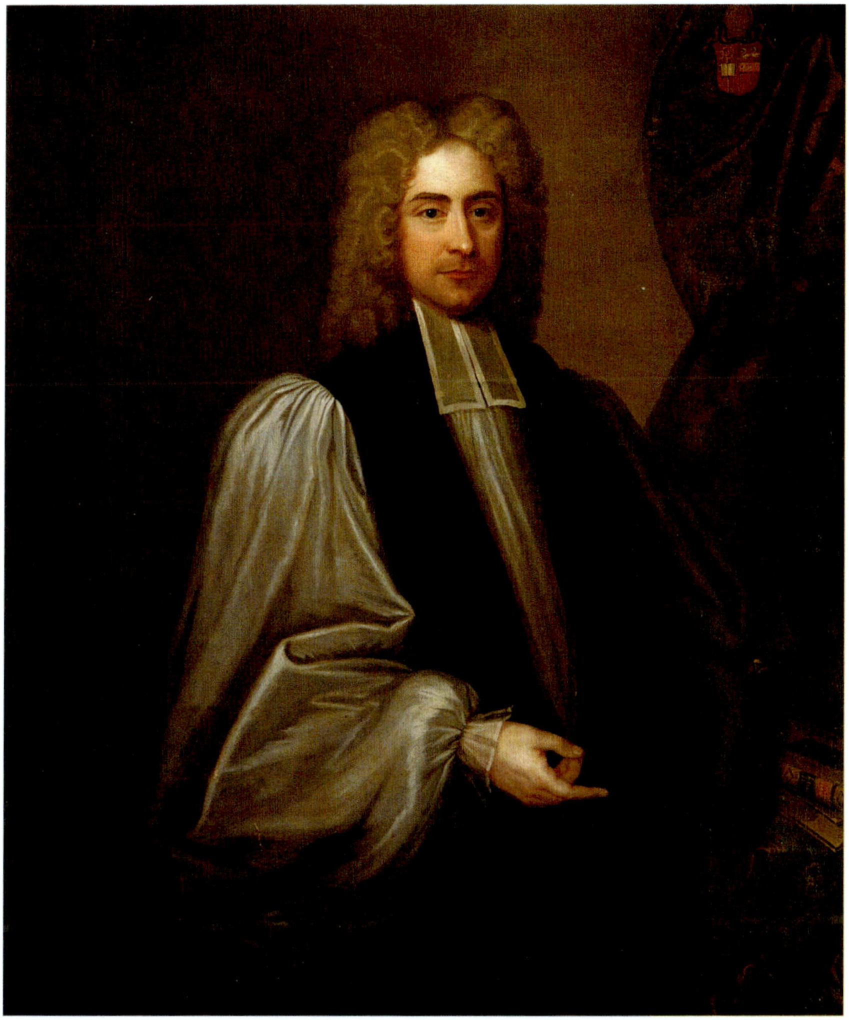

Figure 3.19 James Stewart, *Portrait of Charles Cobbe* (c.1750), oil on canvas, 126.5 × 110 cm
Source: Private collection. Photo credit: © Hugh Cobbe.

an attractive service, particularly in the realm of bespoke ordering and maintenance, but they were not the only options for Irish patrons. Throughout the century, auctions and, less frequently, lotteries offered further opportunities for buying plate in Ireland and, in terms of the market overall, second-hand plate remained an attractive option, not least for reasons of cost and sentiment. The evidence from customs ledgers clearly shows that, particularly during the 1740s and 1750s, sizable cargoes of British plate were being imported into Ireland, with large dinner services for Irish grandees causing spikes in the data in individual years. By the second half of the century, the availability of lighter plate and plated wares was reflected in a decline in the volumes of British plate bound for the Irish capital. Ultimately, the customer's choice was a subjective one. However, there was a unique value system linked to plate, which certainly encouraged its purchase. So, having looked at where Irish clients could go to buy their silverware, it now remains to consider why they bought it.

Notes

1 Brian FitzGerald, ed., *Correspondence of Emily, Duchess of Leinster*, vol. 1 (Dublin: Stationery Office, 1949), 416.
2 See, for example, Claire Walsh, 'Shop Design and the Display of Goods in the Eighteenth Century', MA thesis, Royal College of Art, London, 1993.
3 Ibid., 87.
4 Ibid.
5 Sarah Foster, 'Going Shopping in Georgian Dublin' (MA thesis, Royal College of Art, London, 1995), 75–76.
6 Walsh, 'Shop Design and the Display of Goods in the Eighteenth Century', 6–7. As Walsh notes, throughout the century the term 'warehouse' was used as a synonym for 'shop', 105.
7 Ibid. Those were the words of ceramic retailer Josiah Wedgwood, who also largely eschewed newspaper advertising.
8 Ibid. See also Geoffrey Wills, 'Stafford Briscoe, a London Silversmith', *Apollo* 117 (January 1983): 50–54.
9 Newspaper advertisements were ideal when it came to attracting the custom of country residents who made seasonal or intermittent visits to the capital. Apart from general notices advertising stock, goldsmiths also advertised changes of address, or their decision to cease trading. This cumulative material represents a rich source of evidence, which has previously been neglected. Very small numbers of engraved trade cards survive for goldsmiths and jewellers from eighteenth-century Dublin. For the more extensive numbers extant for eighteenth-century London, see Ambrose Heal, *The London Goldsmiths, 1200–1800* (Cambridge: Cambridge University Press, 1935). For the relative costs of different types of advertising in the eighteenth century, see Julia Muir, 'Printing Persuasion' (MA thesis, Royal College of Art, London, 2002), 25.
10 This is was more visible in the second half of the eighteenth century as the trade in both countries was expanding and Sheffield plate also became commercially available.
11 *Hibernian Chronicle*, 30 September 1782. No mention is made of Terry's involvement in the sale of imported goods in the literature on Irish silver, including the recent retrospective assessment of the achievements of Cork goldsmiths. See John Bowen and Conor O'Brien, *Cork Silver and Gold* (Cork: Crawford Gallery, 2005).
12 This was the claim of John Hector, goldsmith and jeweller, in 1774. See Alfred Cox Prime, ed., *The Arts and Crafts in Philadelphia, Maryland and South Carolina* (Philadelphia: Walpole Society, 1929), 69. He seems to have been trading mainly in small things like jewellery and buckles, which explains the latter promise. Hector was also appealing to patriotic 'lovers and encouragers of American manufactures to support him'.
13 Accounts of Richard Edgeworth, 12 December 1747, Ms. 1517:178, National Library of Ireland.
14 Accounts of Richard Edgeworth, February 1747–48, Ms. 1517: 198, 217, National Library of Ireland.
15 Accounts of James Stewart, 1784–86, Ms. D/3167/2/48, no. 342 (MIC/509/1), Public Record Office of Northern Ireland.
16 Accounts of Richard Johnston, 1783, Ms. D/1594/185, Public Record Office of Northern Ireland.
17 Account of His Grace, the Archbishop of Dublin (Robert Fowler), 16 September 1781, John Wakelin and William Taylor Gentleman's Ledger 1777–87, Garrard Ledgers, V&A.
18 Helen Clifford, *Silver in London: The Parker and Wakelin Partnership* (New Haven and London: Yale University Press, 2004), 138.
19 Ibid., 145–50. On the use of credit in the luxury trades in eighteenth-century Paris, see Gillian Lewis, 'Producers, Suppliers, and Consumers: Reflections on the Luxury Trades in Paris, c.1500 to c.1800', in *Luxury Trades and Consumerism in Ancien Régime Paris*, ed. Robert Fox and Anthony Turner (Aldershot: Ashgate, 1998), 287–99.

20 The eminent London goldsmith Philip Rundell was the source of the latter expression. He commented wryly that 'if we could collect our just debts then indeed we might be rich'; quoted in Clifford, *Silver in London*, 145. He did not have particular cause for concern – according to the title of his memoirs, he had 'by Industry and Perseverance accumulated the immense fortune of One Million and a Half'. See George Fox, *Memoirs of the Late Philip Rundell Esq.* (London: J. Fairbairn, 1827).
21 Arthur Dobbs, *An Essay on the Trade and Improvement of Ireland* (Dublin: Printed by A. Rhames, for J. Smith and W. Bruce on the Blind-Key 1729), 42.
22 Ibid.
23 There were certainly instances of fraudsters acquiring goods from goldsmiths on credit by appearing to be gentlemen. For a warning of such a fraudster operating in England but published in an Irish newspaper, see *Belfast News Letter*, 9–12 October 1787.
24 *Saunders' News-Letter*, 11–14 December 1767. D'Olier also invited any individual to whom he was indebted to deliver their accounts as well.
25 *Saunders' News-Letter*, 2–5 December 1768.
26 *Hibernian Journal*, 27–30 November 1772.
27 *Saunders' News-Letter*, 17–19 May 1775.
28 He also advertised the sale of a 'most elegant' second-hand tureen for 'one third under the cost'.
29 *Public Gazetteer*, 19–22 March 1763.
30 Ibid.
31 On behalf of Matthew Boulton to Jeremiah D'Olier, 12 March 1783, Ms. 3782/3/14: 86, Birmingham City Archives. However, as chapter 2 demonstrated, he did employ a Dublin agent to help him ensure that clients were trustworthy. A letter of 1783 states, in relation to two Dublin customers, 'I hope that you have been able to be fully satisfied respecting those gentlemen.' Ibid., 89.
32 Clifford, *Silver in London*, 148.
33 On the vogue for exhibitions in the eighteenth century, see Hilary Young, ed., *The Genius of Wedgwood* (London: V&A, 1995), 118–33; and Richard Altick, *The Shows of London* (Cambridge, MA: Harvard University Press, 1978).
34 Charles Topham Bowden, *A Tour through Ireland* (Dublin: Printed by W. Corbet, No. 57, Great Britain-Street, 1791), 52.
35 Material Relating to the Dublin Goldsmith Robert Calderwood, Ms. 3269: 11, National Library of Ireland.
36 *Faulkner's Dublin Journal* (*FDJ*), 1 September 1796. The season also brought considerable business to Dublin shops. See Pole Cosby, 'Autobiography of Pole Cosby of Stradbally', *Kildare Archaeological Society Journal* 5 (1906–8): 435; and Tighernan Mooney and Fiona White, 'The Gentry's Winter Season', in *The Gorgeous Mask*, ed. David Dickson (Dublin: Trinity College Dublin, 1987), 1–16. The Dublin jeweller William Moore wrote to Matthew Boulton in the second half of the century urging him to send goods expediently in time for the meeting of parliament. Moore qualified that the latter would bring 'all the quality of the Kingdom' to town. See William Moore to Matthew Boulton, n.d., Miscellaneous Correspondence Letter Box M2, Item 70, Birmingham City Archives.
37 This is borne out by a range of contemporary newspaper advertisements, personal accounts and period correspondence. See, for example, Balfour Accounts, Ms. 9534, National Library of Ireland; Toby Barnard, *Making the Grand Figure: Lives and Possessions in Ireland, 1641–1770* (New Haven and London: Yale University Press, 2004); and Rosemary Ffolliott, 'Captain Balfour's Auction, 15th March 1741/42', *The Irish Ancestor* 16 (1984): 21–31.
38 Barnard, *Making the Grand Figure*, 145.
39 Cynthia Wall, 'The English Auction: Narratives of Dismantlings', *Eighteenth-Century Studies* 31 (1997): 2.
40 The itinerary of the socialite in Charles Jenner's *Town Eclogues* involved a heady round of 'routs, assemblies, auctions, operas, plays, subscription balls and visits without end', culminating in a frail appearance at Mr Christie's auction. Quoted in Wall, 'The English Auction', 2.
41 Iain Pears, *The Discovery of Painting: The Growth of Interest in the Arts in England, 1680–1768* (New Haven and London: Yale University Press, 1988), 106.
42 Máire Kennedy, 'Book Mad: The Sale of Books by Auction in Eighteenth-Century Dublin', *Dublin Historical Record* 54 (2001): 48. Ultimately, legislation was required, both to

regulate auctions and to benefit from the revenue they accrued. A statute of 1797 enforced strict controls and was followed by a series of later statutes.

43 In 1790, an anonymous contributor to the *Freeman's Journal* complained: 'There are not greater deceptions on the public than the present kind of book auctions in this city, to which the people are deluded under the imagination of acquiring cheap books.' The writer advised that 'no gentleman should disgrace his library with such abominable productions; which no book-seller in Dublin would dare offer for sale'; quoted in Kennedy, 'Book Mad', 49. For a favourable opinion of one Dublin auctioneer, see Topham Bowden, *A Tour through Ireland*, 56–57. For a hilarious fictional account of the auction spectacle in an Irish novel, see Henry Brooke, *The Fool of Quality*, vol. 2 (Dublin: Printed for the autor [*sic*] by Dillon Chamberlaine, in Dame Street, facing Fownes' Street, 1766), 142, 148–50.

44 *Hibernian Journal*, 5–7 October 1774.

45 *Hibernian Magazine*, 26 January 1787. The particular incident in question concerned a businesswoman who had visited a wholesale merchant in Dublin and ordered goods to the value of 'some hundred pounds'. Claiming to be in a great hurry, she had her goods dispatched, and without opening them, she sent them 'invoice and all' to an auction room in the centre of the city. After collecting the money they fetched, she rapidly absconded.

46 *Journal of the House of Commons of the Kingdom of Ireland* 12 (15 February 1787), 198.

47 Comparable concerns were raised in an English context. See Pears, *The Discovery of Painting*, 65.

48 For references to auctions in the textile industry, see, for example, *Journal of the House of Commons of the Kingdom of Ireland* 12 (2 March 1787), 215–16. For ceramic auctions, see Peter Francis, *Irish Delftware* (London: Jonathan Horne, 2000), 57. Francis suggests that, with the outbreak of the Seven Years' War in 1756, British porcelain factories like Bow and Chelsea may have used auctions in Ireland to clear stockpiles, despite the fact that they already had good wholesale customers there.

49 *FDJ*, 29 March–1 April 1746. An earlier notice in *Faulkner's Dublin Journal*, 27–31 July 1742, indicates that the scope of Manjoy's business as a retailer included not only silversmiths' and jewellers' work, but also furniture, cutlery cases and other items, at least some of which were English. Susanna Manjoy's name does not occur either in Douglas Bennett, *Irish Georgian Silver* (London: Cassell, 1972), or Douglas Bennett, *Collecting Irish Silver* (London: Souvenir Press, 1984). A Benjamin Manjoy, goldsmith and freeman, who died in 1715, but for whom plate was assayed until 1731, is listed, in addition to Dorothy Manjoy, who is identified as his widow and, it is indicated, continued his business after his death.

50 *FDJ*, 11–14 August 1759.

51 See Bennett, *Irish Georgian Silver*, 315–16.

52 *FDJ*, 25–28 December 1742.

53 The latter were not averse to supplementing their own stock, when prices proved advantageous. It appears that, as in London, small jewellers may have been exempt from assaying in Dublin. However, as foregoing examples have shown, some jewellers did act as more general retailers for goldsmiths' work.

54 *FDJ*, 11–14 February 1769.

55 Ibid.

56 *FDJ*, 9–11 February 1775.

57 Indenture of Thomas Atkinson with Thomas Johnston, 1753 (?), Company of Goldsmiths of Dublin, Ms. 97: 1 (back of ledger), Dublin, Assay Office.

58 This is based on the assumption that the Thomas Johnston mentioned in the apprenticeship ledger was the watchmaker of the same name listed in Bennett, *Irish Georgian Silver*, 312. The notice in *Faulkner's Dublin Journal* described him as a watchmaker and clockmaker.

59 *FDJ*, 7–9 October 1784.

60 Ibid.

61 See Constantia Maxwell, *Dublin under the Georges, 1714–1830* (Dublin: Gill & Macmillan, 1946), 290. For additional references to ballooning in Dublin, see *FDJ*, 5–7 February 1784; 10–12 February 1784; and 14–16 July 1785. Dublin sheriffs frequently employed general auctioneers in cases following bankruptcy. In January 1784, the effects of the late Surgeon General William Buxton were auctioned. The sale included items of plate as well as a valuable collection of books. See Kennedy, 'Book Mad', 59.

62 *FDJ*, 30 June–2 July 1778.

63 The way the advertisement is phrased is particularly interesting. The reference to 'highly chased' silver implied that it was decorated with labour intensive craftsmanship, which represented one tier of value. It was also described as being in the present taste, implying that it was fashionable, although in reality, by that date neoclassical silver was already in vogue. The underlying implication was that a bargain might be had.

64 Cullen mentions the failure of Mitchell's business in 1778. This coincides with the auction notice for the sale of his property in that year. See Louis Cullen, 'The Dublin Merchant Community', in *Cities and Merchants: French and Irish Perspectives on Urban Development, 1500–1900*, ed. Paul Butel and Louis Cullen (Dublin: Trinity College Dublin, 1986), 155.

65 However, surviving examples of Irish silver from the 1760s and 1770s also show that there was a tendency during this period to chase some older plain items of silver. I am grateful to Thomas Sinsteden for this comment.

66 Peter Cameron, 'Henry Jernegan, Charles Frederick Kandler and the Client Who Changed His Mind', *Silver Society Journal* 8 (1996): 487–502.

67 Minute of 15 September 1767, Company of Goldsmiths of Dublin, Ms. 5, Dublin, Assay Office.

68 Ibid.

69 A decision was reached that the master and wardens of the guild would meet the lord mayor to inform him of the negative repercussions of the scheme, both for the public and the trade, and seek its suppression.

70 Minute of 3 June 1771, Company of Goldsmiths of Dublin, Ms. 5: 218, Dublin, Assay Office.

71 The master warden employed the weight of a parliamentary statute. The statute of which 'the said Manly', the organiser of the lotter, was informed was a statute of George II, c. 8. This was an Act for the more effectual preventing of excessive and deceitful gaming. See E.M. Johnston-Liik, *History of the Irish Parliament 1692–1800*, 6 vols. (Belfast: Ulster Historical Foundation, 2002), 433.

72 Minute of 24 November 1774, Company of Goldsmiths of Dublin, Ms. 5: 288, Dublin, Assay Office.

73 It was agreed that, before openly opposing the perpetrators, guild representatives should try to secure a ticket. Rather than a participatory measure, this was obviously an attempt to obtain evidence to support their case against the scheme. The Company of Goldsmiths of London made a rash decision in 1711 to try to clear debts by selling the residue of its plate collection and using the proceeds to buy lottery tickets. See J.S. Forbes, *Hallmark: A History of the London Assay Office* (London: Goldsmiths Company and Unicorn Press, 1999), 167.

74 Anon., *A Descriptive Catalogue of the Several Splendid Pieces of Mechanism and Jewellery in Mr. Cox's Museum, Now Exhibiting at the Great Room, in William Street, Dublin* (Dublin, 1774). On Cox's visit to Dublin, see Alison FitzGerald, '"Astonishing Automata": Staging Spectacle in Eighteenth-Century Dublin', *Irish Architectural and Decorative Studies* 10 (2007): 18–34.

75 Ibid.

76 Ibid.

77 Ibid. It was by no means the first display of mechanised exhibits in Dublin. In February 1737, Richard Edgeworth had paid 6s 6d for himself and a companion 'To see the Clockwork Statues'. Accounts of Richard Edgeworth, 20 February 1737, Ms. 1512: 73, National Library of Ireland. See also *Saunders' News-Letter*, 16–18 November 1767. Marcia Pointon has argued that the emphasis on painting over 'those visual media that had the greatest impact on metropolitan audiences' has led to the neglect of individuals like Cox in historical analyses. See Marcia Pointon, 'Dealer in Magic: James Cox's Jewelry Museum and the Economics of Luxurious Spectacle in Late Eighteenth-Century London', in *Economic Engagements with Arts*, ed. Neil de Marchi and C.D.W. Goodwin (Durham: Duke University Press, 1999), 433.

78 See, for example, *Dublin Intelligencer*, 30 June 1711; and *Hibernian Chronicle* [Cork], 7–11 October 1779.

79 Edward Law, 'Some Provincial Irish Silver Lotteries', *Journal of the Silver Society* 7 (1995): 412–16.

80 Julie Anne Lambert, *A Nation of Shopkeepers: Trade Ephemera from 1654 to the 1860s in the John Johnson Collection* (Oxford: Bodleian Library, 2001), 22 notes that Charles Corbett, bookseller and publisher of the *Whitehall Evening Post* and owner of a lottery office,

was forced to give up his business in 1776, ruined by the sale of a £20,000 lottery ticket. For substantial prizes in an Irish lottery, see *Handbill Advertising the 'First Irish Lottery for 1798'*, Ms. 33,734, National Library of Ireland.

81 A full list of the prizes is given in Law, 'Some Provincial Irish Silver Lotteries', 415.

82 Ibid. This was the cost of a single ticket.

83 Similar events took place in Britain and in the colonies. In 1727, a lottery of 'silver and goldwork, wrought by Simeon Soumain of New York, Goldsmith' was advertised in the *New York Gazette*.

84 See, for example, Anon., *The Wonderful Advantages of Adventuring in the Lottery Or, The History of John Doyle* (Dublin: Sold by William Watson, [1797]).

85 Maria Edgeworth, *Popular Tales* (London: Printed for J. Johnson, St. Paul's Church-Yard, 1804). The story entitled *The Lottery* is dated 1799.

86 Ibid., 20. George Cooper, who visited Dublin in 1799, emphasised the negative effects of lotteries. Commenting on the prevalence of lottery offices in the city of Dublin, he remarked that 'these shops are adorned with every thing which can catch the eye, and delude the mind of the unwary'; quoted in Sarah Foster, 'Going Shopping in Georgian Dublin' (MA thesis, Royal College of Art, London, 1995), 37.

87 Prince Hoare, *The Pedantic Apothecary Quizzed, or Lottery Prize, of 2, 5, 3, 8, A Farce in Two Acts. Performed at the Theatres Royal, London and Dublin* (Dublin: Printed by John Whitworth, No. 14, Exchange-Street, c.1795). In eighteenth-century Ireland, lotteries were also used to raise revenue. See, for example, an Act of 1779–80, 19 & 20 George III, c.5: *An Act for establishing a lottery and for granting to his Majesty a sum of two hundred thousand pounds to be raised thereby and for such other purposes as are therein mentioned*. A surviving ticket from one lottery promises the bearer a 'prize arising to the same number in the State Lottery pursuant to the scheme published by the Grand Lodge of Ireland for the relief of distressed Freemasons, the Widows and Orphans of such'; Album III, John Johnson Collection, Bodleian Library, Oxford.

88 See, for instance, George Berkeley, *The Querist* (Dublin: Printed by R. Reilly, on Cork-Hill, 1735); Thomas Prior, *A List of the Absentees of Ireland, and the Yearly Value of Their Estates and Incomes Spent Abroad. With Observations on the Present State and Condition of That Kingdom* (Dublin: Printed for R. Gunne in Capel-Street, 1729).

89 David Dickson, 'Second-City Syndrome', in *Kingdoms United?*, ed. S.J. Connolly (Dublin: Four Courts Press, 1998), 96–97.

90 A.C. Elias, *Memoirs of Laetitia Pilkington*, 2 vols. (Athens: University of Georgia Press, 1997), 63. Laetitia Pilkington was formerly the wife of Matthew Pilkington, whose influential publication, *The Gentleman's and Connoisseur's Dictionary of Painters*, was published in 1770. Following their scandalous divorce in 1738, she produced a very lively volume of *Memoirs* (1748–54), written while she lived in London.

91 Quoted in Mairead Reynolds, 'Wedgwood in Dublin, 1772–1777', *Irish Arts Review* (*IAR*) 1 (1984): 36. The principal protagonist in Maria Edgeworth's novel *Ormond* was commended for his 'patriotic' decision to winter in Dublin rather than in London. See Maria Edgeworth, *Ormond* (Belfast: Appletree Press, 1992), 159.

92 FitzGerald, *Correspondence of Emily, Duchess of Leinster*, 85. It is worth noting that the social mobility of many of the patrons of plate was such that they moved between London and Dublin, facilitating the placing of orders with English retailers.

93 See Elaine Barr, *George Wickes, Royal Goldsmith 1698–1761* (London: Studio Vista/Christie's, 1980), 197–205; and Michael Snodin, ed., *Rococo Art and Design in Hogarth's England* (London: V&A, 1984), 104, 116.

94 It would appear that the Calderwood set were cast from moulds taken from one of the Wickes candlesticks. See Timothy Schroder, *British and Continental Gold and Silver in the Ashmolean Museum* (Oxford: Ashmolean Museum, 2009), 174.

95 Louis Cullen, *An Economic History of Ireland since 1660* (London: Batsford, 1987), 37.

96 Ibid., 40.

97 This refers only to quantities of silver submitted to the assay office at Goldsmiths' Hall, Dublin. See Thomas Sinsteden, 'Four Selected Assay Records of the Dublin Goldsmiths Company', *Silver Society Journal* 11 (1999): 143–58; Thomas Sinsteden, 'Surviving Dublin Assay Records, part 2. 1708–48', *Silver Studies* 16 (2004): 87–103.

98 FDJ, 16–19 August 1729.

99 Ibid.

100 See Cullen, *An Economic History of Ireland*, 49.
101 Ibid., 51.
102 This is also reflected in the lower volume of plate hallmarked in Dublin over this extended period. I am grateful to Thomas Sinsteden for this comment.
103 This statistic was arrived at by calculating daily volumes submitted to the office between January and December 1753, based on the information in assay book, 27 March 1752–1 August 1755, Company of Goldsmiths Ms. 19, Dublin, Assay Office.
104 James Lomax, 'Royalty and Silver: The Role of the Jewel House in the Eighteenth Century', *Silver Society Journal* 11 (1999): 133–40.
105 Cullen, 'The Dublin Merchant Community', 159.
106 William Cooke, *Memoirs of Samuel Foote Esq*., 3 vols. (London: Richard Phillips, 1805), vol. 2: 114.
107 For example, the curvilinear accents and elaborate chasing of a full blown rococo style candlestick would have required a heavier gauge metal than a columnar candlestick in a neoclassical style, whose constituent parts could be stamped out and soldered together.
108 This is confirmed by the advertisements of Dublin goldsmiths specifying the sale of plated goods, the fact that the Dublin Society was offering premiums in the manufacture of plated wares in the 1780s, and that in the three years preceding March 1779 the annual value of plated ware imported from Britain was more than twice the value of imported wrought plate.
109 Wickes' client was still the Earl of Kildare at the time that the service was ordered. However, the dinner service is generally referred to as the Leinster dinner service. See, for example, Barr, *George Wickes*, 197–205. The ledgers survive from Wickes' start in his Panton Street premises in 1735.
110 For more on Synge and his expenditure, see Marie-Lou Legg, *The Synge Letters* (Dublin: Lilliput Press, 1996).
111 Account of Joseph Leason [*sic*], 16 August 1742, George Wickes, Gentleman's Ledger 1740–48, Garrard Ledgers, V&A.
112 See Thomas Sinsteden, *Russborough: Served in Splendour* (Alfred Beit Foundation, 2014). Leeson also bought some very fine silver from Dublin goldsmiths, notably Robert Calderwood, later on. See ibid., 6–7.
113 A tureen from the service is in the Garrard collection. See Joseph McDonnell, 'Irish Rococo Silver', *IAR* 13 (1997): 83.
114 Account of Joseph Leason [*sic*], 16 August 1742, George Wickes, Gentleman's Ledger 1740–48, Garrard Ledgers, 1742, V&A.
115 Account of Joseph Leason [*sic*], 12 August 1743, George Wickes, Gentleman's Ledger 1740–48, Garrard Ledgers, 1742, V&A.
116 At this stage in his life he would hardly have had much used plate to trade in, unless he had elected to trade in inherited pieces.
117 The circumstances which led to this design dissemination do not appear to be documented.
118 Johnston-Liik, *History of the Irish Parliament*, vol. 6: 116–17.
119 Nonetheless, he was still representative of elite consumption.
120 Account of Sir Thomas Prendergast, 26 December 1754, George Wickes and Samuel Netherton, Gentleman's Ledger 1750–54, Garrard Ledgers, V&A.
121 Account of Sir Thomas Prendergast, 7 November 1759, George Wickes and Samuel Netherton, Gentleman's Ledger 1750–54, Garrard Ledgers, V&A.
122 FDJ, 10–14 February 1761.
123 Account of Sir Thomas Prendergast, 1 April 1752, George Wickes and Samuel Netherton, Gentleman's Ledger 1750–54, Garrard Ledgers, 1752, V&A.
124 Prior, *A List of the Absentees of Ireland*, 35.
125 On clergy, see Toby Barnard, *A New Anatomy of Ireland* (New Haven and London: Yale University Press, 2003), 81–115.
126 Account of the Right Reverend, The Lord Bishop of Elphin, 7 November 1759, George Wickes and Samuel Netherton Gentleman's Ledger, 1756–60, Garrard Ledgers, V&A.
127 Account of His Grace the Archbishop of Dublin (Robert Fowler), 16 September 1781, John Wakelin and William Taylor, Gentleman's Ledger, 1777–87, Garrard: Ledgers, V&A.
128 Quoted in Reynolds, 'Wedgwood in Dublin', 36.
129 Ibid. The latter, according to Wedgwood, was a consequence of 'a wrong entry as they will scarcely know how to specify them'.

130 A.P. Ledger, ed., *Derby Porcelain, English Competitors, Chinamen and Trade Practices 1786–1796* (forthcoming). I am grateful to Hilary Young for giving me access to this material.
131 Ibid.
132 Ibid.
133 Ibid.
134 Minutes of the Irish Customs Board, Ms. CUST 1/159: 92, National Archives, Kew.
135 Minutes of the Irish Customs Board, Ms. CUST 1/163: 22, National Archives, Kew.
136 Minutes of the Irish Customs Board, Ms. CUST 1/154: 87, National Archives, Kew.
137 Ibid. The fact that the parties involved could not discern whether the plate was English or Irish is interesting.
138 In 1762, the Cork goldsmith William Reynolds advertised, that a parcel of plate, which he had for sale, was 'nearly as good as new'; *Cork Evening Post*, 4 November 1762.
139 On the significance of the second-hand trade in early modern Europe, see B. Blondé et al., *Fashioning Old and New*, no. xviii of *Studies in European Urban History, 1100–1800* (Turnhout, Belgium: Brepols, 2009).
140 David Mitchell, *Goldsmiths, Silversmiths and Bankers* (London: Sutton, 1995), 12. The modest growth referred to was relative to the cities' burgeoning wealth and population.
141 'Glass-House Clerk', *The Plate-Glass-Book, By a Glass-House Clerk. To which is Added, The Compleat Appraiser. Consisting of Useful Tables, With their Explanation For the Valuing of Brass, Copper, Pewter, Iron, Damask, Paper and Linen Furniture, Liquors, Plate, &c., By an Eminent Broker lately deceased* (London: Printed for the Author, 1757). See also Vanessa Brett, 'The Compleat Appraiser: An Eighteenth-Century Manual and the Valuing of Plate', *Silver Society Journal* 15 (2003): 2–4.
142 Ellenor Alcorn, *English Silver in the Museum of Fine Arts, Boston* (Boston: Museum of Fine Arts, 2000), 72–75.
143 Stana Nenadic, 'Middle-Rank Consumers and Domestic Culture in Edinburgh and Glasgow 1720–1840', *Past and Present* 145 (1994): 122–56.
144 Wills, 'Stafford Briscoe'.
145 Accounts of the Flower family, 25 April 1741, Ms. 11, 467, National Library of Ireland, includes a receipt for a dozen silver plates in 1741.
146 See, for example, in *FDJ*, 3–5 January 1756.
147 For a useful survey of market prices for silver, see John J. McCusker, *Money and Exchange in Europe and America 1660–1775* (Chapel Hill: University of North Carolina Press, 1978).
148 'Glass-House Clerk', *The Plate-Glass-Book*, 186.
149 Account of Sir Thomas Prendergast, 29 August 1754, George Wickes and Samuel Netherton's Gentleman's Ledger 1750–54, Garrard Ledgers, V&A.
150 McCusker, *Money and Exchange in Europe and America*, 17.
151 Account of Sir Thomas Prendergast, 1752, George Wickes and Samuel Netherton's Gentleman's Ledger 1750–54, Garrard Ledgers, V&A. The rate he was credited with ranged from 4s 10d to 5s 7d.
152 *Saunders' News-Letter*, 21 March 1777.
153 Letter from William King to Lady Beresford, 13 November 1712, Ms. 750/4: 66, Trinity College Dublin.
154 *FDJ*, 3 October 1793.
155 Philippa Glanville, 'The Silver of John, Fourth Duke of Bedford', *Apollo* 127 (June 1988): 413.
156 Ibid., 417.
157 Ibid., 416.
158 Accounts of Charles Cobbe, Archbishop of Dublin (private collection). I am grateful to Hugh Cobbe for permission to consult this ledger.
159 In 1742, Archbishop Cobbe had played a key role in the arrangements for the premier of Handel's *Messiah* in Dublin. See Alistair Laing, *Clerics and Connoisseurs* (London: English Heritage, 2001) 41.
160 Alec Cobbe, 'Developing the Cobbe Museum at Hatchlands Park', in *The Cobbe Cabinet of Curiosities*, ed. Arthur MacGregor (New Haven and London: Yale University Press, 2015), 408–10. I am grateful to Toby Barnard for this reference.
161 *Saunders' News-Letter*, 11 April 1786.
162 *Hibernian Journal*, 2 March 1791.

4 Silver and its meaning in Georgian Ireland

Lucia thinks happiness consists in state,
She weds an idiot; but she eats in plate.[1]

This excerpt from a poem published in Dublin in 1727 illustrates how readily silver was associated with status. The theme of the ill-matched couple was a common one in literary and visual culture during this period, and ownership of plate implied a certain social standing. It was valued for many reasons: for its associations with money, as a form of social currency in gift exchange and as a mark of distinction.[2] Toby Barnard has cautioned against applying an overly prescriptive approach to the study of luxury consumption in eighteenth-century Ireland.[3] There is a danger of ascribing calculated motives to purchases that were prompted by all sorts of instincts. Nevertheless, the intrinsic value of plate was understood and commented upon by contemporaries, whose attitudes go some way to revealing why it was acquired, used, displayed and valued.

Concepts of value: contemporary links between plate and money

There is evidence to suggest that the absence of a mint in Ireland, the circulation of a bewildering variety of coins which were frequently in short supply and the regular failure of banks prior to 1760 provided one motivation for buying plate during the late seventeenth and early eighteenth century. While the Bank of England was founded in 1694 and the Bank of Scotland a year later, it was 1782 before the Bank of Ireland was established. The emergence of deposit banking systems in England released consumers from what Helen Clifford has called 'investment purchasing and a hoarding mentality', and the slower development of banking in Dublin than in London may well have encouraged this outlook to endure longer in an Irish context.[4] A Dublin pamphlet published in 1721 parodied the failed campaign to establish an Irish national bank, and in particular the Irish MP Oliver St George, who was to be one of its managers.[5] St George was a regular buyer of plate, amassing at least 3,933 oz. between 1695 and 1729.[6] His accounts show that even wealthy patrons employed a range of purchase strategies as needs and opportunities arose. He bought new and second-hand, bespoke and at auction, in Dublin and in London. He followed a pattern of favouring Huguenot goldsmiths, which suggests that he was keen to secure value for money as well as good craftsmanship. During the same period a number of elite English patrons also favoured Huguenots.[7] St George's accounts suggest his alertness to the intrinsic value of his plate. A number of notations register small losses of metal through wear or engraving; he also differentiated in his accounts between pieces that were sterling and the higher Britannia standard, legal in England between 1697 and 1720.

In their infancy banks were certainly viewed with caution. In his autobiography Pole Cosby from Co. Laois noted the failure of one Dublin bank, and then his own arrangements for securing his plate when travelling to England. Clearly, he was not taking any chances:

> The plate which I did not carry with me, about £160 worth I put into a large deal box and Will. Holdbrooke and I that night before we went off buried it in the cellar under the big stairs next to the big parlour, my reasons for hiding it in this manner was that perhaps had I entrusted it with anyone in the country some accident might have happened to it, nor did I think it much securer had I left it with a banker in Dublin, and by hiding it under ground I was sure to find it as I left it safe and unabated.[8]

While foreign coins circulated in eighteenth-century England, the whole issue of money flow was more fractious in Ireland. In the absence of a mint, Ireland was dependent on the inflow of specie from England and a mixture of motley coinage which was validated as legal tender out of necessity.[9] The pamphlet war that erupted in 1722, when an English ironmonger was given a patent to coin copper halfpence for Ireland, included references to the perception that the strength of a nation's economy was linked to its supply of precious metal.[10] In Swift's *Drapier's Letters*, the author refers directly to the intrinsic value of silver coin, condemning the exchange of 'fourscore and ten thousand pounds in good gold and silver' for 'trash that will not be worth above eight or nine thousand pounds real value'.[11] A contemporary print on the same subject mocked the exchange of 'British dross for Irish plate' (Fig. 4.1).

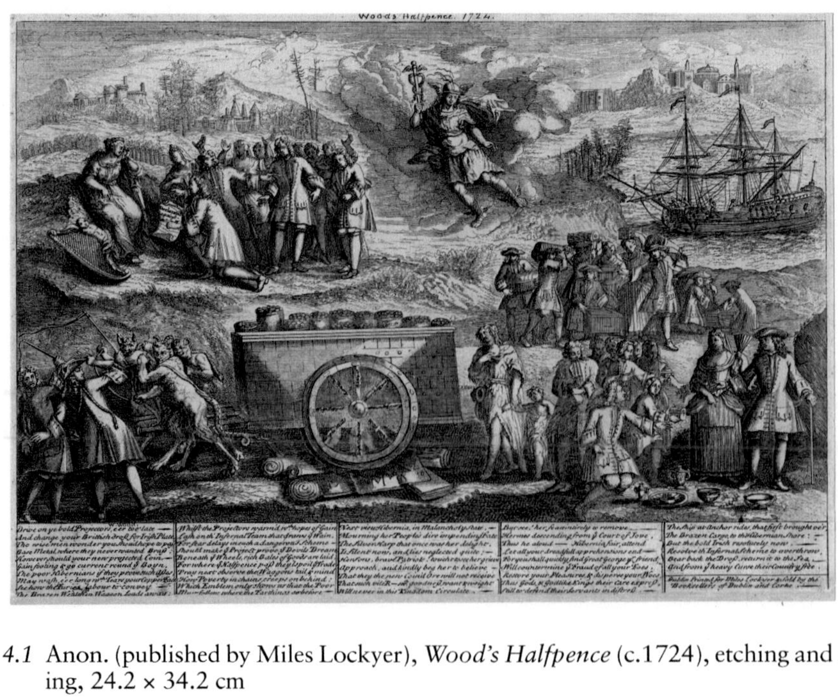

Figure 4.1 Anon. (published by Miles Lockyer), *Wood's Halfpence* (c.1724), etching and engraving, 24.2 × 34.2 cm

Source: British Museum, London. Photo credit: © The Trustees of the British Museum.

This is not to suggest that large purchases of plate in late seventeenth- and early eighteenth-century Ireland were always viewed as a form of investment. Simply, in a climate where banking was in its infancy and coin was frequently in short supply, it made rational sense to put money into plate.[12] The same was true of North America, which like Ireland was often supplying raw materials, importing finished manufactures and battling coinage crises. Before the establishment of banks there, colonists continued in what Gandy Fales has called 'the Old World practice of turning their unidentifiable silver and gold coins into plate'.[13]

At least in the form of plate, as opposed to coin, silver was less likely to leave the country. In a representation to the Revenue Commissioners of England in 1717, Sir Isaac Newton referred to the quantities of silver stored in the country in the form of plate. He advised against recommending that plate be coined, as he reckoned that silver was 'safer from exportation in the form of plate, than in the form of money, because of the greater value of the silver and fashion together'.[14] Eighteenth-century goldsmiths' accounts frequently distinguish between the cost of metal and the cost of fashioning.

The price of silver fluctuated during the course of the eighteenth century. As late as 1737, an Irish broadsheet juxtaposed plate and banking as two avenues through which to make a profit from hoarding undervalued silver. The author clearly suggested that in Ireland the shortage of silver coin was being exacerbated by its use in the manufacture of plate.[15] In 1697, to prevent coin being melted down by goldsmiths at a time when silver and coin were in short supply, the British government raised the standard for wrought silver from 11 oz., 2 dwt. (sterling) to 11 oz., 10 dwt. (Britannia).[16] This law remained in force until 1720 but was not implemented in Ireland.

As chapter 1 showed, a number of Dublin goldsmiths openly advertised their demand for particular types of coins.[17] A poem describing the triennial procession of Dublin's trade guilds refers directly to their practice of using coin in the manufacture of plate:

> Next march the goldsmiths who can form and mould
> In sundry shapes and forms the ductile gold;
> Men call them traitors, rebels and what not
> Nor king nor queen they spare, all goes to pot;
> The splendid shilling either bent or broken,
> And given by parting lover for a token,
> No pity meets; in the devouring fire
> Monarchs and chamber pots and rings expire.[18]

In 1717, Oliver St George gave the Dublin goldsmith Peter Gervais thirty-one pieces of Turkish gold as part payment for his wife's 'attire'.[19] He noted how the metal he supplied was 'above sterling', yet the objects that he received in return were neither 'touched' nor warranted sterling.[20] In November 1730, when a Danish East India ship, the *Golden Lyon*, was stranded off the Irish coast, a Limerick goldsmith used the opportunity to buy a quantity of Danish silver for £30.[21] Later in the century, a surviving billhead for the Dublin goldsmith William Keen indicates his willingness to accept foreign coin as part payment for finished goods (Fig. 4.2). In 1779, a Mr Harman reduced his bill from £31 3s 5d to £3 19s 22d by trading in a gold box, some coin, lace, buttons and dollars when buying a silver basket, some plated candlesticks, a cruet frame and cutlery.

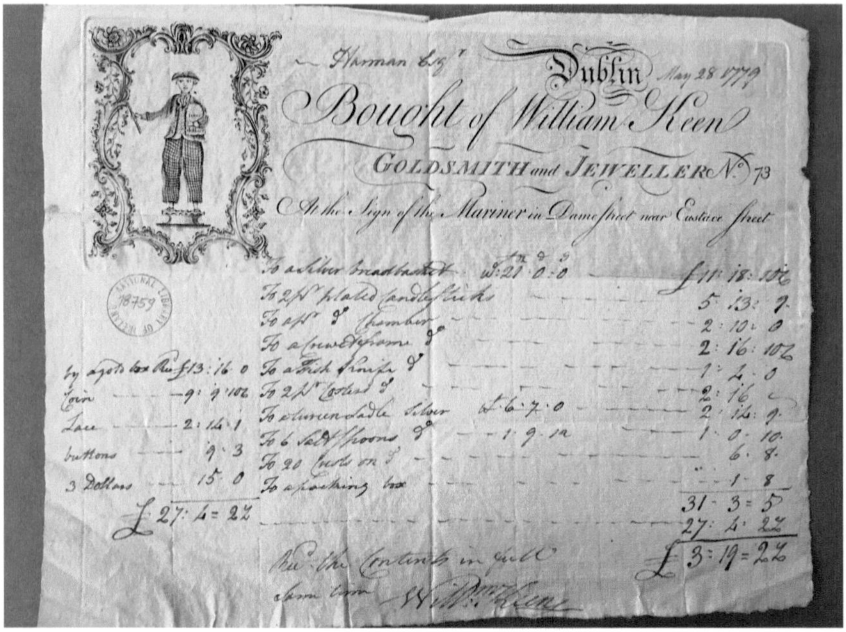

Figure 4.2 Billhead of William Keen (handwritten receipt for 1779), engraving, 19.5 × 24 cm
Source: National Library of Ireland, Dublin. Photo credit: © National Library of Ireland.

The fact that plate could be easily converted into cash in times of need was a factor which influenced some, at least, to buy it before deposit banking and other forms of investment had become well established. Conversely, there were also cases where stolen plate was used to make counterfeit money. In 1782, a house in Dublin's Abbey Street was burgled and a considerable quantity of plate stolen. The investigating officers recovered instruments and guidelines for coining, 'directions for robbers and house breakers', 'run down silver', and 'in the whole three hundred ounces of melted silver'.[22]

American newspapers for this period report cases where goldsmiths were implicated in counterfeiting. In July 1761, the *New York Mercury* published an account of one craftsman who had hanged himself in jail after being committed on suspicion of making Spanish dollars.[23] In the eighteenth century, links between ready money and plate were underscored in all sorts of contexts. For instance, James Warren and William Archdall were among the Dublin goldsmiths who advertised the sale of money weights. Archdall made and sold 'all sorts of money scales'.[24] In early modern Europe the trade was also associated with banking – a number of goldsmiths operated as bankers. In 1708, the Dublin goldsmith Thomas Bolton loaned his guild £200 at a rate of 7 per cent towards the cost of developing their new premises on Werburgh Street.[25]

In the case of silver tokens, goldsmiths' work actually served as a form of currency offering entry to various cultural venues. A surviving ticket for admission to Rathfarnham Castle probably came from Matthew Boulton's Soho manufactory (Fig. 4.3).[26] Tokens were also issued for some Dublin theatres. Daniel Beaufort recorded in his

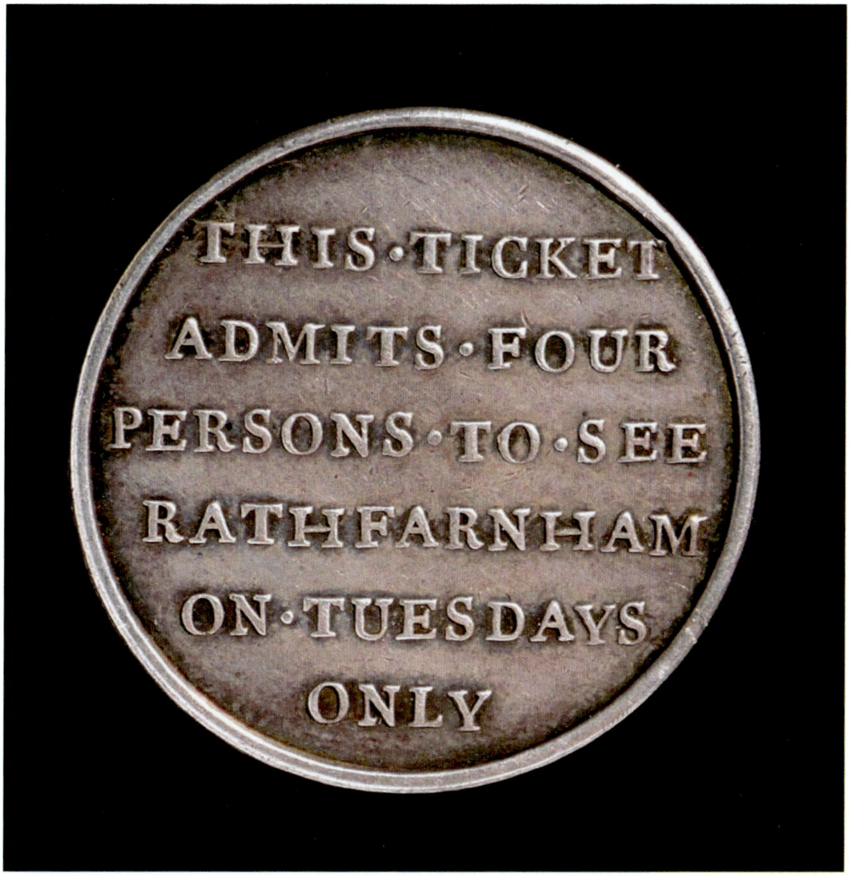

Figure 4.3 Admission ticket to Rathfarnham Castle (late eighteenth century)
Source: Private collection. Photo credit: Author's collection.

journal how he had ended the year 1789 at a performance of *The Suspicious Husband*. An acquaintance had provided him with 'a silver pass for two'.[27] Jonah Barrington's memoirs recall his early interest in the theatre, encouraged by his grandmother who had 'silver tickets of admission'.[28]

As shown in the Introduction, surviving records for eighteenth-century Ireland reveal the spending patterns of an elite that was, by definition, atypical. The data from Dublin assay records indicates the popularity among Irish consumers of relatively small silver items, but the shortage of probate inventories for middle-class consumers in Ireland makes it difficult to profile the consumption of goods by class. As Toby Barnard has shown,

> silver was possessed by others outside the select covey of peers, bishops and members of parliament regularly in Dublin . . . In a number of provincial residences, between 10 and 16 per cent of the value of the contents resided in the silver.[29]

Lorna Weatherill's analysis of English probate inventories has shown that between 1675 and 1725 ownership of silver was widespread in England, particularly in London.[30]

A cache of eighteenth-century wills for Dublin's Quaker community offers one useful window on the consumption patterns of Dublin's middle class. The frequency with which plate is mentioned in these wills, given that Quakers 'had a testimony to plainness of speech, behaviour and apparel', is somewhat unexpected.[31] Almost half of more than a hundred wills examined for the period between c.1690 to c.1760 refer directly to silverware. Some single out particular objects as bequests, and many include inventories, the majority of which specify silver objects (Table 4.1).[32] The goods listed in the inventories (the property of linen drapers, merchants, bricklayers and multiple other tradesmen) were not confined to small things, but include large items like cups, tankards and porringers – goods that would have been readily available in other materials at a fraction of the cost.[33] Evidently, a proportion of Dublin's Quaker community regarded plate as a sound purchase.[34]

In an analysis of Quakerism and visual culture between 1650 and 1750, Marcia Pointon proposes that Friends did not actually acquire or possess luxury goods.[35] The Dublin evidence indicates that this was clearly not the case. An alternative theory is that they did not advertise their ownership of goods by writing about them.[36] However, as Table 4.1 shows, a number of Dublin Quakers singled out particular items of plate in their wills.[37] The merchant Joseph Gill bequeathed a two-handled cup to his wife, and a tankard and spoons to one daughter.[38] Undoubtedly, luxury goods presented particular problems for Quakers. By the late seventeenth century, the incipient consumerism of some Irish Friends had prompted repeated injunctions against ostentation in clothing, furniture and interiors.[39] The fact that they were not deterred from acquiring silver hints at its wider consumption among Dublin's middle class. One reason why may be found by considering how ostentation was actually interpreted. An analysis of Quaker possessions in eighteenth-century Philadelphia has identified that 'heavier gauges and weights of domestic silver, plainly decorated porcelain, and clothes of fine imported fabrics sewn in simpler, less ostentatious styles could be found in the households of the wealthier Quaker elders and their devout children.'[40]

Table 4.1 Silver objects specified in Dublin Quaker inventories, c.1690–c.1760[41]

Object Type	*Quantity*	*Object Type*	*Quantity*
Buckle	3	Salver	2
Button/Stud	2?	Saucepan	2
Cann	10	Scoop	1
Caster	1	Server	1
Chalice	1	Spoon	207
Cream Pot	1	Tankard	13
Cups (Varia)	29	Tea Strainer	1
Mustard Pot	2	Tongs	3?
Pepper Box	7	Waiter	1
Porringer	7	Watch	7
Salt	14	(Not specified)	12

Source: Quaker Wills and Estate Inventories, Mss. MMIIL1, MMIIL2, Religious Society of Friends, Historical Library Dublin.

Evidently it was ornament rather than raw material, which was more problematic.[42] This corresponds with Pointon's view that it was 'what objects become, as well as what they were made of, that is significant'.[43]

Plate as social currency: the value of silverware in an 'economy of gifts'

In 1758, Richard Edgeworth recorded a payment to the Dublin goldsmith James Warren of just over £3, for 'for 2 small silver casters intended as a present to the Revd. Mr. Norris at Drogheda'.[44] Richard Norris was his son's schoolmaster, and a few years earlier Edgeworth had bought (possibly in England) two pairs of sleeve buttons and a pair of silver buckles 'as presents for the 3 Master Dewes, my son's school fellows'.[45]

The exchange of gifts was an integral feature of polite society in this period. Whether surplus produce from a country estate, souvenirs of travel, or tokens to mark special occasions, gifts represented a particular sort of currency.[46] In redressing the emphasis on female consumption in eighteenth-century Britain, Margot Finn has highlighted the role of men in a range of consumer activities.[47] She focuses on the fact that, as well as purchasing luxury goods for their own use, they invested in gift exchange among patrons, friends, neighbours and family members. Daniel Beaumont has argued that expenditure which might be perceived as extravagant was in fact an essential social lubricant among the gentry.[48] In his study of the gentry of the King's and Queen's Counties between 1690 and 1760, Beaumont concludes that the giving of gifts represented a vital form of hospitality and a reflection of social prestige. In eighteenth-century Ireland, gifts of plate were bestowed in political contexts by institutions, guilds and corporations, in professional contexts by grateful employers to employees and in personal contexts between relatives and friends. A complicated set of conventions arose from the exchange of goods, but how did a gift of plate alter the way in which it was valued?

James Carrier draws on the anthropological work of Marcel Mauss to illustrate that 'parties in a gift relationship' are ultimately obligated to one another.[49] Gifts may be given freely, 'yet they are obligatory because they are induced by expectation and belief.'[50] Political gifts of plate in eighteenth-century Ireland cannot have been understood purely as tokens of appreciation. They also served as subtle reminders of the donor's interests. A gold freedom box presented by the Guild of St. Luke to James, Earl of Kildare in 1755 includes an inscription testifying to the guild's gratitude and indebtedness to Kildare 'for his distinguished love of his country' (Fig. 4.4). In reality, a mutual obligation existed between donor and recipient in contexts like these; Kildare was not indifferent to that fact.[51] Guild support was important to political candidates, and objects like these were reminders. Writing to his wife prior to receiving the box, the Earl had expressed some reservation:

> I had a message this morning from the Corporation of Cutlers, Painters and Printers, who are in one, to know when I would be waited upon in form with my Freedom in a gold box; and next Monday at twelve is appointed. I am in distress how I am to receive them, for I shall be abused for taking state upon me, which I don't choose to do; and if I don't take the same it will affront them. The first I heard of it was in the papers, that it was voted me.[52]

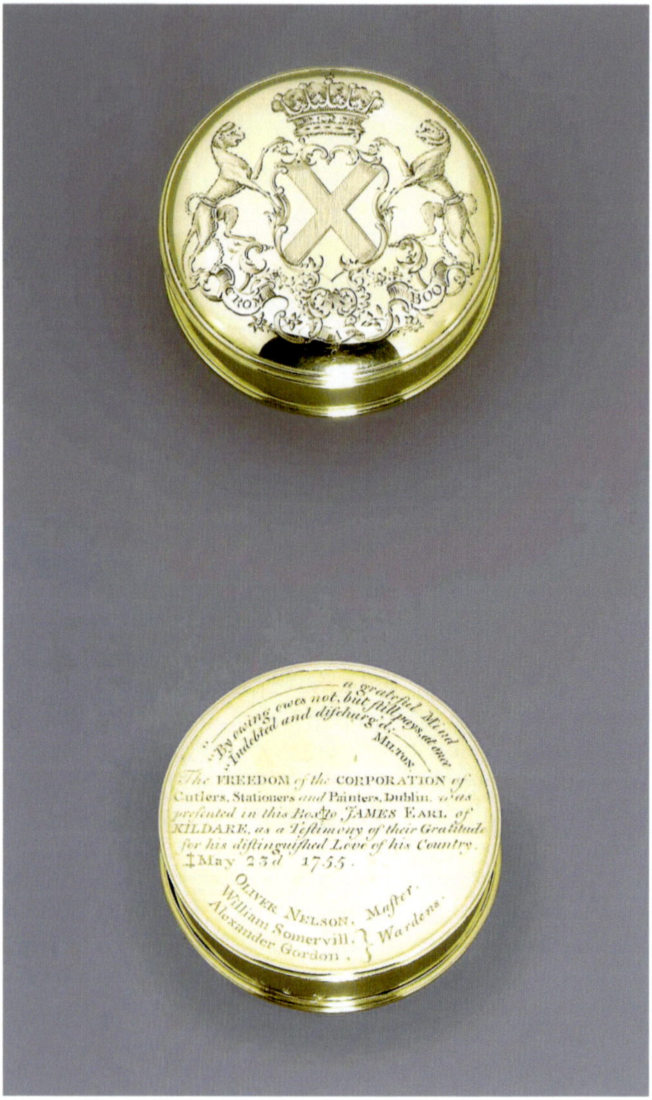

Figure 4.4 Maker's mark 'TW', *Freedom box presented by the Dublin Guild of St Luke to James FitzGerald, 20th Earl of Kildare in 1755* (1754), gold, 6.4 cm diam

Photo credit: © Christie's Images.

Some guilds commissioned idiosyncratic objects rather than the more conventional gold or silver boxes when honorary freedom was being bestowed. In 1768 the Dublin tailors' guild presented the Duke of Leinster and his son, the Marquess of Kildare, with engraved gold thimbles (Fig. 4.5). During the same period, the guild of bricklayers and plasterers presented the Marquess with an ornamental silver trowel. These objects were singled out for mention in nineteenth-century catalogues of the family's

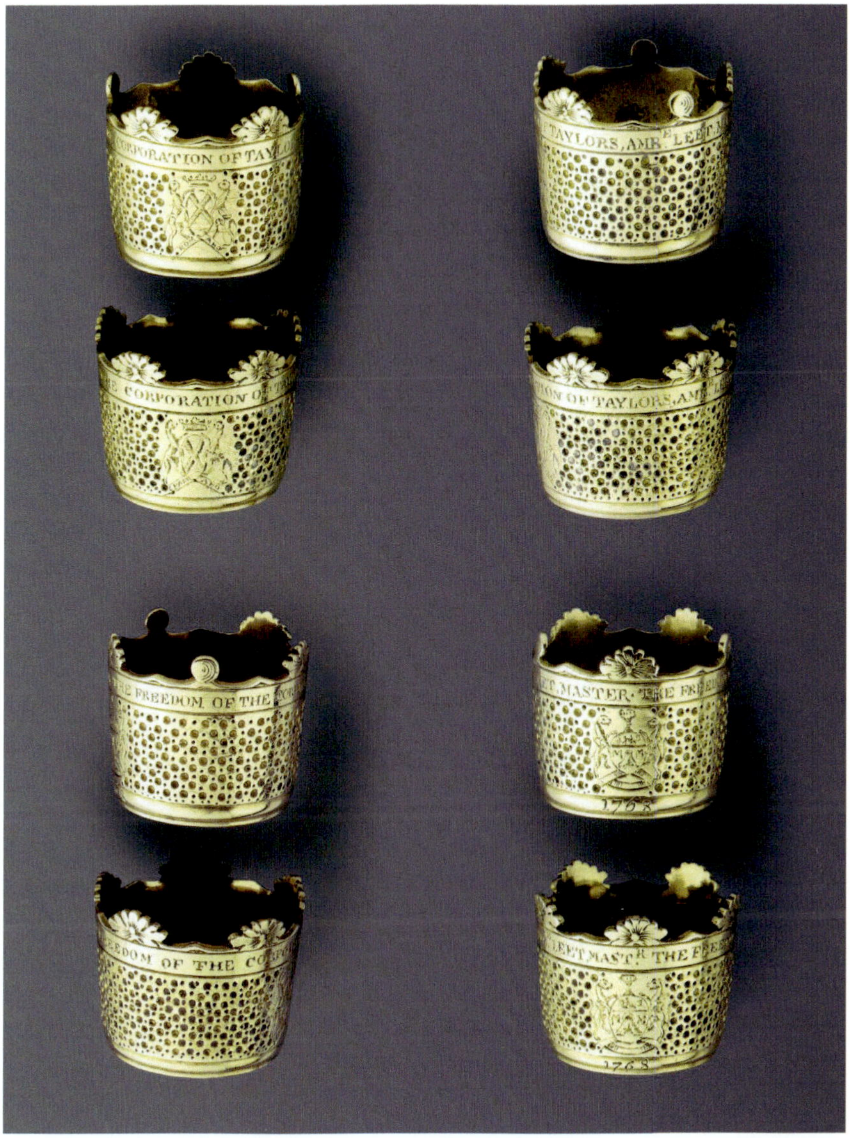

Figure 4.5 Unmarked, *Pair of thimbles (from multiple viewpoints) presented by the Dublin Tailors' Guild to James FitzGerald, 1st Duke of Leinster, and his son, William FitzGerald, Marquess of Kildare* (c.1768), gold, 1.5 cm (h)

Photo credit: © Christie's Images.

possessions, indicating the way in which they were valued not just for what they were worth in monetary terms.[53]

Another who received goldsmiths' work in the line of political duty was James Stewart of Killymoon (Figs. 4.6–4.7). After returning from a grand tour in 1768, Stewart was elected MP for Co. Tyrone. He retained his seat for thirty-two years, followed

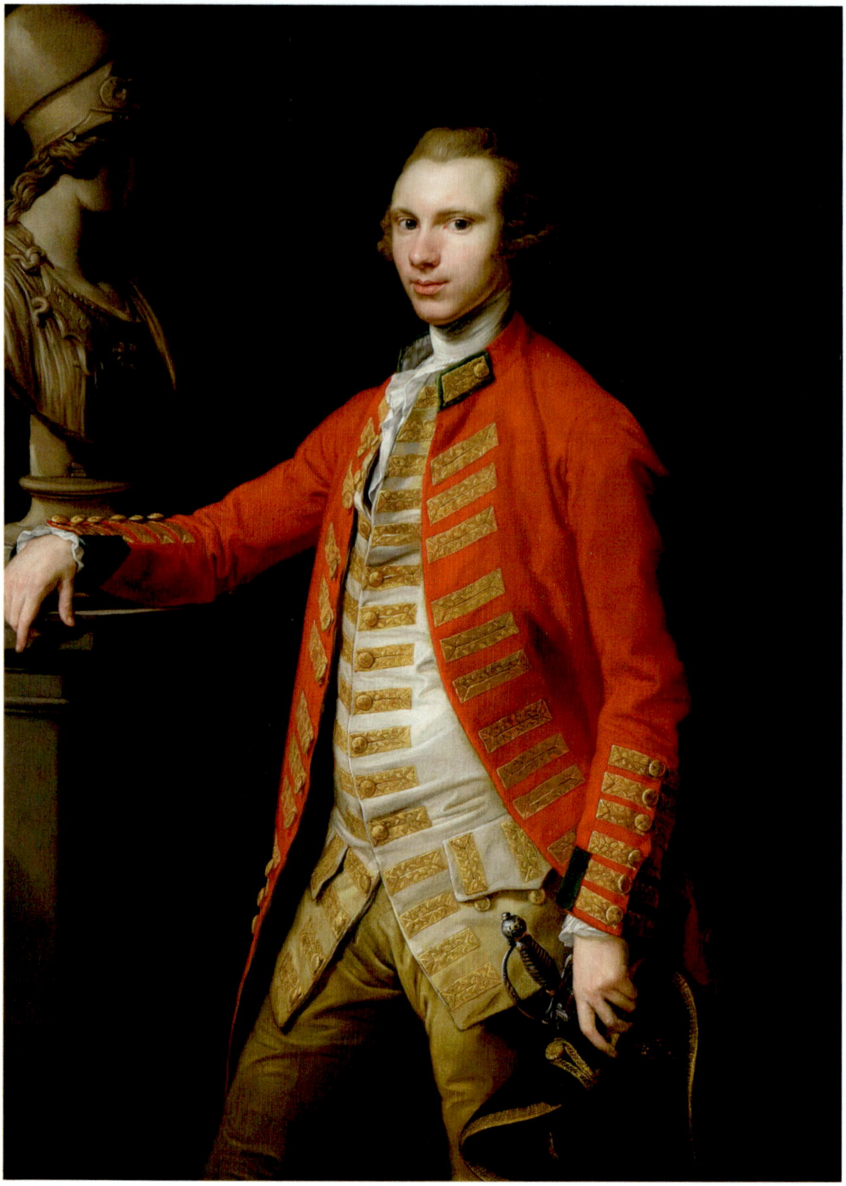

Figure 4.6 Pompeo Batoni, *Portrait of James Stewart of Killymoon* (1767), oil on canvas, 137 × 99 cm

Source: Ulster Museum, Belfast. Photo credit: © Ulster Museum.

by twelve years at Westminster. The Marquess of Kildare, who had encountered him in Italy, wrote that he had known of 'no gentleman better liked than he has been in every town he has passed through'.[54] Stewart became a leading spokesman in the Irish Parliament for the interests of northern Presbyterians and promoted legislation

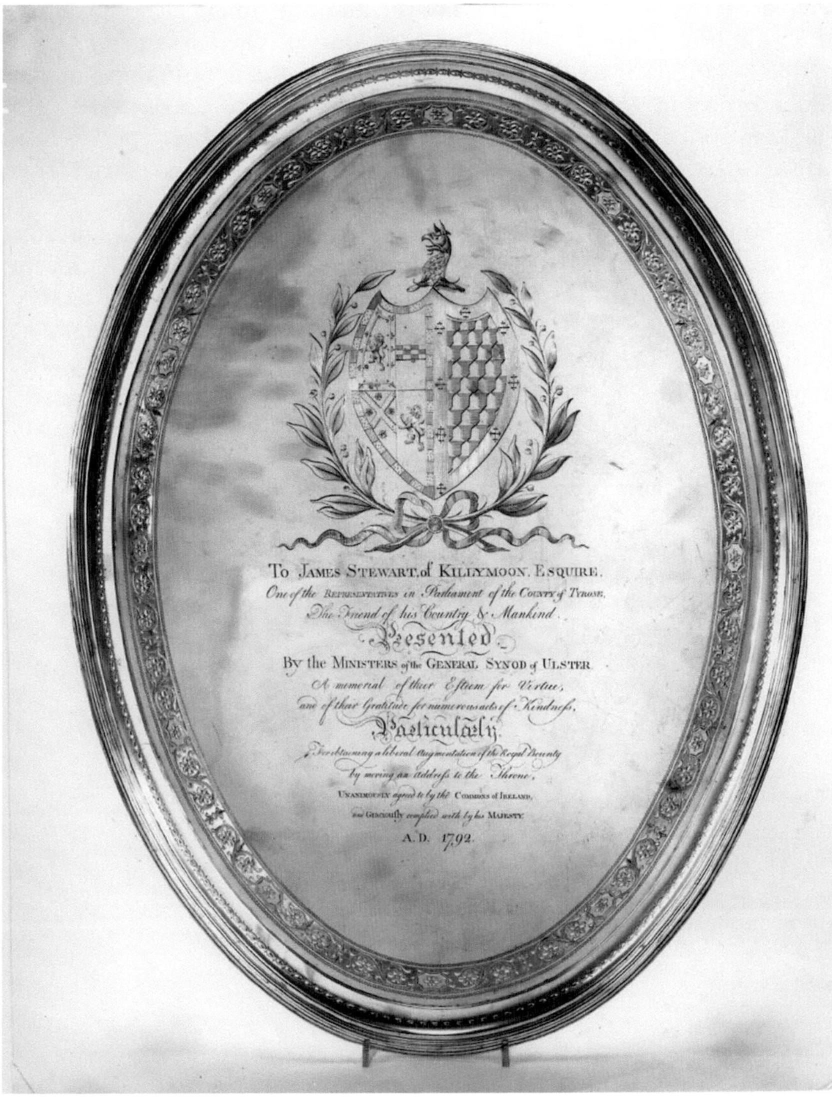

Figure 4.7 Richard Williams, *Salver presented to James Stewart of Killymoon by the General Synod of Ulster* (1792), silver

Source: Ulster Museum, Belfast. Photo credit: © Ulster Museum.

to remove the penal laws that oppressed them. In 1782, he was responsible for a bill retrospectively legitimising previously illegal marriages between Presbyterians conducted by Presbyterian clergy. The Ulster Presbyterians acknowledged his loyal support. In August 1809, Stewart received a letter informing him that, at the last meeting of the Cookstown Synod, 'an address with a piece of plate as a token of gratitude and esteem' had been 'unanimously rated' to him.[55]

Silver objects given to recognise professional achievement could be particularly highly valued by the recipients.[56] The lawyer and MP Jonah Barrington rushed to show off a gold box given to him by the Marquess of Ormonde in 1794.[57] He was delighted that he had been acknowledged in 'so public and honourable a manner', and handed the box around for his colleagues to admire.[58] In the previous decade, Amyas Griffith had received an engraved silver cup from the Belfast brewers.[59] When his circumstances changed, and Griffith had to sell his cup, he expressed particular regret at having to part with an object which clearly meant a lot to him.[60]

Church accounts reveal the extent to which plate was donated or purchased in eighteenth-century Dublin. During the first three decades of the eighteenth century, an average of twenty-five items of plate per decade were bought or donated to parishes in the diocese of Dublin.[61] Occasionally, nuns from genteel families made generous presentations. In 1719, elaborate altar candlesticks were donated to the Dominican Convent in Channel Row by the prioress Julia Browne.[62] She also bought a silver chandelier at the end of her term in office (Fig. 4.8).[63] Supplied by the Dublin goldsmith John Hamilton, it is a rare survival for this type of object in Irish silver of the period. Two members of the same order also presented a magnificent chandelier to their Galway Community in 1742, apparently inspired by Browne's example (Figs. 4.9–4.10).[64]

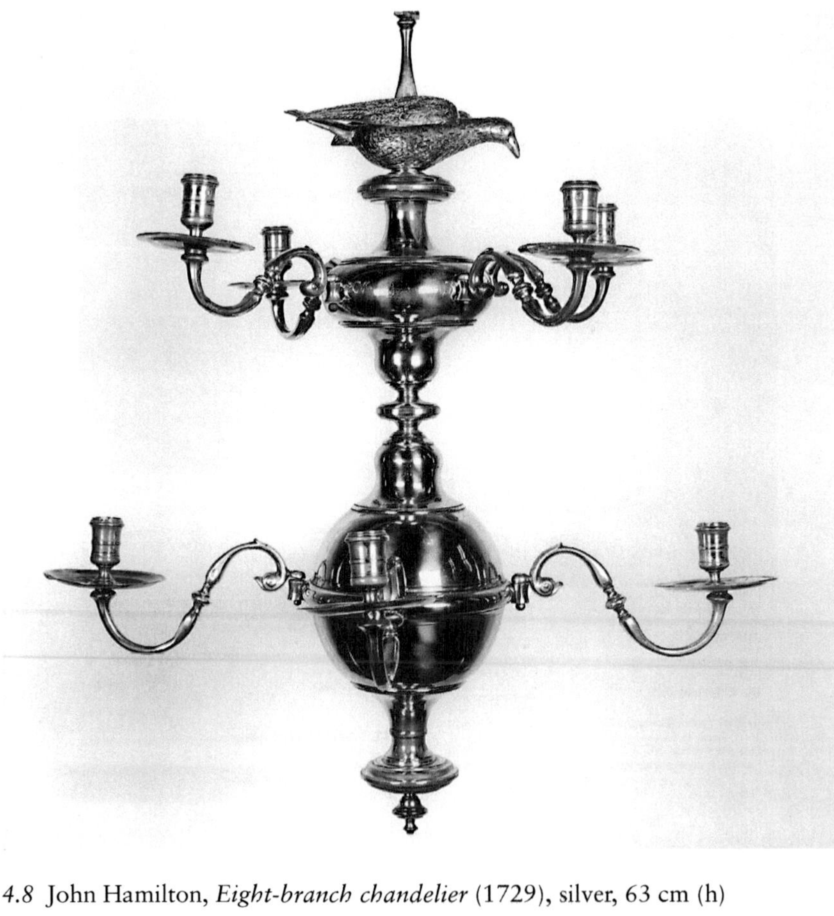

Figure 4.8 John Hamilton, *Eight-branch chandelier* (1729), silver, 63 cm (h)

Source: Congregation of Dominican Sisters in Ireland. Photo credit: © Saint Patrick's College, Maynooth.

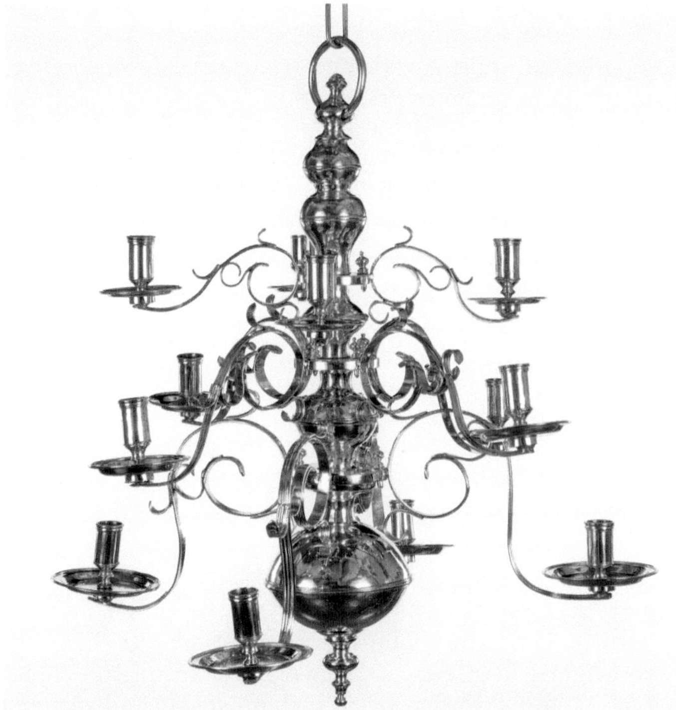

Figure 4.9 Attrib. Mark Fallon, *Chandelier* (Galway ? c.1742 or earlier), silver, 59.7 cm (h)

Source: Winterthur Museum, Delaware. Bequest of Henry Francis du Pont. Photo credit: © Winterthur Museum.

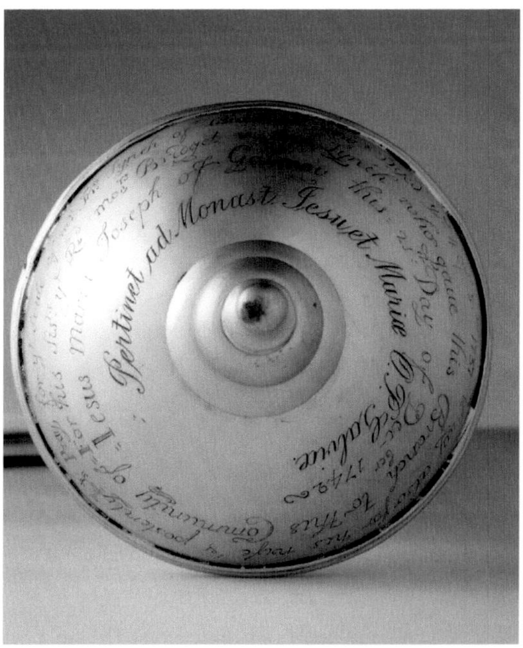

Figure 4.10 Attrib. Mark Fallon, *Chandelier* (Galway ? c.1742 or earlier), silver, 59.7 cm (h). Detail of the base of the chandelier.

Source: Winterthur Museum, Delaware. Bequest of Henry Francis du Pont. Photo credit: © Winterthur Museum.

Later in the century, the Irish-born buckle maker James Gee commented on 'the dozen silver candlesticks' which he had seen on an altar in Cook Street, and which suggested to him that the blanket poverty of Irish Catholics had been exaggerated.[65]

Gifts, whether in private or public contexts, certainly constituted a distinct form of social currency. Those who were in a position to travel, or who had contacts overseas, used their opportunities to help and remember others.[66] When Archbishop William King was arranging to source second-hand plate in London, he asked his contact, Lady Beresford, to remember his friend and physician too.[67] It is often difficult to determine whether plate acquired for others was bought on order or as gifts. For example, in 1789, James Alexander, later Lord Caledon, purchased an épergne for his son-in-law while on a trip to London; whether or not it was a gift is unclear.[68] Alexander spent large sums of money with the goldsmiths' firms of Courtauld and Cowles and Rundell and Bridge. However, on this occasion he favoured the recently appointed royal goldsmiths Jefferys and Jones.[69] The German novelist Sophie van la Roche had visited their shop three years earlier and had described it with enthusiasm:

> We visited Messrs Jeffries silver store . . . whose stock must be worth millions. It was all illuminated, and from this room, full of sparkling gold and silver moulds and vessels with two of its walls lined with large mirrors, there is a magnificent view into two brightly lit streets . . . I have never seen silver moulded into such noble, charming, simple forms; never in such profusion and with the added pleasure of comparing the work of previous generations with up-to-date modern creations, whereby the client's taste and artist's workmanship may be criticised.[70]

During the same period, the Irish banker William Digges La Touche kept a meticulous account book of his expenditure. Outgoings were entered under key headings, like travel and lodging, sums disbursed for others, and gifts.[71] La Touche, who had been educated in England, settled in Ireland in the 1780s, married Grace Puget, daughter of the London banker John Puget, and became a partner in La Touche's Bank in Dublin.[72] Trips to England offered opportunities for shopping. In 1786, he settled an account with Philip Rundell for a silver tea urn given to his in-laws.[73] At a cost of almost £50, this was a generous gift. He also bought jewellery and small trinkets in London for favourite in-laws. His accounts for 1787 include items bought from the London jeweller Thomas Gray, who was also patronised by Lord Molesworth.[74] In *Sense and Sensibility*, Jane Austen created a scene in Gray's shop where the Miss Dashwoods

> found so many people before them in the room, that there was not a person at liberty to attend their orders; and they were obliged to wait. All that could be done was to sit down at the end of the counter which seemed to promise the quickest succession.[75]

Undoubtedly, bonds were strengthened through gift exchange. In the case of heirlooms their meaning in sentimental terms often superseded their material worth. The English peer Lord Newdigate specified that all his household goods and plate should 'be left in the said house [that is Arbury Hall] and be held and enjoyed herewith as Heir Looms'.[76]

Amanda Vickery's research on eighteenth-century consumption suggests that women were more likely to attach sentimental meaning to objects.[77] Drawing on evidence from English wills, she has concluded that it was rare for men to specify objects, with the exception of occasional references to livestock or tools. Vickery proposes that as the more frequent inheritors of personal property rather than 'real property' in the form of land, women attached greater significance to moveable goods, which were ultimately theirs to bestow.[78] This theory is not borne out by the Dublin Quaker wills. While most refer to plate in generalised terms, of almost 10 per cent which to refer to specific silver objects, the majority belonged to male testators.[79]

In 1747, the merchant Joseph Fade bequeathed a silver tankard to his sister, while a niece was left his 'shell punch bowl ribbed with silver and the ladle thereto belonging'.[80] His contemporary, John Barclay, left his wife £25 worth of his plate. She was allowed to choose it, though he specified that his silver punch bowl and his largest silver cup were to go to his son.[81] Another named object was his personal Bible in which was recorded the birth of each of his children. This suggests that the objects singled out were valued above and beyond their material worth.

As chapter 3 suggested, when plate was bought second-hand, the provenance of an object could increase its appeal. For example, the fact that Charles Cobbe recorded that a few modest silver items among his general plate were bought at the late Dean Swift's auction suggests that their association was as important as, if not more important than, their material worth or usefulness to him.[82] The aura of the past may also have been on Charles Agar's mind when he acquired his dinner service second-hand in 1779. Agar, Archbishop of Cashel and first Earl of Normanton, had bought a house on St Stephen's Green in 1775. Four years later, he took the opportunity to buy a silver service to set the tone for his political entertaining in Dublin. The service was purchased from a 'Mrs Tisdall' at a cost of £856, and a friend congratulated him for acquiring 'a handsome service of plate on the easiest of terms'.[83] The fact that the service was valued at the same amount almost two decades later implies that he had not got an exceptional bargain.[84] Mrs Tisdall was the widow of the recently deceased attorney general, and this association probably appealed to Agar.

Buyers of second-hand plate often removed crests, coats of arms and other traces of earlier owners. Yet in the context of gifts and bequests, inscriptions or heraldic devices could add to an object's personal value. The will of Dublin Quaker Isaac Ashton mentions five separate bequests of plate each distinguished by initials marked 'in cypher'.[85] During the 1740s, Blayney Townley Balfour purchased items for his orphaned nephew in keeping with the boy's mother's wishes.[86] In doing so, he was preserving part of Billy Balfour's identity. The objects included a gold snuffbox engraved with the family arms, and a soup dish that had been singled out from the family plate. Like the snuffbox, which was engraved, the dish was selected for its particular meaning and association; it had served as a christening vessel for members of the family. In an analysis of the evocative potential of objects, Marius Kwint argues that objects serve memory in three main ways: by furnishing recollection and constituting an individual's picture of the past, by stimulating memory and by acting as records.[87] The Balfour soup bowl clearly was chosen for these reasons, for a value that could not be quantified in pounds, shillings and pence.[88]

In the case of mourning jewellery, small gold and silver items acquired very personal associations (Fig. 4.11). Susanna Maria Johnston, a spinster cousin of the Dublin goldsmith Robert Calderwood, was evidently keen that close-knit bonds of friendship would endure beyond her lifetime. She left several sums of money

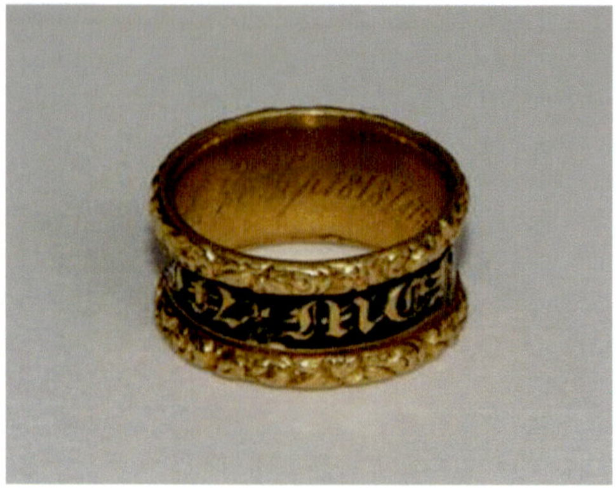

Figure 4.11 Eighteenth-century gold mourning ring. An inscription on the inside of the ring commemorates John FitzGerald of Waterford who died on 6 September 1818.

Source: Private collection. Photo credit: Author's collection.

to different individuals for specially commissioned rings and her intentions were unambiguous:[89]

> I have requested Mr. Calderwood to direct the making of the rings and shall leave some of my hair to put under the stones of them, which I believe will give them a value to my friends.[90]

Hair jewellery held potent meaning as an aide-memoire. As Marcia Pointon puts it, 'hair escapes from the idea of death'.[91] Cash was transient and quickly spent; a ring, by contrast, furnished memories. One Dublin jeweller even anticipated his clients' concern that 'false hair' might be used in hair devices.[92] He reassuringly offered to finish pieces in the presence of his customers.

Concepts of value: plate and status

One of the most obvious reasons for buying plate was as a signifier of prestige or status. According to the German sociologist Max Weber, 'stratification by status goes hand in hand with a monopolisation of ideal and material goods and opportunities.'[93] Thorstein Veblen has stressed the importance for status of 'the unremitting demonstration of the ability to pay'.[94] The connections between plate and status in eighteenth-century Ireland operated at a variety of levels. To visitors, the use and display of plate served as indicators of a host's means, rank and taste. Its power as a signifier also encouraged emulative spending. Privileged patrons, keen to reinforce their own notions of taste copied what others owned. Those below them on the social ladder seized chances to buy small luxuries or cheaper versions of expensive items. The particular social structure of Ireland, and opportunities for upward mobility, created a series of self-made men who, from relatively modest backgrounds, found themselves in positions of wealth and influence. For these, the association of plate with gentility, as well as with status, must have seemed attractive.

Pierre Bourdieu has emphasised the strategies used by different status groups to distinguish themselves from one another through patterns of consumption. He identifies a distinction between economic and intellectual capital, the former referring to financial wealth, the latter including the appreciation of artistic endeavour and the ability to make cultural distinctions.[95] As a commodity that had an intrinsic value, and also a design and display value, plate satisfied both sides of this equation. The fact that it acted as a form of distinction in eighteenth-century Ireland is borne out by a range of contemporary comments. Laetitia Pilkington noted how Dean Swift

> placed himself at the head of his table opposite to a great pier glass, under which was a marble sideboard, so that he could see in the glass whatever the servants did at it; He was served entirely in plate, and with great elegance.[96]

She was less impressed when the dean mislaid an expensive corkscrew and assumed that she had stolen it:

> The Dean then missing his golden bottle-screw told me, very sternly, 'he was sure I had stolen it': I affirmed, very seriously, 'I had not': upon which he looked for it and found it where he himself had laid it; 'tis well for you' says he, 'that I have got it, or I would have charged you with theft': 'why, pray, sir, should I be suspected more than any other person in the company?' 'For a very good reason', says he, 'because you are the poorest'.[97]

Swift, if Pilkington is to be believed, felt uneasy when social boundaries were threatened or blurred. He complained when one of his servants bought a pair of silver buckles, rather than 'going, as he ought, to the alehouse or a whore' and had 'grown very proud upon it'.[98] Neil McKendrick has argued that the lack of sufficient differentiation between the various sectors of English society during the eighteenth century encouraged a type of mass consumption, which led to fears of the kind that Pilkington ascribed to Swift.[99] In *The Fool of Quality*, published in Dublin in 1766, Lady Maitland defends the value of clothing, over and above 'mere decency and comfort':

> Were it not for the various distinctions of dress, it would be impossible to point out the several orders of men throughout the respective subordinations that are necessary to society. Without this useful expedient, we should be in utter confusion, we should not know who was who; we should not know to whom respect or obedience was due, nor be able to ascertain the prince from the peasant.[100]

Travelling throughout Ireland in the late eighteenth century, Daniel Beaufort used references to goods in his journals to make succinct judgments on matters of taste and largesse. Of Westport House in 1787 he remarked, 'dinner on plate; and two great side boards one at each end of a room 38 feet long and 24 wide; which remain there during breakfast & all day – with glasses & c'.[101] Soon afterwards, he noted of Lord Moira's hospitality, that his cook was French and that they dined well, adding that they 'eat on plate', but with 'tallow candles'.[102] The hostelry of a Mr Weir in Carrickfergus, where Beaufort stayed in 1787, had pewter spoons but wax candles, while he wrote of Lord Clanbrassil's that the 'table is rather in French cookery . . . wax candles, & plate for finish course but Queensware the second'.[103]

When clients ordered plate they sometimes referred to what others owned. This may have simply been for clarity and to facilitate the process, but could also indicate a degree of emulation. The Archbishop of Dublin's order with John Wakelin and William Taylor in 1781 included items similar to those owned by Lord Salisbury. 'Large antique fluted tureens and covers' were to imitate the 'shape of Salisbury's but the covers fluted', while three pairs of 'fluted and beaded' candlesticks with 'nozels like Salisbury's' complemented the tureens.[104] The dinner service, evidently in a neoclassical style, was shipped from Chester to Dublin at a cost of almost £1,000, inclusive of silver, manufacture and transport. This included seventy-two plates, engraved 'very neatly' with the archbishop's arms and mitre, and thirty-four round and oval dishes.

Sean Connolly has drawn parallels between the criteria that determined social position in Ireland and England during the late seventeenth and early eighteenth centuries.[105] Both countries, he argues, were characterised by 'the undefined gradations within landed society, the ambiguous status of non-landed wealth', and 'an interchange of personnel between the worlds of land and trade'.[106] However, Connolly also suggests that, partly on account of the smaller size of Ireland's landed elite, greater opportunities existed for upward mobility. Among the avenues to social advancement in eighteenth-century Ireland were offices in the church, the political establishment, and the armed services. Connolly cites the example of the Cust family of Co. Armagh, who used moderate appointments in the Revenue to build up a landed estate worth above £1,600 per annum.[107] Nathaniel Clements, who succeeded Luke Gardiner as deputy vice-treasurer and deputy paymaster-general of Ireland in 1755, exemplifies someone who rose from relatively modest origins to a position of wealth and influence. For men like him, plate was significant for its connotations not just of status, but also of gentility. Mary Delany observed how Clements and his wife had 'set out in life very young, and very humble, though both of good families' and, to judge from 'the magnificence of their living', had 'gathered together an immense fortune'.[108] Archbishop Stone wrote of Clements in 1753:

> He has the command of the money in the treasury, which he lends in large and small sums; and by those means has more people in his power than any other officer; and no power has been more constantly nor vigorously executed than his.[109]

As well as receiving gifts and presentation pieces, Clements also bought significant amounts of plate. According to Mary Delany, the couple excelled their counterparts in furniture and equipage, with Hannah Clements' elegance rivalling the finest English ladies.[110] An inventory compiled in 1775 itemises several thousand ounces of plate owned by her husband shortly before his death.[111] There was a generous dinner service, with plates both 'old' and 'new', a series of tureens, and a complete épergne weighing almost 200 oz.[112] Some of the pieces were in the rococo style and probably bought during Clements' rise to power in the first half of the century. These included four large shell-shaped dishes and a large silver jug. The jug was supplied by Robert Calderwood and included rocaille ornament.[113] Clements also possessed some silver-gilt, a further sign of prosperity. In contrast, one old spoon, described as for the housekeeper's use, recalls Jonathan Swift's (Fig. 4.12) advice in his *Directions to Servants*:

> If you are allowed a large silver spoon for the kitchen, have the bowl of it be worn out with continual scraping and stirring, and often say merrily, 'This spoon owes my master no service.'[114]

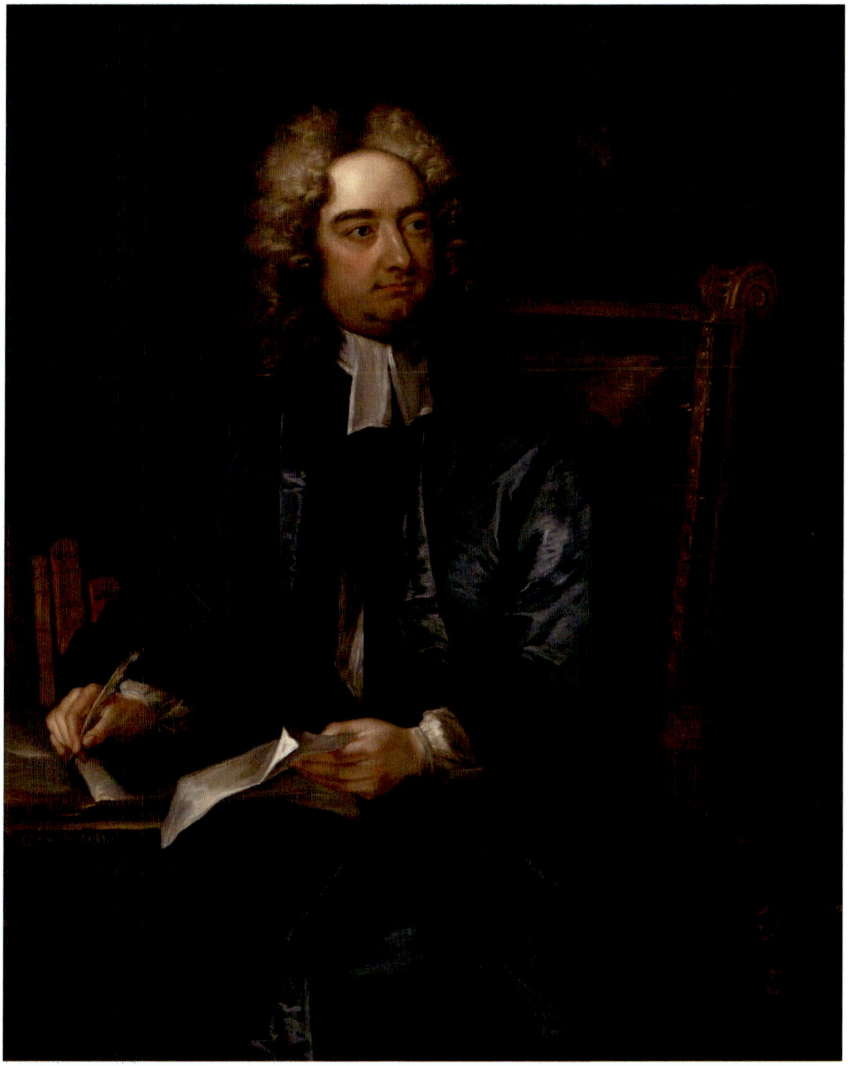

Figure 4.12 Charles Jervas, *Portrait of Jonathan Swift* (c.1718), oil on canvas, 123.2 × 97.2 cm

Source: National Portrait Gallery, London. Photo credit: © National Portrait Gallery, London.

Like many of his contemporaries, Clements bought in Dublin and in London. In 1753, the year that Stone had remarked upon his power, he placed an order with the London goldsmiths' firm of Wickes and Netherton.[115] It was mainly for flatware, which could easily have been bought in Dublin. Nevertheless, there must have been a particular cachet in buying from the goldsmiths to the Prince of Wales.[116]

The lucrative East India trade created nouveau riche nabobs, described by the dramatist Samuel Foote as

> new gentlemen, who from the caprice of fortune, and a strange chain of events, have acquired immoderate wealth, and rose to uncontrolled power abroad, find it difficult to descend from their dignity, and admit of any equal at home.[117]

Plate must have held particular appeal for these newly wealthy men. In an analysis of the symbolic character of consumer goods in eighteenth-century England, Grant McCracken argues that, with the increased importance placed on fashion during the course of the eighteenth century, patina, 'a physical and symbolic property of consumer goods', was eclipsed by novelty.[118] Reflecting a larger pattern of consumer change, new and fashionable goods became more desirable than those traditionally associated with prestige. Nevertheless, for nabobs seeking to establish themselves in the high ranks of polite society, an impressive collection of plate, the archetypal trapping of old, established wealth, must still have seemed attractive.

The Ulster merchant James Alexander provides one such example. Having secured a large fortune through his service with the East India Company, Alexander returned to Ireland in 1772.[119] He was obviously keen to procure a peerage, and set about improving his aristocratic credentials. After buying an estate from the absentee Earl of Orrery, he engaged the Dublin architect Thomas Cooley to develop Caledon House in Co. Tyrone in a fashionable but restrained neoclassical style. Daniel Beaufort noted that the 'great house' was 'finely situated' and commanded a pleasing view at the meeting of three counties.[120] During the same period, he shopped in London to equip himself with appropriate plate for a 'gentleman of large property & good character'.[121] In 1772, the year that he returned to Ireland, he spent over £1,000 in London with the firm of Courtauld and Cowles. His purchases included a range of tableware, including tureens and dishes, a fine épergne, candlesticks, waiters and cutlery.[122] The cutlery included green-handled knives and forks. Though apparently uncommon in London, these were popular with Irish retailers (Fig. 4.13).[123] No silver dining plates were mentioned in the order. However, Alexander's trade connections would certainly have facilitated the purchase of export porcelain.

In 1773, he returned to Courtauld and Cowles. As well as buying new items, he also had pieces mended and certain items engraved.[124] They were not the only London firm

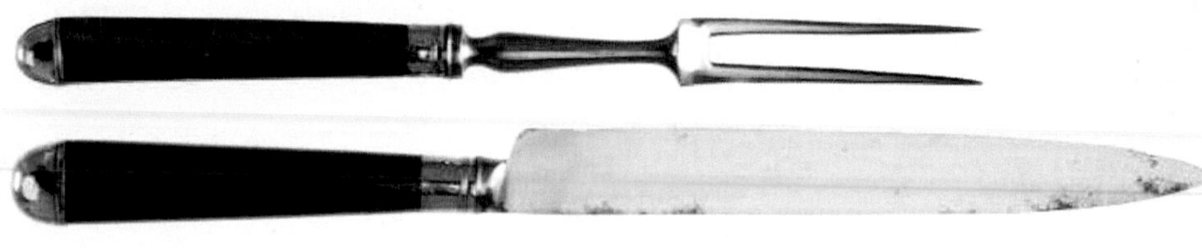

Figure 4.13 Knife and fork, steel blade and prongs, with green ivory handles (c.1790)

Source: Worshipful Company of Goldsmiths, London. Photo credit: © Worshipful Company of Goldsmiths, London.

he patronised. Having ordered goods from Jefferys and Jones during the late 1780s, he turned the following decade to the 'great leviathan of the trade', Philip Rundell and his partner John Bridge.[125] Alexander had been elevated to the peerage as Earl of Caledon in 1790.[126] This clearly necessitated further expenditure. In 1794 his order from Rundell and Bridge reflects his desire for flexibility when entertaining. Four of the table dishes bought could divide to 'serve occasionally for eight'.[127] Five of the packing bags alone were roughly equivalent to the cost of twelve china cups bought in Dublin two years later.[128]

The value of display

The display potential of plate was clearly one reason why it was bought. A contemporary servants' guide advised:

> In setting out your side-board and side-table, you must study convenience, neatness and grandeur, as you cannot think that ladies and gentlemen have splendid and costly things without wishing them to be seen or set out to the best advantage.[129]

While a tasteful display could certainly impress, it was all about getting the balance right; excessive formality or too showy a display could be criticised. In 1736, Lord Orrery remarked that Lord Kildare made 'a much better show of his plate than of his virtues'.[130] A French traveller who toured Ireland in the 1790s criticised the 'too ceremonious hospitality' he experienced:

> Surely it is a curious compliment to oblige a traveller to remain so long in a little town, where he has neither friend nor acquaintance, in order that he may, at last, have the pleasure to see much beautiful silver shining beautifully on the sideboard, servants in livery, and a huge piece of beef on the end of the table with hungry executioners round it.[131]

Servants' guides often included table layouts which helped staff with etiquette.[132] They give an indication of the number of accoutrements that could be needed to entertain in style.[133] A rare manuscript dinner book from the mid-eighteenth century provides exceptional evidence of elite consumption in an Irish context (Figs. 4.14a–c).[134] Between 1740 and 1751, the table layouts, dishes and often the guests of Robert Jocelyn were recorded in his household book. Having served as solicitor and then attorney general of Ireland, Jocelyn was appointed lord chancellor in 1727.[135] In this position he acted as lord justice and 'treated with all the state and ceremony accorded to the viceroy'.[136] During the period covered by the dinner book he had a town house on St Stephen's Green, and a residence at Mount Merrion. Jocelyn mixed with Ireland's elite, a fact reflected in the tone of his hospitality. In 1747, the guests for one meal were annotated simply as '12 Lords' – a table not many Dubliners could host. The soirée included a first course of nineteen dishes, including 'badger flambé', fricasseed frogs and lambs ears' ragout, followed by a further nineteen dishes, including set custard and fricasseed snails. Fricasseed snails were among the delicacies parodied by Hogarth a few years earlier in his print *Taste in High Life* (Fig. 4.15), satirising fashionable excess.[137]

The scale of Jocelyn's entertaining varied quite considerably, so he needed a wide range of tableware.[138] On some occasions four dishes per course sufficed. A lavish

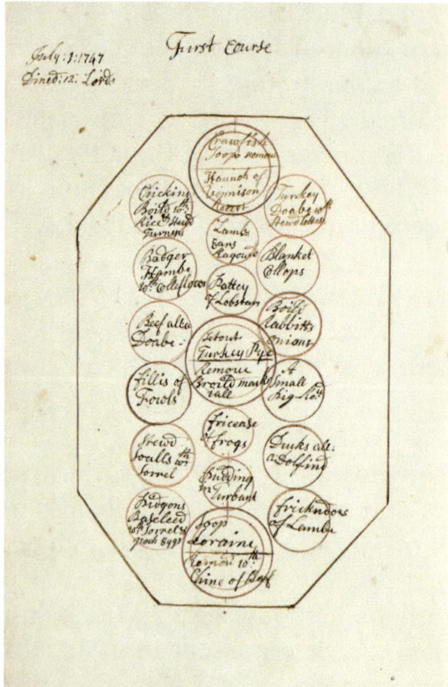

Figure 4.14a

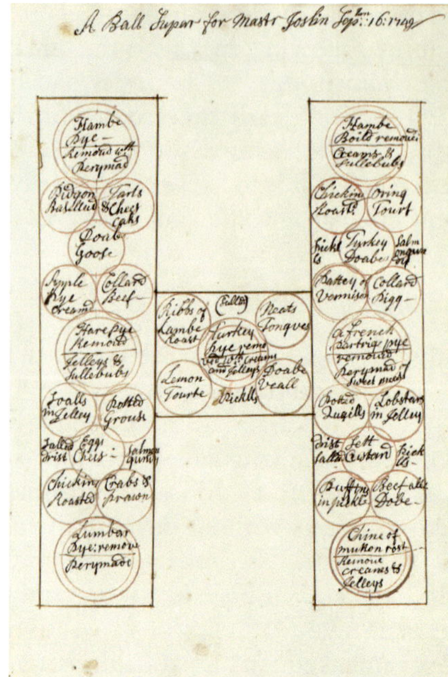

Figure 4.14b

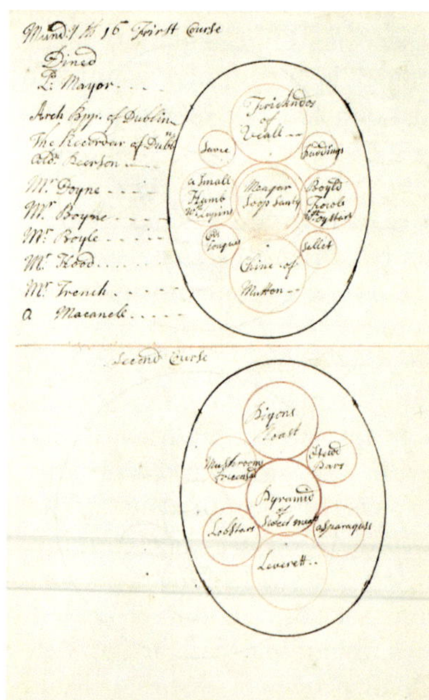

Figure 4.14c Table layout from the manuscript dinner book of Robert Jocelyn, Dublin (mid-eighteenth century)

Source: The Winterthur Library. Photo credit: © The Winterthur Library: Joseph Downs Collection of Manuscripts and Printed Ephemera.

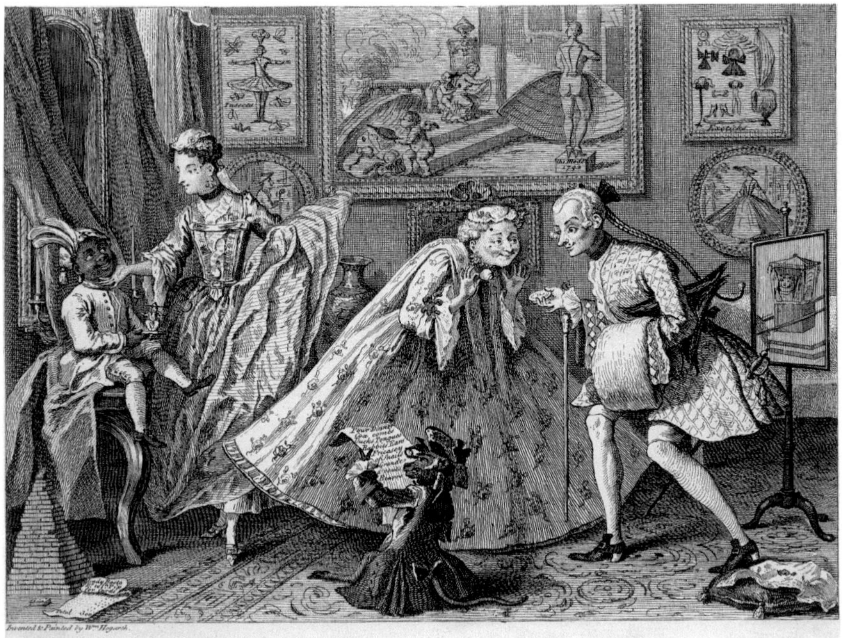

Figure 4.15 William Hogarth, *Taste in High Life* (1746), etching, 20.5 × 26.3 cm
Source: V&A. Photo credit: © V&A.

supper 'in the great parlour' necessitated a grand display of over two dozen dishes, arranged in formation as a cold buffet. The margin notes for the layout specified that the 'table must be 12 foot long, 2 foot: 8 inches broad each, the middle part 6 foot'.[139] A meal described as a 'ball supper for Master Jocelyn' was close to the date of his son's eighteenth birthday and required him to put on a show of magnificence.[140]

The Duke of Devonshire, who served as lord lieutenant, Lord Leinster, and Lord Bessborough were among the eminent guests that Jocelyn entertained. Bessborough dined with him on a number of occasions. An inventory contemporary with the dinner book suggests that Bessborough could reciprocate in style.[141] Listing numerous items of plate, it includes five pairs of candlesticks, three pairs of sconces, four dozen plates and twenty dishes. A number of the items were gilt and Bessborough patronised some of Dublin's leading craftsmen.[142] He owned silver by Robert Calderwood and John Hamilton as well as items bought in England. Links between the two countries were constantly being stressed.[143]

Few could match the spending power of patrons like Jocelyn or Bessborough. Nevertheless, small silver goods could be proudly shown off in different ways. Chapter 2 indicated that large quantities of buckles were assayed in Dublin during the late eighteenth century. These were the kind of things that could be quickly appraised by contemporaries. James Alexander spent almost £12 on a showy pair in 1775, but there were options available in every price category.[144] Similarly, watches, toothpick cases, pencil boxes and other small portable goods could be displayed to advantage. *The History of*

John Juniper includes a caricatured description of a schoolmaster who believes that his silver watch, 'an appendage to the dignity of his character', has been stolen:

> As his watch was too necessary an appendage to the dignity of his character to be left behind on such an occasion; for he did not wear it in common, to save it from being worn out, as soon as he was dressed, he went to his bureau, for that and some money, to defray the expense of his journey. But how great was his astonishment, his consternation of soul, to find the drawer where he kept his treasure, empty. He instantly raised an outcry that brought the whole house about him, to whom he lamented his loss, in the most moving terms. 'His watch! – his new watch, with a case of sterling silver! – his watch, that had cost him two whole guineas and an half, and was not a penny the worse for wearing – was gone – lost – stolen – and gone for ever – he should see it no more.'[145]

Claudia Kinmonth has shown that Irish country dressers frequently had rectangular slots cut into eye-level shelves for the display of spoons. The number of slots could vary according to the wealth of the household. Even if a family could not afford silver, this way of displaying spoons was more satisfying than storing them in drawers.[146] A servant's guide published in Dublin in the early nineteenth century suggests that owners were not the only ones to enjoy displaying plate. Servants were warned against exposing silver to risk by displaying it in vulnerable positions while cleaning or caring for it, in a desire to show how much they had been entrusted with.[147] Some servants, it seems, vicariously enjoyed ownership of plate.

The value which plate offered in personal, economic and social terms made it an attractive acquisition on many levels. In the late seventeenth and early eighteenth centuries, it acted as a store of value, prior to the firm establishment of deposit banking in Ireland. Its prevalence in Dublin Quaker inventories suggests that it was regarded as a sound asset and a reflection of honest industry. These also show the prevalence of small silver goods in middle-class inventories. Undoubtedly, ownership of plate implied gentility, conferred a measure of status, and had great display potential. Dublin may have differed from London in terms of the logistics and scale of production, but similar values encouraged the purchase of plate in both cities. As Lorna Weatherill has observed so astutely in her analysis of English inventory evidence:

> There were many reasons why people wanted to own material goods, some practical, some financial, some psychological, [making] once and for all conclusions both impossible and intellectually dishonest. There is no single answer.[148]

Notes

1 Edward Young, *Love of Fame, the Universal Passion. In Seven Characteristical Satires* (2nd ed., Dublin: Printed by S. Powell, for George Ewing, at the Angel and Bible in Dame Street, 1728), 7.

2 For more on attitudes to plate in eighteenth-century England, see Helen Clifford, 'Of Consuming Cares: Attitudes to Silver in the Eighteenth Century', *Silver Studies* 12 (2000): 53–59; John Culme, *Attitudes to Old Plate 1750–1900* (London: Sotheby's, 1985); Philippa Glanville, *Silver in England* (London: Unwin Hyman, 1987). Toby Barnard, *Making the Grand Figure: Lives and Possessions in Ireland, 1641–1770* (New Haven and London: Yale University Press, 2004), 122–51 treats this subject from an Irish perspective.

3 Barnard, *Making the Grand Figure*, 123.
4 Clifford, 'Of Consuming Cares', 53. For a good history of perceptions of sterling in a monetary context, see Nicholas Mayhew, *Sterling: The Rise and Fall of a Currency* (London: Allen Lane, 1999). Undoubtedly, the upheavals of the seventeenth century, with settlers fleeing twice to Britain, made silver objects convenient currency for converting into cash when in exile. Barnard, *Making the Grand Figure*, 140 cites the example of Sir John Temple, who 'invested some of his profits from the law and office in Charles II's Dublin in silver [which] served him as currency when he was driven from the kingdom in 1688'.
5 *An Account of the Short Life, Sudden Death, and Pompous Funeral of Michy Windybank, Only Child to Sir Oliver Windybank* (Dublin, 1721). He had voted in favour of the proposed bank. E.M. Johnston-Liik, *History of the Irish Parliament*, vol. 6 (Belfast: Ulster Historical Foundation, 2002), 216.
6 Alison FitzGerald, 'Oliver St George's Passion for Plate', *Silver Studies* 22 (2007): 51–61.
7 J.F. Hayward, *Huguenot Silver in England 1688–1727* (London: Faber & Faber, 1959).
8 Pole Cosby, 'Autobiography of Pole Cosby of Stradbally', *Kildare Archaeological Society Journal* 5 (1906–8): 266. The trip was in 1733. The failure of bankers increased hostility among the 'country' interest to paper money, the moneyed interest and all associated with it, comparable to attitudes in England. There were obviously practical fears which caused Pole Cosby not to entrust his plate to a banker, but others, like Archbishop King and Bishop Synge, still elected to do so. For more on banking in Ireland, see Louis Cullen, *Anglo-Irish Trade, 1660–1800* (Manchester: Manchester University Press, 1968); Louis Cullen, 'Landlords, Bankers, and Merchants: The Early Irish Banking World', in *Economists and the Irish Economy, from the Eighteenth Century to the Present Day*, ed. Antoin Murphy (Dublin: Irish Academic Press, 1984), 25–44.
9 For the differing scales of values accorded to foreign coin, see Joseph Johnston, 'Irish Currency in the Eighteenth Century', *Hermathena* 52 (1938): 3–26; James Simon, *An Essay towards an Historical Account of Irish Coins* (Dublin: Printed by S. Powell for the Author, 1749); M.S.D. Westropp, 'Notes on Irish Money Weights and Foreign Coin Current in Ireland', *Proceedings of the Royal Irish Academy* 33 (1916): 43–73. The likelihood, not only of wear to that currency but also additional debasement through clipping, was increased by its limited availability and therefore repeated circulation. On the practice of clipping, see John Styles, 'Our Traitorous Money Makers: The Yorkshire Coiners and the Law, 1760–83', in *An Ungovernable People: The English and Their Law in the Seventeenth and Eighteenth Centuries*, ed. John Brewer and John Styles (London: Hutchinson, 1983), 172–250. John Styles has also indicated to the author that, according to mint solicitor's accounts in Britain, the group who introduced the illegal practice of clipping to London in the 1740s were Irish.
10 The French minister Colbert believed that 'everyone agrees that the might and greatness of a state are measured by the quantity of plate it possesses'; quoted in Clifford, 'Of Consuming Cares', 54. Peter Fürhing has noted that 'during the Régence in France (1715–23) the fear that silver was going to be used as a refuge for capital was instrumental in the renewal of the earlier sumptuary laws forbidding the production of silver above a certain weight; as a result commissions for silver declined, although only temporarily.' See Truman, *Sotheby's Concise Encyclopaedia of Silver* (London: Conran Octopus, 1996), 90.
11 Jonathan Swift, *A Letter to the Shopkeepers, Tradesmen, Farmers and Common People of Ireland, Concerning the Brass Half-Pence Coined by Mr. Woods*. By M.B. Drapier (Dublin: Printed by J. Harding, 1724), 4.
12 Plate offered additional value over coin in terms of display.
13 Martha Gandy Fales, *Joseph Richardson and Family, Philadelphia Silversmiths* (Middletown, CT: Wesleyan University Press, 1974), 7. The author clarifies that 'this practice provided the owner not only with useful and beautiful objects attesting to his prosperity, but with a means of identification (through marks and engraving) should the silver be lost or stolen.'
14 John Gilbert, ed., *Calendar of Ancient Records of Dublin*, 19 vols. (Dublin: Dollard, 1889–1944), vol. 8: 589–90. Newton served as warden and then master-worker at the Royal Mint. While the shortage of coin was particularly acute in Ireland, it was also a controversial issue in England. A number of eighteenth-century English commentaries clearly express

the link between plate and coinage as determinants of a nation's wealth. See, for example, Anon., 'An Essay towards finding the balance of our whole trade annually from Christmas of 1698 to Christmas 1719', in G.N. Clark, *Guide to English Commercial Statistics 1696–1782* (London: Offices of the Royal Historical Society, 1938), 133.

15 *Short Reasons Why Our Gold-Money in Ireland Should Not Be Lowered* (Dublin, 1737). I am grateful to Robert Heslip for information on numismatic matters and for drawing my attention to this source.

16 On the history of sterling, see also J.S. Forbes, *Hallmark: A History of the London Assay Office* (London: Goldsmiths Company and Unicorn Press, 1999), and Nicholas Mayhew, *Sterling: The History of a Currency* (New York: Wiley, 1999).

17 Provincial goldsmiths sometimes marked their work with the word 'dollar'.

18 Andrew Carpenter, ed., *Verse in English from Eighteenth-Century Ireland* (Cork: Cork University Press, 1998). 107. The procession, which took place on 1 August, was known as 'the riding of the franchises' and each of the Dublin trade guilds would be represented. The reference in the verse to 'traytors' is particularly telling. As late as 1755, William Fitzwilliam wrote from Dublin to his brother commenting on the dearth of coin due to a recent bank collapse. He remarked, 'There is a scarcity of specie and if any one here takes from a bank above twenty-five pounds in specie, they are ready to vote him an enemy to his country'; William Fitzwilliam to his brother Lord Fitzwilliam, 8 April 1755, Ms. 97/46/1/2/7/54, National Archives, Dublin.

19 Accounts of Oliver St George, 10 February 1717, Ms. C110/46/198–99, National Archives, Kew.

20 Ibid. This example underscores the value of assaying as a unique form of customer assurance. The use of terminology is interesting, since sterling was a standard applicable to silver as opposed to gold.

21 Johnston-Liik, *History of the Irish Parliament*, vol. 3: 551. It is not made plain whether this was silver coin or plate.

22 *Hibernian Journal*, 25 March 1782, cited in Brian Henry, *Dublin Hanged: Crime, Law Enforcement and Punishment in late Eighteenth-Century Dublin* (Dublin: Irish Academic Press, 1994), 116. Henry notes that in the period 1771–1821, 81 instances of coining operations and 20 trials were reported in the *Hibernian Journal*. However, 'wild estimates circulated that 800 coiners' were actually operating in Dublin. For further information on coining, see John Brewer and John Styles, eds., *An Ungovernable People* (London: Hutchinson, 1983).

23 Rita Susswein Gottesman, *The Arts and Crafts in New York, 1726–76* (New York: New York Historical Society, 1938), 47. For another case, see ibid., 49.

24 *Faulkner's Dublin Journal* (*FDJ*), 19–23 August 1740; and 29 September–1 October 1768. For a list of Dublin goldsmiths involved in the manufacture of money weights, see Westropp, 'Notes on Irish Money Weights', 66.

25 John McCormack, 'The Sumptuous Silver of Thomas Bolton', *Irish Arts Review Yearbook* (*IAR*), 11 (1995): 116.

26 Matthew Boulton to Earl of Ely, 9 December 1775, Ms. 3782/1/10: 259, Birmingham City Archives.

27 Diary of Daniel Beaufort, 31 December 1789, Ms. 4031: 160, Trinity College Dublin.

28 Jonah Barrington, *Personal Sketches of His Own Times* (3rd ed., London: George Routledge and Sons, 1869), 367.

29 Barnard, *Making the Grand Figure*, 149.

30 Lorna Weatherill, *Consumer Behaviour and Material Culture in Britain 1660–1760* (London: Routledge, 1988), 26–27 and 29–30.

31 Joan Kendell, 'The Development of a Distinctive Form of Quaker Dress, *Costume* 9 (1985): 58.

32 The wills and inventories used for this purpose are held in the Quaker Historical Archive and Library, Dublin, Mss. MMIIL1, MMIIL2. As well as wills, the material analysed includes deeds of settlement and inventories, which include similar information. Not all of the wills are followed by inventories but for the purposes of clarity the same date span has been given for inventories as for wills in Table 4.1. Thirty-five out of fifty-one that include inventories specify silver objects. Those that did not include plate in some cases did not specify any other household goods.

33 For a useful introduction to Dublin Quaker wills, see Beryl Eustace and Olive Goodbody, *Quaker Records Dublin: Abstracts of Wills* (Dublin: Stationery Office, 1957).
34 Of course, some of the items mentioned in the wills would also have been inherited.
35 Marcia Pointon, 'Quakerism and Visual Culture 1650–1800', *Art History* 20 (1997): 397–431. The basis for this suggestion is the dearth of references to consumer goods in their personal correspondence and diaries. Pointon does, however, qualify the problem with this conclusion, since so many expressions of concern were being issued to Quakers in respect of luxury goods.
36 Ibid., 423.
37 In contrast, they were reluctant to have pictures.
38 Will of Joseph Gill of the City of Dublin, Merchant, 1741, Ms. MMIIL2: 127, Quaker Historical Archive and Library, Dublin. A second daughter, Isabella, was to receive a 'fine old fashioned chest of drawers which was her mother's and also three silver tablespoons marked I G I'.
39 Barnard, *Making the Grand Figure*, 117. See also Richard Greaves, *Dublin's Merchant-Quaker: Anthony Sharp and the Community of Friends, 1643–1707* (Stanford, CA: Stanford University Press, 1998), 209–11.
40 Jack Lindsay, *Worldly Goods: The Arts of Early Pennsylvania, 1680–1758* (Philadelphia: Philadelphia Museum of Art, 2000), 77. Nevertheless, ownership of plate did present a problem for some devout Quakers. Gandy Fales, *Joseph Richardson and Family*, 67 cites the aversion of one Philadelphia Quaker to the customary use of silver vessels 'in which there is a manifest conformity to outward show and greatness'. For an alternative perspective on Quaker ownership of luxury goods, see Lindsay, *Worldly Goods*, 75.
41 One hundred and sixteen wills form the basis for the analysis in this section. Fifty-one of those refer to plate. Thirteen specify silver objects. Fifty-one had accompanying inventories, thirty-five of which mention plate.
42 While the majority of Dublin testators assessed had relatively modest amounts of plate, there were individuals whose goods seem clearly to contravene Quaker principles. An extensive array of valuable goods willed by Katherine Forbes of Dublin in 1758 included a gold enamelled buckle and gilded tankard, gilded porringer and cover. Will of Katherine Forbes of Eustace Street, 1758, Ms. MMIIL2: 289–94, Quaker Historical Archive and Library, Dublin.
43 Pointon, 'Quakerism and Visual Culture', 401. This also accords with Barnard's finding that rich woods were used in furniture owned by Irish Quakers during this period. Barnard, *Making the Grand Figure*, 117.
44 Accounts of Richard Edgeworth, 6 January 1758: National Library of Ireland, Ms. 1524: 52.
45 Accounts of Richard Edgeworth, 23 May 1754, National Library of Ireland, Ms. 1521: 33.
46 Margot Finn refers to gift-giving as a comparatively neglected 'tier of acquisition', one which reinforced bonds, and reflected a value in social terms. Margot Finn, 'Men's Things: Masculine Possession in the Consumer Revolution', *Social History* 25 (2000): 143.
47 Ibid. This accords with Barnard's observation in an Irish context that 'ceramics, like textiles, bewitched through their look. Busy men confessed to a weakness'. Barnard, *Making the Grand Figure*, 131.
48 Daniel Beaumont, 'The Gentry of the King's and Queen's Counties: Protestant Landed Society, 1690–1760' (PhD thesis, Trinity College Dublin, 1999).
49 James Carrier, *Gifts and Commodities: Exchange and Western Capitalism since 1700* (London: Routledge, 1995), 21. The following analysis does not discount the view that gifts of plate were also frequently prompted by the straightforward motive of pleasure.
50 Ibid.
51 The inscription included the words: 'A grateful mind by owing owes not, but still pays, at once indebted and discharged'. A decade later, the minutes of the goldsmiths' guild record their decision to address James FitzGerald, then Duke of Leinster, requesting that his son, the Marquess of Kildare, should offer himself as a parliamentary candidate. Their justifications included the belief that the 'Illustrious House of Leinster' had 'nothing more at heart than to promote the interest and prosperity of this city'. Minute of 16 September 1767, Company of Goldsmiths of Dublin, Ms. 5: 140, Dublin, Assay Office.
52 Brian FitzGerald, *Correspondence of Emily, Duchess of Leinster*, 3 vols. (Dublin: Stationery Office, 1949–57), 25. The earl's letter was dated 24 May 1755. Evidently, the guild

anticipated a favourable response as the inscription on the box states that it was presented the previous day.

53 Anon., *Notes on the Pictures, Plate, Antiquities, etc. at Carton, Kilkea Castle, 15 Dominick Street Dublin, and at 6 Carlton House Terrace, London* (Dublin, 1871), 6. See also Alison FitzGerald, 'Desiring to "Look Sprucish": Objects in Context at Carton', in *Aspects of Irish Aristocratic Life: Essays on the FitzGeralds of Kildare and Carton House*, ed. Terence Dooley, Patrick Cosgrove, and Karol Mullaney-Dignam (Dublin: University College Dublin Press, 2014), 100–109.

54 John Ingamells, *A Dictionary of British and Irish Travellers in Italy, 1701–1800* (New Haven and London: Yale University Press, 1997) 897. For further information on Stewart, see Johnston-Liik, *History of the Irish Parliament*, 339–42; Ann Stewart, *James Stewart of Killymoon, An Irishman on the Grand Tour* (Belfast: Ulster Museum, 1999).

55 John Pollock to James Stewart, 1 August 1809, Ms. D3167/2/215, Public Record Office of Northern Ireland.

56 It is hard to know whether gifts like these were bonuses that the recipient could decently convert to cash, or were more valued as testimonies of esteem to be publicly displayed.

57 Barrington, *Personal Sketches of His Own Times*, 123. The box was given to acknowledge his help in contesting a legal case.

58 Ibid.

59 Amyas Griffith, *Miscellaneous Tracts* (Dublin, 1788), 11.

60 Ibid., 65. Mary St George willed a silver cup to a female servant in 1746, though this was, strictly speaking, a legacy rather than a gift. The servant was to receive the cup only if still living with St George at the time of her death. Will of Mary St George, 18 August 1746, Ms. D/235/23, Public Record Office of Northern Ireland (PRONI).

61 I am grateful to the late Dr John Crawford for sharing the results of his research on communion plate in Dublin between 1600 and 1900. In contrast to this, there were periods when no church plate at all was acquired, for example, in the years between 1791 and 1800. A letter published in the *Hibernian Journal*, 31 May–3 June 1771, lamented that one Kennedy, a churchwarden in St Paul's parish who had responsibility for the church plate, had retained it until the rector agreed to pay him money owed. The rector was evidently forced to borrow communion plate as a result. Raghnall Ó Floinn, ed., *Franciscan Faith: Sacred Art in Ireland, AD 1600–1750* (Dublin: Wordwell, 2011); J.J. Buckley, *Some Irish Altar Plate* (Dublin: Royal Society of Antiquaries of Ireland, 1943); and Charles A. Webster, *The Church Plate of the Diocese of Cork, Cloyne and Ross* (Guy & Co., 1909).

62 Joseph McDonnell, *Ecclesiastical Art of the Penal Era* (Maynooth: St Patrick's College, 1995), 30–32.

63 Ibid.

64 For further information on this piece, see Gordon St George Mark, 'A Silver Chandelier from Galway', *Bulletin of the Irish Georgian Society* (*BIGS*) 25 (1982): 19–24.

65 Appendix to *The Life and Times of James Gee of Walsall, 1746–1827* (Walsall Local History Centre), 106–7.

66 This could also work within the country, as individuals with Dublin links used them to accommodate those at some remove. In 1792, one Dublin retailer advertised the supply of table services of Queensware, 'ready packed for the Country, at two Guineas per set'. *Hibernian Journal*, 20 June 1792.

67 William King to Lady Beresford, 8 November 1712, Ms. 750/4: 64, Trinity College Dublin.

68 Account of James Alexander with Jefferys and Jones, 12 June 1789, Ms. D2433/B/1/1/23, PRONI; and Plate Account of James Alexander n.d. [1789], Ms. D 2433/B/1/1/19, PRONI. It seems very likely that his son-in-law had actually ordered it, since the latter account refers to plate bought 'on account' for himself and Langford Heyland. Heyland had recently married Caledon's illegitimate daughter and, either way, this suggests his support of the union. Others were less favourable in their comments on the relationship. Mrs McTier wrote to her brother Dr William Drennan that Langford Heyland is to be married 'to a bastard of nabob Alexander's – young and ugly, with £10,000'; Johnston-Liik, *History of the Irish Parliament*, vol. 3: 77.

69 Arthur Grimwade, *London Goldsmiths 1697–1837* (3rd ed., London: Faber & Faber, 1990), 560–61, 565.

70 Ibid., 560.

71 Domestic and Private Account Book of William George Digges La Touche, 1781–98, Ms. 19,898, National Library of Ireland. I am grateful to Gaye Kennedy for drawing my attention to this manuscript.
72 Sergio Benedetti, *The La Touche Amorino, Canova and His Fashionable Irish Patrons* (Dublin: National Gallery of Ireland, 1998). For further information on the La Touche family, see David Dickson and Richard English, 'The La Touche Dynasty', in *The Gorgeous Mask*, ed. David Dickson (Dublin: Trinity College Dublin, 1987), 17–30.
73 Accounts of William George Digges La Touche, 12 June 1786, Ms. 19,898: 1, National Library of Ireland.
74 Ibid., 11. He returned both to Rundell and Gray again. His English accounts for 1792 include £14 8s 9d spent with Gray on 'Presents' (Ibid., 41). Account of the Rt Hon. Lord Viscount Molesworth with Thomas Gray, January–August 1789, Leitrim Papers, Ms. 33,839, National Library of Ireland.
75 Quoted in Walsh, 'Shop Design and the Display of Goods', 121. Over a period of months in 1789, Molesworth acquired various personal items including buckles, 'a sandlewood smelling bottle' and 'a red leather purse with silver edges'. Bill from Thomas Gray to Richard, Viscount Molesworth, 1789, Ms. 33,839, National Library of Ireland.
76 Clifford, 'Of Consuming Cares', 58.
77 See, for example, Amanda Vickery, 'Women and the World of Goods: A Lancashire Consumer and Her Possessions, 1751–81', in *Consumption and the World of Goods*, ed. John Brewer and Roy Porter (London: Routledge, 1994), 274–305.
78 Ibid. In Ireland Pole Cosby of Stradbally chose to sell off household goods in preference to a small area of land when in need of funds. See Beaumont, 'The Gentry of the King's and Queen's Counties', 78.
79 As previously indicated, of 116 wills surveyed, 51 referred to plate. Thirteen specified particular objects and of those eight of the testators were male. While it could be argued that precise descriptions were employed to avoid ambiguity, such specificity suggests a more than mundane awareness of the goods that were singled out. See Barnard, *Making the Grand Figure*, 119.
80 Will of Joseph Fade of the City of Dublin Merchant, 1747, Ms. MMIIL2: 231, Quaker Historical Archive and Library, Dublin. The tankard had belonged to their father.
81 Will of John Barclay of the City of Dublin Merchant, 1750, Ms. MMIIL2, Quaker Historical Archive and Library, Dublin, 246.
82 Account Book of Charles Cobbe, 1760s (private collection). Naturally, this was in addition to the likelihood that buying plate second-hand might have proved cost effective too. Swift's fame was also a factor.
83 Anthony Malcomson, *Archbishop Charles Agar: Churchmanship and Politics in Ireland, 1760–1810* (Dublin: Four Courts, 2002), 380–81.
84 Ibid.
85 Will of Isaac Ashton of Kevin Street, Dublin, 1755, Ms. MMIIL2: 281, Quaker Historical Archive and Library, Dublin. John Fitzgibbon, Lord Clare, enumerated in considerable detail the plate that he wished his wife to have for her lifetime, before it descended to their son Richard 'to become his absolute property'. Will of Lord Clare, 11 December 1800, Ms. T3244/11/1, PRONI. I am grateful to Christine Casey for this reference. Fitzgibbon itemised the service of plate and plated articles that he used at his house at Mount Shannon, specifying that on 'the greater part thereof' his wife's arms were quartered with his.
86 Balfour Family Accounts, Ms. 9534: 79; Ms. 10,279, loose folios, National Library of Ireland.
87 Marius Kwint, Christopher Breward, and Jeremy Aynsley, eds., *Material Memories: Design and Evocation* (Oxford: Berg, 1999), 3. For an analysis of the emotional power of objects, see Anna Moran and Sorcha O'Brien, eds., *Love Objects* (London: Bloomsbury, 2014).
88 A further example of engraved items of plate having particular significance as heirlooms can be found in the Leitrim Papers. In his will Robert, fourth Earl of Leitrim [d.1892], gave his wife various heirlooms. These would inevitably go to the person who inherited the Newtown Gore estate. In Ms. 33,866, National Library of Ireland, there is a list of items selected by the Countess, including '1 small round box Coat of Arms the Gift of Merchants Dublin to Nath.l Clements Esq with Freedom of Corporation 1755'.

89 Material relating to Robert Calderwood, Goldsmith of Dublin, Ms. 3269: 99–101, National Library of Ireland.
90 Ibid., 100.
91 Marcia Pointon, 'Materializing Mourning: Hair, Jewellery and the Body', in *Material Memories*, ed. Kwint et al., 46. See also Nigel Llewelyn, *The Art of Death* (London: Reaktion Books, 1991).
92 *Hibernian Journal*, 18 November 1791.
93 James Carrier, *Gifts and Commodities*, 2.
94 Ibid.
95 Pierre Bourdieu, *Distinction: A Social Critique of the Judgement of Taste* (Cambridge, MA: Harvard University Press, 1984).
96 A.C. Elias Jr, ed., *Memoirs of Laetitia Pilkington*, 2 vols. (Athens: University of Georgia Press, 1997), 27.
97 Ibid., 31. This connection between plate and social status is reiterated in *The Fool of Quality* when the home of a bogus gentleman is searched and the house is found 'richly furnished, a library full of choice books above stairs, a buffet full of massy plate, and everything in order as if prepared for the reception of a family of distinction'. Henry Brooke, *The Fool of Quality*, vol. 1 (Dublin, 1766), 170–71.
98 Elias, *Memoirs of Laetitia Pilkington*, 281. Buckles offered great value in terms of their potential for display and show.
99 Neil McKendrick, John Brewer, and J. H. Plumb, *The Birth of a Commercial Society* (London: Europa, 1982), 11; 15–16.
100 Brooke, *The Fool of Quality*, vol. 2: 269–70.
101 Daniel Beaufort, 'Journal of a Tour throughout Ireland', 1787, Ms. 4027: 33, Trinity College Dublin. Perhaps the outmoded fashion of displaying vessels on impressive sideboards was the cause of his exclamation. This form of display, when silver was involved, was also associated with a desire to showcase visible wealth.
102 Ibid., 58. Beaufort was also struck by Lord Moira's great collection of curious shells and noted, 'He has many valuable medals.'
103 Daniel Beaufort, 'Journal of a Tour throughout Ireland', 1787, Ms. 4028: 49; 68, Trinity College Dublin. The memoirs of Jonah Barrington record how he visited an inn at Hallymount, and deduced that the curtains in his room had previously been owned by 'some greater personage'. He observed how the marks of the embroidery on crimson silk remained after having being picked out, he assumed, 'to sell the silver'. Barrington, *Personal Sketches of His Own Times*, 278.
104 Garrard Ledgers, 16 September 1781, John Wakelin and William Taylor Gentleman's Ledger 1777–87, Garrard Ledgers, V&A.
105 S.J. Connolly, *Religion, Law and Power: The Making of Protestant Ireland 1660–1760* (Oxford: Oxford University Press, 2000).
106 Ibid., 63.
107 Ibid., 61.
108 Quoted in Desmond FitzGerald, 'Nathaniel Clements and Some Eighteenth-Century Irish Houses', *Apollo* (October 1966), 314.
109 Ibid. See also Anthony Malcomson, *Nathaniel Clements: Politics, Fashion and Architecture in Mid-Eighteenth-Century Ireland* (Dublin: Four Courts, 2014).
110 One of the most telling testimonies of Clements' meteoric rise to wealth was a remark made by the Countess of Kildare to her husband, in a letter of June 1757. Writing from Holland House to the earl, then at Carton, she commented of Clements that the only woman of whom she might be jealous was his wife. She teased her husband about the possibility that he might fall in love with Hannah Clements, and she added, 'If you do, Mr Clements shall be my lover, and then I may afford to new-set my diamonds as often as I please'; FitzGerald, *Correspondence of Emily, Duchess of Leinster*, 49–51.
111 Nathaniel Clements' inventory of plate, 1775, Ms. 33,575, National Library of Ireland. Nathaniel Clements' will, dated a few months earlier than the inventory, specifies that his wife was to receive 800 oz. of his plate, of her own choosing 'together with her Watch Strings, Jewels and all other Ornaments of her person usually worn by her'; Copy will of Nathaniel Clements, 19 May 1775, and codicil, 24 May 1777, Ms. 9,621, National Library of Ireland.

112 All sorts of tableware were listed in the inventory, from sauceboats and breadbaskets to cups, goblets, candlesticks and urns.
113 Joseph McDonnell, 'Irish Rococo Silver', *IAR* 13 (1997): 81. The jug was sold by Sotheby's on 24 July 1975 (lot 205) and the weight was catalogued as 55 oz., 13 dwt. Allowing for the wear of silver over time, this suggests that the Calderwood piece is the item referred to in the inventory as the weight correlates with the surviving object.
114 Jonathan Swift, *Directions to Servants* (Dublin: George Faulkner, 1745), 31.
115 Account of Nathaniel Clements, 13 October and 20 December 1753, George Wickes and Samuel Netherton Gentleman's Ledger 1750–54, Garrard Ledgers, V&A.
116 Clements also ordered jewellery from England. An entry in the ledgers of the London jeweller Peter Webb records the sale of '50 fine Brill.ts in Knots' to 'Nat. Clemments Eqr of Dublin' for the sum of £27; London jeweller's accounts of Peter and Arthur Webb, 15 December 1739 (?), Ms. C 108/284: 17, National Archives, Kew.
117 Lord Macaulay observed in 1773 that these men were frequently neither from 'ancient nor opulent families'; quoted in Diana Scarisbrick, *Jewellery in Britain 1066–1837* (Norwich: Michael Russell, 1994), 231.
118 Grant McCracken, *Culture and Consumption* (Bloomington: Indiana University Press, 1990), 31.
119 For more on Alexander, see Johnston-Liik, *History of the Irish Parliament*, vol. 3: 77–79.
120 'Journal of a Tour throughout Ireland 1787', Ms. 4028: 77, Trinity College Dublin. The estate had been purchased for £96,400 and Caledon used his fortune to develop estates to the value of £600,000.
121 William Hunt, ed., *The Irish Parliament in 1775* (Dublin: Hodges, Figgis, Longmans, Green, 1907), 1.
122 Receipt from Courtauld and Cowles to James Alexander, 3 May 1773, Ms. D2433/B/1/1/2, PRONI.
123 Sarah Foster, 'Going Shopping in Georgian Dublin' (MA thesis, Royal College of Art, London, 1995), 83.
124 Receipt from Courtauld and Cowles to James Alexander, 19 September 1773, Ms. D2433/B/1/1/1, PRONI.
125 Rundell was referred to thus by his contemporary and competitor Joseph Brasbridge in the latter's autobiography; Joseph Brasbridge, *The Fruits of Experience* (2nd ed., London, 1824), 172. Receipt from Rundell and Bridge to James Alexander, 11 February 1791, Ms. D2433/B/1/1/25, PRONI; and Receipt from Rundell and Bridge to James Alexander, 1794, Ms. D2433/B/1/1/30, PRONI.
126 Johnston-Liik, *History of the Irish Parliament*, vol. 3: 77–79.
127 Receipt from Rundell and Bridge to James Alexander, 26 May 1794, Ms. D2433/B/1/1/30, PRONI.
128 Receipt from James Donovan to James Alexander, 6 June 1796, Ms. D/2433/B/1/7, PRONI. These were described as coffee cans and saucers and purchased from Donovan's on George's Quay. An advertisement in *Faulkner's Dublin Journal*, 11–13 May 1773, highlighted the sale at Donovan's of 'all types of china, glass and earthenware at the lowest prices'.
129 Thomas Cosnett, *The Footman's Directory and Butler's Remembrancer* (London: Simpkin & Marshall, 1825), 76–77.
130 Barnard, *Making the Grand Figure*, 139.
131 John Stevenson, ed., *A Frenchman's Walk through Ireland*, 1796–7 (Dublin: Hodges and Figgis & Co. 1917), 21.
132 These include cookery books as opposed to texts on the upkeep of a house.
133 See, for example, Cosnett, *The Footman's Directory*. Also, *The Lady's Companion* (Dublin, 1767). A number were published in mid-eighteenth-century England aimed specifically at a middle-class audience and adapted from courtly French cuisine. See Sarah Richards, *Eighteenth-Century Ceramics* (Manchester: Manchester University Press, 1999), 158–59.
134 Dinner book of Robert Jocelyn, 1740–51, Ms. 219, Winterthur Library, Joseph Downs Collection. Alison FitzGerald, 'Taste in High Life: Dining in the Dublin Townhouse', in *The Dublin Townhouse: Form, Function, Finance*, ed. Christine Casey (Dublin: Four Courts, 2009), 120–28.

135 For further information on Jocelyn, see F. E. Ball, *History of the County of Dublin*, 6 vols. (Dublin, 1902–20), vol. 1: 14, 44, 131; vol. 2: 54, 61, 86–90; and Johnston-Liik, *History of the Irish Parliament*, 488–90.
136 Ball, *History of the County of Dublin*, vol. 2: 87.
137 Jenny Uglow has proposed that the monkey in the foreground, apparently mocking the humans, is perusing a 'fantastical' menu of 'cocks combs, ducks tongues, rabbits ears, fricassey of snails [and] grande beurre d'oeufs'. Jenny Uglow, *Hogarth: A Life and a World* (London: Faber & Faber, 1997), 371–74. For the dissemination of Hogarth's prints within the decorative arts, see Lars Tharp, *Hogarth's China: Hogarth's Painting and Eighteenth-Century Ceramics* (London: Merrell Holberton, 1997). While Hogarth certainly intended to satirise fashionable excess, the menu he employed may not have been as fantastical as Uglow is suggesting.
138 William King addressed this need for flexibility much earlier in the century when he wrote that he sometimes had need for 'only two dishes Sometimes 4 Sometimes 5 and Sometimes 9 for a service and therefore in that way must have Sevll.'; William King to Lady Beresford, 16 October 1712, Ms. 750/4: 66, Trinity College Dublin.
139 Dinner book of Robert Jocelyn, 1740–51.
140 Ibid.
141 Schedule No. 1 of Lord Bessborough's Plate in Dublin Taken the Seventh Day of March 1743 (private collection). I am grateful to Daniel Beaumont for sharing the contents of this document with me.
142 Jonah Barrington, recalling the 'enjoyments of winter' in eighteenth-century Ireland, conjured up a novel function for candlesticks. He recalled how, in the aftermath of the hunt, 'A fox's brush stuck into a candlestick, in the centre of the table, was worshipped as a divinity!'; Barrington, *Personal Sketches of His Own Times*, 40.
143 Silver sauce tureens made by the Dublin goldsmith Robert Breading in 1786 mirror the design of soup tureens supplied by Boulton to Jocelyn's son some years previously. See Sotheby's sale catalogue, London, 8 June 1995, lot 73.
144 Receipt from Courtauld and Cowles to James Alexander, 1773–1775, Ms. D2433/B/1/1/2, PRONI. The Duke of Rutland, Viceroy of Ireland between 1784 and 1787, was noted for his luxurious tastes. One letter from an envoy dispatched to France assures him that 'the handsomest shoe buckles possible to be had in Paris shall be sent by the cook (diamonds apart)'; quoted in Joseph Robins, *Champagne and Silver Buckles* (Dublin: Lilliput Press, 2001), 73.
145 Charles Johnstone, *The History of John Juniper* (Dublin: Printed for S. Price et al. 1781), 197–98.
146 Claudia Kinmonth, *Irish Country Furniture, 1700–1950* (New Haven and London: Yale University Press, 1993), 113–15.
147 Cosnett, *The Footman's Directory*, 63. Vulnerable places for the display of plate by servants included cleaning it in view of street-front windows.
148 Weatherill, *Consumer Behaviour*, 200.

5 The silver trade in post-Union Ireland

Over the course of the period 1714 to 1837, Dublin's silver trade changed significantly, not least in terms of the way in which goods reached the consumer. In the early eighteenth century, newspaper advertisements by the city's goldsmiths appeared infrequently, their use of other forms of printed advertising was limited, imports of plate from England were comparatively insubstantial, and commodities like Sheffield plate and English porcelain had not yet been invented. Yet by 1828, a group describing themselves as 'the working silversmiths and jewellers of Dublin' gave evidence, as part of a parliamentary inquiry, claiming that while it had been common in the past for manufacturers to have street-front shops selling goods made on their premises, now 'the working men and shopkeepers' were 'two distinct classes' – craftsmen had become, in effect, journeymen to the keepers of 'show shops'.[1] While the accuracy of their evidence must be questioned, and individual circumstances varied considerably, this chapter will consider the fate of the silver trade in post-Union Ireland, the different concerns of those who were predominantly makers and those who were primarily shopkeepers, and the extent to which England's more technologically advanced and larger trade in silver and plated wares directly affected the manufacture and sale of these goods in Ireland by the end of the Georgian era.

Attitudes to Union

In 1800, the Dublin goldsmiths' guild consulted their members and agreed that a 'union with Great Britain would be a total subversion of a constitution under which the nation [had] so rapidly risen to wealth and prosperity.'[2] They composed a memorial to parliament claiming that the proposed Union would be 'pregnant with innumerable ills to the Empire'.[3] This was not surprising. Theirs was one of the city's most prestigious artisan industries and one that had flourished during the previous century.[4] The idea that MPs and peers might desert the capital once Ireland no longer had her own parliament understandably caused their members concern. Manufacturers worried about further competition from imports in a free market economy, but for retailers, opportunities to buy English goods, potentially at competitive prices, were attractive. The belief that Ireland's 'prosperity' would be compromised by Union recurred among the arguments put forward by opponents. In one of many anti-Union prints (Fig. 5.1) a personification of Ireland laments the fact that her 'unfeeling monster' of a husband (England) would marry the devil's daughter for the chance of financial gain. In truth, all sorts of vested interests coloured the rhetoric: over half the anti-Union pamphlets came from members of the legal profession, keen

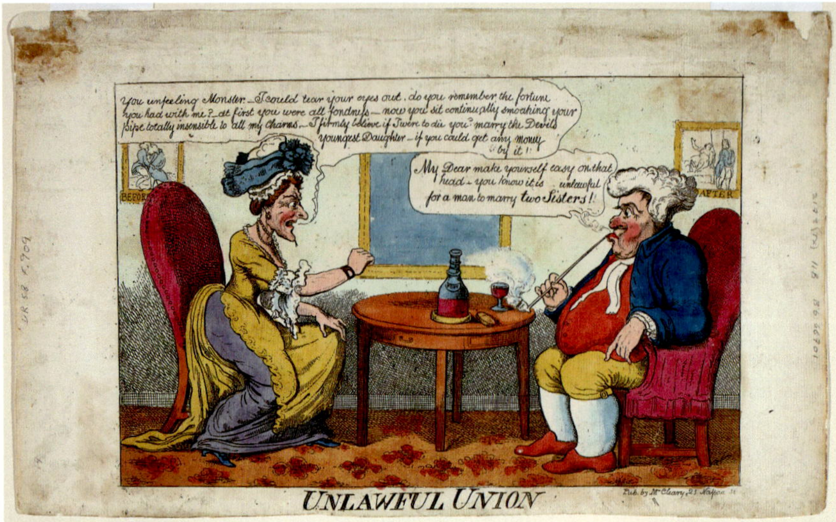

Figure 5.1 Anon, *Unlawful Union* (c.1790–1801), hand-coloured etching, 20.7 × 31.7 cm

Source: National Library of Ireland. Photo credit: © National Library of Ireland.

to protect their own interests.[5] So, were the goldsmiths' fears legitimate – and did they play out in practice?

One way to assess this is to examine assay records for the period, to identify the extent to which the scale and nature of demand for goods changed over time. As chapter 2 has shown, the silver trade was buoyant in Dublin in the late 1780s, with over 80,000 oz. sent to the assay office for hallmarking in 1788. By 1810, this figure had increased to over 113,000 oz., a volume which counters the pessimism of working goldsmiths, but also reflects the fact that 'wartime prosperity, shared by rentier, merchant and the rural consumers of Dublin's goods and services, had masked the dislocating effects of the parliamentary exodus' in the early nineteenth century.[6] As Dickson has suggested, while anti-Unionists feared that Dublin's artisanal industries would collapse from the dual consequences of losing an elite clientele and gaining unfettered competition from English producers, 'in the event, some of the luxury trades flourished in the post-Union generation'.[7]

The 1810 assay returns for silver may have been strong, but it would be a very different story just a few decades later. Middle-class consumers had gradually become increasingly important to the trade. In 1810, a visitor to the city remarked:

> The truth is, a physician here is almost at the pinnacle of greatness: there are few resident nobility or gentry since the union and the professors of law and medicine may be said to form the aristocracy of the place.[8]

Even before the Union, contemporaries noted the impact of the new urban elite. Writing in 1799, while the anti-Unionists were predicting doom, William Stevens reckoned that the overwhelming number of residents in Dublin's 'new streets and great squares' were 'men of profession, men in office, opulent merchants'.[9]

Consumer profile is certainly reflected in the types of goods that were being submitted to the assay office during this period. The prevalence of flatware and small items of domestic plate indicates not just the greater availability of competing alternatives in other materials, but also the significance of a middle-class clientele who had different requirements from the nobility.[10] The same pattern is evident in other branches of trade. For painters, the prosperity of the middling and upper middle class meant a boost to the market for comparatively affordable pictures in media like watercolour and print.[11] This is not to imply that there was no appetite for impressive silverware in Ireland during the early nineteenth century; on the contrary, Douglas Bennett has argued that some affluent members of Dublin's bourgeoisie in the early nineteenth century fuelled a taste for ornate silver with elaborate flat chasing, *repoussé* work and applied cast decoration, specifically designed to impress. A silver teapot in the collection of the National Museum of Ireland, bearing the mark of the Dublin goldsmith William Nowlan (Fig. 5.2), illustrates the sort of showy ornament that was popular among those with money to spend.[12] As Bennett remarks:

> The decoration of all silver was almost a ritual during this period, and it is nothing short of a miracle that so many plain pieces have survived from previous generations; all sorts of objects were re-chased to suit later tastes.[13]

Inevitably, the Act of Union and the beginning of a new century has been seen as a watershed; in reality, changes in patterns of patronage evolved more gradually, and the negative effects of Union were not immediately apparent. As Brian Boydell notes in relation to music: 'The first quarter of the nineteenth century was really a period of

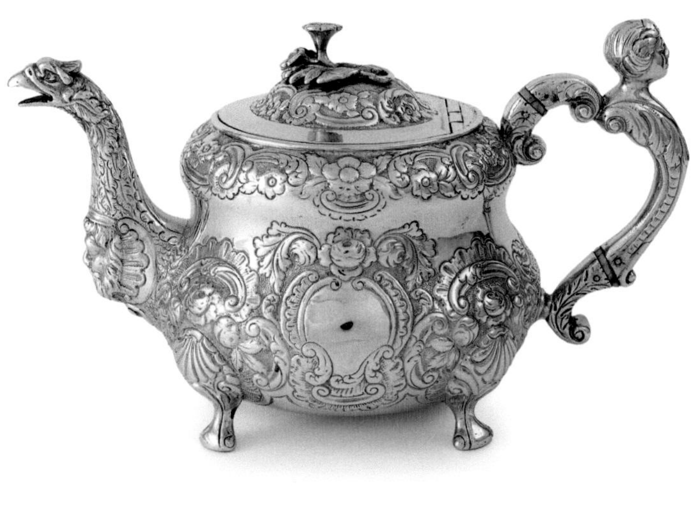

Figure 5.2 William Nowlan, *Teapot* (1817), silver, 18.5 cm (h)

Source: National Museum of Ireland, Dublin. Photo credit: © National Museum of Ireland.

transition from aristocratic patronage to the gradual crystallization in the second half of the century of largely middle class support for music in Irish urban society.'[14] The same pattern can be seen in the silver trade, although the importance of middle-class consumers is evident well before the early nineteenth century.

In 1810, the goldsmiths' guild lobbied for the repeal of Union, a pattern that would recur as the century progressed.[15] They claimed that 'ten years of patient trial' had confirmed their fears, and that the Union had deprived Ireland of her nobility, 'drained her of her wealth, withdrawn from her people the protecting guardianship and residence of the highest orders, extinguished her manufactures and loaded her with enormous debt'.[16] Undoubtedly, by the early nineteenth century there were particular challenges for manufacturing goldsmiths, even if the assay figures for 1810 suggest otherwise. While the goldsmiths had long faced competition from English counterparts, their challenges were exacerbated by the availability of die-stamped, mass-produced objects and component parts from England, a market that could compete strongly in terms of large-scale production. The removal of a 10 per cent duty on imported silverware was also an issue for Ireland's precious metal workers, and the departure of an elite sector of their clientele a real worry.[17] By 1821, there were only thirty-four peers, thirteen baronets and five members of parliament with residences in the city; as one writer put it, the absence of 'three hundred bacchanals whose sun set daily in claret' was keenly felt.[18] Arguably, the silver trade was more dependent on the nobility and gentry than were other Dublin trades, and this was an issue that would be highlighted in later anti-Union rallies by its members.

An increase in the duty payable on Irish-made gold and silverwares also acted as an impetus to fraud.[19] In 1822, referring to 'a great decrease in silverwork' going through the assay office 'for a considerable time past', guild minutes recorded that some shopkeepers were selling goods at such reduced prices that the silver must not have been sterling, and duty on the objects could hardly have been paid.[20] Guild officials also reckoned that there was 'a considerable quantity of illegal plate in some of the principal towns in Ireland', but in a period when its power had been eroded, the guild did not have the funds to proceed consistently and effectively with prosecutions.[21] Pressure on the makers of small wares with modest profit margins may have been a factor in the illicit export of spoons from Dublin through Liverpool at this time. The goldsmith Jacob West, an upstanding member of the trade, reckoned that silver spoons were being illegally exported from Dublin to Liverpool to a considerable extent.[22] There was scope for small things like spoons to be carried over in bags without paying the additional export duty, and it was evidently commercially viable for some, at least, to do so.[23]

According to Dublin assay books, by 1821 the annual assay quota was just short of 79,000 oz., a considerable dip from the total for 1810 and part of a downward trend that would continue until mid-century.[24] While countering an overly simplistic perspective of the impact of Union, David Dickson refers to 'a hollowing out of the city's manufacturing economy in the post-Union years', particularly in 1815 to 1817, 'when post-war depression and appalling harvests led to soaring unemployment in most trades within the city'.[25]

The overwhelming majority of objects assayed in 1821 (95 per cent) comprised cutlery, ladles and tongs; these were commodities suited by virtue of their design and functionality to metal, they were accessible to the middle-class and elite markets in terms of cost, and they were more essential than showier types of goods like dish rings or épergnes. Continuing a pattern that had persisted from the early eighteenth century, a small number of workshops were responsible for the lion's share of production. Among the major workshops active in the early nineteenth century were those of Edward Power, Richard Sawyer and James Le Bas (Fig. 5.3).[26] However, the maker and the seller had gradually separated from each other over time and, increasingly, many craftsmen were at the mercy of big shopkeepers. An analysis of the assay records for 1821 (Table 5.1) shows that not more than a dozen makers were dominating production that year; they in turn supplied prominent retailers, and depended upon them for work. James Le Bas submitted 5 per cent of the volume assayed in 1821. He had come to Dublin from London at the beginning of the nineteenth century and established one of the principal workshops in the city. Despite his comparative success, the guild still recorded the following entry in 1817:

> James Le Bas, 3 plate workers, one jobber and one polisher, has no apprentice and for the last three years has not had as much work in the silver manufacture as would keep these men in constant employment, but faith he carries on gold beating business and has employed in that branch four men and one boy.[27]

While Le Bas submitted some small items for assaying, he was classed by the guild as a large worker. In 1821 his output included coffee pots, ewers and dishes, as well as a variety of ecclesiastical plate.[28] In many cases he employed casters, chasers, gilders and polishers with specialist skills. This sort of collaboration is illustrated in guild minutes, where a case implicating him in an attempt to avoid full duty payments is

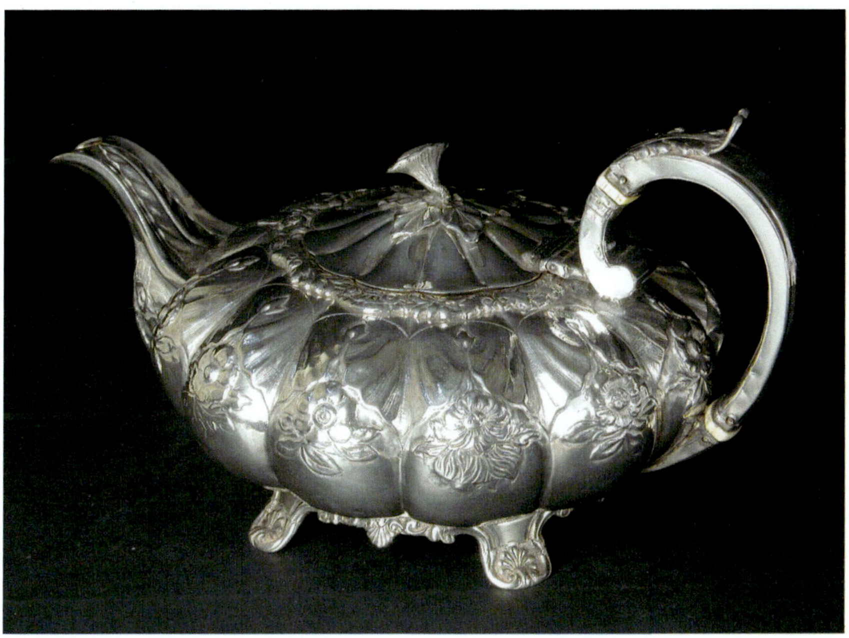

Figure 5.3 James Le Bas, *Teapot* (1827), silver, 16.3 x 28 cm

Source: Hanbury Hall, Worcestershire. Photo credit: © National Trust/Claire Reeves.

Table 5.1 Total of gross weight of goods submitted to the Dublin assay office for assaying and hallmarking in 1821

Goldsmith's surname	*oz.*	*dwt.*
Bergin	4,250	15
Brady	4,911	
Cummins/Cumyng	4,986	
Eades	10,106	
Fray	3,218	
Le Bas	3,548	
Marsh	5,941	5
Neville	9,089	
Nowlan, W.	5,021	6
Smith/Smyth	9,807	
Others	17,899	
Total	78,777	6

Source: Assay Book, 2 May 1820–29 July 1826, Company of Goldsmiths of Dublin Ms. 29, Dublin, Assay Office.

recorded.[29] He was suspected of adding embellishments to objects after they had been assayed and the duty (based on weight) had been paid. One of the objects examined in the course of the guild's investigation was a dish cover made by Le Bas' workmen. In the course of evidence, it emerged that William Middleton had made the cover, Kean Mahony had provided the handle, Owen Reilly had cast the ornaments and John Macklin had chased the piece.[30] If goldsmiths like Le Bas were affected by a slump in the market, their journeymen and employees were even more vulnerable. When Le Bas was investigated, a number of his workers were questioned. Kean Mahony claimed that he had resisted reporting his employer, afraid of compromising his own chances of further work in the city. However disingenuous this claim may have been, there is no doubt that the manufacturing sector was hierarchical, and journeymen could not afford to fall out with employers. As well as supplying shops in Dublin, Le Bas also sent work to Belfast. The silversmith James Carruthers, with a shop on Belfast's Castle Street, received work from him fully finished and did not manufacture goods for sale himself.[31]

Divisions within the trade, and the varying circumstances of its members, can be seen in responses to changes on the legislation in 1825 in regard to licences.[32] Traders were required to pay a flat fee and erect a sign at their premises to show they that they paid taxes.[33] While this measure had been introduced in 1785, the Commissioners of Excise seem to have exercised some latitude when it came to enforcement.[34] However, when responsibility for the tax transferred from the Commissioners of Excise to the Commissioners of Stamps in 1825, the latter adopted a standardised approach to enforcement. This meant that a prosperous retailer with premises on a busy street was being treated the same as a small maker eking out a living supplying low volumes of goods to a retail shop. That hardly seemed fair.

In 1828, a lobby group of craftsmen petitioned for exclusion from payment of the licence fee, claiming that the Commissioners of Excise had required 'only those who had show shops and were engaged in a direct traffic with the public' to pay.[35] Now vulnerable craftsmen were being threatened with prosecution if they failed to get a licence. The petitioners highlighted the changes that the trade had experienced since the introduction of the Act, and referred specifically to the downturn in local production.[36] They asked the commissioners to consider

> the state of trade formerly in this city and to what it now is: that at the period first referred to there were a number of silversmiths and jewellers engaged in business, who employed more journeymen and others in their respective establishments, than could now be found in the trade collectively; therefore your memorialists respectively submit the peculiar cruelty and hardship in now exacting a tax (in the present wretched state of the trade, and the well-known poverty of all classes of artisans).[37]

Signatories, who included Edward Crofton, James Fray and Henry Flavelle (Fig. 5.4), argued that the requirement for all dealers to have the word 'Licensed' over their doors harked back to a period when it was common for manufacturers to have street-front shops as their premises.[38] Now, with dwindling demand for their wares, and the fact that, as they put it, the working men and shopkeepers of Dublin were 'two distinct classes', it did not seem equitable that 'working men living in back-garret rooms and stable-yards' would be classed in the same category as dedicated shopkeepers.[39] To support their case, they cited the example of London, where makers of small wares were charged low licence fees, despite the 'well-known fact' that, in their opinion, many journeymen there were 'better circumstanced' than independent masters in Dublin.[40] They described how London's manufacturing goldsmiths were 'men of wealth, trading on their own capital', while their counterparts in Dublin could not generally 'proceed in their work, without the material being first advanced by the

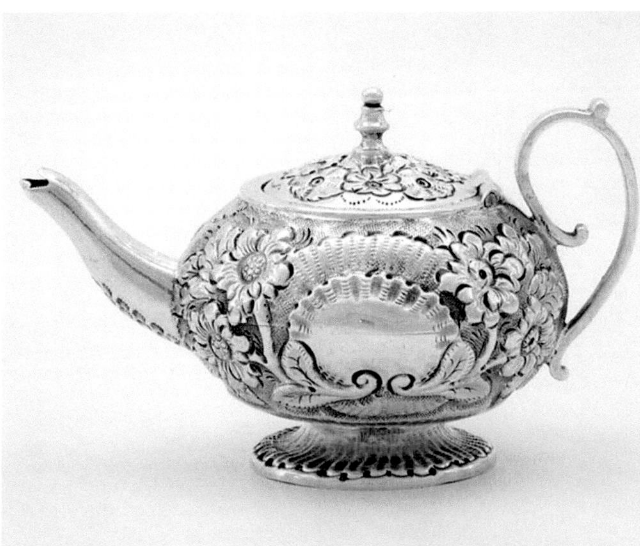

Figure 5.4 Henry Flavelle, *Miniature teapot* (1827), silver, 3.8 × 6.4 cm

Source: Metropolitan Museum of Art, New York. The Joseph M. and Aimee Loeb May Collection, 1963. Photo credit: © Metropolitan Museum of Art.

shopkeeper'.[41] An underlying problem with competition from London must have coloured their arguments. While conditions were certainly very challenging for makers who remained in business, not all artisans were living in straitened circumstances, and the duty figures for the period which, in some cases at least, combine both imported and locally produced plate were still relatively healthy, relative to how they would look by the middle of the century (Appendix 3).

In a nod to the dislocating effects of Union, those lobbying for concessions on the licence fee in 1828 claimed that the 'most wealthy and liberal' of their gentry now lived abroad, that many of those who remained in Ireland purchased their plate and jewellery in London, and that the removal of an import duty meant that their main business was in 'altering and repairing English plate and jewellery' and making up 'trifling orders'.[42] Lord Hartland, of Strokestown, Co. Roscommon, who had been raised to the peerage as a reward for his support of the Union, is an example of an Irish patron who ordered from London during this period, though a receipt of 1814 from Robert Garrard of Panton Street (Fig. 5.5) suggests that he was careful rather than lavish with his money:[43] a large venison dish was plated rather than sterling; a pair of candlesticks was second-hand. The goldsmiths' claim that their wealthiest gentry now lived abroad might have been exaggerated: eighty-seven lay peers had Dublin addresses in 1798, as opposed to just twenty-five in 1824; many would have simply relinquished a Dublin base rather than leave the country.[44]

Fashion was not the only factor which influenced the flow of English plate to Ireland at this stage. By the early nineteenth century, English silver was being imported

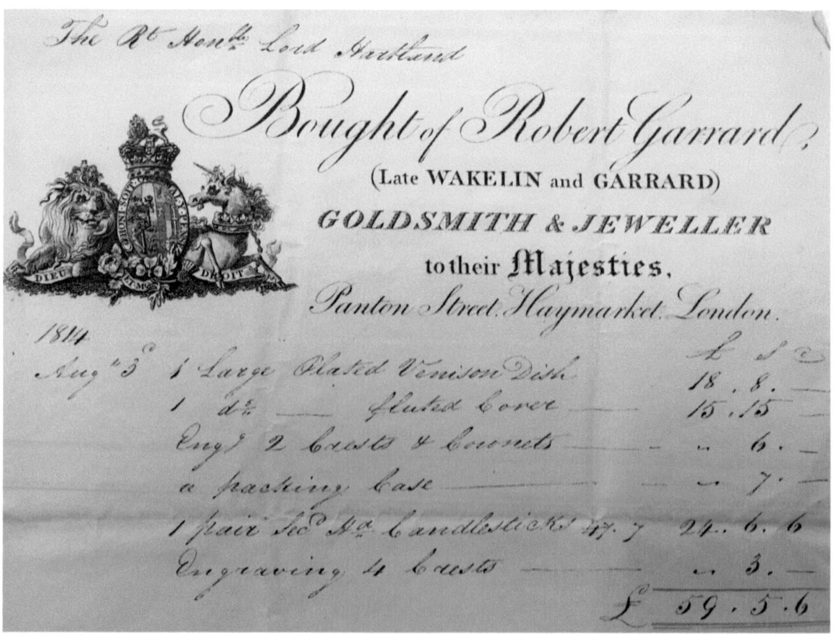

The Rt Honble Lord Hartland

Bought of Robert Garrard,
(Late WAKELIN and GARRARD)
GOLDSMITH & JEWELLER
to their Majesties,
Panton Street, Haymarket, London.

1814

		£	s	d
Aug 3	1 Large Plated Venison Dish	18	8	
	1 do — fluted Cover	15	15	
	Engg 2 Crests & Coronets	..	6	
	a packing Case	..	7	
	1 pair Sd Hd Candlesticks 47.7	24	6	6
	Engraving 4 Crests	..	3	
		£ 59	5	6

Figure 5.5 Account of Lord Hartland with Robert Garrard of Panton Street, London (1814), engraving, 25 × 20 cm

Source: National Library of Ireland, Dublin. Photo credit: © National Library of Ireland.

into Ireland, 'finished' locally, hallmarked at the Dublin assay office and sold as Irish. In other words, there were often cases when Dublin's manufacturing goldsmiths were simply acting as assemblers of die-stamped or prefabricated parts, and objects which had been, at the very least, partially made in England were being hallmarked and sold in Irish shops bearing Dublin 'maker's marks'. This was also a period when leading retailers were not necessarily visible in the guild's assay ledgers, and when some, at least, did not find it fraternally unpatriotic to import, and sell as Irish, goods that had been made in England. Ironically, by the mid-nineteenth century the guild tried to resolve this situation, but by then it was too little too late.

Technology

A fundamental change in the trade, from the second half of the eighteenth century, was the widespread use of metal dies by wholesale manufacturers in England for the large-scale production of silver and plated wares. These dies were expensive to buy, so were suited only in cases where large multiples of individual items were being produced. As techniques for serial production like die-stamping, fly-pressing and transfer printing were developed in England's luxury trades, enterprising retailers like Matthew Boulton in the field of metalwork and Josiah Wedgwood in the field of ceramics looked to expand the markets for their wares. Inevitably, Ireland was an obvious choice. The evidence from Dublin retailers of silver active in the early nineteenth century suggests that, while dies were acquired by them in some cases from England, it was often more cost-effective to import die-stamped components for assembly and finishing. In cases like these, manufacturing goldsmiths were indeed reduced to the status of journeymen to the shopkeepers, as they had claimed. For example, in 1826, the Dublin goldsmith Jacob West, who operated as a major retailer, claimed that, in the case of many articles manufactured using dies, it was more commercially viable for him to buy English manufactured plate than Irish:

> The die of a waiter, perhaps, would cost me £20, and that die will answer to the manufacturer in London to make many from; whereas if it was here there might not be as many sold as that the amount of profit would pay for the die.[45]

West confirmed that his commercial intercourse with England was so streamlined that he could source within four days anything he required and which he regarded as being 'well done in England'.[46] Interestingly, a stock list from the Sheffield firm of Roberts Cadman and Co. shows that West and his partner John Clarke had almost £4,000 of the English manufacturer's products on hand in 1816, including épergnes, coffee urns, teapots and ice pails.[47] A later order from 'Messrs West and Son' to the London firm of Barnard states that an elaborate silver candelabrum with an agricultural theme, costing almost £140, was acquired from the London supplier but hallmarked in Dublin.[48] This was most likely for the firm of Matthew West, whose premises were in Skinner Row. However, the description implies that it did not carry Barnard's mark.[49]

Clearly, in the case of major Dublin retailers like Jacob West and William Law, both of whom had backgrounds in manufacturing and were members of the Dublin goldsmiths' guild, decisions were made during the late eighteenth and early nineteenth century to distance themselves from the manufacturing side of the trade. As West explained, 'being a shopkeeper and a manufacturer' were 'not compatible at all together'.[50] Instead, these prominent retailers provided metal to in-house or outworkers along with specific orders, advanced them capital for the payment of duty, and in some cases stamped their own retailer's mark alongside that of the maker. For West, this meant that the maker would be 'accountable for all being right', in other words, the retailer could refuse goods if they did not suit.[51] This arrangement left him free to call upon, as needed, a network of makers with specialist skills, a model which recalls the example of London firms like Parker and Wakelin.[52] Surviving objects show West's retailer's mark alongside the 'maker's marks' of John Egan, James Fray and Richard Whitford.[53] Working in this way also freed retailers to cultivate political and commercial interests, which could be commercially advantageous. Elected alderman in 1821, West claimed on his billhead from this period that his firm were goldsmiths and jewellers to Their Majesties, as well as to His Royal Highness the Duke of Sussex, His Excellency the Lord Lieutenant, His Grace the Duke of Leinster and the University (Fig. 5.6).[54] He held the office of lord mayor in 1829 and a few years later, along with other traders, added his name to a public notice acknowledging the Duke of Leinster's patriotic patronage.[55] Evidently, he saw nothing unpatriotic in his own wholesale trade with England. William Law's shop featured as the site of a popular panorama exhibited in Leicester Square in London in 1809 (Fig. 5.7), and he exported plated goods to North America.[56] His shop supplied a number of examples of impressive testimonial and presentation plate in the early nineteenth century, likely due to his well-appointed premises, solid connections and long period in business. Just as Law and West saw commercial benefits to accessing the English market, so too did counterparts in other industries. Hutton's, a firm manufacturing gigs and jaunting cars, was one of those keen to see Union duties completely abolished; for the goldsmiths' trade,

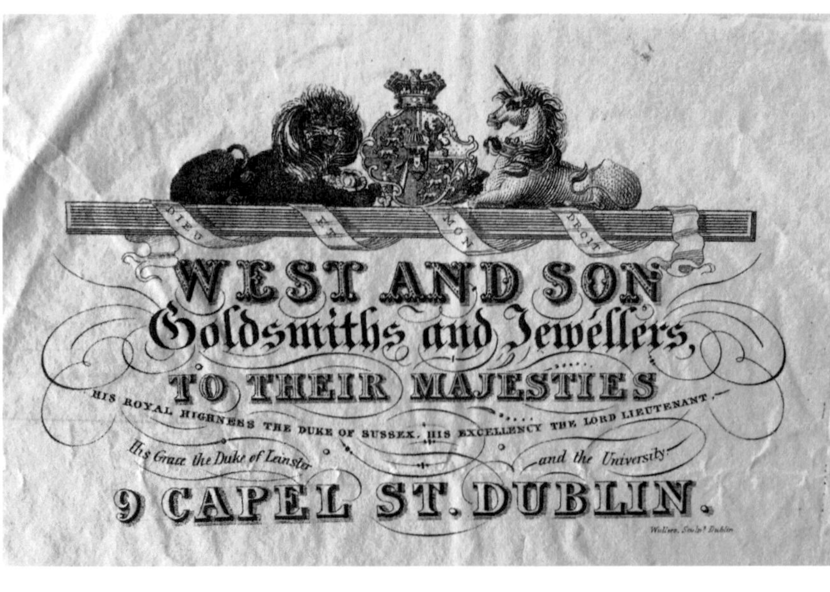

Figure 5.6 Billhead for West and Son, 9 Capel Street, highlighting clients such as 'the University' (handwritten receipt dated 1832), engraving, 20 × 13 cm

Source: National Library of Ireland. Photo credit: © National Library of Ireland.

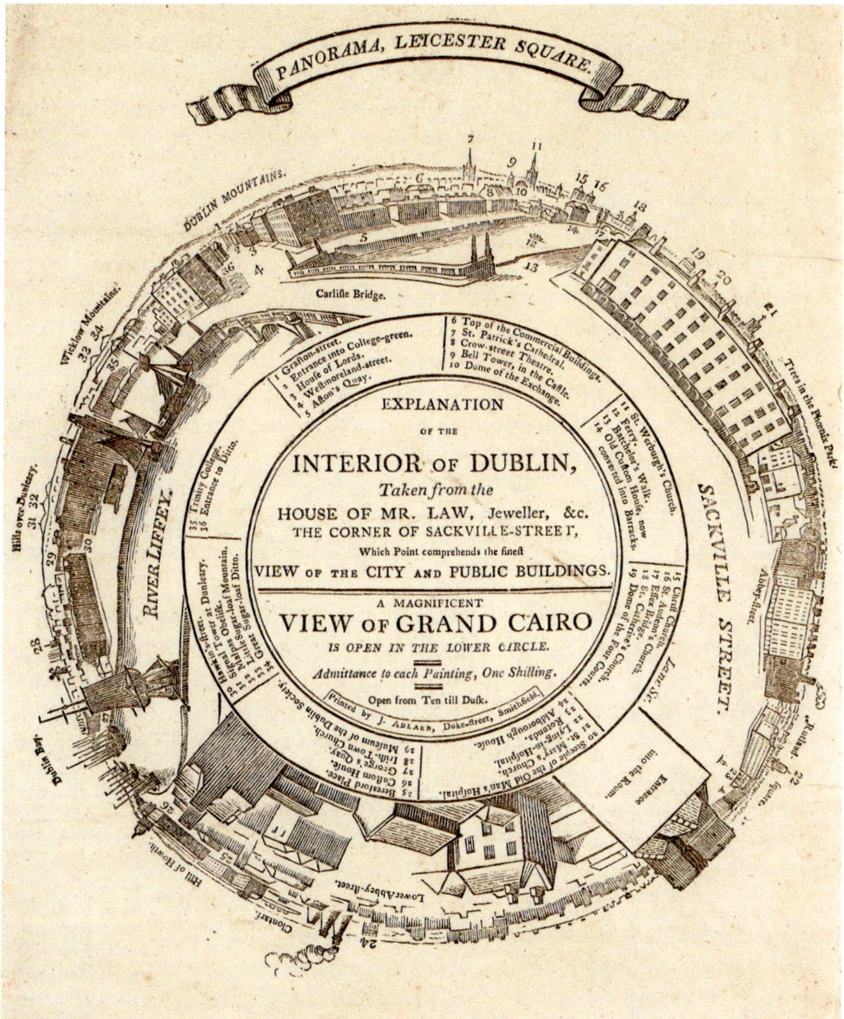

Figure 5.7 Henry Aston Barker, *Explanation of the Interior of Dublin taken from the House of Mr. Law, Jeweller* (1809), engraving, 28.7 × 22.6 cm

Source: National Library of Ireland, Dublin. Photo credit: © National Library of Ireland.

however, there were tensions between those who directly profited from commerce with England and those who were manufacturers.[57]

Journeymen to the keepers of 'show shops'?

Throughout the eighteenth century, there had been prominent goldsmiths who orchestrated both the manufacture and sale to the public of a wide variety of goods. These included people like Thomas Bolton and Robert Calderwood, who ran thriving workshops and sold the output from their own shops but who were vouching for these goods by registering them in their own names at the assay office and marking them with their own 'maker's marks'. As a result of this practice, their names were linked to impressive volumes of plate in the assay ledgers. As previously indicated, modern silver research has demonstrated that the quantities of plate linked to makers like these could not have been the work of individuals, but must have been the work of apprentices and journeymen for whom a master took responsibility. What changed from at least the second half of the eighteenth century, driven by new technology, was a business model in the Dublin silver trade like those exemplified by West and Law, where there could be a greater degree of separation between the maker and the shopkeeper. In other words, a prominent shopkeeper might advance materials to a maker, expect the maker to enter the goods for assaying himself, and might ultimately mark the products of their shop with their own retailer's mark (alongside that of the maker). Inevitably, for shopkeepers like these, profit would take precedence over safeguarding the interests of workers, though some, like William Law, would claim to consult their employee's interests. In 1797 Law, who by then had moved to his impressive premises on Sackville Street, offered a discount of 10 per cent on goods up to the value of 40 shillings, stating that his motive was 'to keep a number of ingenious artists in the habit of industry'.[58] Jacob West would later acknowledge that the imposition of licences on small makers was unfair, but ultimately these men were businessmen and that dictated their priorities.[59]

Law, for instance, exemplifies the model of a goldsmith who started out as a maker, moved increasingly to more prominent and prestigious locations as his business expanded, and ultimately sidelined his manufacturing training to front a major shop. Apprenticed to William Townsend in 1765, he started out in Cole Alley, a minor street close to Dublin Castle, before taking on more high-profile premises on Castle Street, Parliament Street and ultimately Sackville Street.[60] He brought his son into the business, had his trade card altered to mark the partnership and used a retailer's mark to identify some of the products of his shop. He also used a trade label announcing his firm as Law and Son, Goldsmith and Jewellers to His Majesty. All the while he kept up contact with England, importing wares and apparently, in some cases, supplying English clients. A nineteenth-century description of the Sackville Street premises illustrated on his trade card describes how 'on each side of the entrance there was a window, consisting of a single sheet of glass, inside of which a most magnificent display of costly plate, gems, and watches tacitly demanded and obtained the admiration of all spectators.'[61]

Law, like West, cultivated strong contacts with England. Although he had trained in Dublin, early advertisements refer to his experience in both England and Ireland. He imported English goods for sale in his shop and his trade card, with a ship prominently located in the middle distance, hints at tantalising goods arriving from overseas.[62] In 1826, Richard Williams, one of Law's employees, gave evidence as part of a parliamentary inquiry and his testimony provides further insights into Law's professional activities.[63] Williams claimed that Law did not manufacture his own articles but employed workmen who also supplied other shops. This is borne out by the example of surviving objects which show Law's retailer's mark alongside the maker's marks of William Nowlan, Edward Power, Thomas Townsend and James Le Bas.[64]

According to Williams, Law (like Jacob West) provided makers with silver, paid the duty on the finished work and kept a current licence. Occasionally, he bought objects in London to have them replicated in Dublin but, because of the cost, he kept dies only for things which were 'in general use' and in 'the general run of work'.[65] He also sent silver to at least one client in America and exported 'a great deal of plated ware' to the United States.[66] Guild records provide another perspective on his business. Though his name does not appear in the assay records for 1821, those of some of his suppliers do, illustrating how by this period the division between maker and seller could be more pronounced. William Nowlan, one of the more prolific makers that year, was one of Law's outworkers. A tea canister assayed in 1821 bearing both of their marks is now in the collection of the Sterling and Francine Clark Collection in Williamstown, Massachusetts (Fig. 5.8).

When it came to fashionable or well-appointed shops, the owner appears to have been identified as the 'brand' in a number of cases. This concept was well established in the eighteenth century, where visitors to shops in London and Paris describe goods bought as much as for their association with an 'à la mode' shop as for their inherent craftsmanship, usefulness or aesthetic appeal. Even in the medieval apprenticeship system, it was the master who was responsible for winning business for a shop, and therefore it is hardly surprising that in the case of fashionable Dublin shops, like Jacob West's on Capel Street or William Law's on Sackville Street, descriptions of goods purchased there imply that the owner of the shop was in fact the maker of the goods they

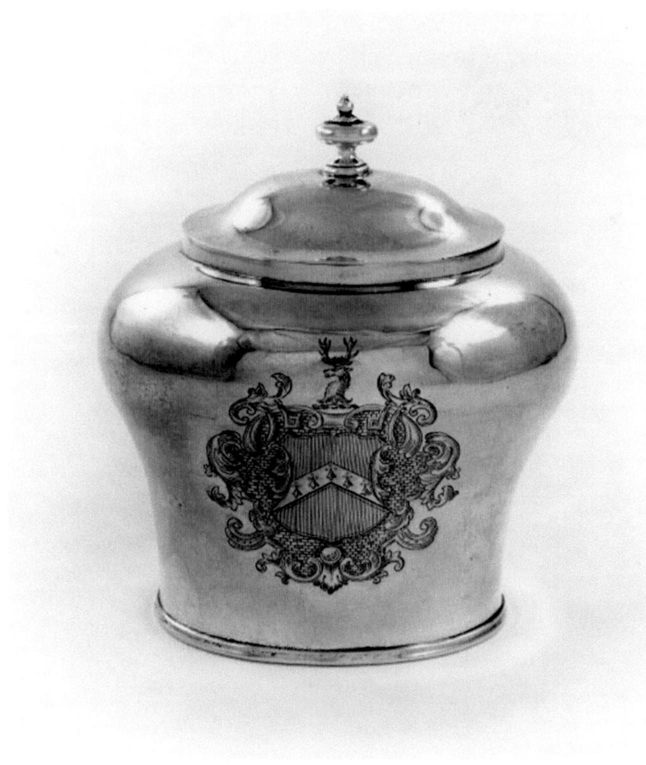

Figure 5.8 William Nowlan (maker) and William Law (retailer), *Tea canister* (1825), silver, 14.6 × 10.3 cm

Source: Sterling and Francine Clark Art Institute, Williamstown, Massachusetts. Photo credit: © Sterling and Francine Clark Art Institute.

sold. In 1833, a public dinner was held to mark the presentation of a testimonial to Thomas M. Gresham by the citizens of Kingstown (now Dun Laoghaire, Co. Dublin), acknowledging his role in resisting the extension of a local railway line. The *Freeman's Journal* describes the testimonial as

> a magnificent vase and salver, *tastefully executed* by the Messrs. Law of Sackville-street in silver – the former of a beautiful modernized Grecian figure, splendidly chased, and finished with superior skill; the latter upwards of four feet in circumference, tastefully sculptured, and having an appropriate inscription on its centre.[67]

More elaborate examples of plate produced through Law's partnership can be seen in a pair of presentation salvers (Fig. 5.9) made for Sir Stapleton Cotton (Lord Combermere) in 1823, during a period when Cotton was commander-in-chief in Ireland. In his earlier role as governor of Barbados and commander-in-chief of the West Indies (1817 to 1820), he had been awarded by the people of Barbados a gift of plate worth a thousand guineas, to be made up as he pleased. Perhaps some of these funds were used to commission the Irish salvers which were later exhibited in London. However, they also offer useful insights into networks of specialised craftsmen.[68] One of the most striking aspects of the salvers, apart from the costly use of silver gilt, is the elaborate chasing which ornaments them. While Nowlan is credited via his mark as the maker, and Law likewise as the retailer, the chasing was carried out by a lesser-known figure, Henry Teare. Teare, as chapter 2 showed, had been

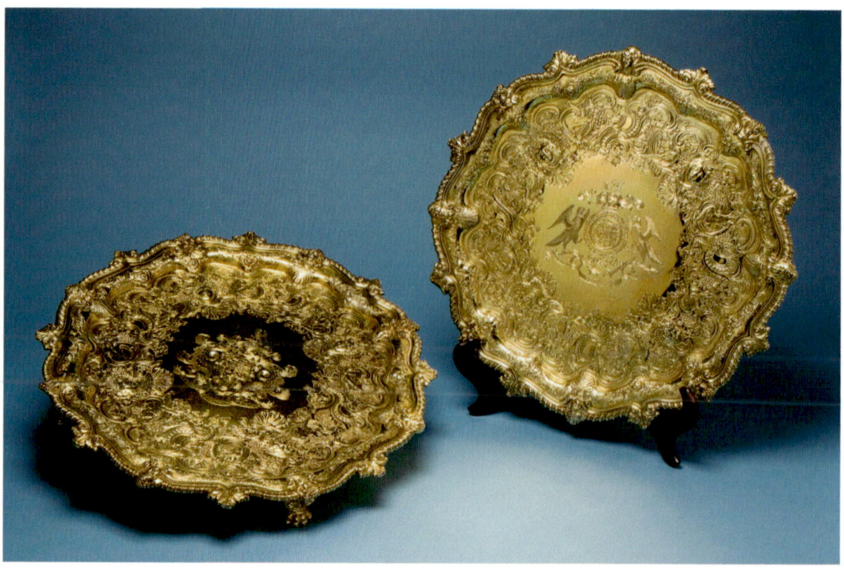

Figure 5.9 William Nowlan, *Pair of salvers* (1823), silver gilt, 47.5 cm diam
Source: Red McCombs Collection, San Antonio, Texas. Photo credit: © Al Renton.

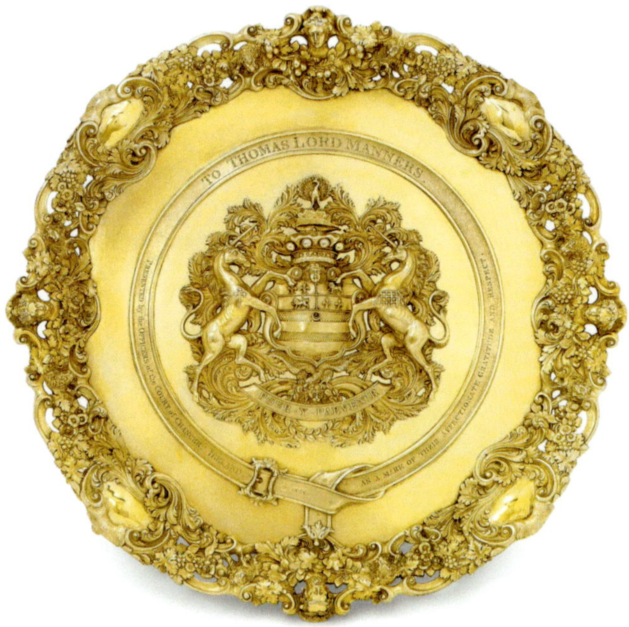

Figure 5.10 James Fray, *Charger* (1828), silver gilt, 68.6 cm diam
Photo credit: © Christie's Images.

trained at the Dublin Society's School of Ornament, along with others who went on to excel in this particular specialisation, like Edward Lorenzo Percy. These men benefited from the design training at the Dublin Society Schools, yet are relatively invisible in contemporary sources. Percy was responsible for the exceptional chasing on a silver-gilt charger presented by the Officers and Court of Chancery of Ireland to Thomas Manners, Lord Chancellor of Ireland, in 1828 (Fig. 5.10).[69] The piece was made by James Fray, who operated out of 39 Bride Street, but was supplied by Charles Stewart and Sons of Dame Street.[70] The reverse of the piece is signed 'Stewart and Sons fecerunt Dame St. Dublin'.[71] Fray was also responsible for an impressive set of salvers retailed by Jacob West, one of which was engraved with a view of the Custom House (Fig. 5.11).[72]

One of West's neighbours on Capel Street was the goldsmith William Mooney. Mooney described himself variously in advertisements during the 1820s as a 'manufacturing silversmith, goldsmith and jeweller' and a 'goldsmith, jeweller and watchmaker'.[73] He succeeded John Kavanagh in business and took over his premises at 32 Capel Street. In January 1820, when he appeared to be starting out in business, he advertised that he had in stock the best articles in each branch of his business, 'some of them manufactured by him and the rest carefully selected from the most respectable

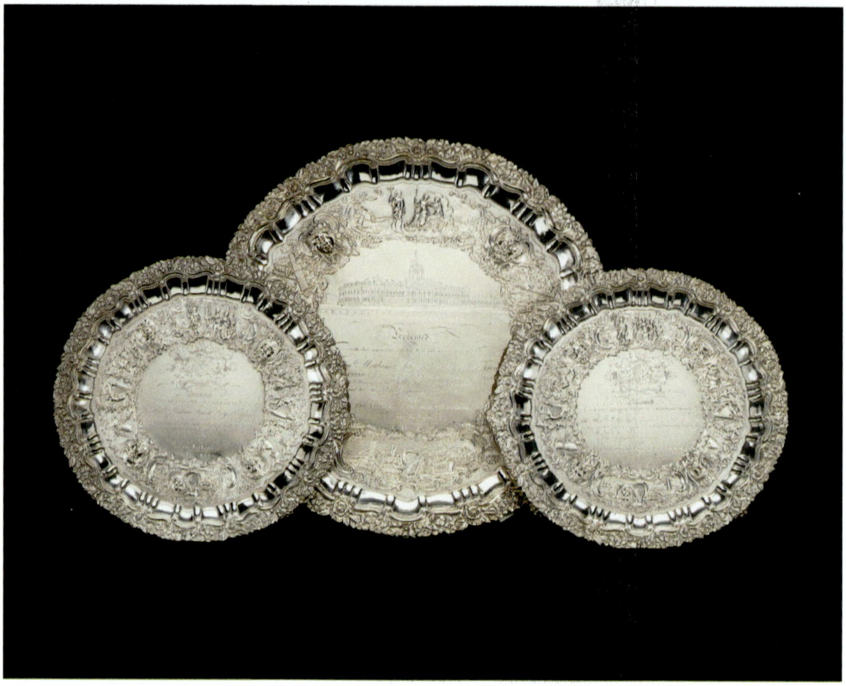

Figure 5.11 James Fray, *Set of salvers* (1824), silver, one 64 cm diam, two 45 cm diam
Photo credit: © Christie's Images.

London warehouses'. In terms of plated wares and 'fancy goods', he said that he had 'the newest patterns and fashion', which he had 'purchased for cash within the last two months'.[74] Another revenue stream was provided by the hire of plate and plated wares. A later advertisement stated that he had 'a separate stock of plate and plated ware for lending out at dinner and supper parties on a moderate commission'.[75]

While some retailers shipped die-stamped components from England during this period, and others had English models copied by local makers, there were those who simply bought in English stock and hoped to turn it over quickly to recoup their costs. The Dublin goldsmith Edward Egerton advertised in 1800 that he was importing the latest fashions in Sheffield plate and was visiting the Ballinasloe Fair for the convenience of his country customers.[76] Three years earlier, he had offered to sell his plated goods at 'fifteen per cent under first cost' due to 'the present distress' of his business.[77] This example of offering plated goods (i.e. Sheffield plate) and smaller wares at a discount for ready money was a pattern that is evident in newspaper advertisements from at least the late eighteenth century onwards. In a number of cases this practice is discernible where goods had been imported; it applied even to high-status goods like plate, where traditionally customers had expected lengthy terms of credit.

In an effort to move stock and draw in ready money, merchants offered various discounts. In the 1780s, Richard D'Olier of Dame Street offered a 5 per cent discount on 'the greatest variety of plate and plated ware . . . spoons and a few articles excepted'.[78]

In the 1790s, John Ash advertised the arrival of jewellery, plate and plated wares from London, all on sale 'for ready money only'.[79] His newspaper notice claimed that, since his profits were so small, it was 'entirely out of his power to keep accounts, or run the risk of giving long credit and contracting bad debts'.[80] Whether because of moving premises, quitting business or simply trying to drum up interest, offering discounts was a way to generate sales. William Morgan, watchmaker, goldsmith and jeweller, moved from Ormond Quay to Grafton Street in 1809. As a way of publicising the move, advertising new goods and clearing old stock, he offered a discount of 15 per cent on jewellery, watches and plated goods for cash, and 5 per cent on silver goods.

There were also cases where clients were given discounts on large orders. In 1817, an audacious pair of thieves fraudulently obtained £140 worth of plate from the goldsmith Matthew West.[81] One of the conmen, dressed as a livery servant, entered West's shop on Skinner Row and asked if his master, Captain Marmaduke Wilson, had been in. The so-called servant claimed that Wilson was on his way to buy some plate and gave a detailed description of him. Shortly afterwards, a person posing as Wilson entered the shop and asked to see some second-hand plate. When the goods were selected, the 'gentleman' asked for a bill to be made out to his wife for payment, requested a discount for cash and, citing a war wound which had been already mentioned by his accomplice, asked West to transcribe his instructions and sign them with his initials 'MW', which, not unexpectedly, were the same as the conman's. West duly transcribed the following: 'Dear Maria, I have bought some second-hand plate, of which, I think you will approve. Send me by bearer, £140.' He initialled the note as requested 'MW' (for Marmaduke Wilson) and waited for the cash to be delivered. After closing up shop that evening (the basket of goods unclaimed and the cash not received), West returned home to find that the note had been delivered to his own wife Maria, who, thinking it was intended for her from her husband, had passed the cash to the conmen.[82]

Early nineteenth-century billheads for West describe his stock at the 'Sign of the Golden Chalice, No. 15 Skinner Row' as including 'all kinds of gold, silver and jewellery' and 'a great variety of second-hand plate' (Fig. 5.12).[83] By 1826, when he was in business with his son, he advertised his clients as including the Lord Lieutenant and Duke of Leinster.[84] He also used a retailer's mark alongside that of the maker's mark of his suppliers. These included Richard Whitford, John Egan, Christopher Eades and Philip Weekes.

As shown in the Introduction, it made sense for retailers of Sheffield plate, and English metalware more generally, to target Ireland as a prime location for offloading stock. The articles of agreement between the Sheffield firm of Roberts Cadman and Co. and their Dublin agent Patrick Moore, drawn up in the early nineteenth century, specify as much. Moore undertook to look after 'such silver and silver plated goods or other goods, wares and merchandizes . . . as they shall think proper to entrust with him', and to 'sell the same goods, wares and merchandizes to the best advantage and for the most profit and at as short a credit' as he could.[85] For this, the firm would pay him 'six pounds for every one hundred pounds for the net (but not gross) amount of all goods, wares and merchandizes and also on the price of fashion of all silver goods'.[86]

Similarly, a pattern book for Samuel Roberts of the same firm, dating to the 1830s, opens with a handwritten list of towns and cities in England, Scotland and Ireland which had clearly been identified as ready markets.[87] Westport, Waterford and Kilkenny were among the Irish locations; the names of sixteen individual clients and firms

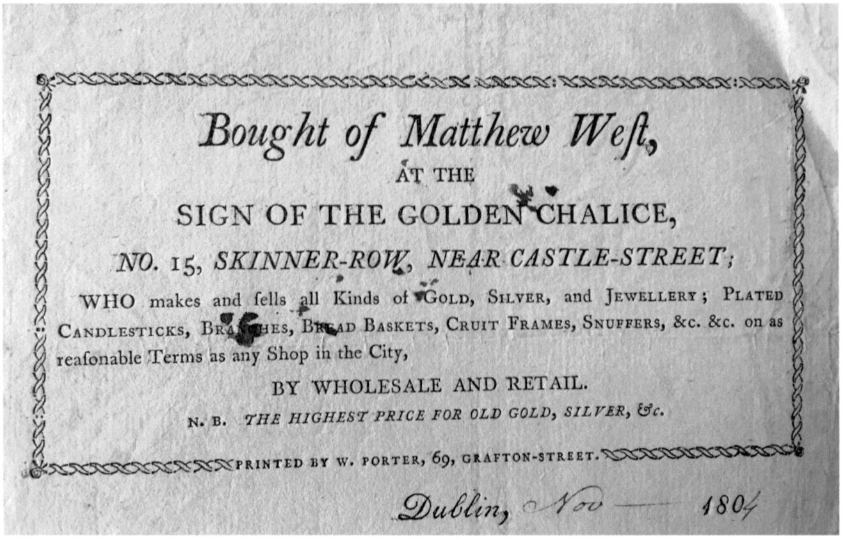

Bought of Matthew Weſt,
AT THE
SIGN OF THE GOLDEN CHALICE,
NO. 15, *SKINNER-ROW, NEAR CASTLE-STREET;*
WHO makes and ſells all Kinds of GOLD, SILVER, and JEWELLERY; PLATED CANDLESTICKS, BRANCHES, BREAD BASKETS, CRUIT FRAMES, SNUFFERS, &c. &c. on as reaſonable Terms as any Shop in the City,
BY WHOLESALE AND RETAIL.
N. B. *THE HIGHEST PRICE FOR OLD GOLD, SILVER, &c.*
PRINTED BY W. PORTER, 69, GRAFTON-STREET.
Dublin, Nov — 1804

Figure 5.12 *Billhead for Matthew West, Sign of Golden Chalice* (handwritten receipt dated 1804), engraving, 19 × 16 cm

Source: National Library of Ireland. Photo credit: © National Library of Ireland.

were listed for Dublin alone. These included Matthew West and Son, Jacob West and Co., William Law and Son, and John Twycross and Son. Clearly, Roberts was in a position to supply a very extensive range of silver and plated wares. One extensive list in the pattern book specifies 'articles made in silver or plated', alongside a sketch of an argyle (gravy-warmer) (Fig. 5.13).[88] The drawings include an elaborately decorated tea kettle, with an elegant hand using it to replenish a nearby teapot (Fig. 5.14).

Douglas Bennett has written that English retailers' outlets in Dublin contributed to the difficulties of local craftsmen during the nineteenth century.[89] One of the most prominent of these was the firm of Waterhouse and Co., who had a shop on Dame Street.[90] In 1842, they placed advertisements in the *Freeman's Journal* to promote their stock of jewellery and watches and highlight a large consignment of silver and plated wares recently arrived from their warehouse in Sheffield. They cannily advised that, since the government duty on all plate manufactured in Ireland would shortly be increased by 5d per oz.,

> they would particularly recommend their friends and the public to avail themselves of the very limited interval afforded them of purchasing those articles of daily use, viz. table and dessert spoons and forks, tea, egg, salt and mustard spoons, fish knives, sugar tongs, etc., 6s 10d per oz.; also the most beautiful tea and coffee sets at 9s per oz.[91]

This example encapsulates a number of the central themes in this analysis: the exponential increase in the range and variety of domestic goods which were available in Ireland from the eighteenth century, the impact of plated wares as alternatives to silver

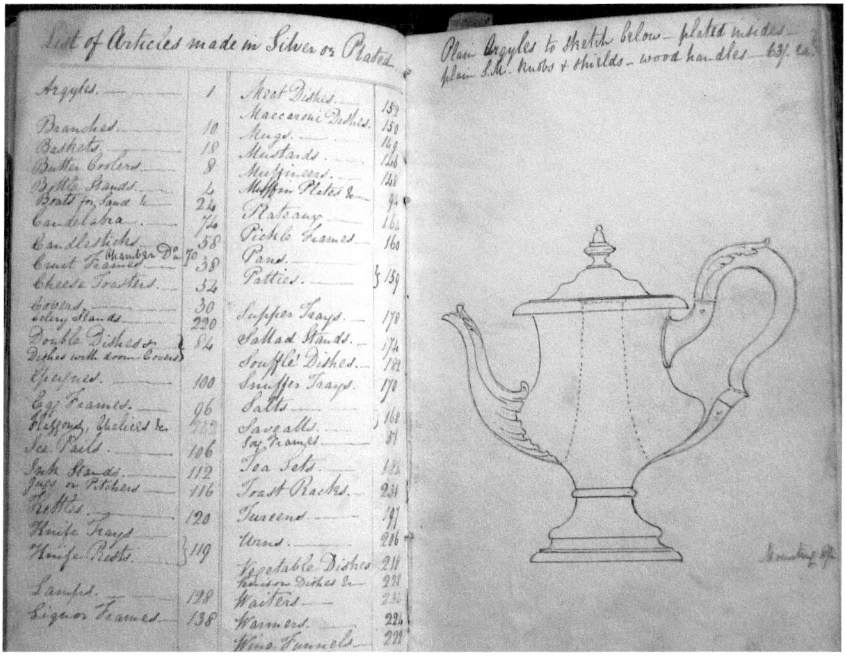

Figure 5.13 Samuel Roberts' pattern book, notation: 'List of Articles made in Silver or Plated' (c.1830)

Source: Sheffield Archives. Photo credit: © Sheffield City Council, Libraries Archives and Information: Sheffield Archives: SIS/7.

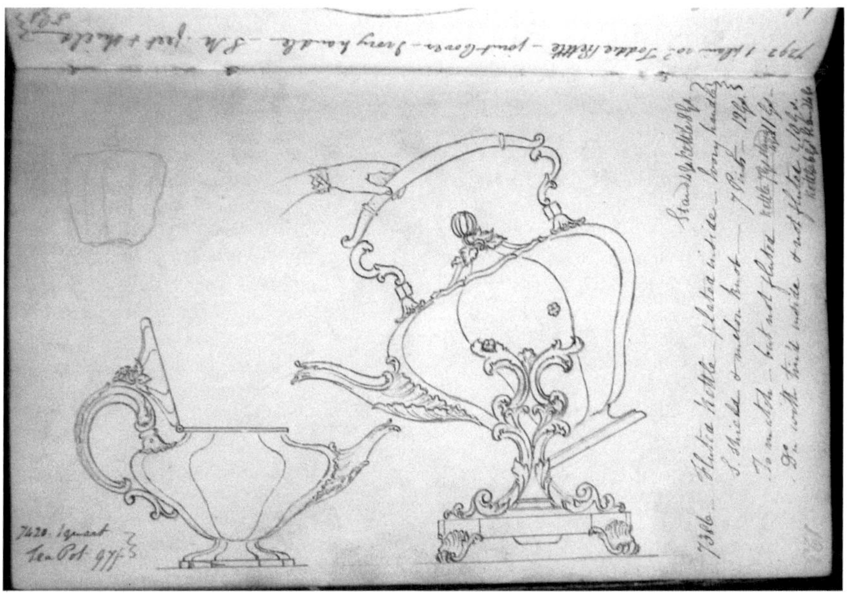

Figure 5.14 Samuel Roberts' pattern book, Drawing of a tea kettle (c.1830)

Source: Sheffield Archives. Photo credit: © Sheffield City Council, Libraries Archives and Information: Sheffield Archives: SIS/7.

equivalents, the way in which printed advertising fuelled appetites for need-nots as well as must-haves, and the reality that London plate and English plated wares frequently appealed to Irish consumers over locally made equivalents.

Notes

1 *Seventeenth Report of the Commissioners of Inquiry into the Collection and Management of the Revenue Arising in Ireland, Scotland etc.*, HC 1828 (8), xv, 104–5.
2 Minute of 28 January 1800, Company of Goldsmiths of Dublin, Ms. 6: 282, Dublin, Assay Office.
3 Ibid., 284.
4 Inevitably, there were peaks and troughs caused by economic vicissitudes, taxes and competition from other sectors of the market such as porcelain, glass and Sheffield plate.
5 David Dickson, *Dublin: The Making of a Capital City* (London: Profile Books, 2014), 261.
6 David Dickson, 'Death of a Capital? Dublin beyond the Union', in *Two Capitals: London and Dublin 1500–1840*, ed. Peter Clark and Raymond Gillespie (Oxford: Oxford University Press, 2001), 111–31.
7 Dickson, *Dublin*, 280. Dickson cites silverwork as one of the trades that flourished in the post-Union generation. However, while the volumes of silver being assayed in 1810 were healthy, a significant downturn was evident by the 1840s. See Appendix 3.
8 John Gamble, *Sketches of History, Politics and Manners in Dublin and the North of Ireland in 1810* (London, 1826), 29.
9 William Stevens, *Hints to the People, Especially to the Inhabitants of Dublin* (Dublin: Printed by H. Fitzpatrick, 1799), 18–19, cited in Dickson, *Dublin*, 274–75.
10 As previously indicated, only a small number of the eighteenth-century assay books kept by the Company of Goldsmiths of Dublin itemise individual objects submitted.
11 Anne Crookshank, 'The Visual Arts, 1603–1740', in *A New History of Ireland*, vol. 4, ed. T. W. Moody and W. E. Vaughan (Oxford: Oxford University Press, 1986), 538.
12 Douglas Bennett, 'James Le Bas 1772–1845', *Antique Collector* (August 1974): 38. Also, Douglas Bennett, '19th-Century Silver', *Dublin Historical Record* 28 (1974), no. 1: 17–20. Nowlan is typical of a manufacturing goldsmith who supplied a number of prominent retailers during this period, while his own workshop was located on Whitefriar Street, convenient to the assay office but outside the fashionable hub around Dublin Castle.
13 Douglas Bennett, *Irish Georgian Silver* (London: Cassell, 1972), 158.
14 Brian Boydell, 'Music before 1700', in *A New History of Ireland*, vol. 4, ed. Moody and Vaughan, 606.
15 Minute of 15 October 1810, Company of Goldsmiths of Dublin, Ms. 7: 113–16, Dublin, Assay Office.
16 Ibid., 114.
17 *Seventeenth Report of the Commissioners*, HC 1828 (8), xv, 105.
18 Gillian O'Brien, '"What Can Possess You to Go to Ireland?": Visitors' Perceptions of Dublin, 1800–30', in *Georgian Dublin*, ed. Gillian O'Brien and Finola O'Kane (Dublin: Four Courts, 2008), 23.
19 See Bennett, *Irish Georgian Silver*, 52. The duty on Irish-made gold and silver wares was raised from 6d to 1s per oz.; 45 George III, c.19 [UK] (25 March 1805).
20 Minute of 29 January 1822, Company of Goldsmiths of Dublin, Ms. 7: 368–69, Dublin, Assay Office.
21 Ibid., 369.
22 *Seventeenth Report of the Commissioners*, HC 1828 (8), xv, 24 and 343.
23 Ibid.
24 Assay Book, 2 May 1820–29 July 1826. Company of Goldsmiths of Dublin, Ms. 29, Dublin, Assay Office. Details were systematically selected from this assay book to form a database that revealed the characteristics of objects submitted for assaying in 1821. The totals did not fall regularly from year to year, but there was a downward trend, compared to the boom years for the trade.
25 Dickson, *Dublin*, 281.

26 These are the names highlighted by Bennett in '19th-Century Silver', 17–20. The assay data for 1821 shows that goldsmiths like Samuel Neville and Christopher Eades were also productive during the period.
27 Bennett, 'James Le Bas', 38–39.
28 The latter included twelve chalices, four ciboria, two 'remonstrances' and two pyx boxes. Curiously, a trowel assayed for him in Dublin was later used by the London goldsmiths Rundell and Bridge to lay the foundation stone of their new premises on Ludgate Hill. This piece was assayed in Dublin c.1814 and later engraved with two salmon, a reference to Rundell and Bridge's shop sign. It has been suggested that they used a second-hand trowel to meet an imminent deadline in terms of the laying of the foundation stone. See http://collections.vam.ac.uk/item/O156495/trowel-bas-james-le/.
29 Minutes of 25 June 1813; 26 June 2013; 5 July 1813; 8 July 1813; 2 February 1815, Company of Goldsmiths of Dublin Ms. 7: 197–204; 235–36, Dublin, Assay Office.
30 Ibid.
31 *Seventeenth Report of the Commissioners*, HC 1828 (8), xv, 347. Interestingly, Carruthers stated that he did not import from England because of the higher duty there. Evidently he had ceased trading by 1828, as in that year John Bryan advertised that he had taken over Carruthers' premises at 5 Castle Street, Belfast, and was selling the latter's stock-in-trade 'at considerably under first cost'. *Belfast News Letter*, 6 May 1828.
32 Duties on Plate Act, 1825 (6 George IV, c.118 (UK) (5 July 1825)).
33 In other words, that they had paid for a licence.
34 For a full transcription of the Act, see Bennett, *Irish Georgian Silver*, 48–49.
35 *Seventeenth Report of the Commissioners*, HC 1828 (8), xv, 104.
36 Ibid.
37 Ibid.
38 Henry Flavelle's name is listed as 'Flaville'. It was not unusual for variant spellings of certain surnames to appear. Other memorialists included Walter Askin, Stephen Cowen, Laurence Keary, Thomas Lowe, Richard Fill, Richard Donnelly, W.H. Moran, James Brady and Geo. Miles.
39 *Seventeenth Report of the Commissioners*, HC 1828 (8), xv, 104.
40 Ibid., 105.
41 Ibid.
42 Ibid.
43 Receipt (Lord Hartland with Robert Garrard, Goldsmith and Jeweller to their Majesties), 3 August 1814. Ms. EPH B847, Ephemera Collection, Prints and Drawings Collection, National Library of Ireland. I am grateful to Honora Faul for drawing my attention to this material.
44 Dickson, *Dublin*, 278.
45 *Seventeenth Report of the Commissioners*, HC 1828 (8), xv, 342.
46 Ibid., 343.
47 Messrs. Roberts, Cadman & Co, Stock on Hands with Clarke and West, 31 January 1816, Sissons Collection, Ms. SIS/10, Sheffield Archive.
48 J.P. Fallon, *House of Barnard: A Notable Family of Manufacturing Silversmiths to the Trade* (Sandy: Bright Pen Books, 2012), 162.
49 There was more than one goldsmith with the surname West operating in Dublin at this time.
50 *Seventeenth Report of the Commissioners*, HC 1828 (8), xv, 340.
51 Ibid.
52 See Helen Clifford, *Silver in London: The Parker and Wakelin Partnership 1760–1776* (New Haven and London: Yale University Press, 2004).
53 West's retailers mark also appeared alongside other 'maker's marks'. See http://www.925-1000.com/forum/viewtopic.php?t=15562 for details of an online research forum on retailer's marks on Irish silver.
54 Gormanston Papers (folder of receipts from silversmiths and jewellers), Ms. 44,413/7, National Library of Ireland. The bill, made out to Richard O'Grady, is dated 1832 but the billhead would have been in general use through this period. West's address is given as 9 Capel Street. In the *Freeman's Journal*, 14 September 1821, Jacob West's Capel Street shop is given as the place to buy commemorative coins to mark the coronation of George IV.

55 *Freeman's Journal and Daily Commercial Advertiser*, 11 February 1831. West and Son, Capel Street, and Matthew West, Skinner Row, were among the Dublin traders associated with this show of support at a time when the duke had been publicly called an absentee.
56 The *Freeman's Journal* of 11 January 1821 includes an advertisement on behalf of Law stating that his plated wares come from 'houses of the first respectability in England'.
57 Dickson, *Dublin*, 285.
58 *Saunders' News-Letter*, 20 May 1797.
59 *Seventeenth Report of the Commissioners*, HC 1828 (8), xv, 344.
60 Register of Apprentices 2 May 1752–7 November 1823, Company of Goldsmiths of Dublin, Ms. 97: 46, Dublin, Assay Office. For Law's commercial addresses see Bennett, *Irish Georgian Silver*, 315.
61 Frank Thorpe Porter, *Gleanings and Reminiscences* (Dublin: Hodges, Foster, 1875), 49. I am grateful to W.E. Vaughan for drawing my attention to this publication. The incident referred to in the subsequent description refers to 1840s after Law's death. The business was continued by his son, trading as William Law and Son.
62 See, for example, *Faulkner's Dublin Journal*, 23–5 February 1786 and 1 September 1796.
63 *Seventeenth Report of the Commissioners*, HC 1828 (8), xv, 345–47.
64 Law's retailer's mark also appears on pieces marked by other manufacturing goldsmiths. See http://www.925–1000.com/IrishRetailers_4.html.
65 *Seventeenth Report of the Commissioners*, HC 1828 (8), xv, 345.
66 Ibid., 346.
67 *Freeman's Journal and Daily Commercial Advertiser*, 8 August 1833. Gresham resisted the extension of the Dublin and Kingstown railway line.
68 Robin Underdahl and Thomas Sinsteden, *The Red McCombs English and Irish Silver Collection* (San Antonio: Institute of Texan Cultures, University of Texas San Antonio, 2010), 236–39. The authors speculate that Lord Combermere may have used the Barbados gift in this way. Henry F. Berry, *A History of the Royal Dublin Society* (London: Longmans, Green, 1915), 130 strengthens the attribution of Teare as the chaser.
69 Berry, *A History of the Royal Dublin Society*, 130.
70 Fray is listed in Bennett, *Irish Georgian Silver*, 306 as registering with the guild in 1813. He became a freeman in 1829 and died in 1842.
71 Christie's, London, 16 November 2010, lot 484. In a meeting of the Repeal Board of Trade in 1843, the Combermere presentation salvers and another testimonial were described as made by Law and Son and West and Son respectively, illustrating how difficult it can be to ascertain the artisans who were was actually responsible for making certain pieces. *Freeman's Journal*, 10 February 1843.
72 Christie's, London, 17 March 1999, lot 47. The salvers were listed in the catalogue as bearing the maker's mark of James 'Fry'.
73 Mooney was advertising in the *Freeman's Journal* from at least 1820. Bennett, *Irish Georgian Silver*, 318 lists him as appearing in street directories from 1827 until at least 1830 but does not list his address.
74 *Freeman's Journal and Daily Commercial Advertiser*, 17 January 1820.
75 *Freeman's Journal and Daily Commercial Advertiser*, 1 February 1821.
76 In newspapers advertisements for this period, Egerton is listed variously as Egerton, Egerton and Pittar and Egerton and Browne with an address at Parliament Street. For example, 'Egerton and Browne, Goldsmiths to his Excellency the Lord Lieutenant, Parliament-street Dublin, beg to inform the Public that they are just returned from England with a large supply of the newest and most fashionable plated goods which are well worth their inspection, manufactured by the first houses in Sheffield (they import no goods from Birmingham). They are supplied as usual with a large assortment of silver goods and jewellery, which they will sell on the most moderate terms'. *Cork Evening Post*, 4 October 1800.
77 *Faulkner's Dublin Journal*, 22 June 1797.
78 *Saunders' News-Letter*, 23 January 1786.
79 *Dublin Evening Post*, 19 March 1791.
80 Ibid.
81 Porter, *Gleanings and Reminiscences*, 45.
82 Allowing for some embellishment in the narrative, it reminds one how perennially vulnerable even established goldsmiths were to fraud.

83 Billhead of Matthew West, 15 Skinner Row, Ms. 8,409 (1), National Library of Ireland. Bennett, *Irish Georgian Silver*, 336 lists Matthew West Jr having premises at 15 Skinner Row; he became a freeman of the goldsmiths' guild in 1804, warden 1808–11, master 1812–13 and died in 1820. Matthew West and Sons registered with the guild in 1827, with a shop at 20 Skinner Row.
84 Folder of receipts from silversmiths and jewellers, Gormanston Papers, Ms. 44,413/7, National Library of Ireland.
85 Records of Roberts, Cadman and Co. Articles of agreement between Patrick Moore, Dublin, and Roberts and Cadman and Co, Sheffield, 1815, Sissons Collection, Ms. SIS/10, Sheffield Archives.
86 Ibid.
87 Samuel Roberts' traveller's pattern book and notes of journeys and merchants in various places, 1830s, Sissons Collection, Ms. SIS/7, Sheffield Archives.
88 Ibid.
89 Bennett, '19th Century Silver', 18.
90 Douglas Bennett, *Collecting Irish Silver* (London: Souvenir Press, 1984), 95–99 provides an account of Waterhouse and Co.
91 *Freeman's Journal*, 2 February 1842. Later that year they advertised the sale of an extensive range of second-hand plate, itemising articles of tableware, though it was not specified if these were of English or Irish manufacture; *Faulkner's Dublin Journal*, 26 September 1842.

Conclusion

Over the course of the Georgian era various patterns of continuity and change can be identified in the goldsmiths' trade of Dublin. Whether as manufacturers, retailers or both, small numbers of goldsmiths consistently dominated the trade. These fortunate individuals often rose to prominence as office holders in the guild and some extended their connections through membership of fraternal organisations such as the Dublin Society, the Royal Irish Academy and the Physico-Historical Society.[1] They depended on extensive networks of artificers, some employed within the workshop, others not. In the absence of business ledgers of the kind surviving for London goldsmiths' firms, it is difficult to be precise about the number of people employed by major workshops and shopkeepers. Apprentices, and sometimes journeymen, can be connected to individual goldsmiths through guild records, but it is much more difficult to reconstruct the web of ancillary craftsmen from chasers to engravers linked to individual goldsmiths and firms.

When the Dublin gold-beater Samuel Guinness married in 1753, *Faulkner's Dublin Journal* described his bride as 'an accomplished young lady with a handsome fortune'.[2] The ceremony was performed at her uncle's country house in Dun Laoghaire.[3] He was the goldsmith Robert Calderwood, whose clients, as has been shown, included the Lord Lieutenant and various members of the nobility. The fact that Calderwood had a country house as well as a shop on Castle Street indicates the kind of lifestyle that could be enjoyed through success in business.[4]

As in London, the increasing separation of the artificer from the customer during the eighteenth century was an inevitable consequence of the rise of big shopkeepers; in Dublin many of the latter sold imported goods alongside those locally produced and advertised this fact in the newspapers. Inevitably, profit would prove more important than patriotism for those shouldering the risk and expenses of running a retail premises, even if some proclaimed the contrary.[5]

Evidence of retail diversification among goldsmiths in Dublin and provincial Ireland is also indicative of the economic realities and pressures of a limited and competitive market. Newspaper advertisements and the accounts of travellers confirm that some Irish goldsmiths tried to drum up extra business by selling such commodities as disparate as coffin ornaments, razor powder or Carolina hats alongside plate. Apart from toymen, who sold a wide range of small luxury goods, this sort of retail diversification was not widespread in a trade associated with exclusivity, but signalled the challenges of running a retail premises in changing circumstances. Even Calderwood, who prospered as a goldsmith, sought out new ways of extending his business interests, establishing a silver-wire manufactory in Dublin and facilitating at least one sale of Chelsea porcelain in Dublin.[6]

When it came to regulating the trade, the distinctive membership structure of Dublin guilds, and the smaller number of practitioners relative to London, made it easier to enforce corporate might during a period of urban transformation. Ireland's quarter-brother system may have discriminated against Catholics and foreigners, but it facilitated guild control. In contrast, the erosion of guild authority in regard to searches for substandard wares came earlier in London. The difference between the two cities is also apparent in the pace at which goldsmith apprenticeship enrolments declined. In London this was evident by the 1720s, whereas in Dublin it was not so marked until the closing decades of the century.

Another example of the divergence between the two countries is the more gradual way that Dublin goldsmiths gained access to new technology like flatting mills, specialist refineries and the facility to produce plated wares. From the 1760s, goldsmiths in both capital cities experienced increased competition from the light, more standardised goods made from silver and Sheffield plate. As shown in chapter 2, it was the 1780s before the Dublin Society moved to offer premiums for innovation in the production of plated wares, and 1779 before the Dublin goldsmiths' guild decided on the need to establish its own flatting mill in or near the city.

Where London goldsmiths largely favoured trade cards and printed handbills over newspaper advertisements, Dublin goldsmiths seem to have advertised more extensively in newspapers. Dublin had an expanding print trade, in which it was alleged to be more inexpensive to advertisers than in London, but cost may not have been the only reason. Many of those advertising were selling imported wares. They needed to highlight the arrival of consignments to potential customers in order to move stock quickly and recoup costs. The extent to which Dublin goldsmiths used newspaper advertising to attract customers from the provinces is difficult to gauge, as is the reach of newspaper advertisements, but some country customers, at least, must have been encouraged to visit the shops touted in the hyperbolic advertisements of Dublin newspapers.

Light goods made from silver and Sheffield plate were imported from England from the second half of the eighteenth century, sold by agents on behalf of wholesale manufacturers like Matthew Boulton, and bought across the counter for cash. As Helen Clifford has shown, London goldsmiths responded to this new demand too, stocking 'slight articles of taste' like 'milk jugs, spoon trays and bottle stands'.[7] Prior to his bankruptcy in 1773,[8] the Dublin retailer Henry Sullivan advertised a variety of imported goods in *Faulkner's Dublin Newsletter*.[9] They included Sheffield plated candlesticks and 'some light English plate curiously wrought as bread baskets, sugar baskets, cruet-stands' as well as various types of cutlery.[10]

Right across the period the demand for second-hand plate was an essential characteristic of the industry. The trade in second-hand goods is increasingly being acknowledged as fundamental to markets for consumers in early modern Europe; silverware represented a distinctive example. Plate was constantly being recycled for reasons of necessity, taste and practicality. Goldsmiths depended on the flow of raw silver and customers, even those with ample means, bought second-hand plate in shops and at auction. Second-hand plate could be cherished for its association with past owners or unsentimentally cashed in – reasons for acquisition and disbursal were as various as the individuals responsible. Fragmentary survival rates for objects, and the tendency for large and impressive pieces to be given pride of place in modern museums, underscores the value of sources like the assay books which provide a much fuller picture of the nature of supply and demand than surviving objects alone.

There was a very significant demand for small items of silverware in Georgian Dublin, confirming the importance of middle- and upper-middle-class customers to Dublin goldsmiths. These clients may not have been able to buy services of plate, but they were a large and increasingly powerful group and they obviously sustained the Dublin goldsmiths' trade.

In the area of design, Irish silver was heavily influenced during this period by developments in London and, indirectly, Paris. Dublin goldsmiths sought to locate themselves within a wider metropolitan dialogue as the rhetoric of their advertising attests. To be sure, there were certain national inflections or forms that were more prevalent in Ireland than elsewhere, but when Dublin goldsmiths raised the question of national identity themselves, it was around issues of economic protectionism rather than seeking to distinguish their work in any material way.

What began simply as an issue of competition from fashionable London goods in the early Georgian period was exacerbated in the mid- to late eighteenth century by the technological expertise and commercial acumen of entrepreneurs like Matthew Boulton and his compatriots in Birmingham and Sheffield, as well as the establishment of English porcelain factories like Chelsea and Bow. This was part of a broader pattern of consumer change, which saw 'old luxuries' augmented, challenged and, in some cases, relegated by 'new luxuries'. Plate, with its ancient association with status and specie, succumbed to new consumer goods, but this was a gradual process.

The fact that Ireland's goldsmiths lagged behind their English counterparts when it came to some of the technological advances of the eighteenth century, and that some of these developments specifically facilitated large-scale serial production, placed them at a distinct disadvantage. This was compounded by consumers who were often seduced by what was new and fashionable, the increased division between those who were makers and those who were sellers, and the negative repercussions of Union.

The impact of parliamentary Union has been vigorously debated. There was a broad consensus both contemporaneously and retrospectively that it would prove detrimental to Dublin's artisanal industries. Inevitably, the reality seems to have been more nuanced. While opinions have varied between the view that Union sounded a swift death knell to the Dublin goldsmiths' trade and the assertion that silverwork flourished in the post-Union generation, a median position is more accurate. Certainly, by 1810 healthy volumes of plate were still being submitted to the Dublin assay office, but a few decades later the situation was very different.

By 1843, Dublin goldsmiths were still calling publicly for the repeal of the Union. At a meeting held at the Corn Exchange, Dublin, in February of that year, representatives of the trade rallied for repeal to rousing cheers and choruses of 'hear, hear' from their supporters.[11] The goldsmith Peter Hughes moved the resolution that he and his counterparts had a duty to fight for reversal of a measure which had been responsible for the 'wholesale decay' of a once flourishing trade. He argued that prior to Union between three and four hundred people had been employed in the trade 'both directly and indirectly', claiming that it had been reduced to thirty members, 'not fifteen of which were fully employed'.[12] Others who contributed to the meeting reckoned that, more than most other trades, goldsmiths were dependent on the nobility and gentry for employment and therefore felt their absence more acutely. By this stage, the decline in the silver trade was very evident, both in terms of locally produced and imported wares. The annual duties collected in each year between 1849 and 1851 were £866, £731 and £817, respectively; two decades earlier it had exceeded £5,000 in individual years (Appendix 3).[13] In contrast, London's returns for the same period ranged between £58,985 and £70,252.[14] It is important to stress, however, that the goldsmiths' trade in London also suffered a significant decline during this period; clearly Union was not the only catalyst. By the middle of the nineteenth century, the manufacture of silverware in London had also appreciably declined. As John Forbes has illustrated,

> in the early 1800s some 800,000 oz. of large and 400,000 oz. of small silver wares (excluding watchcases) were received on average at the Assay Office each year. But by the 1850s these figures had dropped to about 500,000 oz. and 250,000 oz. respectively.[15]

Forbes cites the development of electroplating as a key factor in these dwindling outputs – just as Sheffield plate had challenged silverwares in the second half of the eighteenth century, so electroplating presented a new challenge to manufacturing goldsmiths in the next century.[16] By the 1840s, Waterhouse and Co., the English firm who had established premises in Dame Street in Dublin, was offering Elkington's electroplate, 'received from the patentees in England', alongside their own Sheffield-plated wares.[17] From their stock of English goods, they were claiming to offer the best in terms of novelty, fashion and value and, in terms of the scale of their production, they enjoyed a commercial advantage. This correlates to a period of diminishing returns for silver submitted to the Dublin assay office for hallmarking, and the advertising rhetoric used by Waterhouse is telling. Ultimately, the biggest challenge that Irish manufacturing goldsmiths faced was proximity to England.

Dublin's urban expansion in the post-Union period meant that more households needed furnishing. However, the fact that there was a long decline in the number of townhouses maintained by aristocratic families meant that there was an exodus of many of the most elevated patrons from the city at least, traditionally the 'great customers of plate'.[18] A new moral seriousness deepened by the shock of 1798 and arguably by Union has been associated with the mid-Hanoverian period onwards.[19] It could be that it spread to habits of display, with restraint replacing ostentation, but it is more likely that a combination of political, technological, economic and social factors gradually eroded the demand for Irish-made silver in the first half of the nineteenth century. Writing on the development of Irish industry in the mid-nineteenth century, John Francis Maguire alluded nostalgically to times past:

> If the reader would wish to be satisfied that the silver trade did flourish in Ireland in other days, it is not impossible to convince him that it did. He has but to apply to some friendly jeweller and silversmith, or extensive pawn-broker, in any of our cities or large towns, and induce him to permit a peep at his store of old silver – not meaning thereby old in the sense which we use the term when we speak of old iron; but costly and beautiful articles, in a high state of preservation.

Accounting for his use of the past tense, Maguire explained that a series of factors including famine, Union, and the failure of Irish patrons to shop patriotically had all contributed to the demise of the trade. Providing steadily decreasing figures of duty paid, from £1,183 17s 11d in 1848 to £730 19s 7d in 1851, he argued that the decline was not irreparable.[20] If only people would buy Irish, particularly when it came to the regular demand for presentation plate, the industry might be given a much needed boost. Interestingly, Maguire claimed that church plate was one of the few branches of production which was being provided for at home. He singled out the work of goldsmith John Donegan for particular praise, the latter having exhibited church plate in gold and silver at the Cork Industrial Exhibition of 1852.[21] A spate of church building on the part of the Catholic community of Dublin and throughout the country during the first half of the nineteenth century no doubt provided a boost to Donegan and other manufacturers and retailers of ecclesiastical plate.[22]

Just a few years before Maguire penned his eulogy to the goldsmiths' trade, Henry Flavelle, a former master warden of the goldsmiths' guild, was forced to emigrate with his young family on account of the lack of business.[23] The guild paid tribute to him for his 'past exertions' to promote the welfare and interests of his brethren.[24] In 1853, they agreed to devise the best way of preventing the practice of having plate that was manufactured outside Ireland and hallmarked in Dublin being sold as Irish, vowing to do all in their power to discontinue the practice.[25] They decided to refuse to assay plate in such circumstances, but it was not a straightforward matter to resolve, and by then was arguably too late. While Dublin had been proud of its second-city status relative to London in the eighteenth century, ultimately it was this geographical proximity, not alone to London but to the industrial heartland of England, that would prove so detrimental to the manufacture of plate in Ireland's capital city as the Georgian era drew to a close.

Notes

1 Robert Calderwood became involved with the Physico-Historical Society and the Dublin Society. See Alison FitzGerald, 'Cosmopolitan Commerce: The Dublin Goldsmith Robert Calderwood', *Apollo* (2005): 46. Jeremiah D'Olier was also a member of the Dublin Society.

2 *Faulkner's Dublin Journal* (*FDJ*), 4–7 August 1753.

3 Ibid.

4 Calderwood's counterpart in London, the goldsmith Paul de Lamerie, built up an extensive property portfolio over the course of his career. He had begun speculating in property, as early as 1733, and by the time of his death he owned 45 houses in various parts of London. Helen Clifford, 'Paul de Lamerie, 1688–1751', in *The Jamie Ortiz-Patiño Collection of Silver by Paul de Lamerie* (Sotheby's, New York, 22 April 1998), 18. The example of Samuel Guinness also underscores a frequent pattern of marriage within extended families being linked to specific trades.

5 See, for example, *Saunders' News-Letter*, 20 May 1797.

6 FitzGerald, 'Cosmopolitan Commerce'.

7 Helen Clifford, *Silver in London* (New Haven and London: Yale University Press, 2004), 8.

8 *Saunders' News-Letter*, 19–21 April 1773.

9 *Faulkner's Dublin Journal* (*FDJ*), 15–18 October 1765.

10 Ibid.

11 *Freeman's Journal*, 2 February 1843.

12 Ibid.

13 The rate of duty was 1s 6d per oz. for silver and 17s per oz. for gold. There is a close correlation between the quantities of tax collected and the quantities of plate submitted during this period, indicating a high level of compliance. I am grateful to Thomas Sinsteden for this information.

14 Ibid.

15 J.S. Forbes, *Hallmark: A History of the London Assay Office* (London: Goldsmiths Company and Unicorn Press, 1999), 267. I am grateful to Breda Scott for drawing my attention to this reference.

16 Electroplating, an innovation of the early nineteenth century, is a method of coating metal by electrolytic deposition with chromium, silver or another metal.
17 *Freeman's Journal*, 26 May 1843.
18 David Dickson, *Dublin: The Making of a Capital City* (London: Profile, 2014), 278; Malcolm Baker, 'A Rage for Exhibitions: The Display and Viewing of Wedgwood's Frog Service', in *The Genius of Wedgwood*, ed. Hilary Young (London: V&A, 1995), 124.
19 James Kelly, *Sport in Ireland 1600–1840* (Dublin: Four Courts Press, 2014), 352–53. I am grateful to Toby Barnard for drawing my attention to this source.
20 J.F. Maguire, *The Industrial Movement in Ireland as Illustrated by the National Exhibition of 1852* (Cork, 1853), 134.
21 Ibid., 137. Maguire was mayor of Cork, a city in which the goldsmiths' trade had flourished during the previous century. An advertisement from *The Catholic Directory, Almanac and Registry of Ireland, England, Scotland*, 1865 shows that John Donegan's brother Patrick took over the business on the former's death and supplied a wide range of ecclesiastical wares in precious and non precious metals.
22 Rob Goodbody, ed., *Dublin, Part 3, 1756–1847*, vol. 26 of *Irish Historic Towns Atlas* (Dublin: Royal Irish Academy, 2014), 5.
23 Flavelle was also one of the signatories on the 1828 petition for exclusions from the licence fee. The Pittar family, among the most successful Dublin silver manufacturers of the eighteenth century emigrated, earlier, relocating to India.
24 Minute of 20 November 1848, Company of Goldsmiths of Dublin, Ms. 8: 447–48, Dublin, Assay Office.
25 Minute of 8 August 1853, Company of Goldsmiths of Dublin, Ms. 8: 323, Dublin, Assay Office. Putting this into practice was not a straightforward issue. Guild minutes include a number of references to advice sought from London etc. in this regard. See, for example, Minute of 7 August 1860, Company of Goldsmiths of Dublin, Ms. 10: 60–61, Dublin, Assay Office; Minute of 7 May 1879, Company of Goldsmiths of Dublin, Ms. 10: 145, Dublin, Assay Office.

Appendix 1

Table A.1 Professions recorded for parents or named guardians/relatives of apprentices recorded in the apprenticeship ledgers of the Dublin goldsmiths' guild between 1700 and 1800

Alderman	1	Hairdresser	1
Apothecary	5	Hardware Man	1
Baker	1	Hosier	2
Brazier	3	Innkeeper	4
Brewer	2	Iron Maker	1
Bricklayer	2	Jeweller	5
Buckle Maker	1	Laceman	1
Butcher	1	Lace Weaver	1
Cabinet Maker	1	Lapidary	2
Carpenter	3	Leather Cutter	1
Chandler	5	Mariner	7
Charity School Boy	2	Mathematical Inst. Maker	1
Chaser	2		
Clergyman	15	Merchant	56
Clerk	3	Military	4
Clock Maker	2	Not Specified	115
Clothier	5	Painter	3
Coach Maker	2	Periwig Maker	1
Cook	2	Peruke Maker	1
Cordwinder	2	Pin Maker	1
Distiller	2	Printer	1
Doctor	1	Public Notary	1
Draper	2	Saddler	1
Dyer	3	Seal Cutter	1
Engraver	1	Ship Carpenter	1
Esquire	8	Shoe Maker	8
Farmer	27	Silk Throwster	1
Feltmaker	1	Silversmith	1
Founder	3	Skinner	3
Fuller	1	Slater	2
Gardener	3	Smith	6
Gentleman	169	Soap Boiler	1
Glover	1	Spinster	1
Gold Lace Weaver	1	Stay Maker	3
Goldsmith/In Trade	51	Stocking Weaver	1
Grocer	8	Stone Manufacturer	1
Gunsmith	4	Surgeon	2

(*Continued*)

Table A.1 (Continued)

Sword Cutler	3	Weaver	11
Tailor	12	Wheelwright	1
Tanner	3	Whip Maker	1
Unclear Entry	1	Widow	80
Victualler	4	Wig Maker	1
Vintner	2	Wine Cooper?	1
Watch Engraver	1	Worsted Sorter	1
Watchmaker	1	Yeoman	3

Total: 715

Source: Registers of Apprentice Enrolments incorporating the period 1700 to 1800, Company of Goldsmiths of Dublin, Mss. 95–97, Dublin, Assay Office.

Appendix 2

Table A.2 Proportional breakdown of apprentices among Dublin goldsmiths between 1700 and 1800

Master	*Number of apprentices*	*Master*	*Number of apprentices*
Archdall, William	2	Clarke, John*	1
Austin, John	1	Clifton, John*	3
Balaquier, James	1	Connor, Michael	1
Banks, John	1	Cope, Erasmus	8
Barrett, Edward	6	Cope, Thomas	4
Barrett, John	1	Crab/Crabb, Isaac	1
Barrett, Mary	2	Crampton, John	6
Barry, John	1	Crampton, Thomas	5
Barry, William	2	Cunningham, Hugh	1
Bate, William	3	Currie, William*	10
Beere, George*	3	Cuthbert, John Jr	2
Beere, William*	1	Dalrymple, John	2
Billing, Henry	8	Daniel/Daniell, Henry	3
Billing, Martin	6	Daniel/Daniell, Jane	1
Billing, Robert*	7	Darragh, Charles	2
Billing, Thomas*	1	Deane, Thomas	1
Bingham, Walter	3	Dolittle, William	1
Black, James	1	Doogan/Duggan, William	1
Blundell, Joseph	4	Douglas, John	1
Blundell, Thomas*	8	Douglas/Douglass, James	4
Bolton, Thomas	3	Dowdall, Charles	1
Bomes, David	12	Dowling, Murtagh	3
Bradley, John	3	Dufour, J. M.	1
Breading, Robert	3	Dunn, John	1
Bridgman, Joseph	2	Eaton, Richard	1
Brown, Alexander*	3	Ebbs, John	2
Brown/Browne, Matthias	5	Egerton, Edward	1
Burton, John	2	Finch, Roger	9
Burton, Thomas	2	Forbes, Esther	1
Calderwood, Robert	14	Forbes, Robert	1
Campbell, George	1	Forster, Richard	2
Cassidy, Owen	2	Foster, Richard	1
Chalmers, George	1	Forster, Vere	5
Champion, James I	2	Fowler, Michael	1
Champion, James II	6	Fraigneau, Adam	1

(*Continued*)

Table A.2 (Continued)

Master	*Number of apprentices*	*Master*	*Number of apprentices*
Freboul/Frebon?, John	1	Meekins, Thomas	1
Freeze, John	1	Mockler, Edward	2
Gerard, Mary	2	Moore, John*	10
Gervais, Peter	6	Moore, John & William	1
Gillespy/Gillespie, Charles	5	Mosse, Bartholomew	2
Giraud, Fran.	2	Manjoy/Mountjoy, Benjamin	3
Glanvile/Glanville, Robert	3	Murray, Nathan*	5
Glasco, Philip*	3	Narney, John	1
Goodwin, Andrew	4	Nash, Maurice	1
Gordon, Alexander*	4	Nixon, Joseph	6
Gordon, David	1	Nuttall, Thomas	1
Gradell, Gaspard	1	D'Olier, Isaac*	7
Green, Thomas*	2	Onge, Daniel	4
Gregory, Andrew	2	Orr, Ebenezer	1
Gumley, John	4	Osborne, William	1
Hall, Edward	1	Palet/Pallett, John	3
Hamilton, John	11	Parker, George	5
Harris, John	3	Parker, Thomas	2
Hartwick, Christopher	1	Parsons, Thomas	1
Hopkins, Robert	1	Paterell/Paturel/ Paturle, John	5
Hughes, William	5	Pemberton, Benjamin	1
Humphry, Francis	2	Peter, David*	3
Ince, Robert	1	Pineau, Daniel	9
Isack/Isaacs, Thomas	1	Pitts, Robert	1
Jackson, Joseph	5	Popkins, Bartholomew	4
Johnston, Thomas	2	Popkins, Daniel	2
Jones, Francis	3	Potter, Robert	1
Jones, Thomas	3	Power, William	2
Kehoe, Darby	1	Prendergast, Charles	1
Kindt/Keindt, Christian	4	Racine, Benjamin	2
King, David	3	Racine, Peter	1
Kinnersly, Philip	5	Raper, Edward	4
Kirkpatrick, Martin	3	Raymond, William*	1
Laughlin, John	3	Read, Michael	1
Laughlin, John Jr	4	Richards, Alexander	2
Law, William	1	Ringland, John	1
Lefebure, Anthony	1	Robertson, James	1
Lemaistre, Charles	1	Rose, Robert	1
Lemaistre, Nicholas	3	Ruston, Jonathan	4
Leslie, Charles	2	St. John, John	1
Letablere, John	3	Savill/Saville, William	5
Lilly, Alexander	3	Shephard, Thomas	5
Limarest, Thomas de	3	Sherwin, Henry	2
Lloyd, John*	2	Sherwin, John*	5
Locker, Christopher	1	Simms, Philip	3
Locker, John	4	Sinclare/Sinclair, Alexander	3
Mallory, Cyriac	1	Sinclare/Sinclair, William	6
Manjoy/Monjoy, Dorothy	5	Skinner, Christopher	6
Martin, Mark	5	Skinner, William	1
Matthews, John	5	Slack, Benjamin	2
McCarthy, Christopher	1	Slicer, Edward	4
McCoy, James	1	Smith, Robert*	2

Master	*Number of apprentices*	*Master*	*Number of apprentices*
Standish, Deacon	2	Walsh, Patrick	2
Steele, William	4	Ward, William	1
Stern/Sterne, John*	9	Warren, James	1
Stokes, Benjamin	3	Welding, James	1
Stopleare, William	3	Weldon, Arthur	8
Streeter, William	3	West, John*	3
Sturgys, Edmond	4	West, Matthew	4
Sutton, Thomas	6	Whitefield, John	1
Sutton, William	1	Whitthorne/Whitehorne/ Whithorn, James	5
Taylor, John*	1	Whitthorne, William	1
Taylor, Poole*	3	Whitshed, John	1
Teare, Samuel	2	Williams, Richard	6
Thompson, George	1	Williams, Robert	1
Thompson, Joseph	2	Williamson, Francis	1
Tough, Philip	1	Williamson, John	8
Townsend, Charles	3	Williamson, Thomas*	1
Townsend, William	9	Williamson, William*	10
Tudor, Richard	1	Wilme, Henry	3
Twelves, Mark	1	Wilme, John*	7
Usher, Peter	4	Wilme, William	13
Vialas/Violas, Noah	13	Wilson, Benjamin*	7
Vidouze, James	9	Wilson, Matthew	1
Wade, John	4	Wilson, William	1
Waggoner, Chr.	1	Wingfield, Peter	2
Walker, Joseph	3	Workman, Edward	6
Walker, Matthew	5	Wyer, James	5
Walker, Samuel	1	Young, Simon	3
Walker, Thomas	6	**Total**	**715**

Source: Registers of Apprentice Enrolments incorporating the period 1700 to 1800, Company of Goldsmiths of Dublin, Mss. 95–97, Dublin, Assay Office. It does not take account of apprentices who were 'turnovers' from one master to another. The goldsmiths, jewellers and watchmakers whose names are indicated with an asterisk indicate cases where there was more than one master of that name.

Appendix 3

Table A.3 Gold and silver plate duty collected from March 1730 to March 1869

Rates of duty per oz.:

1730 to 1806: 6d
1807 to 1842: 1s
1843 to 1869: 1s 6d

Year	*Total £*	*Year*	*Total £*	*Year*	*Total £*	*Year*	*Total £*
1730	1,689	1761	1,384	1792	1,905	1823	3,362
1731	851	1762	1,521	1793	1,512	1824	3,860
1732	1,175	1763	1,618	1794	1,612	1825	2,388
1733	946	1764	1,984	1795	1,928	1826	5,108
1734	1,080	1765	1,772	1796	1,865	1827	4,995
1735	936	1766	1,718	1797	1,081	1828	5,616
1736	1,062	1767	1,688	1798	1,138	1829	5,186
1737	1,060	1768	1,870	1799	1,897	1830	4,494
1738	1,098	1769	1,688	1800	2,093	1831	3,887
1739	1,142	1770	1,851	1801	1,839	1832	3,891
1740	1,076	1771	1,654	1802	1,938	1833	3,709
1741	1,062	1772	1,703	1803	2,240	1834	2,801
1742	1,170	1773	1,675	1804	2,375	1835	2,906
1743	1,115	1774	1,646	1805	2,660	1836	3,107
1744	1,198	1775	1,669	1806	2,422	1837	2,073
1745	1,038	1776	1,833	1807	2,796	1838	2,443
1746	949	1777	1,968	1808	5,762	1839	2,491
1747	1,131	1778	1,768	1809	6,209	1840	2,145
1748	1,354	1779	1,658	1810	4,751	1841	1,884
1749	1,288	1780	1,877	1811	3,931	1842	1,941
1750	1,532	1781	1,941	1812	4,888	1843	1,602
1751	1,501	1782	2,049	1813	5,406	1844	1,951
1752	1,606	1783	1,854	1814	4,786	1845	2,342
1753	1,610	1784	1,868	1815	3,818	1846	2,047
1754	1,328	1785	1,801	1816	2,689	1847	1,184
1755	1,235	1786	1,862	1817	3,015	1848	1,016
1756	1,506	1787	2,003	1818	3,968	1849	866
1757	1,150	1788	2,004	1819	3,863	1850	731
1758	1,485	1789	1,855	1820	2,573	1851	817
1759	1,333	1790	1,892	1821	3,072	1852	913
1760	1,335	1791	1,883	1822	3,291	1853	1,059

Year	*Total £*	*Year*	*Total £*	*Year*	*Total £*	*Year*	*Total £*
1855	1,028	1859	1,369	1863	831	1867	809
1856	1,069	1860	1,245	1864	676	1868	896
1857	1,370	1861	1,249	1865	774	1869	885
1858	1,271	1862	843	1866	889		

Source: Report of the Commissioners of Inland Revenue on the duties under their management, for the years 1856 to 1869 inclusive; with some retrospective history, and the complete tables of accounts of the duties from their first imposition, ii, pp. 139–41 [C. 82–1], HC 1870, xx, 517–19. I am grateful to W.E. Vaughan for giving me this information.

Bibliography

PRIMARY SOURCES

Manuscripts

Birmingham city archives

Matthew Boulton Papers

Bodleian library, Oxford

John Johnson Papers (Irish Trade Cards and other Ephemera Album 143).

British Museum, London: Department of Prints and Drawings

Banks Trade Card Collection
Heal Trade Card Collection

Company of Goldsmiths of Dublin

i. Minute books

2 February 1686–30 October 1731, Ms. 1
9 November 1731–1 May 1758, Ms. 2
30 October 1739–20 June 1746, Ms. 3
1746–1 November 1754, Ms. 4
1 May 1760–15 June 1779, Ms. 5
1 August 1779–26 November 1807, Ms. 6
26 November 1807–6 October 1824, Ms. 7
11 October 1824–7 May 1855, Ms. 8
6 August 1855–29 July 1918, Ms. 10

ii. Assay books

16 April 1638–1649; then 1693–10 February 1699, Ms. 13
2 November 1705–31 July 1713, Ms. 14
4 May 1725–30 October 1728, Ms. 15
1729–13 July 1733 [parts torn out], Ms. 16
2 November 1744–13 April 1748, Ms. 17
27 March 1752–1 August 1755, Ms. 19
18 July 1758–November 1758, Ms. 20
3 February 1787–2 February 1789, Ms. 21

1 November 1788–22 January 1799, Ms. 22
31 December 1795–3 July 1802, Ms. 23
11 August 1807–2 February 1818, Ms. 24
2 November 1809–30 October 1817, Ms. 25
29 November 1809–30 July 1811, Ms. 26
2 May 1820–29 July 1826, Ms. 29

iii. Enrolment books and registration books

Apprentices, 1637–June 1703; Freemen and Journeymen, 1656–1702, Ms. 95
Apprentices, September 1704–1 March 1752; Freemen and Quarter brothers, 1703–1760, Ms. 96
Apprentices, 2 May 1752–7 November 1823, Ms. 97
A–Z index 1680–1780, Ms. 94
Freeman and Officers, 1637–c.1779 (18th-century transcript), Ms. 93
Registration Book of Silversmiths under 1784 Act, 1784–1838, Ms. 99

iv. Miscellaneous

Correspondence, Circulars, Bonds and Agreements (18th century), Also Assay Masters 1824–54, Ms. 131
Indentures; Bond of Nathaniel Murray 1774; List of Assay Masters (unsorted papers), Ms. 134
Petitions, 1706–31, Ms. 128

Cork City Archives

Caulfield Indenture Transcripts, 1881, Ms. U225

Dublin City Archives

Wide Streets Commission of Dublin. Minutes, 1758–1830, Ms. WSC/Mins/1–39

Goldsmiths' Company, London

Apprenticeship Books 5–7 1652, 1653, 1659, B39
Enrolment of Apprentices, 1708–63
Gerald Taylor Papers
Total Book, 1782–91

Henry Francis du Pont Museum, Winterthur

Joseph Downs Collection. Dinner Book of Robert Jocelyn, 1740–51, Ms. 219

Marsh's Library, Dublin

Garstin, J. R., Materials Collected Towards the History of Irish Goldsmiths, Late 19th Century, Ms. Z.1.1.18/25

National Archives, Dublin

Fitzwilliam Family Papers, 18th century, Ms. 97/46
Ticher, Kurt, Papers, 20th century, Ms. 2002

National Archives, Kew

Correspondence Relating to the Establishment of an Assay Office in Cork, Ms. 30/9/147
Irish Customs Board. Minutes, CUST 1/154, 159, 165
Ledgers of Imports and Exports from London and the Outports, 1697 to 1780, CUST3
Plate Tax Lists, 1756–62 and 1776, T47/6
St George, Oliver. Accounts, 1661–1731, C110/46
Webb, Peter, and Arthur Webb (London jewellers). Accounts, 1735–93, C108/284–85

National Library of Ireland, Dublin

Balfour Family. Accounts, Mss. 9534, 10,279
Calderwood, Robert. Genealogical Notes on Robert Calderwood, 1918, Ms. 3269
Edgeworth, Richard. Accounts, 1720–70, Mss. 1507–36
Flower Family. Accounts, 1700–50, Mss. 11, 467
Gormanstown Family. Jewellers' and Silversmiths' Receipts, 1781–1932, Ms. 44,413/7
Guild of St Luke. Proceedings, 1677–1728, Ms. 12123; Guild of St Luke. Register of Apprentices, Ms. 12131
Handbill Advertising the 'First Irish Lottery for 1798', Ms. 33,734
Inventory of Nathaniel Clements' Plate, 1775, Ms. 33,575; Nathaniel Clements' Will dated 19 May 1775, and codicil 24 May 1777, Ms. 9,621
Inventory of Plate of James Butler, 2nd Duke of Ormonde, 1 May 1705, Ms. 2521
La Touche, William George Digges. Accounts, 1781–98, Ms. 19.898
Leitrim Family. Papers, 1748–93, Ms. 33,839
Michael Ward in Relation to the Specie Shortage in Ireland, Mid-1720s, Ms. 2256
Petition of Lord Abercorn, Lord Boyne, Sir Ralph Gore, Oliver St George and
Taylor, Sir Thomas. Accounts, Ms. 25, 386
Trade Cards and Billheads, 18th and 19th Century, Boxes 1–3 (Unsorted), Prints and Drawings Department

Private collections

Account Book of Charles Cobbe, 1760s (Cobbe Family)
Inventory of Lord Bessborough's Plate in Dublin, 1743 (Bessborough Family)

Public record office of Northern Ireland

Abercorn Papers, D623/D/4
Annesley Papers, D1503/8/2
Caledon Papers, D2433/B/1/1
Downshire Papers, D607/B
Johnston Papers, D1594/185
Kenmare Papers, D4151/R
Stewart of Killymoon Papers, D3167/2
Will of John Fitzgibbon, Earl of Clare, 11 December 1800, T3244/11/1
Will of Mary St George, 18 August 1746, D235/23

Registry of Deeds, Dublin

Deeds at Large.

Religious Society of Friends, Historical Library, Dublin

Quaker Wills and Estate Inventories, Mss. MMIIL1, MMIIL2

Sheffield Archives

Sissons Collection, SIS/10

Trinity College, Dublin

Beaufort, Daniel, Diaries, 1781–1818, Mss. 4031, 4037, 7941–7942
Beaufort, Daniel, Travel Journals, 1764–1808, Mss. 4024–36
King, William, Correspondence, Ms. 750
Trinity College Muniments, MUN/P

Victoria and Albert Museum, London

Garrard Ledgers, Gentlemen's Ledgers, 1740–87, Archive of Art and Design

Walsall Local History Centre

Gee, James, Autobiography, 1797.

Wilson and Company, Sharrow

Wilson, Joseph (manufacturer of Sheffield plate). Business papers.

Printed primary sources

Account of the Short Life, Sudden Death, and Pompous Funeral of Michy Windybank, Only Child to Sir Oliver Windybank. Dublin, 1721.

Anon. *Notes on the Pictures, Plate, Antiquities, etc. at Carton, Kilkea Castle, 15 Dominick Street Dublin, and at 6 Carlton House Terrace, London*. Dublin, 1871.

Badcock, William. *A New Touch-Stone for Gold and Silver Wares, 1677*. London, 1677.

Barrington, Jonah. *Personal Sketches of His Own Times*. 3rd ed., 2 vols. London, 1869.

Berkeley, George. *The Querist*. Dublin, 1735.

Brasbridge, Joseph. *The Fruits of Experience; or Memoir of Joseph Brasbridge Written in His 80th and 81st Years*. 2nd ed. London, 1824.

Brooke, Henry. *The Fool of Quality*. Dublin, 1766.

Bush, John. *Hibernia Curiosa: A Letter from a Gentleman in Dublin to His Friend at Dover in Kent, Giving a General View of the Manners, Customs, Dispositions, &c. of the Inhabitants of Ireland . . . Collected in a Tour throughout the Kingdom in the Year 1764*. Dublin, 1769.

Campbell, R. *The London Tradesman*. London, 1747.

Case of the Wardens and Assistant of the Company or Mystery of Goldsmiths of the City of London. London, 1773.

Caulfield, Richard, ed. *The Council Book of the Corporation of Cork*. Guildford, 1876.

Chaigneau, William. *The History of Jack Connor*. 2 vols. Dublin, 1752.

Chetwood, William Rufus. *A Tour through Ireland in Several Entertaining Letters*. London, 1748.

Cooke, William. *Memoirs of Samuel Foote Esq*. 3 vols. London, 1805.

Cosby, P. 'Autobiography of Pole Cosby of Stradbally'. *Kildare Archaeological Society Journal* 5 (1906–8): 79–99, 165–84, 253–73, 311–24, and 423–36.
Cosnett, Thomas. *The Footman's Directory and Butler's Remembrancer*. London, 1825.
Defoe, Daniel. *The Compleat English Tradesman*. London, 1727.
Descriptive Catalogue of the Several Splendid Pieces of Mechanism and Jewellery in Mr. Cox's Museum, Now Exhibiting at the Great Room, in William Street, Dublin. Dublin, 1774.
Dobbs, Arthur. *An Essay on the Trade and Improvement of Ireland*. Dublin, 1729.
Dowling, Vincent. *Trials at Large*. Dublin, 1792.
Edgeworth, Maria. *Castle Rackrent; an Hibernian Tale*. 2nd ed. London, 1800.
———. *Popular Tales*. London, 1804.
———. *Ormond*. Belfast: Appletree, 1992.
Elias, A.C. *Memoirs of Laetitia Pilkington*. 2 vols. Athens: University of Georgia Press, 1997.
FitzGerald, Brian. *The Correspondence of Emily, Duchess of Leinster*. 3 vols. Dublin: Stationery Office, 1949–57.
Fox, G. *Memoirs of the Late Philip Rundell Esq. Goldsmith and Jeweller to His Majesty and the Royal Family, Late of the Golden Salmon, Ludgate Hill, London*. London, 1827.
Gamble, John. *Sketches of History, Politics and Manners in Dublin and the North of Ireland in 1810*. London, 1826.
Gilbert, J. ed. *Calendar of Ancient Records of Dublin*. 19 vols. Dublin: Joseph Dollard, 1889–1944.
Glass House Clerk. *The Plate-Glass-Book, By a Glass-House Clerk. To Which Is Added, The Compleat Appraiser. Consisting of Useful Tables, with Their Explanation for the Valuing of Brass, Copper, Pewter, Iron, Damask, Paper and Linen Furniture, Liquors, Plate, &c., by an Eminent Broker Lately Deceased*. London, 1757.
Griffith, Amyas. *Miscellaneous Tracts*. Dublin, 1788.
Hoare, Prince. *Pedantic Apothecary Quizzed, or Lottery Prize, of 2, 5, 3, 8, A Farce in Two Acts. Performed at the Theatres Royal, London and Dublin*. Dublin, [1795?].
Hunt, William, ed. *The Irish Parliament in 1775*. Dublin: Hodges, Figgis, Longmans, Green, 1907.
Johnstone, Charles. *The History of John Juniper*. Dublin, 1781.
Lady's Companion: Or, Accomplish'd Director in the Whole Art of Cookery. Dublin, 1767.
Legg, Marie Lou, ed. *The Synge Letters*. Dublin: Lilliput, 1996.
Mitchel, John, ed. *Irish Political Economy by Jonathan Swift Dean of St. Patrick's and George Berkeley, Bishop of Cloyne*. Dublin, 1847.
Porter, Frank Thorpe. *Gleanings and Reminiscences*. Dublin, 1875.
Prideaux, Walter S. *Memorials of the Goldsmiths' Company Being Gleanings from Their Records between the Years 1335 and 1815*. 2 vols. London, 1896–97.
Prior, Thomas. *A List of the Absentees of Ireland, and the Yearly Value of Their Estates and Incomes Spent Abroad. With Observations on the Present State and Condition of That Kingdom*. Dublin, 1729.
Proceedings of the Dublin Society (Royal Dublin Society after 1821). Dublin, 1764–1800.
Report from the Committee Appointed to Enquire into the Manner of Conducting the Several Assay Offices in London, York, Exeter, Bristol, Chester, Norwich, and Newcastle upon Tyne. London, 1773.
Second Annual Exhibition of Articles of Irish Manufacture, Produce and Invention at the Royal Dublin Society's House, May 1835. Dublin, 1835.
Short Reasons Why Our Gold-Money in Ireland Should Not Be Lowered. Dublin, 1737.
Simon, James. *An Essay Towards an Historical Account of Irish Coins*. Dublin, 1749.
Swift, Jonathan. *A Letter to the Shopkeepers, Tradesmen, Farmers and Common People of Ireland, Concerning the Brass Half-Pence Coined by Mr. Woods. By M.B. Drapier*. Dublin, 1724.
———. *Directions to Servants*. Dublin, 1745.

Topham Bowden, Charles. *A Tour through Ireland*. Dublin, 1791.
Twiss, Richard. *A Tour in Ireland in 1775*. 2nd ed. Dublin, 1776.
Whitshaw, James, *A New Law Dictionary*. London, 1829.
Wonderful Advantages of Adventuring in the Lottery Or, the History of John Doyle. Dublin, 1797.
Young, Edward. *Love of Fame, the Universal Passion. In Seven Characteristical Satires*. 2nd ed. Dublin, 1728.

Newspapers

Belfast News Letter
Clonmel Gazette; or, Hibernian Advertiser
Cork Evening Post
Dublin Courant
Dublin Daily Advertiser
Dublin Evening Post
Dublin Intelligence
Dublin Mercury
Dublin Spy
Dublin Weekly Journal
Faulkner's Dublin Journal
Freeman's Journal
Hibernian Chronicle
Hibernian Journal
Limerick Chronicle
Munster Journal
Pue's Occurrences
Saunders' News-Letter
Star and Fashionable World
Universal Advertiser
Volunteer Journal; or, Independent Gazetteer
Volunteers Journal; or, Irish Herald
Walker's Hibernian Magazine

Parliamentary papers

Parliamentary and other official papers

Journals of the House of Commons of the Kingdom of Ireland, 21 vols., 1796–1802.
Report of the Commissioners of Inland Revenue on the Duties under Their Management, for the Years 1856 to 1869 Inclusive; with Some Retrospective History, and Complete Tables of Accounts of the Duties from Their First Imposition, ii [C. 82–1], HC 1870, xx.
Seventeenth Report of the Commissioners of Inquiry into the Collection and Management of the Revenue Arising in Ireland, Scotland etc., HC 1828 (8), xv.
Third Report of the Commissioners of Inquiry into the Collection and Management of the Revenue Arising in Ireland, HC 1822 (606), xiii.

Calendars of state papers

Calendars of State Papers, Domestic
Calendars of State Papers, Ireland

SECONDARY WORKS

Ahern, Fiona. 'Jane Williams: An Outstanding Cork Silversmith and Her Work'. *Journal of the Cork Archaeological Society* 117 (2012): 31–36.

Alcorn, Ellenor. *English Silver in the Museum of Fine Arts, Boston*, i, *Silver from 1697 Including Irish and Scottish Silver*. Boston: Museum of Fine Arts, 2000.

Altick, Richard. *The Shows of London*. Cambridge, MA: Harvard University Press, 1978.

Appadurai, Arjun. *The Social Life of Things: Commodities in Cultural Perspective*. Cambridge: Cambridge University Press, 1986.

Baker, Malcolm. 'Roubiliac and Cheere in the 1730s and 1740s: Collaboration and Subcontracting in Eighteenth-Century English Sculptors' Workshops'. *Church Monuments* 10 (1995): 90–107.

Ball, Francis Elrington. *A History of the County of Dublin*. 6 vols. Dublin: Alexander Thom, 1902–20.

Barker, Robert. 'Proposals for an Assaying System in Pennsylvania, 1753–1770'. *Silver Society Journal* 2 (1991): 75–79.

Barnard, Toby. *A New Anatomy of Ireland: The Irish Protestants, 1649–1770*. New Haven and London: Yale University Press, 2003.

———. *Making the Grand Figure: Lives and Possessions in Ireland, 1641–1770*. New Haven and London: Yale University Press, 2004.

———. *A Guide to Sources for the History of Material Culture in Ireland, 1500–2000*. Dublin: Four Courts, 2005.

———. 'The Artistic and Cultural Activities of the Caldwells of Castle Caldwell, 1750–1783'. *Irish Architectural and Decorative Studies* 10 (2007): 90–112.

Barquist, David. *Myer Myers: Jewish Silversmith in Colonial New York*. New Haven and London: Yale University Press, 2001.

Barr, Elaine. *George Wickes, Royal Goldsmith 1698–1761*. London: Christie's, 1980.

Barrow, G. L. 'Some Dublin Private Banks'. *Dublin Historical Record* 25, no. 2 (1972): 38–53.

Benedetti, Sergio. *The La Touche Amorino: Canova and His Fashionable Irish Patrons*. Dublin: National Gallery of Ireland, 1998.

Bennett, Douglas. *Irish Georgian Silver*. London: Cassell, 1972.

———. 'James Le Bas 1772–1745'. *Antique Collector*, August 1974, 36–41.

———. *Collecting Irish Silver*. London: Souvenir Press, 1984.

———. *The Company of Goldsmiths of Dublin, 1637–1987*. Dublin: National Museum of Ireland, 1987.

———. *The Silver Collection, Trinity College Dublin*. Dublin: Trinity College Dublin Press, 1988.

Benson, John, and Laura Ugolini, eds. *Cultures of Selling: Perspectives on Consumption and Society since 1700*. Aldershot: Ashgate, 2006.

Berg, Maxine. *The Age of Manufactures, 1700–1820*. London: Routledge, 2004.

———, and Kristine Bruland. *Technological Revolutions in Europe: Historical Perspectives*. Cheltenham: Edward Elgar, 1998.

———, and Helen Clifford, eds. *Consumers and Luxury: Consumer Culture in Europe, 1650–1850*. Manchester: Manchester University Press, 1999.

———, and Elizabeth Eger, eds. *Luxury in the Eighteenth Century. Debates, Desires and Delectable Goods*. Houndmills: Palgrave Macmillan, 2003.

Bermingham, Ann, and John Brewer, eds. *The Consumption of Culture, 1600–1800: Image, Object, Text*. London: Routledge, 1995.

Berry, Christopher. *The Idea of Luxury: A Conceptual and Historical Investigation*. Cambridge: Cambridge University Press, 1994.

Berry, Helen. 'Polite Consumption: Shopping in Eighteenth-Century England'. *Transactions of the Royal Historical Society* 12 (2002): 375–94.

Berry, Henry F. 'The Records of the Dublin Gild of Merchants, Known as the Gild of Holy Trinity, 1438–1671'. *Journal of the Royal Society of Antiquaries of Ireland* 30 (1900): 44–68.

———. 'The Goldsmiths' Company of Dublin'. *Journal of the Royal Society of Antiquaries of Ireland* 31 (1901): 119–33.

———. 'The Ancient Company of Barber Surgeons, or Gild of St. Mary Magdalene, Dublin'. *Journal of the Royal Society of Antiquaries of Ireland* 33 (1903): 217–38.

———. 'The Records of the Feltmakers' Company of Dublin, 1787–1841: Their Loss and Recovery'. *Journal of the Royal Society of Antiquaries of Ireland* 41 (1911): 26–45.

———. *A History of the Royal Dublin Society*. London: Longmans, Green, 1915.

———. 'The Merchant Tailors' Gild, That of St. John the Baptist, Dublin, 1418–1841'. *Journal of the Royal Society of Antiquaries of Ireland* 48 (1918): 19–64.

Black, Antony. *Guilds and Civil Society in European Political Thought from the Twelfth Century to the Present*. London: Methuen, 1984.

Blondé, Bruno, Natasha Coquery, Jon Stobart, and Ilja van Damme. *Fashioning Old and New: Changing Consumer Preferences in Europe, Seventeenth to Nineteenth Centuries*. xviii of *Studies in European Urban History, 1100–1800*. Turnhout, Belgium: Brepols, 2009.

———, Peter Stabel, Jon Stobart, and Ilja van Damme. *Buyers and Sellers: Retail Circuits and Practices in Medieval and Early Modern Europe*. ix of *Studies in European Urban History, 1100–1800*. Turnhout, Belgium: Brepols, 2006.

Borsay, Peter. *The English Urban Renaissance: Culture and Society in the English Provincial Town, 1660–1770*. Oxford: Oxford University Press, 1989.

———. 'The London Connection: Cultural Diffusion and the Eighteenth-Century Provincial Town'. *London Journal* 19 (1994): 21–35.

Bourdieu, Pierre. *Distinction: A Social Critique of the Judgement of Taste*, translated by Richard Nice. Cambridge, MA: Harvard University Press, 1984.

Bowen, John, and Conor O'Brien. *Cork Silver and Gold: Four Centuries of Craftsmanship*. Cork: Crawford Gallery, 2005.

———, eds. *A Celebration of Limerick's Silver*. Cork: Collins Press in Association with the Hunt Museum, 2007.

Boydell, Mary. 'The Origin of the Glass Piggin'. *Irish Arts Review* 3, no. 3 (1986): 22.

Brady, Joseph, and Anngret Simms, eds. *Dublin through Space and Time*. Dublin: Four Courts, 2001.

Braham, Helen. *A Century of Silver: The Courtauld Family of Silversmiths, 1710–1780*. London: Paul Holberton, 2003.

Braudel, Fernand. *The Wheels of Commerce*. ii of *Civilization and Capitalism, Fifteenth to Eighteenth Century*. Berkeley: University of California Press, 1992.

Breen, Timothy H. 'An Empire of Goods: The Anglicization of Colonial America, 1690–1776'. *Journal of British Studies* 25 (1986): 467–99.

———. 'Baubles of Britain: The American and Consumer Revolution of the Eighteenth Century'. *Past and Present* 119 (1988): 73–104.

Brett, Vanessa. 'The Compleat Appraiser: An Eighteenth-Century Manual and the Valuing of Plate'. *Silver Society Journal* 15 (2003): 2–4.

———. *Bertrand's Toyshop in Bath: Luxury Retailing 1685–1765*. Wetherby: Oblong, 2014.

Brewer, John. *Pleasures of the Imagination: English Culture in the Eighteenth Century*. London: HarperCollins, 1997.

———, and Roy Porter, eds. *Consumption and the World of Goods*. London: Routledge, 1993.

———, and John Styles, eds. *An Ungovernable People: The English and Their Law in the Seventeenth and Eighteenth Centuries*. London: Hutchinson, 1983.

Brockliss, Laurence, and David Eastwood, eds. *A Union of Multiple Identities: The British Isles, c.1750–c.1850*. Manchester: Manchester University Press, 1997.

Brown, Peter. *In Praise of Hot Liquors*. York: York Civic Trust, 1995.

———, and Marla Schwarz. *Come Drink the Bowl Dry: Alcoholic Liquors and Their Place in Eighteenth-Century Society*. York: York Civic Trust, 1996.

Buckley, John Joseph. 'Irish Altar Plate'. *Museum Bulletin* 11 (1912): 23–26.
———. *Some Irish Altar Plate: A Descriptive List of Chalices and Patens Dating from the Fourteenth to the End of the Seventeenth Century*. Dublin: Royal Society of Antiquaries of Ireland, 1943.
Burke, Bernard. *A Genealogical and Heraldic History of the Landed Gentry of Ireland*. Rev. ed. London: Harrison and Sons, 1912.
Bury, Shirley. 'The Lengthening Shadow of Rundell's, Part I: Rundell's and Their Silversmiths'. *Connoisseur* 161 (1966): 78–85.
Butel, Paul, and L.M. Cullen, eds. *Cities and Merchants: French and Irish Perspectives on Urban Development, 1500–1900*. Dublin: Trinity College Press, 1986.
Butler, Harriet, and Harold Edgeworth Butler. *The Black Book of Edgeworthstown and Other Edgeworth Memories*. London: Faber and Gwyer, 1927.
Butler, Jon. *Becoming America: The Revolution before 1776*. Cambridge, MA: Harvard University Press, 2000.
Caffrey, Paul. *Treasures to Hold: Irish and English Miniatures, 1650–1850, from the National Gallery of Ireland Collections*. Dublin: National Gallery of Ireland, 2000.
Caldicott, C.E.J., Hugh Gough, and Jean-Paul Pittion, eds. *The Huguenots and Ireland: Anatomy of an Emigration*. Dublin: Glendale, 1987.
Cameron, Peter. 'Henry Jernegan, Charles Frederick Kandler and the Client who Changed His Mind'. *Silver Society Journal* 8 (1996): 487–502.
Campbell, Colin. 'Consumption and the Rhetorics of Need and Want'. *Journal of Design History* 11 (1998): 235–46.
Carpenter, Andrew, ed. *Verse in English from Eighteenth-Century Ireland*. Cork: Cork University Press, 1998.
Carrier, James. *Gifts and Commodities: Exchange and Western Capitalism since 1700*. London: Routledge, 1995.
Carson, Cary, Ronald Hoffman, and Peter J. Albert, eds. *Of Consuming Interests: The Style of Life in the Eighteenth Century*. Charlottesville: University of Virginia Press, 1994.
Casey, Christine. 'Gaetano Brunetti'. *Irish Arts Review Yearbook* January (1988): 244–45.
———, ed. *The Eighteenth-Century Dublin Town House: Form, Function, and Finance*. Dublin: Four Courts, 2010.
———, and Conor Lucey, eds. *Decorative Plasterwork in Ireland and Europe: Ornament and the Early Modern Interior*. Dublin: Four Courts, 2012.
Chaffers, Wilfred J. *Hallmarks on Gold and Silver Plate*. London: J. Davy & Sons, 1863.
Clark, George. *Guide to English Commercial Statistics, 1696–1782*. London: Royal Historical Society, 1938.
Clark, Mary, and Raymond Refaussé. *Directory of Historic Dublin Guilds*. Dublin: Dublin Public Libraries, 1993.
Clark, Peter, and Raymond Gillespie, eds. *Two Capitals, London and Dublin, 1500–1840*. Oxford: Oxford University Press, 2001.
Clarke, Desmond. *The Ingenious Mr. Edgeworth*. London: Oldbourne, 1965.
Clarkson, Leslie, and Margaret Crawford. *Feast and Famine: Food and Nutrition in Ireland, 1500–1920*. Oxford: Oxford University Press, 2001.
Clayton, Michael. *The Collector's Dictionary of the Silver and Gold of Great Britain and North America*. New York: World, 1985.
Clifford, Helen. 'Goldsmiths of Invention: Hidden Connections and Alternative Occupations'. *Silver Society Journal* 9 (1997): 574.
———. 'Paul de Lamerie, 1688–1751'. In *The Jaime Ortiz-Patiño Collection of Silver by Paul de Lamerie*, 10–15. New York: Sotheby's, 1998.
———. 'Concepts of Invention, Identity and Imitation in the London and Provincial Metal-Working Trades, 1750–1800'. *Journal of Design History* 12 (1999): 241–55.
———. 'Of Consuming Cares: Attitudes to Silver in the Eighteenth Century'. *Silver Society Journal* 12 (2000): 53–59.

———. *Silver in London: The Parker and Wakelin Partnership, 1760–1776*. New Haven and London: Yale University Press, 2004.

———. *A Treasured Inheritance: 600 Years of Oxford College Silver*. Oxford: Ashmolean Museum, 2004.

Cokayne, George. *The Complete Peerage of England, Scotland, Ireland, Great Britain and the United Kingdom*. 13 vols. London: St Catherine, 1910–59.

Connolly, S. J. *Kingdoms United? Great Britain and Ireland since 1500: Integration and Diversity*. Dublin: Four Courts, 1999.

———. *Religion, Law and Power: The Making of Protestant Ireland, 1660–1760*. Oxford: Oxford University Press, 2000.

Cox, Nancy. *The Complete Tradesman: A Study of Retailing, 1550–1820*. Aldershot: Ashgate, 2000.

———, and Karin Dannehl. *Perceptions of Retailing in Early Modern England*. Aldershot: Ashgate, 2007.

Cox Prime, Alfred, ed. *The Arts and Crafts in Philadelphia, Maryland and South Carolina, 1721–1785*. Philadelphia: Walpole Society, 1929.

Craig, Maurice. *Dublin, 1660–1860*. Dublin: Allen Figgis, 1969.

Craske, Matthew. 'Plan and Control: Design and the Competitive Spirit in Early and Mid-Eighteenth-Century England'. *Journal of Design History* 12 (1999): 187–216.

Cripps, Wilfrid. *Old English Plate*. London: John Murray, 1878.

Crosskey, Gordon. 'The Early Development of the Plated Trade'. *Silver Society Journal* 12 (2000): 27–38.

Cullen, Louis. *Anglo-Irish Trade, 1660–1800*. Manchester: Manchester University Press, 1968.

———. *An Economic History of Ireland since 1660*. London: Batsford, 1987.

Culme, John. 'Beauty and the Beast: The Growth of Mechanisation in the Trade'. *Proceedings of the Silver Society* 9/10 (1980): 158–65.

———. *Attitudes to Old Plate 1750–1900*. London: Sotheby's, 1985.

———. *The Directory of Gold and Silversmiths, Jewellers and Allied Traders, 1838–1914*. i. London: Antique Collector's Club, 1987.

———. 'The Embarrassed Goldsmith, 1729–1831: Eighteenth-Century Failures'. *Silver Society Journal* 10 (1998): 66–76.

Cunningham, Jessica. 'Dublin's Huguenot Goldsmiths, 1690–1750: Assimilation and Divergence'. *Irish Architectural and Decorative Studies* 12 (2009): 159–85.

Curran, C. P. *Dublin Decorative Plasterwork of the Seventeenth and Eighteenth Centuries*. London: Alec Tiranti, 1967.

Day, Ivan. *Eat, Drink and Be Merry: The British at Table, 1600–2000*. London: Philip Wilson, 2000.

Day, Robert. 'Notice of the Silver Mace of the Corporation of Castlemartyr'. *Journal of the Royal Historical and Archaeological Association of Ireland* 8 (1888): 483.

———. 'Notes on Some Early Examples of Cork Silver'. *Journal of the Royal Historical and Archaeological Association of Ireland* 9 (1889): 127–30.

———. 'Notes and Queries'. *Journal of the Cork Historical and Archeological Society* 12 (1906): 149.

De Castro, John Paul. *The Law and Practice of Hall-Marking Gold and Silver Wares*. London: C. Lockwood & Son, 1926.

Delamer, Ida, and Conor O'Brien. 'Dublin Hallmarks: A Reappraisal'. *Silver Society Journal* 11 (1999): 158–67.

———. *500 Years of Irish Silver*. Bray, Co. Wicklow: Wordwell/National Museum of Ireland, 2005.

De Marchi, Neil, and Craufurd Goodwin, eds. *Economic Engagements with Arts*. Durham, NC: Duke University Press, 1999.

De Munck, Bert. 'Skills, Trust and Changing Consumer Preferences: The Decline of Antwerp's Craft Guilds from the Perspective of the Product Market, c.1500 to c.1800'. *International Review of Social History* 53, no. 2 (2008): 197–233.

———. 'From Brotherhood Community to Civil Society? Apprentices between Guild, Household and the Freedom of Contract in Early Modern Antwerp'. *Social History* 35 (2010): 1–20.

———. 'Guilds, Product Quality and Intrinsic Value: Towards a History of Conventions?' *Historical Social Research/Historische Sozialforschung* 36, no. 4 (2011): 103–24.

———. 'The Agency of Branding and the Location of Value: Hallmarks and Monograms in Early Modern Tableware Industries'. *Business History* 54, no. 7 (2012): 1055–76.

———. 'Artisans, Products and Gifts: Rethinking the History of Material Culture in Early Modern Europe'. *Past and Present* 224 (August 2014): 39–74.

———, Steven L. Kaplan, and Hugo Soly, eds. *Learning on the Shop Floor: Historical Perspectives on Apprenticeship*. New York: Berghahn, 2007.

Dependahl Waters, Deborah, Kristan McKinsey, and Gerard Ward, eds. *Elegant Plate: Three Centuries of Precious Metals in New York City*. New York: Museum of the City of New York, 2000.

Devine, T.M., and David Dickson, eds. *Ireland and Scotland, 1600–1850*. Edinburgh: John Donald, 1983.

Dickson, David, ed. *The Gorgeous Mask: Dublin, 1700–1800*. Dublin: Trinity College Dublin Press, 1987.

———. *Old World Colony: Cork and South Munster, 1630–1830*. Cork: Cork University Press, 2005.

———. *Dublin: The Making of a Capital City*. London: Profile, 2014.

Dooley, Terence, Patrick Cosgrove, and Karol Mullaney-Dignam, eds. *Aspects of Irish Aristocratic Life: Essays on the FitzGeralds and Carton House*. Dublin: University College Dublin Press, 2014.

Douglas, Mary, and Baron Isherwood. *The World of Goods: Towards an Anthropology of Consumption*. London: Routledge, 1996.

Dunlevy, Mairead. 'James Donovan, Emperor of China'. *Irish Arts Review* 2, no. 3 (1985): 28–36.

———. *Jewellery, Seventeenth to Twentieth Centuries*. Dublin: National Museum of Ireland, 2001.

———. *Pomp and Poverty: A History of Silk in Ireland*. New Haven and London: Yale University Press, 2011.

Earle, Peter. *The Making of the English Middle Class*. Berkeley: University of California Press, 1989.

Eatwell, Ann. 'Capital Lying Dead: Attitudes to Silver in the Nineteenth Century'. *Silver Society Journal* 12 (2000): 59–64.

Edgecumbe, Richard. *The Art of the Chaser*. Oxford: Oxford University Press, 2001.

Epstein, Stephen. 'Craft Guilds, Apprenticeship and Technological Change in Preindustrial Europe'. *Journal of Economic History* 58 (1998): 684–713.

———. 'Craft Guilds in the Pre-Modern Economy: A Discussion'. *Economic History Review* 61 (2008): 155–74.

———, and Maarten Prak, eds. *Guilds, Innovation and the European Economy, 1400–1800*. Cambridge: Cambridge University Press, 2008.

Eustace, Beryl, and Olive Goodbody. *Quaker Records, Dublin: Abstracts of Wills*. Dublin: Stationery Office, 1957.

Evans, Joan. 'Huguenot Goldsmiths in England and Ireland'. *Proceedings of the Huguenot Society* 14, no. 4 (1933): 496–554.

Fagan, Patrick. *The Second City: Portrait of Dublin, 1700–1760*. Dublin: Branar, 1986.

———. 'The Population of Dublin in the Eighteenth Century with Particular Reference to the Proportions of Protestants and Catholics'. *Eighteenth-Century Ireland* 6 (1991): 121–56.

———. *Catholics in a Protestant Country: The Papist Constituency in Eighteenth-Century Dublin*. Dublin: Four Courts, 1998.

Fallon, John. *Marks of London Goldsmiths and Silversmiths, c.1697–1837*. London: David & Charles, 1988.

———. *Marks of London Goldsmiths and Silversmiths, 1837–1914*. London: Barrie & Jenkins, 1992.

———. *House of Barnard: A Notable Family of Manufacturing Silversmiths to the Trade*. Sandy: Bright Pen Books, 2012.

Ffolliott, Rosemary. 'Captain Balfour's Auction, 15th March 1741/42'. *Irish Ancestor* 16 (1984): 21–31.

Figgis, Nicola, and Brendan Rooney. *Irish Paintings in the National Gallery of Ireland*. Dublin: National Gallery of Ireland, 2001.

Finn, Margot. 'Men's Things: Masculine Possession in the Consumer Revolution'. *Social History* 25 (2000): 133–55.

FitzGerald, Alison. 'Cosmopolitan Commerce: The Dublin Goldsmith Robert Calderwood'. *Apollo* (September 2005): 46–52.

———. '"Astonishing Automata": Staging Spectacle in Eighteenth-Century Dublin'. *Irish Architectural and Decorative Studies* 10 (2007): 18–34.

———. 'Oliver St George's Passion for Plate'. *Silver Studies* 22 (2007): 51–61.

———. 'The Business of Being a Goldsmith in Eighteenth-Century Dublin'. In *Georgian Dublin*, edited by Gillian O'Brien and Finola O'Kane, 127–35. Dublin: Four Courts, 2008.

———, and Conor O'Brien. 'The Production of Silver in Late Georgian Dublin'. *Irish Architectural and Decorative Studies* 4 (2001): 8–48.

FitzGerald, Desmond. 'Nathaniel Clements and Some Eighteenth-Century Irish Houses'. *Apollo* (October 1966): 314–21.

———. 'Early Irish Trade-Cards and Other Eighteenth-Century Ephemera'. *Eighteenth-Century Ireland* 2 (1987): 115–32.

———, and Anne Crookshank. *Ireland's Painters, 1600–1940*. New Haven and London: Yale University Press, 2002.

———, and James Peill. *Irish Furniture: Woodwork and Carving in Ireland from the Earliest Times to the Act of Union*. New Haven and London: Yale University Press, 2007.

Flavin, Susan. *Consumption and Culture in Sixteenth-Century Ireland: Saffron, Stockings and Silk*. Woodbridge: Boydell & Brewer, 2014.

Fleming, John, and Hugh Honour. *Penguin Dictionary of Decorative Arts*. London: Viking, 1989.

Forbes, J.S. *Hallmark: A History of the London Assay Office*. London: Goldsmith's Co. and Unicorn Press, 1999.

Foster, Roy, and Raymond Gillespie, eds. *Provincial Ireland*. Dublin: Four Courts, 2012.

Foster, Sarah, 'Going Shopping in 18th-Century Dublin'. *Things* 4 (Summer, 1996): 33–61.

———. 'Buying Irish: Consumer Nationalism in Eighteenth-Century Dublin'. *History Today* 47 (1997): 44–52.

———. '"Ornament and Splendour": Shops and Shopping in Georgian Dublin'. *Irish Architectural and Decorative Studies* 15 (2013): 12–33.

Fox, Robert, and Anthony Turner, eds. *Luxury Trades and Consumerism in Ancien Régime Paris*. Aldershot: Ashgate, 1998.

Francis, Peter. *Irish Delftware: An Illustrated History*. London: Jonathan Horne, 2000.

Gadd, Ian Anders, and Patrick Wallis, eds. *Guilds, Society and Economy in London, 1450–1800*. London: Centre for Metropolitan History, 2002.

Gandy Fales, Martha. *Joseph Richardson and Family, Philadelphia Silversmiths*. Middletown, CT: Wesleyan University Press, 1974.

Garstin, John Ribton. 'The Sword and Mace of Kilkenny'. *Journal of the Royal Society of Antiquaries of Ireland* 13 (1903): 209–10.

Gill, Margaret. *A Directory of Newcastle Goldsmiths*. Newcastle upon Tyne: Worshipful Company of Goldsmiths, 1980.

Glanville, Philippa. *Silver in England*. London: Unwin Hyman, 1987.

———. 'The Silver of John, Fourth Duke of Bedford'. *Apollo* 127 (June 1988): 413–17.

———, ed. *Silver*. London: Victoria and Albert Museum, 1996.

———, and Jennifer Faulds Goldsborough. *Women Silversmiths, 1685–1845: Works from the Collection of the National Museum of Women in the Arts*. London: Thames & Hudson, 1990.

———, and Hilary Young, eds. *Elegant Eating*. London: Victoria and Albert Museum, 2002.

Goodbody, Rob. *Dublin, Part 3, 1756–1847*, vol. 26 of *Irish Historic Towns Atlas*. Dublin: Royal Irish Academy, 2014.

Goodway, Eileen. 'The Rapilliart Family: David Willaume, His Son and Their Apprentices'. *Silver Society Journal* 10 (1998): 56–60.

Greaves, Richard L. *Dublin's Merchant-Quaker: Anthony Sharp and the Community of Friends, 1643–1707*. Stanford, CA: Stanford University Press, 1998.

Grimwade, Arthur. *Rococo Silver, 1727–1765*. London: Faber & Faber, 1974.

———. *London Goldsmiths, 1697–1837: Their Marks and Lives from the Original Registers at Goldsmith's Hall and Other Sources*. 3rd ed. London: Faber & Faber, 1990.

Guinness, Henry Seymour. 'Dublin Trade Gilds'. *Journal of the Royal Society of Antiquaries of Ireland* 52 (1922): 143–63.

Hare, Susan. *Touching Gold and Silver: 500 Years of Hallmarks*. London: Worshipful Company of Goldsmiths, 1978.

———, ed. *Paul de Lamerie: At the Sign of the Golden Ball*. London: Worshipful Company of Goldsmiths, 1990.

Hartop, Christopher. *The Huguenot Legacy: English Silver, 1680–1760, from the Alan and Simone Hartman Collection*. London: Thomas Heneage, 1996.

Hayward, J. F. *Huguenot Silver in England, 1688–1727*. London: Faber & Faber, 1959.

———. 'The Earl of Warrington's Plate'. *Apollo* (July 1978): 32–39.

Heal, Ambrose. *London Tradesmen's Cards of the Eighteenth Century*. London: Batsford, 1925.

———. *The London Goldsmiths, 1200–1800*. Cambridge: Cambridge University Press, 1935.

———. *Sign Boards of Old London Shops*. London: Batsford, 1957.

Henry, Brian. *Dublin Hanged: Crime, Law Enforcement and Punishment in Late Eighteenth-Century Dublin*. Dublin: Irish Academic Press, 1994.

Hill, Jacqueline. *From Patriots to Unionists: Dublin Civic Politics and Irish Protestant Patriotism, 1660–1840*. Oxford: Oxford University Press, 1997.

———, and Colm Lennon. *Luxury and Austerity*. Dublin: University College Dublin Press, 1999.

Howard, David. 'Chinese Armorial Porcelain for Ireland'. *Bulletin of the Irish Georgian Society* 29, nos. 3–4 (July–December 1986): 3–24.

Hughes, G. B. 'The Ancient Craft of the Wire-Drawer'. *Country Life* 19 (April 1956): 817–18.

Hylton, R. P. 'Dublin's Huguenot Communities: Trials, Development, and Triumph, 1662–1701'. *Proceedings of the Huguenot Society* 24 (1985): 221–31.

Ingamells, John. *A Dictionary of British and Irish Travellers in Italy, 1701–1800*. New Haven and London: Yale University Press, 1997.

Jackson, Charles J. *English Goldsmiths and Their Marks*. 2nd ed. London: Macmillan, 1921.

Johnston, Joseph. 'Irish Currency in the Eighteenth Century'. *Hermathena* 52 (1938): 3–26.

Johnston-Liik, Edith M. *History of the Irish Parliament, 1692–1800*. 6 vols. Belfast: Ulster Historical Foundation, 2002.

Jowett, Judy. 'The Warning Carriers'. *Silver Studies: The Journal of the Silver Society* 18 (Special Issue 2005).

Kahl, William. 'Apprenticeship and the Freedom of the London Livery Companies, 1690–1750'. *Guildhall Miscellany* 7 (1956): 17–20.

———. *The Development of London Livery Companies*. Cambridge, MA: Harvard University Press, 1960.

Kane, Patricia, ed. *Colonial Massachusetts Silversmiths and Jewellers: A Biographical Dictionary*. New Haven: Yale University Art Gallery, 1998.
Kellett, J. R. 'The Breakdown of Guild and Corporation Control over the Handicraft and Retail Trades of London'. *Economic History Review* 10 (1958): 381–94.
Kelly, James. *Sport in Ireland 1600–1840*. Dublin: Four Courts Press, 2014.
———, and Martyn Powell, eds. *Clubs and Societies in Eighteenth-Century Ireland*. Dublin: Four Courts, 2010.
Kendell, Joan. 'The Development of a Distinctive Form of Quaker Dress'. *Costume* 9 (1985): 58–74.
Kennedy, Máire. 'Book Mad: The Sale of Books by Auction in Eighteenth-Century Dublin'. *Dublin Historical Record* 54 (2001): 48–71.
———. *French Books in Eighteenth-Century Ireland*. Oxford: Voltaire Foundation, 2001.
Kinmonth, Claudia. *Irish Country Furniture, 1700–1950*. New Haven and London: Yale University Press, 1993.
Kirkham, Pat. *The London Furniture Trade, 1700–1870*. London: Furniture History Society, 1988.
———. *The Gendered Object*. Manchester: Manchester University Press, 1996.
Kowaleski-Wallace, Elizabeth. 'Women, China and Consumer Culture in Eighteenth-Century England'. *Eighteenth-Century Studies* 29 (1995–96): 153–67.
———. *Consuming Subjects: Women, Shopping and Business in the Eighteenth Century*. New York: Columbia University Press, 1997.
Kwint, Marius, Christopher Breward, and Jeremy Aynsley, eds. *Material Memories: Design and Evocation*. Oxford: Berg, 1999.
Laffan, William, and Christopher Monkhouse, *Ireland, Crossroads of Art and Design 1690–1840*. Chicago: Art Institute of Chicago, 2015.
Laing, Alistair, ed. *Clerics and Connoisseurs*. London: English Heritage, 2001.
Lambert, Julie Anne. *A Nation of Shopkeepers: Trade Ephemera from 1654 to the 1860s in the John Johnson Collection*. Oxford: Bodleian Library, 2001.
Lane, Joan. *Apprenticeship in England, 1600–1914*. London: University College London Press, 1996.
La Niece, Susan, and Paul Craddock. *Metal Plating and Patination: Cultural, Technical and Historical Developments*. Oxford: Butterworth-Heinemann, 1993.
Law, Edward. 'Some Provincial Irish Silver Lotteries'. *Silver Society Journal* 7 (1995): 412–16.
Lawton, Richard, and Robert Lee, eds. *Urban Population Development in Western Europe from the Late-Eighteenth to the Early-Twentieth Century*. Liverpool: Liverpool University Press, 1989.
Lecky, W.E.H. *History of Ireland in the Eighteenth Century*. 5 vols. London: Longmans Green, 1892.
Lee, Grace Lawless. *The Huguenot Settlements in Ireland*. London: Longmans, Green, 1936.
Lemire, Beverly. 'Consumerism in Pre-Industrial and Early Industrial England: The Trade in Second-Hand Clothes'. *Journal of British Studies* 27 (1988): 1–24.
Lennon, Colm. *Dublin, Part 2, 1610–1756*. No. 19 of *Irish Historic Towns Atlas*. Dublin: Royal Irish Academy, 2008.
———, and John Montague. *John Rocque's Dublin: A Guide to the Georgian City*. Dublin: Royal Irish Academy, 2010.
Leunig, Tim, Chris Minns, and Patrick Wallis. 'Networks in the Pre-Modern Economy: The Market for London Apprenticeships, 1600–1749'. *Journal of Economic History* 71 (2011): 413–43.
Lindsay, Jack. *Worldly Goods: The Arts of Early Pennsylvania, 1680–1758*. Philadelphia: Philadelphia Museum of Art, 2000.
Llewelyn, Nigel. *The Art of Death*. London: Reaktion, 1991.
Lomax, James. 'Royalty and Silver: The Role of the Jewel House in the Eighteenth Century'. *Silver Society Journal* 11 (1999): 133–40.

Mahaffy, J.P. *The Plate in Trinity College Dublin: A History and a Catalogue*. London: Macmillan, 1918.

Malcomson, Anthony. *Archbishop Charles Agar: Churchmanship and Politics in Ireland, 1760–1810*. Dublin: Four Courts, 2002.

———. *Nathaniel Clements: Politics, Fashion and Architecture in Mid-Eighteenth-Century Ireland*. Dublin: Four Courts, 2014.

Maxwell, Constantia. *Dublin under the Georges, 1714–1830*. Dublin: Gill & Macmillan, 1946.

Mayhew, Nicholas. *Sterling: The Rise and Fall of a Currency*. London: Allen Lane, 1999.

McCabe, Patricia. 'Trappings of Sovereignty: The Accoutrements of the Lord Chancellor of Ireland'. *Irish Architectural and Decorative Studies* 5 (2002): 48–73.

McCormack, John. 'The Sumptuous Silver of Thomas Bolton, 1658–1736'. *Irish Arts Review* 11 (1995): 112–16.

McCracken, Grant. *Culture and Consumption: New Approaches to the Symbolic Character of Consumer Goods and Activities*. Bloomington: Indiana University Press, 1990.

McCullough, Niall. *A Vision of the City: Dublin and the Wide Streets Commissioners*. Dublin: Dublin Corporation, 1991.

McCusker, John J. *Money and Exchange in Europe and America, 1660–1775*. Chapel Hill: University of North Carolina Press, 1978.

McDonnell, Joseph. *Irish Eighteenth-Century Stuccowork and Its European Sources*. Dublin: National Gallery of Ireland, 1991.

———. 'The Influence of the French Rococo Print in Eighteenth-Century Ireland'. *Bulletin of the Irish Georgian Society* 36 (1994): 63–75.

———, ed. *Maynooth Bicentenary Art Exhibitions: Ecclesiastical Art of the Penal Era*. Maynooth: Saint Patrick's College, 1995.

———. 'Irish Rococo Silver'. *Irish Arts Review Yearbook* 13 (1997): 78–87.

McEvansoneya, Philip. 'A Colourful Spectacle Restored: The State Coach of the Lord Mayor of Dublin'. *Irish Arts Review Yearbook* 17 (2001): 80–88.

MacGregor, Arthur, ed. *The Cobbe Cabinet of Curiosities*. New Haven and London: Yale University Press, 2015.

McKendrick, Neil, John Brewer, and J.H. Plumb, eds. *The Birth of a Commercial Society: The Commercialisation of Eighteenth-Century England*. London: Europa, 1982.

McKillop, A.D. 'Samuel Richardson's Advice to an Apprentice'. *Journal of English and Germanic Philology* 42 (1943): 40–54.

McParland, Edward. 'The Wide Streets Commissioners: Their Importance for Dublin Architecture in the Late 18th–Early 19th Century'. *Bulletin of the Irish Georgian Society* 15, no. 1 (1972): 1–31.

Mitchell, David. 'Dressing Plate by the "Unknown" London Silversmith "WF"'. *Burlington Magazine* (June 1993): 386–400.

———, ed. *Goldsmiths, Silversmiths and Bankers: Innovation and the Transfer of Skill, 1550–1750*. London: Sutton, 1995.

Moffat, Valerie. '"A Map of Her Jurisdiction": The Account Books of Meliora Adlercron, of Dawson Street, Dublin, 1782–94'. *Irish Architectural and Decorative Studies* 15 (2012): 128–49.

Monkhouse, Christopher. 'A Chinoiserie Dish Ring by Charles Townsend'. *Irish Architectural and Decorative Studies* 17 (2014): 70–79.

Montague, John. 'A Shopping Arcade in Eighteenth-Century Dublin: John Rocque and the Essex Street "Piazzas"'. *Irish Architectural and Decorative Studies* 10 (2008): 225–45.

Moody, T.W., F.X. Martin, and F.J. Byrne, eds. *A New History of Ireland, ix. Maps, Genealogies, Lists. A Companion to Irish History, pt. ii*. Oxford: Oxford University Press, 1984.

Moran, Anna. 'Selling Waterford Glass in Early Nineteenth-Century Ireland'. *Irish Architectural and Decorative Studies* 6 (2003): 56–89.

———. 'Merchants and Material Culture in Early Nineteenth-Century Dublin: A Consumer Case Study'. *Irish Architectural and Decorative Studies* 11 (2008): 140–65.

———, and Sorcha O'Brien, eds. *Love Objects*. London: Bloomsbury, 2014.
Mui, Hoh-Cheung, and Lorna Mui. *Shops and Shopkeeping in Eighteenth-Century England*. Montreal: McGill-Queen's University Press, 1989.
Murdoch, Tessa, ed. *The Quiet Conquest: The Huguenots, 1685–1985*. London: Museum of London, 1985.
———, ed. *Beyond the Border: Huguenot Goldsmiths in Northern Europe and North America*. Brighton: Sussex Academic Press, 2008.
Murphy, Antoin, ed. *Economists and the Irish Economy, from the Eighteenth Century to the Present Day*. Dublin: Irish Academic Press, 1984.
Nenadic, Stana. 'Middle-Rank Consumers and Domestic Culture in Edinburgh and Glasgow, 1720–1840'. *Past and Present* 145 (1994): 122–56.
North, Michael, and David Omrod, eds. *Art Markets in Europe, 1400–1800*. Aldershot: Ashgate, 1999.
Norton, Lucy, ed. *Saint-Simon at Versailles*. London: Book Club Associates, 1980.
O'Brien, Conor. 'The Evolution of Silver Dish Rings'. *Collectors' Guide* (January 1977): 71–75.
O'Brien, Gerard, ed. *Catholic Ireland in the Eighteenth Century: Collected Essays of Maureen Wall*. Dublin: Geography Publications, 1989.
O'Brien, Gillian, and Finola O'Kane, eds. *Georgian Dublin*. Dublin: Four Courts, 2008.
O'Flanaghan, Patrick, Cornelius G. Buttimer, and Gerard O'Brien. *Cork: History and Society*. Dublin: Geography Publications, 1993.
Ó Floinn, Raghnall, ed. *Franciscan Faith: Sacred Art in Ireland, 1600–1750*. Dublin: Wordwell, 2011.
Ogilvie, Sheilagh. 'Guilds, Efficiency and Social Capital: Evidence from German Proto-Industry'. *Economic History Review* 57 (2004): 286–333.
———. 'Rehabilitating the Guilds: A Reply'. *Economic History Review* 61 (2008): 175–82.
O'Regan, Philip. *Archbishop William King of Dublin (1650–1729) and the Constitution in Church and State*. Dublin: Four Courts, 2000.
Pears, Iain. *The Discovery of Painting: The Growth of Interest in the Arts in England, 1680–1768*. New Haven and London: Yale University Press, 1988.
Penzer, Norman. 'The Hervey Silver at Ickworth'. *Apollo* 65 (February 1957): 38–43; and *Apollo* 65 (March 1957): 133–37.
Pointon, Marcia. 'Quakerism and Visual Culture, 1650–1800'. *Art History* 20 (1997): 397–431.
———. *Strategies for Showing: Women, Possession and Representation in English Visual Culture, 1665–1800*. Oxford: Oxford University Press, 1997.
Pollard, Michael. *A Dictionary of Members of the Dublin Book Trade, 1550–1800*. London: Bibliographical Society, 2000.
Powell, Martyn. *The Politics of Consumption in Eighteenth-Century Ireland*. London: Palgrave Macmillan, 2004.
Quickenden, Kenneth, Sally Baggott, and Malcolm Dick, eds. *Matthew Boulton: Enterprising Industrialist of the Enlightenment*. Aldershot: Ashgate, 2013.
Reynolds, Mairead. 'Wedgwood in Dublin, 1772–1777'. *Irish Arts Review* 1 (1984): 36–9.
Richards, Sarah. *Eighteenth-Century Ceramics: Products for a Civilised Society*. Manchester: Manchester University Press, 1999.
Riello, Giorgio. *A Foot in the Past: Consumers, Producers and Footwear in the Long Eighteenth Century*. Oxford: Oxford University Press, 2005.
Robins, Joseph. *Champagne and Silver Buckles*. Dublin: Lilliput, 2001.
Ryder, Michael. 'The Bank of Ireland, 1721: Land, Credit and Dependency'. *Historical Journal* 25 (1982): 557–82.
Sargentson, Carolyn. *Merchants and Luxury Markets: The Marchands Merciers of Eighteenth-Century Paris*. London: Victoria and Albert Museum, 1996.
Scarisbrick, Diana. *Jewellery in Britain, 1066–1837*. Norwich: Michael Russell, 1994.
Schroder, Timothy. *The Francis E. Fowler, Jr. Collection of Silver*. Los Angeles: University of California Press, 1991.

———. *British and Continental Gold and Silver in the Ashmolean Museum*. Oxford: Ashmolean Museum, 2009.
Scott, Katie. *The Rococo Interior: Decoration and Social Spaces in Early Eighteenth-Century Paris*. New Haven and London: Yale University Press, 1995.
Sekora, John. *Luxury: The Concept in Western Thought, Eden to Smollett*. Baltimore: Johns Hopkins University Press, 1977.
Severne McKenna, Francis. *Chelsea Porcelain: The Red Anchor Wares*. Leigh-on-Sea: F. Lewis, 1951.
Shammas, Carole. *The Pre-industrial Consumer in England and America*. Oxford: Oxford University Press, 1990.
Sinsteden, Thomas. 'Four Selected Assay Records of the Dublin Goldsmiths' Company'. *Silver Society Journal* 11 (1999): 143–58.
———. 'Surviving Dublin Assay Records, Part 2, 1708–48'. *Silver Studies: The Journal of the Silver Society* 16 (2004): 87–103.
———. *Russborough: Served in Splendour*. Alfred Beit Foundation, 2014.
———. 'Victory Bowl'. *Magazine Antiques* (March/April 2015): 94–97.
Skinner, David. *Wallpaper in Ireland, 1700–1900*. Tralee: Churchill, 2014.
Smith, Roger. 'James Cox, c.1723–1800: A Revised Biography'. *Burlington Magazine* 142 (June 2000): 344–53.
Snodin, Michael, ed. *Rococo Art and Design in Hogarth's England*. London: Victoria and Albert Museum, 1984.
Sotheby's Sale Catalogue. *The Panter Collections: The Superb Collection of Early Irish Silver*. London: J. Davy, 1929.
Stewart, Ann. *James Stewart of Killymoon: An Irishman on the Grand Tour, 1766–68*. Belfast: Ulster Museum, 1999.
St. George Mark, Gordon. 'A Silver Chandelier from Galway'. *Bulletin of the Irish Georgian Society* 25 (1982): 19–24.
Stroeker, Natasha. *Second-Hand Markets for Consumer Durables*. Amsterdam: Thesis Publications, 1995.
Stubbs, W. C. 'The Weavers' Guild, the Guild of the Blessed Virgin Mary, Dublin, 1446–1840'. *Journal of the Royal Society of Antiquaries of Ireland* 49 (1919): 60–88.
Susswein Gottesman, Rita. *The Arts and Crafts in New York, 1726–1776*. New York: New York Historical Society, 1938.
———. *The Arts and Crafts in New York, 1777–1799*. New York: New York Historical Society, 1954.
Sweeney, Tony. *Irish Stuart Silver: Catalogue Raisonné*. Dublin: Edmund Burke, 1995.
Tann, Jennifer. *Birmingham Assay Office, 1773–1993*. Birmingham: Assay Office, 1993.
Taylor, Elise. 'Silver for a Countess's Levee: The Kildare Toilet Set'. *Irish Arts Review* 14 (1998): 115–24.
Teahan, John. *Irish Silver*. Dublin: Stationery Office, 1979.
———. *Irish Silver from the Seventeenth to the Nineteenth Century*. Washington, DC: Smithsonian, 1982.
Thorpe, Ruth. *Women, Architecture and Building in the East of Ireland, c.1790–1840*. Dublin: Four Courts, 2013.
Ticher, Kurt. *Irish Silver in the Rococo Period*. Shannon: Irish University Press, 1972.
———. 'Three Huguenot Goldsmiths in Dublin in the Early 1700s'. *Quarterly Bulletin of the Irish Georgian Society* 15 (1972): 73–80.
———. 'Galway Silver in a Dominican Convent'. *Antique Dealer and Collector's Guide* (October 1977): 71–74.
———, Ida Delamer, and William O'Sullivan. *Hall-Marks on Dublin Silver, 1730–1772*. Dublin: National Museum of Ireland, 1968.

Tinto, Margarita. 'The "Llibres de Passantia" of the Silversmiths of Barcelona, Sixteenth to Nineteenth Centuries'. *Jewellery Studies* 6 (1993): 29–37.

Townshend, Francis. 'Irish Silver, Decoration and Re-Decoration'. *Quarterly Bulletin of the Irish Georgian Society* 8 (1965): 10–39.

Truman, Charles, ed. *Sotheby's Concise Encyclopaedia of Silver*. London: Conran Octopus, 1996.

Turpin, John. 'The School of Ornament of the Dublin Society in the Eighteenth Century'. *Journal of the Royal Society of Antiquaries of Ireland* 116 (1986): 38–50.

———. 'French Influence on Eighteenth-Century Art Education in Dublin'. *Eighteenth-Century Ireland* 5 (1990): 105–16.

———. *A School of Art in Dublin since the Eighteenth Century*. Dublin: Gill and Macmillan, 1995.

Uglow, Jenny. *Hogarth: A Life and a World*. London: Faber & Faber, 1997.

Underdahl, Robin, and Thomas Sinsteden. *The Red McCombs English and Irish Silver Collection*. San Antonio: Institute of Texan Cultures, University of Texas San Antonio, 2010.

Veblen, Thorstein. *The Theory of the Leisure Class*. (1899). New York: Dover, 1994.

Vickery, Amanda. *The Gentleman's Daughter: Women's Lives in Georgian England*. New Haven and London: Yale University Press, 1998.

———. *Behind Closed Doors: At Home in Georgian England*. New Haven and London: Yale University Press, 2010.

Wall, Cynthia. 'The English Auction: Narratives of Dismantlings'. *Eighteenth-Century Studies* 31 (1997): 1–27.

Wall, Maureen. 'The Catholic Merchants, Manufacturers and Traders of Dublin, 1778–1782'. *Reportorium Novum* 2, no. 2 (1960): 298–323.

Wallis, Patrick. 'Apprenticeships and Training in Pre-modern England'. *Journal of Economic History* 68 (2008): 832–61.

Walsh, Claire. 'Shop Design and the Display of Goods in Eighteenth-Century London'. *Journal of Design History* 8 (1995): 157–76.

Ward, Joseph. *Metropolitan Communities: Trade Guilds, Identity and Change in Early Modern London*. Stanford, CA: Stanford University Press, 1997.

Weatherill, Lorna. *Consumer Behaviour and Material Culture in Britain, 1660–1760*. London: Routledge, 1988.

Webb, John. *The Guilds of Dublin*. Dublin: Three Candles, 1929.

Webster, Charles. *The Church Plate of the Diocese of Cork, Cloyne and Ross*. Cork: Guy, 1909.

Wees, Beth Carver. *English, Irish and Scottish Silver at the Sterling and Francine Clark Art Institute*. New York: Hudson Hills Press, 1997.

Westropp, M.S.D. 'The Goldsmiths of Cork'. *Cork Historical and Archaeological Society Journal* 12 (1906): 37–43.

———. *National Museum of Ireland, Dublin: General Guide to the Art Collections*, Part 6 *Metalwork*. Dublin: Stationery Office, 1914.

———. 'Notes on Irish Money Weights and Foreign Coin Current in Ireland'. *Proceedings of the Royal Irish Academy* 33 (1916): 43–73.

———. 'The Cork Goldsmiths, Silversmiths, Jewellers, Watchmakers and Apprentices'. *Cork Historical and Archaeological Society Journal* 31 (1926): 8–13.

———. 'The Goldsmiths of Limerick'. *North Munster Antiquarian Journal* 1 (1936–39): 159–62.

Willemson, Gitta. *The Dublin Society Drawing Schools: Students and Award Winners, 1746–1876*. Dublin: Royal Dublin Society, 2000.

Wills, Geoffrey. 'Stafford Briscoe: A London Silversmith'. *Apollo* 117 (January 1983), 50–54.

Wyse Jackson, Robert. *Irish Silver*. Cork: Mercier, 1972.
Young, Hilary, ed. *The Genius of Wedgwood*. London: Victoria and Albert Museum, 1995.
———. *English Porcelain, 1745–95: Its Makers, Design, Marketing and Consumption*. London: Victoria and Albert Museum, 1999.

Unpublished theses

Beaumont, Daniel. 'The Gentry of the King's and Queen's Counties: Protestant Landed Society, 1690–1760'. PhD thesis, Trinity College Dublin, 1999.
Foster, Sarah. 'Going Shopping in Georgian Dublin: Luxury Goods and the Negotiation of National Identity'. MA thesis, Royal College of Art, London, 1995.
Freundel, Werner John. 'The Production and Commissioning of London-Made Private Carriages: 1740–1800'. MA thesis, Royal College of Art, London, 1999.
Hidaka, K. 'Gold and Silver Thread in Jacobean London, 1603–1625'. MA thesis, Royal College of Art, London, 1998.
Moran, Anna. 'Manufacturing Mythology? Waterford Glass in the Early Nineteenth Century'. MA thesis, Royal College of Art, London, 2002.
Muir, Julia. 'Printing Persuasion: Advertising Goods in Eighteenth-Century England'. MA thesis, Royal College of Art, London, 2000.
Packer, Emma. 'Refining the Goldsmith: The London Goldsmiths' Trade Seen through Inventories, 1695–1732'. MA thesis, Royal College of Art, London, 1992.
Walker, M.J. 'The Extent of the Guild Control of Trades in England, c.1660–1820: A Study Based on a Sample of Provincial Towns and London Companies'. PhD thesis, University of Cambridge, 1985.
Walsh, Claire. 'Shop Design and the Display of Goods in the Eighteenth Century'. MA thesis, Royal College of Art, London, 1993.
Whelan, Edward. 'The Dublin Patriciate and the Reception of Migrants in the Seventeenth Century'. PhD thesis, National University of Ireland, Maynooth, 2008.

Index

For Product Safety Concerns and Information please contact our EU representative GPSR@taylorandfrancis.com Taylor & Francis Verlag GmbH, Kaufingerstraße 24, 80331 München, Germany

Batch number: 10722104

Printed by Printforce, the Netherlands